SOFTWARE ENGINEERING CONCEPTS

McGraw-Hill Series in Software Engineering and Technology

Consulting Editor

Peter Freeman, *University of California, Irvine*

Cohen: *Ada as a Second Language*
Fairley: *Software Engineering Concepts*
Jones: *Programming Productivity*
Kolence: *An Introduction to Software Physics*
Pressman: *Software Engineering: A Practitioner's Approach*

SOFTWARE ENGINEERING CONCEPTS

Richard E. Fairley

School of Information Technology
Wang Institute of Graduate Studies
Tyngsboro, Massachusetts

McGraw-Hill Book Company

New York   St. Louis   San Francisco   Auckland   Bogotá   Hamburg
London   Madrid   Mexico   Montreal   New Delhi
Panama   Paris   São Paulo   Singapore   Sydney   Tokyo   Toronto

This book was set in Times Roman by Interactive Composition Corporation.
The editors were Debbie K. Dennis and Sheila H. Gillams;
the production supervisor was Charles Hess.
The cover was designed by Suzanne Haldane.
The drawings were done by ECL Art.
R. R. Donnelley & Sons Company was printer and binder.

SOFTWARE ENGINEERING CONCEPTS

7890 DOCDOC 89

ISBN 0-07-019902-7

Library of Congress Cataloging in Publication Data

Fairley, R. E. (Richard E.), date
    Software engineering concepts.

    (McGraw-Hill series in software engineering and
technology)
    Includes bibliographical references and indexes.
    1. Electronic digital computers—Programming.
2. Computer programs.   I. Title.   II. Series.
QA76.6.F35   1985   001.64′2   84-12210
ISBN 0-07-019902-7

To Janie

CONTENTS

PREFACE

During the past decade, increasing attention has been focused on the technology of computer software. As computing systems become more numerous, more complex, and more deeply embedded in modern society, the need for systematic approaches to software development and software maintenance becomes increasingly apparent. Software engineering is the field of study concerned with this emerging technology.

Primary goals for this text are to acquaint students with the basic concepts and major issues of software engineering, to describe current tools and techniques, and to provide a basis for evaluating new developments. Many different techniques are presented to illustrate basic concepts, but no single technique receives special attention. Individual instructors may choose to emphasize particular techniques, depending on local circumstances, the backgrounds of their students, and their own interests.

The text is written for juniors, seniors, graduate students, and practitioners of software engineering. Those with more experience in the software field will profit more from the material. Minimal preparation for the material includes a course in data structures and exposure to system software concepts.

The layout of the text follows the traditional software life cycle: an introductory chapter is followed by chapters on planning, cost estimation, and requirements definition. These are followed by chapters on design, implementation issues, and modern programming languages. Chapters on quality assessment and software maintenance conclude the text. This layout should not be taken as an indication that the phased life-cycle approach to software development is the only method presented in the text. The use of prototypes and successive versions is emphasized throughout the text and in the term project material, which is presented in the appendix.

It is strongly recommended that a course in software engineering incorporate a term project. The project should involve team participation and preparation of various software engineering documents. This provides a focal point for the course and allows students to practice various techniques in the different phases of the project. The appendix provides numerous project suggestions, a schedule of project milestones, and formats for the project documents.

During the semester project, teams of three or four students per team prepare a requirements definition, architectural and detailed design specifications, a test plan, a user's manual, and documented source code for their software products. Because they are working against fixed deadlines imposed by the semester calendar, students are required to define three versions of their systems: a prototype, a modest version, and an enhanced version. Versions are defined so that functionality and performance characteristics can be moved between the versions as necessary. This allows a team to meet or exceed project milestones by adding or removing features in the current version of their system. Students are thus confronted with the realities of project deadlines, and they are also able to produce operational software products by semester's end.

Some teams will choose projects that are too ambitious and produce only a prototype. Others will produce all three versions of their product. In any case, it is important that students experience the frustration and satisfaction of integrating their subsystems into well-designed, well-documented functioning software products. If the project is not carried through to implementation, students may not realize the benefits of their analysis, design, test planning, and documentation efforts. Hence, the importance of defining successive versions of their systems. I have found this approach of successive versions to be valuable on "real" software projects that must meet fixed deadlines, and the documents prepared by the students are typical of good software engineering practice. Students thus learn valuable techniques in the process of learning software engineering concepts.

There are two ways to present the material in this text: in the sequence as written, or by first covering Chapters 6, 7, and 8 (programming techniques, programming languages, and quality assessment), followed by Chapters 4 and 5 (requirements definition and software design), followed by Chapters 2 and 3 (planning and cost estimation), followed by Chapter 9 (software maintenance). The latter approach has the advantage of building on the student's knowledge, and terms such as data abstraction and information hiding can be illustrated in an implementation language at the beginning of the course; however, a different approach to the term project is required. In this case, students are given an existing software product to critique and test during the early part of the course. During the latter part of the course they are required to analyze, design, and implement a significant modification to the product.

Both approaches have been used and found to be satisfactory. The author's preference is to present the material in the sequence as written, and to provide implementation language illustrations of terminology as it is introduced. This allows students to define and develop their own term projects following the schedule presented in the appendix. In presenting the material in sequence, the instructor often discusses software cost estimation (Chapter 3) following design (Chapter 5), or at the end of the semester in conjunction with software maintenance (Chapter 9).

I am indebted to the reviewers, namely, Bill Riddle, James Redmond, Tony Wasserman, and Marv Zelkowitz. They found time in their busy schedules to read the text and offer valuable suggestions for improvement. Also, thanks to series editor Peter Freeman for his encouragement and counsel, and thanks to Janice Fairley, who typed the first draft of the manuscript.

I owe a particular debt of gratitude to my students, from whom I have received more than I have given, and to the many researchers and practitioners of software engineering whose ideas and techniques are reported here. I have attempted to acknowledge their contributions where possible. I apologize for any oversights or inaccuracies in my acknowledgments.

Finally, I want to acknowledge the understanding and support of my wife, Janice; she makes it all worthwhile.

Richard E. Fairley

CHAPTER ONE

INTRODUCTION TO SOFTWARE ENGINEERING

INTRODUCTION

This text is concerned with development and maintenance of software products for digital computers. A software product, in contrast to software developed for personal use, has multiple users and often has multiple developers and maintainers. In most cases, the developers, users, and maintainers are distinct entities. Development and maintenance of software products thus requires a more systematic approach than is necessary for personal software.

In order to develop a software product, user needs and constraints must be determined and explicitly stated; the product must be designed to accommodate implementors, users, and maintainers; the source code must be carefully implemented and thoroughly tested; and supporting documents such as the principles of operation, the user's manual, installation instructions, training aids, and maintenance documents must be prepared. Software maintenance tasks include analysis of change requests, redesign and modification of the source code, thorough testing of the modified code, updating of documents and documentation to reflect the changes, and distribution of the modified work products to appropriate user sites.

The need for systematic approaches to development and maintenance of computer software products became apparent in the 1960s. During that decade, third-generation computing hardware was invented, and the software techniques of multiprogramming and time-sharing were developed. These capabilities provided the technology for implementation of interactive, multiuser, on-line, and real-time computing systems. New applications of computers based on the new technology included systems for airline reservations, medical information, general-purpose time-sharing, process control, navigational guidance, and military command and control.

Many such systems were built and delivered, and some of those attempted were never delivered. Among those systems delivered, many were subject to cost overruns, late delivery, lack of reliability, inefficiency, and lack of user acceptance. As computing systems became larger and more complex, it became apparent that the demand for computer software was growing faster than our ability to produce and maintain it.

A workshop was held in Garmisch, West Germany, in 1968 to consider the growing problems of software technology. That workshop, and a subsequent one held in Rome, Italy, in 1969, stimulated widespread interest in the technical and managerial processes used to develop and maintain computer software (NAU76). The term "software engineering" was first used as a provocative theme for those workshops.

Since 1968, the applications of digital computers have become increasingly diverse, complex, and critical to modern society. As a result, the field of software engineering has evolved into a technological discipline of considerable importance.

According to Boehm (BOE76a), software engineering involves "the practical application of scientific knowledge to the design and construction of computer programs and the associated documentation required to develop, operate, and maintain them." As Boehm points out, the term "design" must be interpreted broadly to include activities such as software requirements analysis and redesign during software modification. The IEEE *Standard Glossary of Software Engineering* terminology (IEE83) defines software engineering as: "The systematic approach to the development, operation, maintenance, and retirement of software," where "software" is defined as: "Computer programs, procedures, rules, and possibly associated documentation and data pertaining to the operation of a computer system."

In this text, we use the following definition:

> Software engineering is the technological and managerial discipline concerned with systematic production and maintenance of software products that are developed and modified on time and within cost estimates.

The primary goals of software engineering are to improve the quality of software products and to increase the productivity and job satisfaction of software engineers.

Software engineering is a new technological discipline distinct from, but based on the foundations of, computer science, management science, economics, communication skills, and the engineering approach to problem solving.

Software engineering is a pragmatic discipline that relies on computer science to provide scientific foundations in the same way that traditional engineering disciplines such as electrical engineering and chemical engineering rely on physics and chemistry. Software engineering, being a labor-intensive activity, requires both technical skill and managerial control. Management science provides the foundations for software project management. Computing systems must be developed and maintained on time and within cost estimates; economics provides the foundation for resource estimation and cost control. Software engineering activities occur within an organizational context, and a high degree of communication is required among customers, managers, software engineers, hardware engineers, and other technologists. Good oral, written, and interpersonal communication skills are crucial for the software engineer.

Because software engineering is concerned with development and maintenance of technological products, problem-solving techniques common to all engineering disciplines are utilized. Engineering problem-solving techniques provide the basis for project planning, project management, systematic analysis, methodical design, careful fabrication, extensive validation, and ongoing maintenance activities. Appropriate notations, tools, and techniques are applied in each of these areas. Furthermore, engineers balance scientific principles, economic issues, and social concerns in a pragmatic manner when solving problems and developing technological products. Concepts from computer science, management science, economics, and communication skills are combined within the framework of engineering problem solving. The result is software engineering.

Software engineering and traditional engineering disciplines share the pragmatic approach to development and maintenance of technological artifacts. There are, however, significant differences between software engineering and traditional engineering. The fundamental sources of these differences are the lack of physical laws for software, the lack of product visibility, and obscurity in the interfaces between software modules.

Software is intangible: it has no mass, no volume, no color, no odor—no physical properties. Source code is merely a static image of a computer program, and while the effects produced by a program are often observable, the program itself is not. Software does not degrade with time as hardware does. Software failures are caused by design and implementation errors, not by degradation. Because software is intangible, extraordinary measures must be taken to determine the status of a software product in development. It is easy for optimistic individuals to state that the product is "95 percent complete" and difficult for software engineers and their managers to assess progress and spot problem areas, except in hindsight. Many of the concepts discussed in this text are concerned with improving the visibility of software products.

Because software has no physical properties, it is not subject to the laws of gravity or the laws of electrodynamics. There are no Newton's laws or Maxwell's equations to guide software development. Intangibility and lack of physical properties for software limit the number of fundamental guidelines and basic constraints available to shape the design and implementation of a software product. Software design is comparable to architectural design of buildings in the absence of gravity. Excessive degrees of freedom are both a blessing and a curse to software engineers.

In a very real sense, the software engineer creates models of physical situations in software. The mapping between the model and the reality being modeled has been called the intellectual distance between the problem and a computerized solution to the problem (DIJ72). A fundamental principle of software engineering is to design software products that minimize the intellectual distance between problem and solution; however, the variety of approaches to software development is limited only by the creativity and ingenuity of the programmer. Often it is not clear which approach will minimize the intellectual distance, and often different approaches will minimize different dimensions of the intellectual distance. This discussion is not meant to imply that programming is entirely ad hoc, or that there are no fundamental principles of software engineering; however, the principles and guidelines must always be tempered by the particular situation.

Obscurity in the interfaces between software modules also distinguishes software engineering from the traditional engineering disciplines. A fundamental principle for managing complexity is to decompose a large system into smaller, more manageable subunits with well-defined interfaces. This approach of divide and conquer is routinely used in the engineering disciplines, in architecture, and in other disciplines that involve analysis and synthesis of complex artifacts. In software engineering, the units of decomposition are called "modules." (A precise definition of "software module" is presented in Chapter 5.)

Software modules have both control and data interfaces. Control interfaces are established by the calling relationships among modules, and data interfaces are manifest in the parameters passed between modules as well as in the global data items shared among modules. It is difficult to design a software system so that all the control and data interfaces among modules are explicit, and so that the modules do not interact to produce unexpected side effects when they invoke one another. Unexpected side effects complicate the interfaces between modules and complicate documentation, verification, testing, and modification of a software product. Programmers who intentionally write convoluted programs that have obscure side effects are known as hackers. "Hacker" is not a complimentary term in software engineering.

Finally, the data interfaces between modules must be exact. For instance, the number and types of positional parameters passed between routines must agree in every detail. There is no concept of an "almost" integer parameter or a global array of "almost" proper dimension. Constructing a stable software system is analogous to constructing a skyscraper with the stability of the entire structure depending on an exact fit of every door on every janitor's closet in every subbasement of the building; less than exact fit might cause the entire structure to crash.

During the past decade significant advances have occurred in all areas of software engineering: analysis techniques for determining software requirements and notations for expressing those requirements have been developed; methodical approaches to software design have evolved and design notations have proliferated; implementation techniques have been improved and new programming languages have been developed; software validation techniques have been examined and quality assurance procedures have been instituted; formal techniques for verifying software properties have evolved; and software maintenance procedures have been improved. Management techniques have been tailored to software engineering, and the problems of group dynamics and project communication have been explored. Quantitative models for cost estimation and product reliability have evolved, and fundamental principles of analysis, design, implementation, and testing have been discovered. Automated software tools have been developed to increase software quality, programmer productivity, and management control of software projects. New technical journals have been created, and existing journals devote increasing attention to software engineering topics. International conferences are held on a regular basis.

All this activity should not be interpreted to mean that the problems of software engineering have been solved. In fact, the level of activity in software engineering is indicative of the vast number of problems to be solved. Every technology evolves through the predictable phases of ad hoc invention, development of systematic procedures, and eventual culmination in a routine handbook approach to the discipline. As you read this text, it will become apparent that the technology of software engineering still involves a great deal of ad hoc invention.

1.1 SOME DEFINITIONS

We have defined software engineering as the technological discipline concerned with systematic production and maintenance of software products that are developed and modified on time and within cost estimates. Software engineering differs from traditional computer programming in that engineering-like techniques are used to specify, design, implement, validate, and maintain software products within the time and budget constraints established for the project. In addition, software engineering is concerned with managerial issues that lie outside the domain of traditional programming. On small projects, perhaps involving one or two programmers for one or two months, the issues of concern are primarily technical in nature. On projects involving more programmers and longer time durations, management control is required to coordinate the technical activities.

In this text the term "programmer" is used to denote an individual who is concerned with the details of implementing, packaging, and modifying algorithms and data structures written in particular programming languages. Software engineers are additionally concerned with issues of analysis, design, verification and testing, documentation, software maintenance, and project management. A software engineer should have considerable skill and experience as a programmer in order to understand the problem areas, goals, and objectives of software engineering.

It is sometimes said that software engineering concepts are applicable only to large projects of long duration. On large projects standard practices and formal procedures are essential, and some of the notations, tools, and techniques of software engineering have been developed specifically for large projects. On a small project, one can be more casual, but the fundamental principles of systematic analysis, design, implementation, testing, and modification remain the same, whether for a one-person, one-month project or a 1000-person, 10-year project. The fundamental concepts of software development and maintenance presented in this text are useful on every programming project; however, a few of the techniques discussed are cost-effective only on large projects.

The term "computer software" is often taken to be synonymous with "computer program" or "source code." In this text, "computer software" is synonymous with "software product." Thus, computer software includes the source code and all the associated documents and documentation that constitute a software product. Requirements documents, design specifications, source code, test plans, principles of operation, quality assurance procedures, software problem reports, maintenance procedures, user's manuals, installation instructions, and training aids are all components of a software product. Software products include system-level software as well as application software developed to solve specific problems for end users of computing systems.

As used in this text, "documentation" explains the characteristics of a document. Internal documentation of source code describes the characteristics of the code, and external documentation explains the characteristics of the documents associated with the code. Software engineering is concerned with systematic development and maintenance of documentation and supporting documents as well as the source code.

In this text the terms "developer" and "software engineer" are used interchangeably. The term "customer" is used to denote an individual or organization that initiates procurement or modification of a software product. The term "customer" does not necessarily imply a financial transaction between customer and developer. The customer's organization is usually distinct from the product developer's organization, but sometimes the customer is another division of a parent organization or the person in the next office.

The customer may or may not be the end user of a software product, and the customer, developer, end user, and maintainer may be the same person; however, software products usually have multiple customer representatives, multiple developers, multiple users, and multiple maintainers. Sometimes, a software product is developed to satisfy a perceived marketing opportunity without having a specific customer or group of users in mind.

Software quality is a primary concern of software engineers. Quality attributes of importance for any particular software product are of course dependent on the nature of that product. In some instances, transportability of the software product between machines may be an attribute of prime importance, while efficient utilization of memory space may be paramount in other cases. There are, however, a few fundamental quality attributes that every software product should possess. These include usefulness, clarity, reliability, efficiency, and cost-effectiveness.

The most important quality attribute a software product can possess is usefulness; i.e., the software product must satisfy user needs. This may seem painfully obvious, but delivered software products frequently do not perform the functions expected of them. This problem is symptomatic of poor communication among the customer, the users, and the software engineers. Careful planning, analysis, and customer involvement are required to develop useful software products.

Software reliability is "the ability of a program to perform a required function under stated conditions for a stated period of time" (IEE83). The degree of reliability required of a particular product can be expressed in terms of the cost of product failure. There is obviously a great difference between product failure that results in minor irritation to the user and product failure that results in loss of human life. The amount to be spent on attaining increased reliability is a function of the cost of product failure; however, there is a minimal level of reliability that every software product must possess.

Software products must be clearly written and easy to understand. As we shall see, testing and maintenance activities consume a large portion of most software budgets. The key to making a system testable and maintainable is to make it understandable. Software products must also exhibit conceptual integrity and clarity of purpose to the users. Many of the techniques discussed in this text have the goal of improving both the internal and external clarity of software products.

Next, a software product should be efficient—but only as appropriate for the particular application. In the early days of digital computers, hardware was very expensive and very slow by today's standards, and great emphasis was placed on squeezing the last bit and the last memory cycle from every program; efficiency was the primary quality attribute of computer programs. As software becomes larger and more complex, attributes such as usefulness, reliability, and clarity assume overriding importance for most software products.

On the other hand, there are software products (i.e., real-time systems implemented on microprocessors) that are critically constrained in memory space and execution time. Efficiency remains a primary quality attribute for those systems. Thus, we say that efficiency is a fundamental quality attribute, but as appropriate to the situation.

Finally, a software product must be cost-effective in development, in maintenance, and in use. Development and maintenance efforts devoted to increasing the efficiency and reliability of a software product must be appropriate to the intended applications of the product, and the "creeping elegance" of marginally useful features must be avoided. In use, a software product must perform an existing task using less time or human and machine resources than were required without the product, or it must provide new services that were not feasible without it. Sometimes, a new software product will not perform the intended tasks as expected, but will provide unforeseen options and capabilities that make it attractive on different grounds than originally envisioned.

1.2 SOME SIZE FACTORS

In this section, the level of effort devoted to software development and maintenance is discussed; the distribution of effort among activities is presented; and size categories for software projects are described. The results reported here summarize many different software projects from many different organizations, and they should be viewed only in the statistical sense. Any particular project may deviate considerably from the reported results. On the other hand, these numbers are typical of many projects and provide educated rules of thumb.

1.2.1 Total Effort Devoted to Software

It is estimated that the total amount spent on all aspects of computing in the United States in 1980 was approximately 5 percent of the Gross National Product (GNP), or about $130 billion. It is further estimated that computing revenues will be 8 percent of the GNP by 1985 and 12.5 percent by 1990 (DAT80). In contrast, the U.S. automobile industry contributed 2.3 percent to the GNP in 1980 (USB81). While these figures are impressive, they do not fully convey the growing importance of computing technology in modern society. As computing systems become more numerous and more critical to post-industrial societies, the demand for high-quality software increases at an increasing rate.

Current demand for software technologists exceeds the available supply, and it is estimated that demand will exceed supply by 750,000 to 2,000,000 people by 1990 (SCH81). Thus, a major goal of software engineering is to provide tools and techniques to increase the productivity of the available software engineers.

Figure 1.1 illustrates the changing ratio of expenditures for hardware and software over time. In 1960, the ratio was approximately 80 percent hardware cost to 20 percent software cost. By 1980, the ratio was reversed: approximately 20 percent hardware cost to 80 percent software cost. By 1990, software costs will account for more than 90 percent of the amount spent on computing systems. Also, observe that software maintenance is a large and growing portion of the software effort.

Reasons for the trends illustrated in Figure 1.1 are not hard to determine. Transistors, integrated circuits, and VLSI have resulted in dramatic decreases in hardware costs. On the other hand, software is labor-intensive, and personnel costs are constantly increasing. Similarly, software maintenance is an increasing portion of software cost because with passing time more software accumulates.

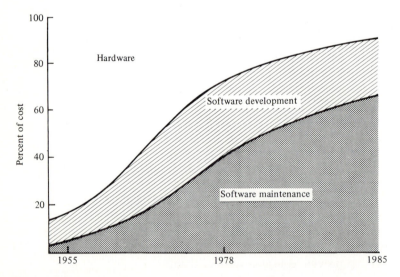

Figure 1.1 Changing hardware-software cost ratio *(from BOE76)*.

Correct interpretation of Figure 1.1 has been a topic of some controversy (BOE83). The figure extrapolates overall hardware/software cost trends in the United States from an Air Force study conducted in 1972. It should not be interpreted as the relative cost of hardware and software for any particular computing system or development project. Another qualification to Figure 1.1 concerns the projected level of software maintenance costs. Use of modern software engineering tools and techniques should result in software products that are easier to maintain; however, the increasing number, size, and complexity of software products may offset the gains from modern technology.

In (BOE83), Boehm estimates that the cost of software for computer manufacturers, software firms, and user organizations in the United States in 1980 was $40.2 billion, or 84 percent of the $47.9 billion spent on computing hardware and software. Note that these numbers are for hardware and software only; the percent of GNP stated above includes all aspects of computing and data processing.

1.2.2 Distribution of Effort

The typical lifespan for a software product is 1 to 3 years in development and 5 to 15 years in use (maintenance). The distribution of effort between development and maintenance has been variously reported as 40/60, 30/70, and even 10/90. This is not surprising when it is understood that maintenance comprises all activities following initial release of a software product.

Software maintenance involves three types of activities: enhancing the capabilities of the product, adapting the product to new processing environments, and correcting bugs. Typical distributions of maintenance effort for enhancement, adaptation, and correction are 60 percent, 20 percent, and 20 percent, respectively. During the development phase of a software product, the distribution of effort is typically 40 percent for analysis and design; 20 percent for implementation, debugging, and unit testing; and 40 percent for integration and acceptance testing. Taking the distribution of effort between development and maintenance to be 40/60 and normalizing total effort to 100 percent results in the distributions presented in Figure 1.2.

Several facts are evident from Figure 1.2. First, software maintenance activities consume more resources than software development activities, although maintenance is spread over a longer time period so that the effort per unit of time is lower. Second, a large percentage of total effort is devoted to software enhancement. Third, testing requires almost half the effort during software development. A major reason for schedule slippage and cost overrun is failure to allot sufficient time and adequate resources for testing.

The fourth observation from Figure 1.2 is that the activities of system testing, enhancement, and adaptation consume three-fourths of total life-cycle effort. Observe that implementation, which is commonly thought to be the predominant activity in software technology, requires less than 10 percent of total life-cycle effort for a typical software product.

It is obvious from this discussion that the goals of analysis, design, and

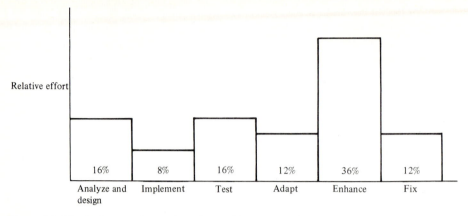

Figure 1.2 Distribution of effort in the software life cycle *(Boehm, Datamation 1973)*.

implementation should be to ease testing and maintenance activities. The benefits of using systematic tools and techniques during software development are thus twofold: first, an increase in quality and productivity during initial product development can be expected; and second, the resulting documentation levels and clarity of the product will permit systematic testing, enhancement, adaptation, and correction.

1.2.3 Project Size Categories

Project size is a major factor that determines the level of management control and the types of tools and techniques required on a software project. The following categories give some indication of software project size. These categories have been adapted from material originally presented by Yourdon (YOU75). They are summarized in Table 1.1.

Trivial projects. A trivial software project involves one programmer working, perhaps part time, for a few days or a few weeks and results in a program of less than 500 statements, packaged in 10 to 20 subroutines. Such programs are often personal software; they are developed for the exclusive use of the programmer and are usually discarded after a few months.

There is little need for formal analysis, elaborate design documentation, extensive test planning, or supporting documents for trivial programs; however, even trivial programs can be improved by some analysis, by systematic design, by structured coding, and by methodical testing. One of the dangers of personal software development (of whatever size) is that a program intended for personal use becomes a software product, but without benefit of the planning and support required for a product.

Small projects. A small project employs one programmer for 1 to 6 months and results in a product containing 1000 to 2000 lines of source code packaged in

Table 1.1 Size categories for software products

Category	Number of programmers	Duration	Product size
Trivial	1	1–4 wks.	500 source lines
Small	1	1–6 mos.	1K–2K
Medium	2–5	1–2 yrs.	5K–50K
Large	5–20	2–3 yrs.	50K–100K
Very large	100–1000	4–5 yrs.	1M
Extremely large	2000–5000	5–10 yrs.	1M–10M

perhaps 25 to 50 routines. Small programs usually have no interactions with other programs. Examples of such programs include scientific applications written by engineers to solve numerical problems; small commercial applications written by data processing personnel to perform straightforward data manipulation and report generation; and student projects written in compiler and operating system courses.

A small project requires little interaction among programmers or between programmers and customers. Standardized techniques and notations, standardized documents, and systematic project reviews should be used even on small projects, but the degree of formality will be much less than is required on larger projects.

Medium-size projects. A project of medium size requires two to five programmers working for 1 to 2 years and results in 10,000 to 50,000 lines of source code packaged in 250 to 1000 routines. Products of medium size have few, if any interactions with other programs. Medium-size programs include assemblers, compilers, small management information systems, inventory systems, and process control applications.

Development of medium-size programs requires interaction among programmers and communication with customers. Thus, a certain degree of formality is required in planning, documents, and project reviews. It is undoubtedly true that the vast majority of software projects, and the resulting programs, are of small or medium size. Most applications programs and many systems programs are developed in 2 years or less by five or fewer programmers. Use of systematic software engineering principles on medium-size projects can result in vastly improved product quality, increased programmer productivity, and better satisfaction of customer needs.

Large projects. A large project requires 5 to 20 programmers for a period of 2 to 3 years and results in a system of 50,000 to 100,000 source statements, packaged in several subsystems. A large program often has significant interactions with other programs and software systems.

Examples of large programs include large compilers, small time-sharing systems, data-base packages, graphics programs for data acquisition and display, and real-time control systems. Communication problems among programmers, managers, and customers often become severe on large projects. A large project generally requires more than one programming team (e.g., three teams of five persons each) and often involves more than one level of management. In addition, there is a great likelihood that there will be some turnover of project personnel during the development cycle. This will require training and indoctrination of new personnel or distribution of the responsibilities of a departed team member among the remaining members.

The size and complexity of a large project make it difficult, if not impossible, to foresee all eventualities during planning and analysis. Changes to the product requirements may be initiated by both customers and developers as the project evolves. Systematic processes, standardized documents, and formal reviews are essential throughout a large project.

Very large projects. A very large project requires 100 to 1000 programmers for a period of 4 to 5 years and results in a software system of 1 million source instructions. A very large system generally consists of several major subsystems, each of which forms a large system. The subsystems typically have complex interactions with one another and with other separately developed systems.

Very large systems often involve real-time processing, telecommunications, and multitasking. Examples of such systems include large operating systems, large data-base systems, and military command and control systems. Brooks reports that the IBM operating system OS/360 was developed by 5000 programmers over a period of 5 years and contained more than 1 million source instructions (BRO75). A recent study forecasts the size of typical operating systems for data processing applications growing to 4 million lines of code by 1990 (SCH81).

Extremely large projects. An extremely large project employs 2000 to 5000 programmers for periods of up to 10 years and results in 1 million to 10 million lines of source code. Extremely large systems consist of several very large subsystems and often involve real-time processing, telecommunications, multitasking, and distributed processing. Such systems often have extremely high reliability requirements and involve life-and-death processes.

Examples of extremely large systems include air traffic control, ballistic missile defense, and military command and control systems. Very few extremely large systems have been built. A U.S. Department of Defense project involving an antiballistic missile system was abandoned a few years ago after computer experts testified before a congressional committee that the necessary software for the system was beyond the capabilities of current technology. It is fair to assume, however, that increasing pressures of modern society and new advances in software technology will result in increasing numbers of extemely large projects in the future.

1.2.4 How Programmers Spend Their Time

In 1964, Bairdain of Bell Labs conducted a time and motion study of 70 programmers to determine how they spent their time (BAI64). The results of that study are presented in Figure 1.3. At first glance, the fact that a typical programmer

Bell Labs Study (1964, 70 Programmers)

Writing Programs	13%
Reading programs and manuals	16%
Job communication	32%
Personal	13%
Miscellaneous	15%
Training	6%
Mail	5%

39% "Other"

Figure 1.3 How programmers spend their time.

spends only 13 percent of the time writing programs appears to be unreasonable, but some analysis indicates that these figures are, in fact, quite reasonable. For example, consider the personal time of 13 percent in Figure 1.3. Assuming 260 potential work days per year (5 × 52 = 260), and assuming 11 paid holidays, 15 paid vacation days, 5 days of sick leave, and 3 days for jury duty, extra vacation, etc., gives a total of 34 days personal time, which is approximately 13 percent of 260. Similarly, 1 hour per day for coffee breaks, personal phone calls, and visits to the restroom plus 13 days travel time results in 39 days, or 15 percent, miscellaneous time. Although this experiment was conducted in 1964, there is no reason to expect the results to have changed.

Major reasons for underestimating the cost of a software project are failure to account for the 39 percent overhead time for programmers (13 + 15 + 5 + 6 = 39) and failure to account for the 48 percent of time spent in job communication and reading of programs and manuals (32 + 16 = 48). To this we would add forgetting to add the 40 to 50 percent of development time required for testing.

Another view of how programmers spend their time on a software project was reported by Boehm (BOE80). The results for two projects are illustrated in Figure 1.4. Note that approximately 40 percent of project effort involved activities such as reading, reviewing, meeting, and fixing.

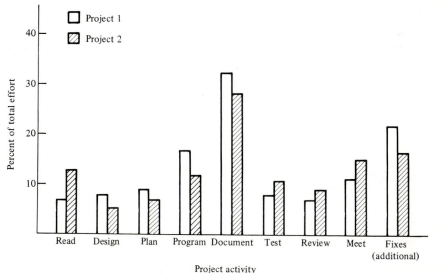

Figure 1.4 Distribution of effort on two software projects *(adapted from BOE81)*.

1.3 QUALITY AND PRODUCTIVITY FACTORS

Development and maintenance of software products are complex tasks. Those who have written only small programs for personal use or homework exercises may find it difficult to understand the importance of systematic activities. The degree of formality and the amount of time spent on various activities will vary with the size and complexity of the product, but systematic activities are, in fact, necessary. There is a fundamental difference between writing a small program for personal use and developing or modifying a software product.

We observe that electrical engineers do not produce electronic circuits by soldering components together. It is absurd to imagine an electrical engineer sitting at a workbench, selecting some components, connecting them together, pausing for a few moments, selecting some more components, interconnecting them, scratching his head, disassembling and rearranging the components, and continuing to build a circuit in this manner. Yet, this is an exact analogy to the way in which many programmers go about the task of constructing a computer program. No analysis, no design, no test planning, and no reviews; just "coding by the seat of the pants." Development and maintenance of high-quality software products requires technical and managerial skills comparable to those in more traditional engineering disciplines.

Software quality and programmer productivity can be improved by improving the processes used to develop and maintain software products. Some factors that influence quality and productivity are listed in Table 1.2 and discussed below. Techniques that address these factors are discussed in subsequent chapters of the text.

Individual ability. Production and maintenance of software products are labor-intensive activities. Productivity and quality are thus direct functions of individual ability and effort. There are two aspects to ability: the general competence of the individual, and familiarity of the individual with the particular application area. Competent data processing programmers are not usually competent in scientific application areas, nor are scientific programmers ordinarily competent system programmers. Lack of familiarity with the application area can result in low productivity and poor quality.

Table 1.2 Factors that influence quality and productivity

Individual ability	Problem understanding
Team communication	Stability of requirements
Product complexity	Required skills
Appropriate notations	Facilities and resources
Systematic approaches	Adequacy of Training
Change control	Management skills
Level of technology	Appropriate goals
Required reliability	Rising expectations
Available time	

By "general level of competence" we mean the basic ability to write correct computer programs. An experiment by Sackman and others conducted in 1968 had the goal of assessing the effect of batch and interactive programming techniques on programmer productivity (SAC68). The experiment involved 12 programmers who implemented two programs each. To everyone's surprise, the individual differences in productivity among the programmers were much greater than the effects of batch versus interactive access to the computer. The results of Sackman's experiment are presented in Figure 1.5. Note that the ratio of coding hours for the worst:best programmer is 25:1 for program 2, and that the ratio of debugging hours is 28:1 for program 1 and 26:1 for program 2. Because the programmers were all familiar with the application areas of the programs in the experiment, the results were interpreted as a measure of the level of competence of individual programmers.

In a subsequent experiment, Sackman observed ratios of 16:1 in programmer productivity. In both experiments, the extremes were due to a small number of very good and very poor performances. Eliminating the extremes results in a more typical variation in programmer productivity of 5:1. Nevertheless, a productivity range of 5:1 or greater is a significant factor in software engineering.

On very large and extremely large projects, the number of programmers is so large that individual differences in programmer productivity will tend to average out. However, the modules developed by weaker programmers may exhibit poor quality and may lag in delivery time. Small and medium-size projects (five or fewer programmers) are extremely sensitive to the ability of the individual programmer.

In programming, as in sports, the general guideline is to utilize outstanding people. However, it is not always possible to hire exceptional individuals. One of the goals of software engineering is to provide notations, tools, and techniques that will enable programmers of good but not outstanding ability to perform their work activities in a competent, professional manner. By investing in better hardware and software tools, organizations can shift software engineering from a labor-intensive to a capital-intensive industry. Nevertheless, individual ability will be a primary factor in quality and productivity into the foreseeable future.

Team communication. Programming has traditionally been regarded as an individual and private activity. Many programmers have low social needs and prefer

Performance Measure	RATIO
Debugging hours #1	28:1
Debugging hours #2	26:1
CPU Sec. for DVMT #1	8:1
CPU Sec. for DVMT #2	11:1
Coding hours #1	16:1
Coding hours #2	25:1
Program size #1	6:1
Program size #2	5:1
Run time #1	5:1
Run time #2	13:1

(Sackman, et al., 1968, 12 Programmers)   **Figure 1.5** Variations in programmer productivity.

to work alone (COU78). Programs are seldom perceived as public documents, and programmers seldom discuss the exact details of their work in a systematic manner. As a result, it is possible for programmers to misunderstand the role of their modules in an evolving system, and to make mistakes that may not be detected until some time later. Many of the recent innovations in software engineering, such as design reviews, structured walkthroughs, and code-reading exercises, have the goals of making software more visible and improving communication among programmers.

On the other hand, increasing product size results in decreasing programmer productivity due to the increased complexity of interactions among program components, and due to the increased communication required among programmers, managers, and customers. Brooks has observed that the number of communication paths among programmers grows as $n(n - 1)/2$, where n is the number of programmers on a project team (BRO75). Thus, increasing the number of team members from three to four to five increases the number of communication paths from three to six to ten. Also, each team member must learn the project and overcome the "learning curve" effect before becoming a contributing team member. This further increases overhead and lowers overall productivity.

In addition, many processes in software development are interdependent and must occur in sequential order. Adding more programmers to an ongoing project may be counterproductive unless there are independent tasks that the new programmers can perform without incurring the overhead required to learn various details of the project. As Brooks states: "Men and months are interchangeable commodities only when a task can be partitioned among many workers with no communication among them. This is true of reaping wheat and picking cotton; it is not even approximately true . . . of programming." Brooks observes that this same principle prevents the production of a baby in 1 month using nine women.

These considerations lead Brooks to formulate his now famous law, which we paraphrase as follows:

BROOKS LAW (modified form):
Adding more programmers to a late project may make it later.

Product complexity. There are three generally acknowledged levels of product complexity: applications programs, utility programs, and system-level programs. Applications programs include scientific and data processing routines written in a high-level language such as FORTRAN, Pascal, or COBOL. Utility programs include compilers, assemblers, linkage editors, and loaders. They may be written in a high-level language such as Pascal or Ada or in assembly language. Systems programs include data communications packages, real-time process control systems, and operating systems routines, which are usually written in assembly language or a high-level systems language such as PL/1 or Ada.

Applications programs have the highest productivity and systems programs the lowest productivity, as measured in lines of code per programmer-day. Utility programs can be produced at a rate 5 to 10 times, and applications programs at a rate 25 to 100 times, that of systems programs. Some typical figures for lines of code per programmer day as a function of project complexity are: less than one line per day for systems programs, 5 to 10 lines per day for utility programs, and 25 to 100 lines per programmer-day for applications programs. We caution that these figures are only rule-of-thumb approximations and should not be regarded as definitive. They are strongly influenced by other factors.

The effort required to develop and maintain a software product is a nonlinear function of product size and complexity. A product that is twice as large or twice as complex as a known product, by whatever measure other than effort, may require 10 times or even 100 times the amount of effort required for the known product. Failure to allow for the nonlinear scaling of size and complexity is a primary reason for cost and schedule overruns on many software projects.

Appropriate notations. In software engineering, as in other technological disciplines, the representation schemes are of fundamental importance. Good notations can clarify the relationships and interactions of interest, while poor notations complicate and interfere with good practice. Programming languages provide concise notations for the implementation phase of software development, but there are no widely accepted notations for stating functional requirements, design specifications, test plans, or performance criteria. Several notations have been developed in these areas, and some are discussed in subsequent chapters of this text; however, there are no universally accepted notations in software engineering that correspond to the schematic diagrams of electrical engineering or the blueprints of civil engineering.

Appropriate notations provide vehicles of communication among project personnel and introduce the possibility of using automated software tools to manipulate the notations and verify proper usage. This can be of great benefit to a particular project, but even greater benefits will accrue when organization-wide and industry-wide adoption of a few well-defined notational schemes occurs.

Systematic approaches. In every field of endeavor there are certain accepted procedures and techniques. The existence of these standard practices is one of the distinguishing characteristics of a professional discipline. Various systematic approaches to software development and maintenance are discussed in this text, but because the field of software engineering is in its infancy, many of our procedures and techniques have not yet matured. Furthermore, it is unreasonable to expect that a single approach to software development and maintenance will ever be adequate to cover all situations. At this point in the evolution of software engineering, it is often not clear which of the various approaches to software development should be used in which situations. However, we are convinced that any one—or a combination—of the methods described in this text is superior to the traditional ad hoc, seat-of-the-pants approach to software development and maintenance.

Change control. In a very real sense software adapts general-purpose computing hardware to particular applications. Sometimes software must compensate for design deficiencies in the hardware, and software is often tailored to satisfy differing requirements of different customers. The flexibility of software is a great strength and also a great source of difficulty in software engineering. Because source code is easily modified, it is not uncommon for difficult issues to be resolved in software, or for the customer to request, and the project manager agree to, seemingly minor changes to the source code. Thus, the software engineer is often caught between an inadequate hardware base and a customer who wants a product "just slightly different" from the standard one.

Requirements can also change due to poor understanding of the problem, or external economic and political factors beyond the control of customer or developer. Some projects experience constantly changing requirements, which can quickly undermine project morale.

Notations and procedures that provide the ability to trace and assess the impact of proposed changes are necessary to make visible the true cost of apparently small changes to source code. These changes often become large when the cost of updating requirements, design documents, test plans, and user's manuals is added. On the other hand, use of appropriate notations and techniques makes controlled change possible without degrading the quality of work products.

The devastating effects of constantly changing requirements can be minimized by planning for change and by formalizing the mechanism of change. Planning for a software project must include plans for change control.

Level of technology. The level of technology utilized on a software project accounts for such factors as the programming language, the machine environment, the programming practices, and the software tools. Modern programming languages provide improved facilities for data definition and data usage, improved constructs for specifying control flow, better modularization facilities, user-defined exception handling, and facilities for concurrent programming.

The machine environment includes the set of hardware and software facilities available for developing, using, and maintaining a software product. Stability and availability of the machine environment exert a strong influence on productivity and quality.

Modern programming practices include use of systematic analysis and design techniques, appropriate notations, structured coding, systematic techniques for examining design documents and source code, and systematic testing. Software tools span the spectrum from elementary tools such as assemblers and primitive debugging aids to fully integrated development environments that incorporate tools for managing and controlling the software development process.

Level of reliability. Every software product must possess a basic level of reliability; however, extreme reliability is gained only with great care in analysis, design, implementation, system testing, and maintenance of the software product. Both human and machine resources are required to obtain increased reliability. This results in decreased productivity when productivity is measured in lines of code produced per programmer-month. Boehm estimates that the productivity ratio between very low and extremely high required reliability is on the order of 2:1 (BOE81).

Problem understanding. Failure to understand the true nature of the problem to be solved is a common and difficult issue. There are several factors that contribute to this lack of understanding. Often the customer does not truly understand the nature of the problem and/or does not understand the capabilities and limitations of computers. Most customers (most people in general) are not trained to think in logical, algorithmic terms, and often do not understand the true nature of their needs.

Often the software engineer does not understand the application area and has trouble communicating with the customer because of differences in educational backgrounds, viewpoints, and technical jargon. Sometimes the customer is not the end user of the system, and the software engineer has no opportunity to investigate the user's problem. Sometimes the true nature of the problem does not become apparent until the software product, or some major portion of it, is constructed and operated. Sometimes the automated solution changes the nature of the problem (for better or worse), and the change may not be apparent until the system is installed. Careful planning, customer interviews, task observation, prototyping, a preliminary version of the user's manual, and precise product specifications can increase both customer and developer understanding of the problem to be solved.

Available time. While it might appear that a software project requiring six programmer-months of effort can be completed by one programmer in 6 months or by six programmers in 1 month, software projects are sensitive not only to total effort but also to elapsed time and the number of people involved. Utilizing six programmers for 1 month will probably be less effective than using one programmer for 6 months because the learning curve for six programmers on a 1-month schedule will occupy a large percentage of the elapsed time, and because the effort required for coordination and communication among six programmers will drastically increase project overhead. On the other hand, using two programmers for 3 months may be more effective than using one programmer for 6 months due to the reinforcement that each programmer gains from the other.

Programmer productivity is also sensitive to the calendar time available for project completion. A well-known rule of thumb states that it takes 2 years to develop a compiler for a new language, regardless of the number of people involved. There is quantitative evidence to suggest that development time cannot be compressed below about 75 percent of the nominal development time regardless of the personnel and resources expended (BOE81). It is not clear that extending development time beyond some reasonable limit (say 2 years for a compiler) makes the project any easier. In fact, some investigators believe that extending a project beyond some nominal duration increases the total effort required. It is clear, however, that the difficulty of a project, and the resulting programmer productivity and software quality, are sensitive functions of the time available for product development or modification.

Determining optimum staffing levels and proper elapsed times for various activities in software product development is an important and difficult aspect of cost and resource estimation.

Required skills. The practice of software engineering requires a vast range of skills. Extracting information from customers in order to establish user needs demands good communication skills, tact, and diplomacy as well as knowledge of the application area. Requirements definition and design activities are conceptual in nature and require good creative problem-solving skills. Implementation of software requires concentrated attention to details; to correctly write a large program is comparable to writing a textbook that has no misspellings, no errors in syntax or punctuation, and absolute consistency in cross-referencing.

Debugging often requires the deductive skills of a Sherlock Holmes. Test planning requires consideration of every conceivable situation, and stress testing requires a destructive, "what if" frame of mind. Preparation of external documents requires good writing skills and the ability to place oneself in the user's or maintainer's position, to anticipate questions and concerns and address them in a straightforward manner. Working with customers and other developers requires good oral and interpersonal communication skills. Finally, all these skills are exercised within a technical and managerial framework; software engineers must be technically competent and possess sufficient social skills to interact with managers, customers, and other engineers.

It is not necessary that every software engineer possess all the requisite skills, but these skills must be present among the members of a programming team. The project manager must assess the abilities of team members and make optimal use of each individual's talents.

Facilities and resources. Studies of factors that motivate programmers have shown that work-related factors, such as good machine access and a quiet place to work, are more important to the typical programmer than status-related factors, such as reserved parking places and keys to the executive restroom (COU78). Most programmers feel that the positive aspects of their jobs are the creative challenges, the variety of tasks, and the opportunities for professional advancement, while the negative aspects of their jobs involve management ineptness, company policies, and organizational bureaucracy. Most programmers receive their motivational rewards from the nature of the work itself and are thus quite sensitive to, and easily frustrated by, poor facilities and inadequate resources. Software project managers must be effective in dealing with the factors that motivate and frustrate programmmers if they are to maintain high product quality, high programmer productivity, and high job satisfaction.

Adequacy of training. Product implementation is only one aspect of software engineering, yet this is the only phase of product development and maintenance taught in many educational institutions. Some institutions offer courses that deal with the topics of analysis and design, testing, maintenance, and software project management techniques, but these institutions are few in number.

Boehm has described the skills most lacking in entry-level programmers (BOE76b). His list includes inability to:

1. Express oneself clearly in English.
2. Develop and validate software requirements and design specifications.
3. Work within applications area.
4. Perform software maintenance.
5. Perform economic analyses.
6. Work with project management techniques.
7. Work in groups.

Reasons for lack of these skills are not hard to find. The full economic and social impact of software engineering has only recently been realized, and there is a predictable time lag between educational supply and industrial demand. Until now, most programmers have been trained as computer scientists, electrical engineers, accountants, or mathematicians, not as software engineers. Computer science education is concerned with providing a basic understanding of the underlying theories and concepts of information and information processing (we interpret these terms in the broadest possible sense), whereas software engineering is concerned with analyzing, designing, constructing, testing, verifying, documenting, operating, and maintaining software products. Universities have traditionally produced computer scientists, and industries have traditionally sought software engineers. This has resulted in entry-level programmers who are poorly prepared to become software engineers.

Management skills. Software projects are often supervised by managers who have little, if any, knowledge of software engineering. Many of the problems in software project management are unique; even managers experienced in management of computer hardware projects find software project management to be difficult due to the differences in design methods, notations, development tools, and issues of concern. Often a software engineer must report to a hardware engineer or an accountant whose only experience with software was an introductory FORTRAN course in which he or she excelled. This is indeed an unfortunate situation for both manager and managee.

On the other hand, the practice of "promoting" technically competent individuals who have little management inclination and no management training into software project management often produces equally unsatisfactory results. Many organizations offer project management training to software engineers to prepare them for project management tasks, but this is not always successful. In part, this may be due to the low social needs of many software people and the need for good social skills in managers.

Appropriate goals. The primary goal of software engineering is development of software products that are appropriate for their intended use. Ideally, every software product should provide optimal levels of generality, efficiency, and reliability. Inordinate effort devoted to marginally useful features and excessive efficiency are as detrimental to programmer productivity as lack of sufficient reliability and efficiency are to product quality. An appropriate trade-off between productivity and quality factors can be achieved by adhering to the goals and requirements established for the software product during project planning.

Rising expectations. The most pervasive problem in software engineering is that of rising expectations. There are two interrelated aspects to rising expectations: first is the concern for how much functionality, reliability, and performance can be provided by a given amount of development effort; and second is the issue of fundamental limitations of software technology. Progress is constantly being made in the development of tools and techniques to improve software quality and programmer productivity; however, the diversity, size, and complexity of software applications are growing at a much faster rate than our ability to cope with the increasing demand.

Dramatic advances in hardware technology have created the expectation that software technology will advance at an equally fast pace. Each report of success in software engineering exerts increased pressure for even higher quality and greater productivity. It is not clear whether our current inability to meet the increasing demand for software is inherent in the nature of software and human problem-solving capabilities or whether it is due to the immaturity of the software engineering discipline.

We are convinced that use of systematic techniques to develop and maintain software products results in increased programmer productivity and improved product quality. Future advances will certainly improve the situation. However, the extent to which the concepts discussed in this text can satisfy constantly rising expectations remains an open question.

Other factors. There are many other factors that influence programmer productivity, including familiarity with, access to, and stability of the computing system used to develop or modify the software; the memory and timing constraint for the software product; experience with the programming language; and data-base size. Walston and Felix (WAL77) and Boehm (BOE81) have conducted studies of many factors that influence quality and productivity. While our discussion is not exhaustive, it does indicate that a large number of factors influence the quality of software products and the productivity of software engineers.

1.4 MANAGERIAL ISSUES

Technical and managerial activities are equally important to the success of a software project. Managers control the resources and the environment in which technical activities occur. Managers also have ultimate responsibility for ensuring that software products are delivered on time and within cost estimates, and that products exhibit the functional and quality attributes desired by the customer. Other management responsibilities include developing business plans, recruiting customers, developing marketing strategies, and recruiting and training employees.

The concerns of project management include methods for organizing and monitoring a project; cost estimation techniques; resource allocation policies; budgetary control; project milestones; assessing progress, reallocating resources, and making schedule adjustments; establishing quality assurance procedures; maintaining control of various product versions; fostering communication among project members; communicating with customers; developing contractual agreements with customers; and ensuring that the legal and contractual terms of the project are observed.

In an effort to identify some of the major problem areas in software project management, Thayer, Pyster, and Wood hypothesized 20 potential problem areas and surveyed 294 individuals for their opinions on the importance of the problem, the nature of the problem (technical, managerial, or both), and the nature of a possible solution to the problem (THA81). Problems were categorized as planning problems, organizing problems, staffing problems, directing problems, and controlling problems.

Some of the problems identified by respondents as important management problems were:

1. Planning for software engineering projects is generally poor.
2. Procedures and techniques for the selection of project managers are poor.
3. The accountability of many software engineering projects is poor, leaving some question as to who is responsible for various project functions.
4. The ability to accurately estimate the resources required to accomplish a software development project is poor.
5. Success criteria for software development projects are frequently inappropriate. This results in software products that are unreliable, difficult to use, and difficult to maintain.
6. Decision rules to aid in selecting the proper organizational structure are not available.
7. Decision rules to aid in selecting the correct management techniques for software engineering projects are not available.
8. Procedures, methods, and techniques for designing a project control system that will enable project managers to successfully control their project are not readily available.
9. Procedures, techniques, strategies, and aids that will provide visibility of progress to the project manager are not available.
10. Standards and techniques for measuring the quality of performance and the quantity of production expected from programmers and data processing analysts are not available.

Some of the methods mentioned for solving these problems were (solutions are not paired with problems):

1. Educate and train top management, project managsrs, and software developers.
2. Enforce the use of standards, procedures, and documentation.
3. Analyze data from prior software projects to determine effective methods.
4. Define objectives in terms of quality desired.
5. Define quality in terms of deliverables.
6. Establish success priority criteria.
7. Allow for contingencies.
8. Develop truthful, accurate cost and schedule estimates that are accepted by management and customer, and manage to them.
9. Select project managers based on ability to manage software projects, rather than on technical ability or availability.
10. Make specific work assignments to software developers and apply job performance standards.

In a subsequent paper, Thayer and colleagues report that a survey of software engineering project personnel failed to show any predominant techniques that could account for either the success or failure of software projects (THA82). Thayer and colleagues point out that while there is some consensus on the nature of problems in software project management, there is little agreement concerning the nature of possible solutions. Although it is widely recognized that technological and managerial issues are equally important in software engineering, improvements in management techniques have not kept pace with advances in technology. Perhaps this is because software engineers believe that management per se is not their task, and professional managers do not have the technical knowledge to deal with managerial problems in software engineering.

Another factor contributing to the problems of software project management is that programmers and managers tend to have differing perceptions. Problem solutions originated by managers are often perceived by the programmers as fixing minor aspects of the situation. Similarly, problems perceived by programmers are often regarded as insignificant by managers.

1.5 OVERVIEW OF THE TEXT

Chapter 1 has provided an introduction to software engineering. Some definitions were presented, and factors that influence software quality and programmer productivity were discussed. Project size categories, the distribution of effort among software development and maintenance activities, and variations in programmer productivity were examined. Project management issues were mentioned, and management problem areas were enumerated.

Chapter 2 presents various considerations involved in planning a software project. Format and contents of the *System Definition* and the *Project Plan* are discussed. The steps required to plan a software project are presented, the resulting work products are discussed, and some factors to be considered in developing project goals and product requirements are indicated. Various life-cycle models are presented and contrasted, and typical documents, milestones, reviews, and audits for a software development project are described. The role of prototypes in software development is discussed. Organizational structures, programming team structures, and mechanisms for assigning and evaluating work activities are presented. Planning for configuration management, quality assurance, independent validation and verification, and phase-dependent tools and techniques are also discussed.

Chapter 3 describes software cost factors and cost estimation techniques. A quantification scheme developed by Boehm is used to indicate the relative influence of various cost factors. Expert judgment, the Delphi technique, and the principal features of the Constructive Cost Model (COCOMO) are presented. Estimation of staffing level using Rayleigh curves and COCOMO is described, and techniques for estimating software maintenance costs are presented.

Chapter 4 is concerned with software requirements definition. The format and contents of a requirements document are described, formal techniques for specifying software requirements are presented, and some notations and automated tools for specifying requirements are discussed.

Chapter 5 considers the topic of software design. Fundamental principles of design are presented, and techniques for both architectural design and detailed design are discussed. Design notations are discussed, and some popular design methods are described and contrasted. Detailed design considerations are provided, and test plans, milestones, inspections, reviews, and design guidelines are discussed.

Chapter 6 discusses implementation issues. Structured coding techniques, coding style, coding standards and guidelines, program unit notebooks, and internal documentation of source code are discussed.

Chapter 7 describes features of modern programming languages that support development and maintenance of software products. Strong type checking, separate compilation, user-defined data types, data encapsulation and data abstraction, flexible scoping rules, generic routines, user-defined exception handling, and concurrency mechanisms are discussed. The Ada programming language is used for purposes of illustration. The deficiencies of Pascal for developing software products are described, and the differing philosophies of type checking and exception handling in PL/1 and Ada are contrasted.

Chapter 8 presents techniques for assessing the quality of software products. Techniques discussed include quality assurance procedures, walkthroughs, inspections, static analysis, symbolic execution, formal verification, unit testing, and system testing.

Chapter 9 examines software maintenance issues. Activities during the development cycle that enhance maintainability of software are discussed, managerial aspects of maintenance are described, source code metrics are presented, and automated tools for maintaining software products are discussed.

1.6 END NOTES

During the past decade a large body of software engineering literature has been generated. In addition to the cited references for Chapter 1, we have included a compilation of important references in software engineering. Texts focused on specific topics, such as design or testing, are referenced in the appropriate chapter. We make no claim to completeness, and we apologize in advance for omissions; however, these texts will lead the interested reader to other references.

Alexander, C.: *Notes on the Synthesis of Form*, Harvard University Press, Cambridge, MA, 1970.

Baker, S.: *The Practical Stylist*, Tho. Crowell, New York, 1977.

Boehm, B., et al.: *Characteristics of Software Quality*, North-Holland, Amsterdam, 1978.

————: *Software Engineering Economics*, Prentice-Hall, Englewood Cliffs, N.J., 1981.

————:"Keeping the Lid on Software Costs," *Computerworld*, January 1982.

Brooks, F.: *The Mythical Man-Month*, Addison-Wesley, Reading, Mass., 1975.

Buckle, J.: *Managing Software Projects*, MacDonald and Janes, London, 1977.

Cleland, D., and W. King: *System Analysis and Project Management*, McGraw-Hill, New York, 1975.

Gunning, R.: *The Techniques of Clear Writing*, McGraw-Hill, New York, 1968.

Horowitz, E.: *Practical Strategies for Developing Large Software Systems*, Addison-Wesley, Reading, Mass., 1978.

Hughes, J., and J. Michtom: *A Structured Approach to Programming*, Prentice-Hall, Englewood Cliffs, N.J., 1977.

Hunke, H. (ed): *Symposium on Software Engineering Environments*, Elsevier North-Holland, Amsterdam, 1981.

Jensen, R., and C. Tonies: *Software Engineering*, Prentice-Hall, Englewood Cliffs, N.J., 1978.

Kernighan, B., and P. Plauger: *Software Tools*, Addison-Wesley, Reading, Mass., 1976.

———— and ————: *The Elements of Programming Style*, McGraw-Hill, New York, 1978.

———— and————: *Software Tools in Pascal*, Addison-Wesley, Reading, Mass., 1981.

Ledgard, H.: *Programming Proverbs*, Hayden Book Co., Rochelle Park, N.J., 1975.

Linger, R., et al.: *Structured Programming*, Addison-Wesley, Reading, Mass., 1979.

McGowan, C., and J. Kelly: *Top-Down Structured Programming Techniques*, Petrocelli/Charter, New York, 1975.

Metzger, P.: *Managing a Software Project*, Prentice-Hall, Englewood Cliffs, N.J., 1973.

Myers, G.: *Reliable Software through Composite Design*, Petrocelli/Charter, New York, 1975.

————: *Software Reliability Principles and Practices*, Wiley, New York, 1976.

Newman, E.: *Strictly Speaking*, Bobbs-Merrill, Indianapolis, Ind., 1974.

Perrin, P., and W. Ebbert: *Writers Guide and Index to English*, Scott-Foresman, Glenview, Ill., 1972.

Pressman, R.: *Software Engineering: A Practitioner's Approach*, McGraw-Hill, New York, 1982.

Riddle, W., and R. Fairley (eds.): *Software Development Tools*, Springer-Verlag, Berlin, 1980.

Shooman, M.: *Software Engineering*, McGraw-Hill, New York, 1983.

Simon, H.: *The Sciences of the Artificial*, MIT Press, Cambridge, Mass., 1981.

Strunk, W., and E. White: *The Elements of Style*, MacMillan, New York, 1979.

Tausworthe, R.: *Standardized Development of Computer Software*, Prentice-Hall, Englewood Cliffs, N.J., 1977.

Tichy, H.: *Effective Writing for Engineers, Managers, and Scientists*, Wiley, New York, 1976.

Wasserman, A., and P. Freeman (eds): *Software Engineering Education*, Springer-Verlag, Berlin, 1976.

Wegner, P. (ed.): *Research Directions in Software Technology,* MIT Press, Cambridge, Mass., 1978.

Weinberg, G.: *The Psychology of Computer Programming,* Van Nostrand Reinhold, New York, 1971.

Yeh, R.: *Current Trends in Programming Methodology,* vols. I through IV, Prentice-Hall, Englewood Cliffs, N.J., 1977, 1978.

Yourdon, E.: *Techniques of Program Structure and Design,* Prentice-Hall, Englewood Cliffs, N.J., 1975.

————: *Managing Software Projects,* Yourdan Press, New York.

Zelkowitz, M.: "Perspectives on Software Engineering," *ACM Computing Surveys,* vol. 10, no. 2, June 1978.

In addition, there are several journals, periodicals, tutorials, and conference proceedings that should become familiar to the student of software engineering. They include:

IEEE Transactions on Software Engineering (TSE)
Communications of the ACM
COMPUTER (IEEE Computer Society)
Software Engineering Notes (ACM SIGSOFT Newsletter)
The Journal of Systems and Software
Software Practice and Experience
SIGPLAN Notices (ACM SIGPLAN Newsletter)
ACM Computing Surveys
Proceedings of the International Conferences on Software Engineering
Tutorials published by the IEEE Computer Society:
Software Design Techniques, edited by Freeman and Wasserman
Models and Metrics for Software Management and Engineering, edited by V. Basili
Structured Testing, edited by T. McCabe
Software Maintenance, edited by G. Parikh and N. Zvengintzov
End User Facilities, edited by J. Larson
Programming Language Design, edited by A. Wasserman
Software Configuration Management, edited by Bryan, Chadbourne, and Siegel
Human Factors in Software Development, edited by B. Curtis
Software Cost Estimating and Life-Cycle Control, edited by L. Putnam
Software System Design, edited by Riddle and Wileden
Software Testing and Validation Techniques, edited by Miller and Howden
Automated Tools for Software Engineering, edited by E. Miller
Software Development Environments, edited by A. Wasserman
Software Design Strategies, edited by Bergland and Gordon
Structured Programming, edited by *Basili and Baker*
Computer System Requirements, edited by K. Thurber
Software Management, edited by D. Reifer
Programmer Productivity, edited by C. Jones

REFERENCES

(BAI64) Bairdain, E.: *Research Studies of Programmers and Programming,* unpublished study, New York, 1964.

(BOE76a) Boehm, B.: "Software Engineering," *IEEE Transactions on Computers,* vol. C-25, no. 12, December 1976.

(BOE76b) Boehm, B.: "Software Engineering Education: Some Industry Needs," in *Software En-*

gineering Education: Needs and Objectives, edited by P. Freeman and A. Wasserman, Springer-Verlag, Berlin, 1976.

(BOE81) Boehm, B.: *Software Engineering Economics,* Prentice-Hall, Englewood Cliffs, NJ, 1981.

(BOE83) Boehm, B.: "The Hardware/Software Cost Ratio: Is It a Myth?" *IEEE COMPUTER,* vol. 16, no. 3, March 1983.

(BRO75) Brooks, F.: *The Mythical Man-Month,* Addison-Wesley, Reading, MA, 1975.

(COU78) Cougar, D., and R. Zawacki: "What Motivates DP Professionals?" *Datamation,* September 1978.

(DAT80) "News in Perspective," *Datamation,* September 1980, p. 124.

(DIJ72) Dijkstra, E.: "Notes on Structured Programming," *Structured Programming,* Academic Press, 1972.

(IEE83) *IEEE Standard Glossary of Software Engineering Terminology,* IEEE Standard 729-1983.

(NAU76) Naur, P., et al. (eds): *Software Engineering: Concepts and Techniques,* Petrocelli/Charter, New York, 1976.

(SAC68) Sackman, H., et al.: "Exploratory Experimental Studies Comparing Online and Offline Programming Performance," *Comm. ACM,* vol. 11, no. 1, January 1968.

(SCH81) Schindler, M.: "The Software Decade," *Electronic Design,* Jan. 8, 1981.

(THA81) Thayer, R., et al.: "Major Issues in Software Engineering Project Management, *IEEE TSE,* vol. SE-7, no. 4, July 1981.

(THA82) Thayer, R., et al.: "Validating Solutions to Major Problems in Software Engineering Project Management," *IEEE COMPUTER,* vol. 15, no. 8, August 1982.

(USB81) U.S. Bureau of the Census, *Statistical Abstract of the United States,* 1981 (102d ed.), Washington, D.C.

(WAL77) Walston, C., and C. Felix: "A Method of Program Measurement and Estimation," *IBM Systems Journal,* vol. 16, no. 1, 1977.

(YOU75) Yourdon, E.: *Techniques of Program Structure and Design,* Prentice-Hall, Englewood Cliffs, N.J. 1975.

EXERCISES

1.1 (*a*) Develop a list of 20 or 30 software quality attributes.

(*b*) Arrange the attributes in hierarchical fashion; i.e., try to describe high-level quality attributes in terms of more fundamental attributes. For example, maintainability is a high-level attribute that can be described in terms of attributes such as modularity, clarity of documentation, etc.

(*c*) Provide a concise definition for each of the quality attributes.

(*d*) What criteria do you use to classify quality attributes as "high-level" or "low-level"?

1.2 (*a*) Tailor your list of quality attributes from Exercise 1.1 to a specific software project (either real or hypothetical) by ranking your list in order of importance for the project.

(*b*) How can attainment of these attributes be determined?

1.3 In an organization or software project of your choice, how does the time and effort devoted to various activities compare with the levels of effort shown in Figure 1.2? If you do not work in a software organization, seek out one and compare their activities with those described in Chapter 1.

1.4 (*a*) How does the organization of your choice measure programmer productivity?

(*b*) Will they share productivity data with you?

(*c*) If not, why not? If so, how do they compare with the data presented in Chapter 1?

1.5 (*a*) Interview programmers and managers in the organization of your choice to determine management problem areas.

(*b*) How do the perceptions of managers and programmers differ?

1.6 (*a*) Add to the list of factors that influence software quality and programmer productivity presented in Table 1.1. Draw on your own experience, the experiences of your colleagues, and the professional programmers in an organization of your choice.

(*b*) Rank the list in order from most important to least important. Provide reasons to justify your ranking.

(*c*) What factors influence your ranking?

(*d*) What can be done in the organization of your choice to ease these problems? Distinguish between what can be done by programmers and what can be done by managers.

1.7 (*a*) Develop a list of skills and traits possessed by excellent programmers.

(*b*) Which of these skills are most lacking in your colleagues? In you?

(*c*) Develop a list of skills and traits possessed by excellent software project managers.

(*d*) Which of these management skills, in your opinion, can be taught in a classroom? Which are best learned "on the job"? Which are inherent in one's personality? Justify your answers.

1.8 Verify the data presented in Section 1.3 by consulting other sources. How do you explain the discrepancies that may be uncovered?

TWO

PLANNING A SOFTWARE PROJECT

INTRODUCTION

Lack of planning is a primary cause of schedule slippage, cost overruns, poor quality, and high maintenance costs for software. Careful planning is required for both the development process and the work products in order to avoid these problems. It is often said that early planning is impossible because precise information concerning project goals, customer needs, and product constraints is not available at the beginning of a software project, but a major purpose of the planning phase is to clarify goals, needs, and constraints. The difficulty of planning should not discourage this most important activity.

A software product becomes better understood as it progresses through analysis, design, and implementation; however, a software project should not be commissioned until enough information is available to permit preliminary planning. It must be recognized that preliminary plans will be modified as the work products evolve; planning for change is one of the key aspects of successful planning.

The steps required to plan a software project are listed in Table 2.1 and discussed in subsequent sections of this chapter.

2.1 DEFINING THE PROBLEM

Every man-made entity is first a concept in someone's mind. Computing systems, like other products of technology, are developed in response to perceived needs. Sources of software product ideas include externally generated customer requirements, internal organizational requirements, marketing plans, and organizational

Table 2.1 Planning a software project

Defining the problem

1. Develop a definitive statement of the problem to be solved. Include a description of the present situation, problem constraints, and a statement of the goals to be achieved. The problem statement should be phrased in the customer's terminology.
2. Justify a computerized solution strategy for the problem.
3. Identify the functions to be provided by, and the constraints on, the hardware subsystem, the software subsystem, and the people subsystem.
4. Determine system-level goals and requirements for the development process and the work products.
5. Establish high-level acceptance criteria for the system.

Developing a solution strategy

6. Outline several solution strategies, without regard for constraints.
7. Conduct a feasibility study for each strategy.
8. Recommend a solution strategy, indicating why other strategies were rejected.
9. Develop a list of priorities for product characteristics.

Planning the development process

10. Define a life-cycle model and an organizational structure for the project.
11. Plan the configuration management, quality assurance, and validation activities.
12. Determine phase-dependent tools, techniques, and notations to be used.
13. Establish preliminary cost estimates for system development.
14. Establish a preliminary development schedule.
15. Establish preliminary staffing estimates.
16. Develop preliminary estimates of the computing resources required to operate and maintain the system.
17. Prepare a glossary of terms.
18. Identify sources of information, and refer to them throughout the project plan.

mission plans. Most software development organizations are very selective in deciding which products to develop; not all targets of opportunity are exploited. The decision to proceed is usually based on the outcome of a feasibility study.

The first step in planning a software project is to prepare, in the customer's terminology, a concise statement of the problem to be solved and the constraints that exist for its solution. The definitive problem statement should include a description of the present situation and the goals to be achieved by the new system.

Note that the customer's problem, from the customer's point of view, is perhaps a payroll problem, an inventory problem, or an air traffic control problem, and not a problem of DMA channels, sorting algorithms, or relational data bases.

Problem definition requires a thorough understanding of the problem domain and the problem environment. Techniques for gaining this knowledge include customer interviews, observation of problem tasks, and actual performance of the tasks by the planner. The planner must be highly skilled in the techniques of problem definition because different customer representatives will have different viewpoints, biases, and prejudices that will influence their perception of the problem area. In addition, customer representatives may not be familiar with the capabilities that a computer can offer in their situation, and customer representatives are seldom able to formulate their problems in a manner that yields to logical, algorithmic analysis.

Sometimes, computing systems are built to remedy a symptom rather than the root cause of a problem. This occurs when the true problem is understood but cannot be solved due to economic, political, or social circumstances, or when the customer is unable to communicate the true problem, or when the planner fails to understand the customer's explanation of the problem.

The second step in planning a software project is to determine the appropriateness of a computerized solution. In addition to being cost-effective, a computerized system must be socially and politically acceptable. To be cost-effective, a new software product must provide the same services and information as the old system using less time and personnel, or it must provide services and information that were impractical without the new system. A system that displaces numerous workers may be economically and technically feasible, but it may not be socially or politically acceptable to the customer.

Having determined, at least in preliminary fashion, that a computerized solution to the problem is appropriate, attention is focused on the roles to be played by the major subsystems of the computing system. A computing system consists of people subsystems, hardware subsystems, and software subsystems plus the interconnections among subsystems. People subsystems include operators, maintenance personnel, and end users. Hardware subsystems include the computing hardware and peripheral devices, and may include other devices such as process control sensors and actuators or tracking antennas and radars. Software subsystems include the software to be developed plus existing software that may be used "as is" or in modified form.

The functions to be performed by each major subsystem must be identified, the interactions among subsystems must be established, and developmental and operational constraints must be determined for each major subsystem. Constraints specify numbers and types of equipment, numbers and skill levels of personnel, and software characteristics such as performance, accuracy, and level of reliability. Precise allocation of functions among hardware, software, and people may be difficult during preliminary planning; it may be necessary to first perform some detailed analysis. Nevertheless, preliminary definition of major subsystem functions should be attempted.

2.1.1 Goals and Requirements

Given a concise statement of the problem and an indication of the constraints that exist for its solution, preliminary goals and requirements can be formulated. Goals are targets for achievement, and serve to establish the framework for a software development project. Goals apply to both the development process and the work products, and goals can be either qualitative or quantitative:

A qualitative process goal: the development process should enhance the professional skills of quality assurance personnel.

A quantitative process goal: the system should be delivered within 12 months.
A qualitative product goal: the system should make users' jobs more interesting.
A quantitative product goal: the system should reduce the cost of a transaction by
    25 percent.

Some goals apply to every project and every product. For instance, every
software product should be useful, reliable, understandable, and cost-effective.
Every development process should deliver work products on time and within cost
estimates, and should provide project personnel with the opportunity to learn new
skills. Other goals, such as transportability, early delivery of subset capabilities,
and ease of use by nonprogrammers, depend on the particular situation.

Requirements specify capabilities that a system must provide in order to solve
a problem. Requirements include functional requirements, performance requirements, and requirements for the hardware, firmware, software, and user interfaces.
Requirements may also specify development standards and quality assurance standards for both project and product. Requirements should be quantified whenever
possible. Quantified requirements such as

1. Phase accuracy shall be within 0.5 degrees.
2. Response to external interrupts shall be 0.25 second maximum.
3. System shall reside in 50K bytes of primary memory, excluding file buffers.
4. System shall be fully operational 95 percent of each 24-hour period.

can be used as the basis for acceptance testing of the delivered system. Qualitative
requirements such as

1. Accuracy shall be sufficient to support mission.
2. System shall provide real-time response.
3. System shall make efficient use of primary memory.
4. System shall be 99 percent reliable.

are often meaningless and can result in misunderstandings and disagreements
between developers and customers. It is difficult to quantify requirements in the
planning phase because usually it is not clear what is needed to solve the problem,
or what can be achieved within the solution constraints. Nevertheless, every effort
should be made to formulate meaningful requirements, and to state the methods that
will be used to verify each requirement.

High-level goals and requirements can often be expressed in terms of quality
attributes that the system should possess. These high-level quality attributes can in
turn be expressed in terms of attributes that can be built into the work products. For
example, reliability can be expressed in terms of source-code accuracy, robustness,
completeness, and consistency. Each of these terms can be carefully defined in
terms of more specific attributes of the source code. For instance, accuracy can be
defined as the extent to which the results produced by the code are sufficiently
precise to satisfy their intended usage. This can be translated into specific require-

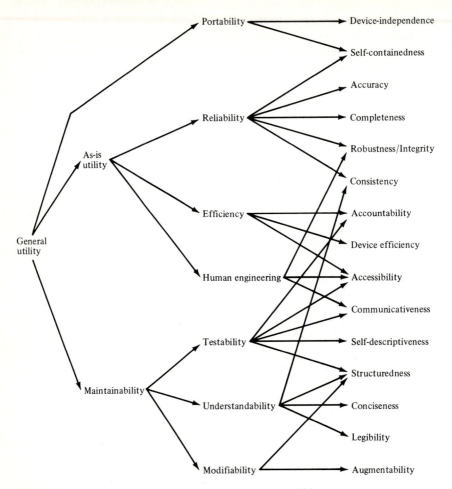

Figure 2.1 Software quality characteristic tree *(Boehm et al., 1976).*

ments for any particular problem. For example, "phase accuracy shall be 0.5 degrees" is an accuracy requirement that can be used to assess the quality of software in a navigation system. A decomposition of quality attributes into source-code characteristics is illustrated in Figure 2.1 (BOE76). Table 2.2 provides definitions for some of the terms used in Figure 2.1 (IEE83).

It is important that high-level acceptance criteria for the system be established during the planning phase. Lack of clearly stated, quantified acceptance criteria can lead to serious misunderstandings between customer and developer. Acceptance criteria must be stated in terms that can be verified by well-defined methods, such as inspection, analysis, or tests to be performed on the resulting work products. Each requirement should include the method that will be used to verify it.

Plans describe the mechanisms to be used in achieving goals and requirements. For instance, the goal of delivering work products on time can be expressed in terms of reaching each project milestone on time. A milestone is a significant event in the

Table 2.2 Glossary of quality attributes (IEE83)

Portability: The ease with which software can be transferred from one computer system or environment to another.

Reliability: The ability of a program to perform a required function under stated conditions for a stated period of time.

Efficiency: The extent to which software performs its intended functions with a minimum consumption of computing resources.

Accuracy: (1) A qualitative assessment of freedom from error. (2) A quantitative measure of the magnitude of error, preferably expressed as a function of the relative error.

Error: A discrepancy between a computed value or condition and the true, specified, or theoretically correct value or condition.

Robustness: The extent to which software can continue to operate correctly despite the introduction of invalid inputs.

Correctness: (1) The extent to which software is free from design defects and from coding defects; that is, fault-free. (2) The extent to which software meets its specified requirements. (3) The extent to which software meets user expectations.

software product life cycle; examples of milestones include completion of requirements analysis, completion of design, and integration and successful testing of all system components.

In order to plan for reaching each milestone on schedule, questions such as the following must be answered:

1. How many milestones are appropriate?
2. When do they occur?
3. What resources are required to reach each milestone?
4. Who will be responsible for achieving the milestones?
5. What must be true to permit achievement of each milestone?
6. Exactly what will constitute achievement of each milestone?

Consideration of these questions will lead into issues such as life-cycle models, cost estimation, and project staffing levels. Tables 2.3 and 2.4 present some factors to

Table 2.3 Some factors to consider in project planning

1. Estimation techniques to be used; accuracy required
2. Life-cycle model, control functions, and reviews
3. Organizational structure
4. Level of formality in specifications, test plans, etc.
5. Level of verification and validation (independent group?)
6. Level of configuration management required
7. Level of quality assurance required
8. Follow-on maintenance responsibilities
9. Tools to be developed and used
10. Personnel recruitment and training

Table 2.4 Some factors to consider in setting project goals

1. New capabilities to be provided
2. Old capabilities to be preserved/enhanced
3. Level of user sophistication
4. Efficiency requirements
5. Reliability requirements
6. Likely modifications
7. Early subsets and implementation priorities
8. Portability requirements
9. Security concerns

consider in establishing goals and requirements for software products and development processes.

2.2 DEVELOPING A SOLUTION STRATEGY

The tendency to adopt the first solution that occurs to us is a major problem in software engineering. One way of avoiding this problem is to first develop a solution strategy. A solution strategy is not a detailed solution plan, but rather a general statement concerning the nature of possible solutions. Strategy factors include considerations such as batch or time-sharing; database or file system; graphics or text; and real-time or off-line processing. A solution strategy should account for all external factors that are visible to the product users, and a strategy should be phrased to permit alternative approaches to product design.

Several strategies should be considered before one is adopted; however, one or more solution strategies must be chosen by the planners in order to perform feasibility studies and prepare preliminary cost estimates. The selected strategy provides a framework for design and implementation of the software product.

Solution strategies should be generated without regard for feasibility because it is not possible for humans to be both creative and critical at the same time. Typically, an unreasonable idea will lead to other ideas, some of which may be very reasonable. Often, the best strategy is a composite of ideas from several different approaches, and the best solution strategy may become apparent only after all the obvious solutions have been enumerated. Idea generation is best done by a group of people who have been trained in the techniques of brainstorming (OSB56).

The feasibility of each proposed solution strategy can be established by examining solution constraints. Constraints prescribe the boundaries of the solution space; feasibility analysis determines whether a proposed strategy is possible within those boundaries. A solution strategy is feasible if the project goals and requirements can be satisfied within the constraints of available time, resources, and technology using that strategy. Some iteration and trade-off decisions may be required to bring feasibility and constraints into balance.

Techniques for determining the feasibility of a solution strategy include case studies, worst-case analysis, simulation, and construction of prototypes. A prototype differs from a simulation model in that a prototype incorporates some components of the actual system. Prototype implementations usually have limited functionality, low reliability, and poor performance characteristics. Prototypes are constructed during the planning phase to examine technical issues and to simulate user displays, report formats, and dialogues. The latter mechanism is particularly valuable for obtaining a better understanding of the customer's needs.

When recommending a solution strategy, it is extremely important to document the reasons for rejecting other strategies. This provides justification for the recommended strategy, and may prevent ill-considered revisions at some later date.

A solution strategy should include a priority list of product features. There are several important reasons for stating product priorities. At some later time in the development cycle it may be necessary to postpone or eliminate some system capabilities due to inconsistencies in the requirements, technical bottlenecks, or time and cost overruns. At that time, it is essential that high-level guidance be available to indicate the priorities of essential features, less important features, and "nice if" features. Without this guidance, a designer or programmer may make serious mistakes in judgment, resulting in customer dissatisfaction with the delivered product. Product priorities are also useful to indicate the manner in which capabilities can be developed and phased into an evolving system. Many software engineers advocate development of systems as a series of successive enhancements to a kernel system. Product priorities are useful in planning the successive versions to be built.

2.3 PLANNING THE DEVELOPMENT PROCESS

As illustrated in Table 2.1, planning the software development process involves several important considerations. The first consideration is to define a product life-cycle model. The software life cycle encompasses all activities required to define, develop, test, deliver, operate, and maintain a software product. Different models emphasize different aspects of the life cycle, and no single life-cycle model is appropriate for all software products. It is important to define a life-cycle model for each software project because the model provides a basis for categorizing and controlling the various activities required to develop and maintain a software product. A life-cycle model that is understood and accepted by all concerned parties improves project communication and enhances project manageability, resource allocation, cost control, and product quality. Life-cycle models discussed here include the phased model, the cost model, the prototype model, and the successive versions model.

2.3.1 The Phased Life-Cycle Model

The phased model segments the software life cycle into a series of successive activities. Each phase requires well-defined input information, utilizes well-defined processes, and results in well-defined products. Resources are required to complete the processes in each phase, and each phase is accomplished through the application of explicit methods, tools, and techniques.

In this text, we consider the phased model to consist of the following phases: analysis, design, implementation, system testing, and maintenance. The basic phased model is presented in Figure 2.2. This model is sometimes called a "waterfall chart," the implication being that products cascade from one level to the next in smooth progression.

Analysis consists of two subphases: planning and requirements definition. Major activities during planning are summarized in Table 2.1. They include understanding the customer's problem, performing a feasibility study, developing a recommended solution strategy, determining the acceptance criteria, and planning the development process. The products of planning are a *System Definition* and a *Project Plan*. The *System Definition* is typically expressed in English or some other natural language, and may incorporate charts, figures, graphs, tables, and equations of various kinds. The exact notations used in the *System Definition* are highly dependent on the problem area. Obviously, one uses different terminology to describe an accounting system than to describe a process control system. The format of a *System Definition* is illustrated in Table 2.5.

The *Project Plan* contains the life-cycle model to be used, the organizational structure for the project, the preliminary development schedule, preliminary cost and resource estimates, preliminary staffing requirements, tools and techniques to be used, and standard practices to be followed. Items to be included in the *Project Plan* are listed in Table 2.6.

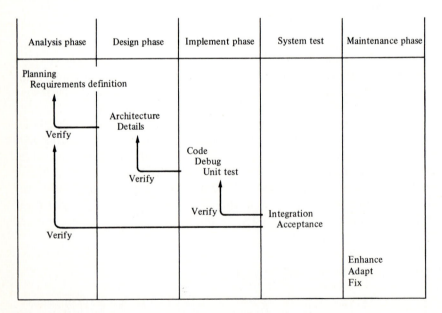

Figure 2.2 The phased model of the software life cycle.

Table 2.5 Format of a *System Definition*

Section 1: Problem definition
Section 2: System justification
Section 3: Goals for the system and the project
Section 4: Constraints on the system and the project
Section 5: Functions to be provided (hardware/software/people)
Section 6: User characteristics
Section 7: Development/operating/maintenance environments
Section 8: Solution strategy
Section 9: Priorities for system features
Section 10: System acceptance criteria
Section 11: Sources of information
Section 12: Glossary of terms

Table 2.6 Format of a *Project Plan*

Section 1: Life-cycle model
            Terminology/milestones/work products

Section 2: Organizational structure
            Management structure/team structure/
            work breakdown structure/statements of
            work

Section 3: Preliminary staffing and resource requirements
            Staffing and resource schedule

Section 4: Preliminary development schedule
            PERT network/Gantt charts

Section 5: Preliminary cost estimate

Section 6: Project monitoring and control mechanisms

Section 7: Tools and techniques to be used

Section 8: Programming languages

Section 9: Testing requirements

Section 10: Supporting documents required

Section 11: Manner of demonstration and delivery

Section 12: Training schedule and materials

Section 13: Installation plan

Section 14: Maintenance considerations

Section 15: Method and time of delivery

Section 16: Method and time of payment

Section 17: Sources of information

During the planning phase cost estimates and work schedules will be preliminary in nature, because it is usually not possible to make accurate estimates without doing some design. Early cost estimates are thus unavoidably preliminary. Current contracting practices often require that final cost and schedule information be provided during the planning phase. This situation, coupled with the competitive nature of business, is a major factor that contributes to cost overruns and late delivery of software products. In recognition of these facts, many organizations use a series of successively refined cost and schedule estimates. Preliminary estimates are prepared during the planning phase. Refined estimates are presented at a preliminary design review, and the final cost and schedule are established at the critical design review. Several different estimates, representing a range of capabilities, may be presented during the reviews. In this manner the customer and developer can negotiate a cost-effective product.

Requirements definition is concerned with identifying the basic functions of the software component in a hardware/software/people system. Emphasis is placed on what the software is to do and the constraints under which it will perform its functions. Deciding exactly how the software will be implemented is deferred until the design phase. The product of requirements definition is a specification that describes the processing environment, the required software functions, performance constraints on the software (size, speed, machine configuration), exception handling, subsets and implementation priorities, probable changes and likely modifications, and the acceptance criteria for the software.

In the phased model, software design follows analysis. Design is concerned with identifying software components (functions, data streams, and data stores), specifying relationships among components, specifying software structure, maintaining a record of design decisions, and providing a blueprint for the implementation phase. Design consists of architectural design and detailed design.

Architectural design involves identifying the software components, decoupling and decomposing them into processing modules and conceptual data structures, and specifying the interconnections among components. Detailed design is concerned with the details of "how to": how to package the processing modules and how to implement the processing algorithms, data structures, and interconnections among modules and data structures.

Detailed design involves adaptation of existing code, modification of standard algorithms, invention of new algorithms, design of data representations, and packaging of the software product. Detailed design is not the same as implementation. Detailed design is strongly influenced by the programming language used to implement the system, but detailed design is not concerned with syntactic aspects of the implementation language or the level of detail inherent in expression evaluation and assignment statements.

The implementation phase of software development involves translation of design specifications into source code, and debugging, documentation, and unit testing of the source code. Modern programming languages provide many features to enhance the quality of source code. These include structured control constructs, built-in and user-defined data types, secure type checking, flexible scope rules, exception handling mechanisms, concurrency constructs, and separate compilation of modules. Some of these features can be simulated in primitive programming languages by use of disciplined programming style.

Errors discovered during the implementation phase may include errors in the data interfaces between routines, logical errors in the algorithms, errors in data structure layout, and failure to account for various processing cases. In addition, the source code may contain requirements errors that indicate failure to capture the customer's needs in the requirements documents, design errors that reflect failure to translate requirements into correct design specifications, and implementation errors that reflect failure to correctly translate design specifications into source code. One of the primary goals of the phased approach to software development is to eliminate requirements and design errors from an evolving software product before implementation begins. As we shall see, it is very expensive to remove analysis and design errors from source code during implementation and system testing.

System testing involves two kinds of activities: integration testing and acceptance testing. Developing a strategy for integrating the components of a software system into a functioning whole requires careful planning so that modules are available for integration when needed. Acceptance testing involves planning and execution of various types of tests in order to demonstrate that the implemented software system satisfies the requirements stated in the requirements document.

Following acceptance by the customer, the software system is released for production work and enters the maintenance phase of the phased life-cycle model. Maintenance activities include enhancement of capabilities, adaptation of the software to new processing environments, and correction of software bugs.

The phased model of the software life cycle presented in Figure 2.2 is admittedly simplistic. There are no milestones in the model, no mention of the documents generated or the reviews conducted during the development process, no indication of the relative effort devoted to each phase, no indication of the role of prototypes in software development, no indication of quality assurance activities, and only cursory indication of the constant verification of work products that must occur throughout the life cycle; and the process of software development is not linear.

Software development never proceeds in a smooth progression of activities as indicated in the waterfall chart. There is more overlap and interaction between phases than can be indicated in a simple two-dimensional representation. Nevertheless, the phased model of the software life cycle is a valid model of the development process in situations where it is possible to write a reasonably complete set of specifications for the software product at the beginning of the life cycle. This typically occurs when the developers have previously developed similar systems.

2.3.2 Milestones, Documents, and Reviews

Another view of the software life cycle that emphasizes the milestones, documents, and reviews throughout product development is illustrated in Figure 2.3. As a software product evolves through the development cycle, it is often difficult, if not

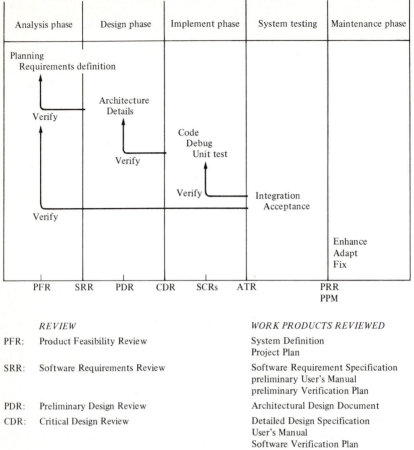

Analysis phase	Design phase	Implement phase	System testing	Maintenance phase

Planning
Requirements definition

Architecture
Details

Verify

Code
Debug
Unit test

Verify

Verify

Integration
Acceptance

Verify

Enhance
Adapt
Fix

PFR	SRR	PDR	CDR	SCRs	ATR	PRR
						PPM

	REVIEW	*WORK PRODUCTS REVIEWED*
PFR:	Product Feasibility Review	System Definition Project Plan
SRR:	Software Requirements Review	Software Requirement Specification preliminary User's Manual preliminary Verification Plan
PDR:	Preliminary Design Review	Architectural Design Document
CDR:	Critical Design Review	Detailed Design Specification User's Manual Software Verification Plan
SCR:	Source Code Review	Walkthroughs & Inspections of the Source Code
ATR:	Acceptance Test Review	Acceptance Test Plan
PRR:	Product Release Review	All of the Above.
PPM:	Project Post-Mortem	Project Legacy

Figure 2.3 Reviews and milestones in the phased life-cycle model.

impossible, for project managers and project team members to assess progress, to determine resources expended, to predict schedule delays, or to anticipate problem areas. Establishing milestones, review points, standardized documents, and management sign-offs can improve product visibility. The development process becomes a more public activity and the product becomes more tangible. This in turn can result in improved product quality, increased programmer productivity, and better morale among the project team members.

The following discussion presents typical documents, project milestones, reviews, and sign-offs used in the phased model of software development. Some of the terminology is adapted from the *IEEE Standard for Software Quality Assurance*

Plans; however, our categorization is not the same as that of the IEEE Standard (BUC79).

1. A *System Definition* and *Project Plan* are prepared, using the formats of Tables 2.5 and 2.6. A product feasibility review is then held to determine the feasibility of project continuation. The outcome of the review may be termination of the project, redirection of the project, or continuation of the project as presented in the *System Definition* and *Project Plan*. Redirection of the project may involve some reworking of the *System Definition* and *Project Plan* and another feasibility review.
2. A preliminary version of the *User's Manual* is prepared. The preliminary *User's Manual* provides a vehicle of communication between customer and developer. It is prepared using information from the *System Definition* as well as the results of prototype studies and mock-ups of user displays and reports. Often the capabilities described in the preliminary *User's Manual* become part of the product requirement specification. The outline of a typical *User's Manual* is illustrated in Table 2.7.
3. A *Software Requirement Specification* is prepared. The requirement specification clearly and precisely defines each essential requirement for the software product, as well as the external interfaces to hardware, firmware, other software, and people. Each requirement should be defined so that it can be verified by a method such as inspection, demonstration, analysis, or testing. The format of a *Software Requirement Specification* is illustrated in Table 2.8; content is discussed in Chapter 4.
4. A preliminary version of the *Software Verification Plan* is prepared. The preliminary version states methods to be used, and the results to be obtained, in verifying each of the requirements stated in the *Software Product Specification*. The outline of a *Software Verification Plan* is illustrated in Table 2.9.

Table 2.7 Outline of the *User's Manual*

Section 1: Introduction

        Product overview and rationale
        Terminology and basic features
        Summary of display and report formats
        Outline of the manual

Section 2: Getting started

        Sign-on
        Help mode
        Sample run

Section 3: Modes of operation

        Commands /dialogues/reports

Section 4: Advanced features

Section 5: Command syntax and system options

Table 2.8 Format of a *Software Requirement Specification*

Section 1:	Product overview and summary
Section 2:	Development/operations/maintenance environments
Section 3:	External interfaces and data flow
	User displays/report formats
	User command summary
	High-level data flow diagrams
	Logical data sources/sinks
	Logical data stores
	Logical data dictionary
Section 4:	Functional specifications
Section 5:	Performance requirements
Section 6:	Exception conditions/exception handling
Section 7:	Early subsets and implementation priorities
Section 8:	Foreseeable modifications and enhancements
Section 9:	Acceptance criteria
	Functional and performance tests
	Documentation standards
Section 10:	Design guidelines (hints and constraints)
Section 11:	Sources of information
Section 12:	Glossary of terms

5. A Software Requirements Review is held to ensure the adequacy of the *System Definition*, the *Project Plan*, the *Software Requirement Specification*, the *Software Verification Plan*, and the preliminary *User's Manual*.

Attendees at the Requirements Review (and the project feasibility review) typically include the planning and analysis team, customer representatives, representatives from the product development group, and quality assurance representatives. Major goals of a requirements review are to ensure that everyone agrees on terminology, to ensure that everyone interprets the specifications in the same way, and to expose problem areas. Problems are recorded by a secretary for later resolution; verbal agreements are forbidden. Depending on the size and nature of the project, the number of people involved in a review may range from three or four to ten or twelve. Smaller groups are of course easier to coordinate, but the appropriate people must be included to ensure the adequacy of the review. Following a preliminary requirements review, the planning and analysis team works with the customer, the developers, and the quality assurance group to resolve problems. When all major issues are settled,

Table 2.9 Outline of a *Software Verification Plan*

Section 1:	Requirements to be verified
Section 2:	Design verification plan
Section 3:	Source-code test plan
Section 4:	Test completion criteria
Section 5:	Document verification plan
Section 6:	Tools and techniques to be used

a final requirements review is held and the requirements documents are approved by a formal sign-off from the customer's organization and the developer's organization. In many instances, the approved documents form a contract for product development. Often, further changes to the requirements can be made only by written request from the customer and with the written agreement of the developer, or vice versa.

6. The design team, which may or may not be the same as the analysis team, creates the *Software Design Specification* in two stages. First the architectural design document is created, then, following a preliminary design review, the detailed design specification is generated. Information contained in the architectural and detailed design specifications is illustrated in Tables 2.10 and 2.11.

7. A preliminary design review is held to evaluate the adequacy of the architectural design in satisfying the *Software Product Specification*. More than one review may be required to resolve problems, and a formal sign-off is required of the project manager.

8. Following completion of detailed design, a critical design review is held. The purpose of the critical design review is to determine the acceptability of the *Software Design Specification*. A formal sign-off is required of the project manager.

9. During the design phase, the *Software Verification Plan* is expanded to include methods that will be used to verify that the design is complete and consistent with respect to the requirements, and to verify that the source code is complete

Table 2.10 Content of an architectural design specification

—Data flow diagrams for the software product
—Conceptual layout of data structures and data bases
—Names, dimensional units, and other attributes of data objects
—Name and functional description of each module
—Interface specifications for each module
—Interconnection structure of the modules
—Interconnections among modules and data structures
—Timing constraints
—Exception conditions

Table 2.11 Content of a detailed design specification

—Physical layout of data structures and data bases
—Data dictionary specification of all concrete data objects
—Detailed algorithms for each new module to be written
—Adaptations required for existing code that will be reused
—Specific programming techniques required to solve unique problems
—Initialization procedures
—Legality checks and exception handling
—Packaging of modules into the physical implementation

Table 2.12 Format of an *Acceptance Test Plan*

Section 1: Requirements to be verified
Section 2: Test cases for each requirement
Section 3: Expected outcome of each test case
Section 4: Capabilities demonstrated by each test

and consistent with respect to the requirement specifications and the design specifications.

10. A software verification review is held to evaluate the adequacy and completeness of the verification plan and to review the preliminary *Acceptance Test Plan*. The *Acceptance Test Plan* includes the actual test cases, expected results, and capabilities to be demonstrated by each test. The acceptance plan is initiated during the design phase and completed during product implementation. The outline of an *Acceptance Test Plan* is illustrated in Table 2.12.

11. During the implementation phase, source code is written, debugged, and unit tested, observing standard practices in the following areas:

—Logical structure   —Comments
—Coding style   —Debugging
—Data layout   —Unit testing

12. During implementation, source-code reviews are held. The purpose of code reviews is to ensure that all code has been reviewed by at least one person other than the programmer who wrote it before it is added to an evolving software product. A formal sign-off is required of the reviewer.

13. During product evolution, inspections and walkthroughs are conducted to verify the completeness, consistency, and suitability of the work products. Items audited may include requirement specifications, design documents, source code, and test cases. (Walkthroughs and inspections are discussed in Chapter 8.) In addition, in-process audits of work products may be conducted by the Quality Assurance group.

14. The *User's Manual,* the *Installation and Training Plans,* and the *Software Maintenance Plan* are completed during the implementation phase. Depending on the nature of the product, installation and customer training may be quite simple or quite involved. Adequate time and resources for installation and training must be allotted in the development schedule. Maintenance may or may not be a contractual responsibility of the development organization. In some cases, the development organization produces a maintenance plan for their own use or that of the customer, and in other cases the customer may elect to develop the maintenance plan. Software maintenance issues are discussed in Chapter 9.

15. Prior to product delivery, a final acceptance review is performed. The final review confirms that all requirements specified in the product requirement specification have been met, and verifies that the source code and all external

Table 2.13 Format of a *Project Legacy*

Section 1: Project description
Section 2: Initial expectations
Section 3: Current status of the project
Section 4: Remaining areas of concern
Section 5: Activities/time log
Section 6: Technical lessons learned
Section 7: Managerial lessons learned
Section 8: Recommendations for future projects

---

documents are complete, internally and externally consistent, and ready for delivery. Formal sign-offs of the final acceptance review are required of the developer and customer organizations. A *Software Verification Summary* is prepared. It describes the results of all reviews, audits, inspections, and tests conducted throughout the development cycle.

16. Finally, a *Project Legacy* is written. The legacy summarizes the project and provides a record of what went well and what went wrong during the project. A common failing of software development organizations is not to allot time or resources for preparation of the *Project Legacy*. It is difficult for an organization to profit from past successes and learn from past mistakes unless the project is reviewed and summarized in the *Project Legacy*. The outline of a typical legacy report is presented in Table 2.13.

Not all the activities outlined in this discussion are necessary for every software product; however, the discussion indicates the range of milestones, documents, and reviews that may occur during product development. The phased model of software development is not intended to preclude activities such as prototyping during analysis and design or to preclude the start of implementation prior to the completion of design. The phased model is intended to provide a framework in which orderly and systematic activities can occur.

2.3.3 The Cost Model

Another view of the software life cycle can be obtained by considering the cost of performing the various activities in a software project. The cost of conducting a software project is the sum of the costs incurred in conducting each phase of the project. Costs incurred within each phase include the cost of performing the processes and preparing the products for that phase, plus the cost of verifying that the products of the present phase are complete and consistent with respect to all previous phases.

Modifications and corrections to the products of previous phases are necessary because the processes of the current phase will expose inaccuracies, inconsistencies, and incompleteness in those products, and because changes in customer requirements, schedules, priorities, and budget will dictate modifications.

The cost of producing the *System Definition* and the *Project Plan* is the cost of performing the planning function and preparing the documents, plus the cost of verifying that the *System Definition* accurately states the customer's needs and the cost of verifying that the *Project Plan* is feasible.

The cost of preparing the *Software Requirement Specification* includes the cost of performing requirements definition and preparing the specification document, plus the cost of modifying and correcting the *System Definition* and the *Project Plan*, plus the cost of verifying that the *Software Requirement Specification* is complete and consistent with respect to the *System Definition* and the customer's needs.

Similarly, the cost of design is the cost of performing the design activities and preparing the design specification and the test plan, plus the cost of modifying and correcting the *System Definition*, the *Project Plan*, and the *Software Requirement Specification*, plus the cost of verifying the design against the requirements, the *System Definition*, and the *Project Plan*.

The cost of product implementation is the cost of implementing, documenting, debugging, and unit testing the source code, plus the cost of completing the *User's Manual*, the verification plan, the maintenance procedures, and the installation and training instructions, plus the cost of modifying and correcting the *System Definition*, the *Project Plan*, the *Software Requirement Specification*, the *Design Specification*, and the *Verification Plan*, plus the cost of verifying that the implementation is complete, consistent, and suitable with respect to the *System Definition*, the *Software Requirement Specification*, and the design documents.

The cost of system testing includes the cost of planning and conducting the tests, plus the cost of modifying and correcting the source code and the external documents during system testing, plus the cost of verifying that the tests adequately validate the product.

Finally, the cost of software maintenance is the sum of the costs of performing product enhancements, making adaptations to new processing requirements, and fixing bugs. Each of these activities may involve modifying and correcting any or all of the supporting documents and running a large number of test cases to verify the correctness of the modification. The cost of conducting a software project is summarized in Figure 2.4.

Given this view of the software life cycle, it is not difficult to understand why modifications or corrections to the *Software Requirement Specification* and design documents in subsequent phases of the life cycle are so costly. Not only must the documents be modified, but all intermediate work products must also be updated, and in each subsequent phase more people and more details must be coordinated. Figure 2.5 illustrates the relative cost to make a change as a function of the phase in which the change is made (BOE76). Observe that it is perhaps 100 times as costly to make a change to the requirements during system testing as it is to make the change during requirements definition. Also note that the data in Figure 2.5 are presented in semilogarithmic format; the straight-line plot indicates an exponential rise in cost.

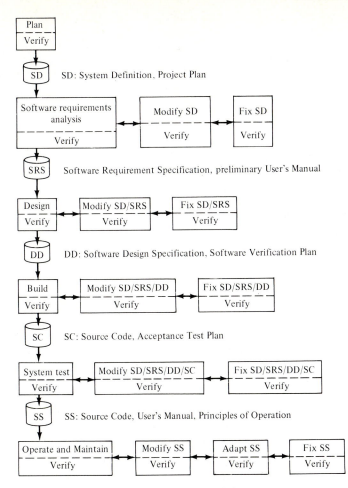

Figure 2.4 The cost model of the software life cycle *(ALF82)*.

2.3.4 The Prototype Life-Cycle Model

Still another view of software development and maintenance is presented in Figure 2.6. This model emphasizes the sources of product requests, the major go/no-go decision points, and the use of prototypes. A prototype is a mock-up or model of a software product. In contrast to a simulation model, a prototype incorporates components of the actual product. Typically, a prototype exhibits limited functional capabilities, low reliability, and/or inefficient performance.

There are several reasons for developing a prototype. One important reason is to illustrate input data formats, messages, reports, and interactive dialogues for the customer. This is a valuable mechanism for explaining various processing options to the customer and for gaining better understanding of the customer's needs.

The second reason for implementing a prototype is to explore technical issues

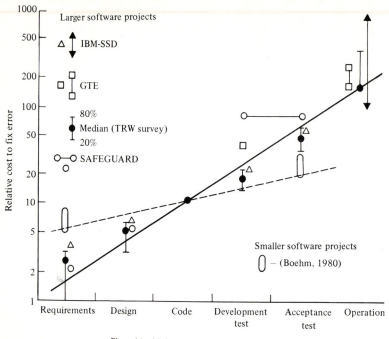

Figure 2.5 Relative cost to make a change.

in the proposed product. Often a major design decision will depend on, say, the response time of a device controller or the efficiency of a sorting algorithm. In these cases, a prototype may be the best, or only, way to resolve the issue.

The third reason for developing a prototype is in situations where the phased model of analysis → design → implementation is not appropriate. The phased model is applicable when it is possible to write a reasonably complete set of specifications for a software product at the beginning of the life cycle. Sometimes it is not possible to define the product without some exploratory development, and sometimes it is not clear how to proceed with the next enhancement to the system until the current version is implemented and evaluated. The approach of exploratory development is often used to develop algorithms to play chess, to solve maze problems, and to accomplish other tasks that require simulation of intelligent behavior; however, we hasten to add that prototyping is not limited to these situations (SEN82).

The nature and extent of prototyping to be performed on a particular software project is dependent on the nature of the product. New versions of existing products can most likely be developed using the phased life-cycle model with little or no prototyping. Development of a totally new product will probably involve some prototyping during the planning and analysis phase, or the product may be developed by iterating through a series of successive designs and implementations. This

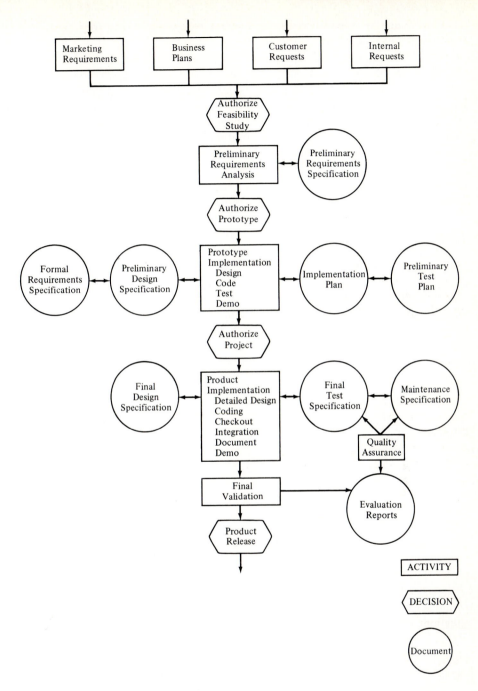

Figure 2.6 An alternate life-cycle model.

latter technique is referred to as the method of successive versions, which is illustrated in Figure 2.7 and discussed below.

As Brooks says, it is nearly impossible to "get it right" the first time, and we should always plan to "throw one away" (BRO75). Gunther suggests that a prototype version of a software product be considered Version 1 of the product. According to Gunther, the prototype should be developed to the point of system testing and, perhaps, on-site evaluation by the customer (GUN78). Development of Version 2, which is the first release of the product, follows system testing of Version 1. Gunther states that development of Version 2 tends to proceed rapidly, with little overall wasted effort. He cites Brooks's caution against the "second system effect," in which software engineers tend to encumber the clean design of Version 1 with marginally useful frills (we refer to this phenomenon as "creeping elegance").

2.3.5 Successive Versions

Product development by the method of successive versions is an extension of prototyping in which an initial product skeleton is refined into increasing levels of capability. In this approach, each successive version of the product is a functioning system capable of performing useful work. Figure 2.7a illustrates the analysis phase followed by iterative design, implementation, and assessment of successive versions. The dashed line indicates that assessment of Version I may dictate the need for further analysis before designing Version $I + 1$.

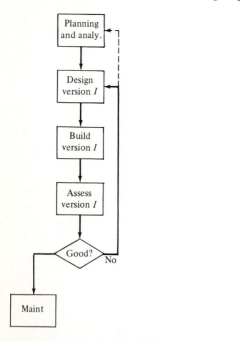

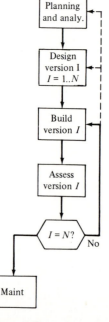

Figure 2.7a Design & implementation of successive versions.

Figure 2.7b Analysis & design followed by implementation of successive versions.

In Figure 2.7b, Versions 1 through N of the product are designed prior to any implementation activities. In this case, the characteristics of each successive design will have been planned during the analysis phase. The dashed lines in Figure 2.7b indicate that implementation of the Ith version may reveal the need for further analysis and design before proceeding with implementation of Version $I + 1$. Our method of successive versions is similar, but not identical, to the method of iterative enhancement (BAS75).

In reality, the development cycle for a software product is a composite of the various models presented in this section. Particular organizations and particular projects may adopt the structure of one particular model, but elements of each model are likely to be found in every project. For instance, it is not uncommon for software projects to adopt a phased model as the basic framework for the project and to incorporate prototyping and development of successive versions into the model.

To summarize, there are several possible life-cycle models. We have discussed four: the phased model, the cost model, the prototype model, and the successive versions model. Typical documents to be generated during a software development cycle were discussed. Not all the documents described need be generated for every product, but supporting documents are required for every software product regardless of the life-cycle model used. A minimal set of supporting documents for a software product includes a statement of requirements, a design specification, a test plan, and a user's manual. Determining the appropriate documents, development schedules, milestones, and reviews for a software project is a major activity during the planning phase. Adopting a product life-cycle model provides standardized terminology for the project, and increases the visibility of work products. This can result in improved software quality, increased programmer productivity, better management control, and improved morale. We observe that every life-cycle model, however inadequate or simplistic, is preferable to no model.

2.4 PLANNING AN ORGANIZATIONAL STRUCTURE

During the lifetime of a software product, various tasks must be performed. The tasks include planning, product development, services, publications, quality assurance, support, and maintenance (GUN78). The planning task identifies external customers and internal product needs, conducts feasibility studies, and monitors progress from beginning to end of the product life cycle. The development task specifies, designs, implements, debugs, tests, and integrates the product. The services task provides automated tools and computer resources for all other tasks, and performs configuration management, product distribution, and miscellaneous administrative support. The publications task develops user's manuals, installation instructions, principles of operation, and other supporting documents. The quality assurance task provides independent evaluation of source code and publications prior to releasing them to customers. The support task promotes the product, trains users, installs the product, and provides continuing liaison between users and other tasks. The maintenance task provides error correction and minor enhancement throughout the productive life of the software product. Major enhancements and adaptation of the software to new processing environments are treated as new development activities in this scheme.

Several variations on this structure are possible. For example, the quality assurance task might provide configuration management, the maintenance task might provide user liaison, and the support task might be handled by the marketing department. Methods for organizing these tasks include the project format, the functional format, and the matrix format.

2.4.1 Project Structure

Project format. Use of a project format involves assembling a team of programmers who conduct a project from start to finish; project team members do product definition, design the product, implement it, test it, conduct project reviews, and prepare the supporting documents. Some project team members may stay with the product during installation and maintenance, and some team members may go on to new projects while retaining responsibility for maintenance of the delivered product. Project team members typically work on a project for 1 to 3 years and are assigned to new projects on completion of the current one.

Functional format. In the functional approach to organization, a different team of programmers performs each phase of the project, and the work products pass from team to team as they evolve. Thus, a planning and analysis team develops the *System Definition* and *Project Plan* and passes these documents to a product definition team, who performs software requirements analysis and prepares the *Software Requirement Specification*. The *Requirement Specification* is passed to a design team, who designs the product to conform with the *System Definition* and *Requirement Specification*. An implementation team implements, debugs, and unit tests the product, and passes it to a system testing team. A quality assurance team certifies the quality of all work products. A separate maintenance team maintains the product during its useful life.

A typical variation on the functional format involves three teams: an analysis team, a design and implementation team, and a testing and maintenance team. In this scheme, a support group provides publications, maintains the facilities, and provides installation and training. Team members are periodically rotated from function to function to provide career development and to relieve the tedium of overspecialization. The functional format requires more communication among teams than the project format, but it also allows personnel to become specialists in particular roles and results in more attention to proper documentation because of the increased need for clear communication.

Matrix format. In matrix organizations, each of the functions described above has its own management team and a group of specialist personnel who are concerned only with that function. The matrix format is illustrated in Figure 2.8. Each

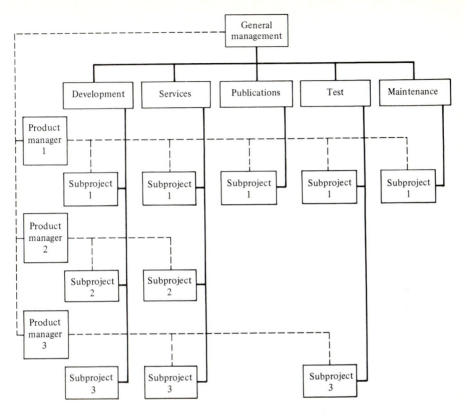

Figure 2.8 Product-function matrix organization *(adapted from (GUN78))*.

development project has a project manager concerned only with that project. The project manager is organizationally a member of the planning function or the development function. The project manager generates and reviews documents and may participate in design, implementation, and testing of the product.

Each functional group participates in each project. For example, software development team members belong organizationally to the development function but work under the supervision of a particular project manager. In a similar way, testing personnel belong to the testing function, publications personnel belong to the publication function, and so forth, but each works on one or more projects under the supervision of one or more project managers.

In matrix organizations, everyone has at least two bosses, and the need to resolve ambiguity and conflict is the price paid for project accountability (GUN78). In spite of the problems created by matrix organizations, they are increasingly popular because special expertise can be concentrated in particular functions, which results in efficient and effective utilization of personnel. Also, project staffing is eased because personnel can be brought onto a project as needed, and returned to their functional organization when they are no longer needed. In a well-managed organization, the workload is balanced so that individuals returning to their functional organization are assigned to other projects, or perhaps spend some time in their functional organization for training and acquisition of new skills.

2.4.2 Programming Team Structure

Every programming team must have an internal structure. The best team structure for any particular project depends on the nature of the project and the product, and on the characteristics of the individual team members. Basic team structures include the democratic team, in which all team members participate in all decisions; the chief programmer team, in which a chief programmer is assisted and supported by other team members in the same way that a chief surgeon is assisted and supported by an anesthesiologist, assisting surgeons, and nurses; and the hierarchical team, which combines aspects of the democratic team and the chief programmer team. Variations in these basic forms are also possible.

A large project may utilize several programming teams. In this case, each team should have responsibility for a well-defined functional unit that communicates with other units through well-defined interfaces. Regardless of the team structure used, each team should be limited to no more than five to seven team members. This limit controls the number of communication paths within the team and permits effective coordination of each team member's work activities.

Characteristics of the various team structures and considerations involved in planning a team structure are discussed in the following paragraphs.

Democratic teams. The idealized democratic team was first described by Weinberg as the "egoless team" (WEI71). The management structure and communication paths in an egoless team are illustrated in Figure 2.9. In an egoless team, goals are set and decisions made by group consensus. Group leadership rotates from member to member based on the tasks to be performed and the differing abilities of the team members. Work products (requirements, design, source code, user's manual, etc.) are discussed openly and are freely examined by all team members.

A democratic team differs from an egoless team in that one team member is designated team leader and occupies the position of first among equals. The team leader position does not usually rotate among team members in a democratic team because a team functions best when one individual is responsible for coordinating

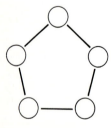

(a) Structure

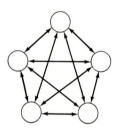

(b) Communication paths

Figure 2.9 Egoless programming team structure and communication paths *(MAN81)*.

team activities and for making final decisions in situations where consensus cannot be reached.

Advantages of the democratic team structure include the opportunity for each team member to contribute to decisions, the opportunity for team members to learn from one another, and the increased job satisfaction that accrues from good communication in an open, nonthreatening work environment. Mantei suggests that the democratic team is well suited to difficult, long-term research and development projects (MAN81). In some organizations, democratic teams stay together for several years and may work on several different projects.

Democratic team structures have the disadvantages of the communication overhead required to reach decisions, the requirement that all team members must work well together, and the weakening of individual responsibility and authority that may occur. Less individual responsibility and authority can result in less initiative and less personal drive from team members.

Chief programmer teams. In contrast to democratic teams, chief programmer teams are highly structured. The management structure and communication paths of chief programmer teams are illustrated in Figure 2.10. The chief programmer designs the product, implements critical parts of the product, and makes all major technical decisions. Work is allocated to the individual programmers by the chief programmer. The programmers, who number between two and five, write code and debug, document, and unit test it.

A program librarian maintains program listings, design documents, test plans, etc., in a central location and, in a batch environment, prepares job runs and retrieves output. The back-up programmer serves as consultant to the chief programmer on various technical problems; provides liaison with the customer, the publications group, and the quality assurance group; and may perform some analysis, design, and implementation under supervision of the chief programmer.

The chief programmer is assisted by an administrative program manager, who handles administrative details, such as time cards, sick leave, and vacation schedules. The emphasis in a chief programmer structure is thus to provide complete technical and administrative support to the chief programmer, who has responsibility and authority for development of the software product.

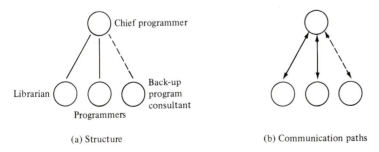

(a) Structure   (b) Communication paths

Figure 2.10 Chief programmer team structure and communication paths *(MAN81)*.

Chief programmer teams have the advantages of centralized decision making and reduced communication paths; however, the effectiveness of a chief programmer team is quite sensitive to the chief programmer's technical and managerial abilities. The chief programmer structure can also result in low morale among the subordinate programmers.

Two situations where chief programmer teams are effective are, first, in data processing applications where the chief programmer has responsibility for sensitive financial software packages and the packages can be written by relatively unskilled programmers; and second, in situations where one senior programmer and several junior programmers are assigned to a project. In the latter case, the goal is often to train the junior programmers in an apprenticeship setting, and to evolve the team structure into a hierarchical or democratic team when the junior programmers have obtained enough experience to assume responsibility for various project activities.

Hierarchical team structure. The hierarchical team structure occupies a middle position between the extremes of democratic teams and chief programmer teams. The management structure and communication paths in a hierarchical team are illustrated in Figure 2.11. In a hierarchical team, the project leader assigns tasks, attends reviews and walkthroughs, detects problem areas, balances the workload, and participates in technical activities.

Hierarchical structure limits the number of communication paths in a project, while permitting effective communication among team members who need to communicate with one another. Hierarchical teams are particularly well suited to development of hierarchical software products because each major subsystem in the hierarchy can be assigned to a different programming team. It has been observed on more than one occasion that the structure of software products tends to resemble the structure of the teams that develop them. If a hierarchical product is to have three major subsystems, it is reasonable to have three teams organized in hierarchical fashion, with each team leader reporting to the project leader. The number of immediate subordinates at each level in a hierarchy should be limited to five to

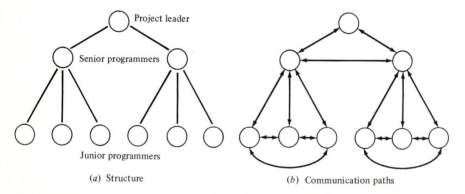

(a) Structure   (b) Communication paths

Figure 2.11 Hierarchical programming team structure and communication paths *(MAN81)*.

seven people to permit effective communication and supervision of work activities. Thus, a large project may have several levels in the hierarchy.

A major disadvantage of a hierarchical structure is that the most technically competent programmers tend to be promoted into management positions. This is generally regarded as desirable by the programmer being promoted because more prestige and a higher salary are associated with higher levels in the hierarchy. Unfortunately, "promotion" of the best programmer may have the doubly negative effect of losing a good programmer and creating a poor manager. The technically competent programmer may coincidentally have good management skills, but there is no reason to assume that a competent programmer will have the best communication skills or the best ability to organize and direct the work activities of other people (i.e., not all good programmers are good software engineers).

In summary, we have discussed three basic programming team structures: the democratic structure, the chief programmer structure, and the hierarchical structure. Variations on these structures are possible. For example, a large project might be organized as a hierarchy of chief programmer teams, or each member of a democratic team might be the project leader of a hierarchical team that is responsible for a subsystem of the software product.

2.4.3 Management by Objectives

Given a project format and a team structure, it is also necessary for the project leader to establish methods for directing and controlling the activities of individuals assigned to the project. An effective technique for assigning work activities is development of written job descriptions for each project member. This reduces misunderstandings and false assumptions of both manager and managee.

At the beginning of a project, project members should develop their own written job descriptions based on their understanding of the project and their role in it. The job descriptions are then modified in consultation with the project leader so that everyone has a clear understanding of project responsibilities and individual work assignments.

Management by objectives (MBO) is a related technique that is increasingly popular in software organizations. Using MBO, employees set their own goals and objectives with the help of their supervisor, participate in the setting of their supervisor's goals, and are evaluated by meeting concrete, written objectives. Tangible, clearly achievable objectives are set for periods of 1 to 3 months. MBO is well suited to the milestones and intermediate work products of software engineering, and to the temperament of highly skilled and self-motivated software engineers.

Management by objectives can be applied at all levels of an organization, and can include both product-oriented objectives, such as completion of design or testing, and self-improvement objectives, such as skills to acquire and preparations for advancement. Both job-oriented skills and career-oriented goals are agreed to by supervisor and subordinate, placed in writing, and evaluated at the end of an agreed-upon time period. The general theory of MBO is presented in (HUM73) and (BAT66). Gunther discusses the application of MBO to software projects (GUN78).

While MBO is an increasingly popular technique, it is sometimes criticized as a cumbersome, bureaucratic exercise. In our experience, the criticism is usually justified, not because the concept of MBO is faulty, but because the local implementation of MBO is often incorrect. Typical problems with MBO include requiring employees to state excessive numbers of objectives (20 or 30) and making the reporting period too long (6 months or more). Objectives for software projects should be specific, few in number, and achievable in a short time period (say 1 to 3 months). Furthermore, objectives should be phrased so that attainment of an objective can be readily determined.

2.5 OTHER PLANNING ACTIVITIES

Other planning activities include planning the configuration management and quality assurance functions, planning for independent validation and verification, and planning phase-dependent tools and techniques. Each of these activities is discussed in turn.

2.5.1 Planning for Configuration Management and Quality Assurance

Configuration management is concerned with controlling changes in work products, accounting for the status of work products, and maintaining the program support library, which is the central repository for all project information. Quality assurance develops and monitors adherence to project standards, performs audits of the processes and work products, and develops and performs the acceptance tests, perhaps in conjunction with the customer.

During the planning phase, the configuration management and quality assurance procedures to be used are specified, and the tools needed to perform configuration management and quality assurance are identified and acquired. During the design phase, configuration management and quality assurance of the requirements and design specifications are performed, adherence to project standards is monitored, and the tools needed to perform configuration management and quality assurance are used. During the implementation and testing phases, configuration management and quality assurance of requirements, design specifications, and source code are performed. During the testing phase, acceptance testing and preparation of test results are performed. During the planning phase, these activities should be planned and adequate resources should be budgeted to permit successful configuration management and quality assurance.

2.5.2 Planning for Independent Verification and Validation

On some critical software projects, an independent organization may provide verification and validation of work products. Verification ensures that various work products are complete and consistent with respect to other work products and customer needs. Thus, an external organization might verify that the design specifications are complete and consistent with respect to the *System Definition* and the *Software Product Specifications,* and that the source code is complete and consistent with respect to the design specifications and the requirements. Validation is concerned with assessing the quality of a software system in its actual operating environment. Validation typically involves planning and execution of test cases. On projects using independent verification and validation, test cases are developed and executed by the independent organization. Independent verification and validation results in high-quality software products; however, the cost of performing independent verification and validation may be as much as 25 percent of the development cost. The benefits must be judged in terms of the high cost.

2.5.3 Planning Phase-Dependent Tools and Techniques

Automated tools, specialized notations, and modern techniques are often used to develop software requirement specifications, architectural and detailed designs, and the source code. In addition, automated testing tools may be used for unit testing, system testing, and acceptance testing. Management tools such as PERT charts, Gantt charts, work breakdown structures, and personnel staffing charts may be used to track and control progress. Use of these tools, techniques, and notations typically requires lead time for procurement and training. They must be anticipated during the planning phase.

2.5.4 Other Planning Activities

Other planning activities include preparing preliminary cost estimates for product development, establishing a preliminary development schedule, establishing preliminary staffing levels, and developing preliminary estimates of the computing resources and personnel required to operate and maintain the system. These activities are discussed in Chapter 3.

2.6 SUMMARY

Planning is a necessary, yet often neglected, aspect of software product development. Careful planning is required for both the development process and the software product. The results of planning are expressed in the *System Definition* and the *Project Plan.*

In this chapter, we have discussed the steps required to plan a software project, and have indicated some factors to be considered in developing project goals and plans. The importance of a life-cycle model was indicated, and several models were presented. Typical documents, milestones, reviews, and audits for a software development project were described, and the formats of the documents were illustrated. The role of prototypes in software development was discussed, and the phased model and successive versions model of the life cycle were contrasted.

Every software development project must have an organizational structure, a team structure, and a mechanism for assigning and evaluating work activities. The project, functional, and matrix organizational structures were presented; democratic team, chief programmer team, and hierarchical team structures were described; and written job descriptions and management by objectives were discussed.

Additional planning activities, such as planning for configuration management, quality assurance, independent validation and verification, and phase-dependent tools and techniques, were discussed. The important activities of cost estimation and estimation of staffing levels and development schedules are discussed in Chapter 3.

REFERENCES

(ALF82) Alford, M: Private communication.

(BAS75) Basili, V., and A. Turner: "Iterative Enhancement, A Practical Technique for Software Development," *IEEE TSE,* vol. SE-1, no. 4, December 1975.

(BAT66) Batton, J.: *Beyond Management by Objectives,* American Management Association, 1966.

(BOE76) Boehm, B.: "Software Engineering," *IEEE Trans. on Computers,* vol. C-25, no. 12, December 1976.

(BOE78) Boehm, B., et al.: *Characteristics of Software Quality,* North-Holland, Amsterdam, 1978.

(BRO75) Brooks, F.: *The Mythical Man-Month,* Addison-Wesley, Reading, Mass., 1975.

(BUC79) Buckley, F.: "A Standard for Software Quality Assurance Plans," *COMPUTER,* vol. 12, no. 8, August 1979.

(GUN78) Gunther, R.: *Management Methodology for Software Product Engineering,* Wiley Interscience, New York, 1978.

(HUM73) Humble, J.: *How to Manage by Objectives,* American Management Association, 1973.

(IEE83) *IEEE Standard Glossary of Software Engineering Terminology,* IEEE Standard 729-1983.

(MAN81) Mantei, M.: "The Effect of Programming Team Structure on Programming Tasks," *CACM,* vol. 24, no. 3, March 1981.

(OSB56) Osborn, A.: *Your Creative Power,* Scribner, New York, 1956.

(SEN82) "Software Engineering Notes: Special Issue on Rapid Prototyping," *ACM SEN* vol. 7, no. 5, December 1982.

(WEI71) Weinberg, G.: *The Psychology of Computer Programming,* Van Nostrand Reinhold, 1971.

EXERCISES

2.1 Interview programmers and managers in a software organization of your choice to determine how their planning for a software project agrees or disagrees with Table 2.1.

2.2 (*a*) Obtain a requirements document for a software project. Examine it for the presence or absence of verifiable requirements.

(*b*) Are the methods stated for verifying the requirements adequate to verify them?

(*c*) Select some requirements in the document and state better methods for verifying them.

(*d*) Identify requirements that are imprecise and/or ambiguous.

(*e*) Rephrase the imprecise and/or ambiguous requirements in verifiable terms, and specify the verification technique.

2.3 (*a*) Compare the life-cycle models used in a software organization of your choice with those presented in Section 2.3.

(*b*) Does the organization have one model for all projects, or is a model developed for each project? Why?

2.4 (*a*) Compare the documents, reviews, audits, and sign-offs used in a software organization of your choice with those presented in Figure 2.3.

(*b*) How do the format and contents of the documents differ from those described in Chapter 2?

2.5 Interview project managers and programmers to determine their views on the use of prototypes. Are prototypes used? In what circumstances? If not, why not?

2.6 (*a*) Investigate the management methods used in a software organization of your choice. Are projects conducted using project, function, or matrix management, or by a combination of these techniques?

(*b*) Are different methods used on different projects? Why or why not?

(*c*) Are the people involved satisfied with the methods being used? In answering this question, distinguish between managers and programmers.

(*d*) Seek out programmers and managers who have worked within different organizational structures and determine their attitudes concerning various approaches.

2.7 (*a*) Conduct an investigation similar to that described in Problem 2.6, but this time focus on programming team structure. Contrast democratic teams, chief programmer teams, hierarchical teams, and variations on these basic structures.

(*b*) How are project leaders selected in a software organization of your choice?

2.8 (*a*) Identify one or more software organizations that utilize management by objectives. Interview managers and programmers in the organization to determine how MBO is adapted to that organization.

(*b*) Identify positive and negative aspects of MBO in that organization. Observe that different people have different perceptions of MBO.

THREE

SOFTWARE COST ESTIMATION

INTRODUCTION

Estimating the cost of a software product is one of the most difficult and error-prone tasks in software engineering. It is difficult to make an accurate cost estimate during the planning phase of software development because of the large number of unknown factors at that time, yet contracting practices often require a firm cost commitment as part of the feasibility study. This, coupled with the competitive nature of business, is a major factor that contributes to the widespread cost and schedule overruns of software projects.

In recognition of this problem, some organizations use a series of cost estimates. A preliminary estimate is prepared during the planning phase and presented at the project feasibility review. An improved estimate is presented at the software requirements review, and the final estimate is presented at the preliminary design review. Each estimate is a refinement of the previous one, and is based on the additional information gained as a result of additional work activities. Sometimes several product options and associated costs are presented at the reviews. This allows the customer to choose a cost-effective solution from a range of possible solutions.

Customers sometimes fund the analysis phase and the preliminary design phase on separate contracts in order to arrive at accurate cost and schedule estimates. Contracts for analysis and preliminary design are sometimes awarded to multiple software development organizations by the customer, who then chooses an organization to develop the software product on the basis of the analysis and preliminary design competitions.

**Table 3.1 Major factors that
influence software cost**

Programmer ability
Product complexity
Product size
Available time
Required reliability
Level of technology

Major factors that influence software costs are listed in Table 3.1 and discussed in the following section.

3.1 SOFTWARE COST FACTORS

There are many factors that influence the cost of a software product. The effects of most of these factors, and hence the cost of a development or maintenance effort, are difficult to estimate. Primary among the cost factors are the individual abilities of project personnel and their familiarity with the application area; the complexity of the product; the size of the product; the available time; the required level of reliability; the level of technology utilized; and the availability, familiarity, and stability of the system used to develop the product. Each factor is discussed in turn.

3.1.1 Programmer Ability

In Chapter 1, we discussed a well-known experiment conducted in 1968 by Harold Sackman and colleagues. The goal was to determine the relative influence of batch and time-shared access on programmer productivity. Twelve experienced programmers were each given two programming problems to solve, some using batch facilities and some using time-sharing. The resulting differences in individual performance among the programmers were much greater than could be attributed to the relatively small effect of batch or time-shared machine access. The differences between best and worst performance were factors of 6 to 1 in program size, 8 to 1 in execution time, 9 to 1 in development time, 18 to 1 in coding time, and 28 to 1 in debugging time. These results are summarized in Figure 1.5. On one program, the best and worst performances were by the two programmers who had the most experience (11 years). In a subsequent experiment, Sackman observed a productivity variation of 16 to 1 (SAC68).

As we observed in Chapter 1, the wide variability among programmers was due to a small number of extreme performances in both directions. Eliminating those cases results in a more typical variation in programmer productivity of 5 to 1. Nevertheless, variability of 5 to 1 in programmer productivity is a significant factor in cost estimation. On very large projects, the differences in individual programmer ability will tend to average out, but on projects utilizing five or fewer programmers, individual differences in ability can be significant.

3.1.2 Product Complexity

There are three generally acknowledged categories of software products: applications programs, which include data processing and scientific programs; utility programs, such as compilers, linkage editors, and inventory systems; and system-level programs, such as data-base management systems, operating systems, and real-time systems. Applications programs are developed in the environment provided by a language compiler such as FORTRAN or Pascal. Interactions with the operating system are limited to job control statements and run-time support facilities provided by the language processor. Utility programs are written to provide user processing environments and make sophisticated use of operating system facilities. Systems programs interact directly with the hardware. They typically involve concurrent processing and timing constraints.

Brooks states that utility programs are three times as difficult to write as applications programs, and that systems programs are three times as difficult to write as utility programs (BRO74). His levels of product complexity are thus 1–3–9 for applications–utility–systems programs.

Boehm uses three levels of product complexity and provides equations to predict total programmer-months of effort, PM, in terms of the number of thousands of delivered source instructions, KDSI, in the product (BOE81). Programmer cost for a software project can be obtained by multiplying the effort in programmer-months by the cost per programmer-month. The equations were derived by examining historical data from a large number of actual projects. These projects were large enough that individual differences in programmer productivity tended to average out. In Boehm's terminology, the three levels of product complexity are organic, semidetached, and embedded programs. These levels roughly correspond to applications programs, utility programs, and systems programs:

$$\text{Applications programs:} \quad PM = 2.4*(KDSI)**1.05$$

$$\text{Utility programs:} \quad PM = 3.0*(KDSI)**1.12$$

$$\text{Systems programs:} \quad PM = 3.6*(KDSI)**1.20$$

Graphs of these equations are presented in Figure 3.1. From the graphs, it can be observed that the ratio of programmer-months is roughly 1 to 1.7 to 2.8 for development of a 60,000-line applications program, utility program, and systems program, respectively. Thus, these equations state that roughly twice as much effort is required to develop a utility program, and roughly three times as much effort is required to develop a systems program, as is required to develop an applications program of 60K lines. It can be observed in Figure 3.1 that the ratios grow larger with larger programs.

The development time for a program, as given by Boehm, is

$$\text{Applications programs:} \quad TDEV = 2.5*(PM)**0.38$$

$$\text{Utility programs:} \quad TDEV = 2.5*(PM)**0.35$$

$$\text{Systems programs:} \quad TDEV = 2.5*(PM)**0.32$$

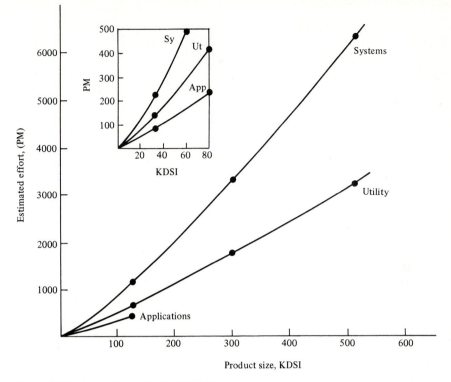

Figure 3.1 Cocomo effort estimates *(BOE81)*.

Graphs of these equations are presented in Figure 3.2. From these graphs, it is obvious that development time is roughly the same for all three types of systems.

For example, a 60 KDSI program can be developed in approximately 18 months, regardless of its complexity level. We interpret this to mean that there are more opportunities for parallel activity in the development of a utility program or a systems program than in the development of an applications program of corresponding size, or perhaps scheduling of work activities is done differently on applications projects.

Given the total programmer-months for a project and the nominal development time required, the average staffing level can be obtained by simple division. For our 60 KDSI program, we obtain the following results:

Applications program: 176.6 PM/17.85 MO = 9.9 programmers

Utility program: 294 PM/18.3 MO = 16 programmers

Systems program: 489.6 PM/18.1 MO = 27 programmers

These figures represent average staffing levels. Only a few people are required during analysis and architectural design, and perhaps 125 to 150 percent of average

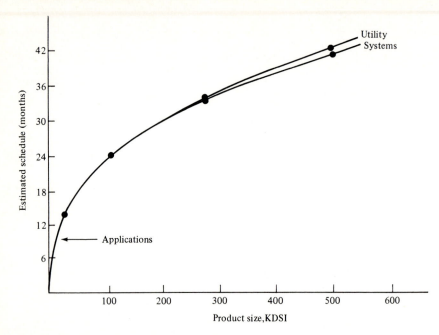

Figure 3.2 Cocomo schedule estimates *(BOE81)*.

staffing will be required during the implementation phase. Staffing-level estimation is discussed in Section 3.3.

It must be emphasized that these results are presented only for purposes of illustration. These equations should not be used to estimate software effort without careful reading of Boehm to understand the assumptions and limitations of the method. Also, recall that the independent variable in these equations is delivered source instructions. The estimates are thus no better than our ability to estimate the final number of instructions in the program. This is a difficult estimate to make in the planning phase.

One of the common failures in estimating the number of source instructions in a software product is to underestimate the amount of housekeeping code required. Housekeeping code is that portion of the source code that handles input/output, interactive user communication, human interface engineering, and error checking and error handling. Housekeeping code often amounts to more than 50 percent and sometimes as much as 90 percent of the source code in a software product. It is usually easier to estimate the amount of code needed to manipulate data and perform calculations than to estimate the amount of housekeeping code. Estimates based on the former value can be misleading when used to estimate total lines of source code.

3.1.3 Product Size

A large software product is obviously more expensive to develop than a small one. Boehm's equations indicate that the rate of increase in required effort grows with

Table 3.2 Effort and schedule estimators (BOE81)

Effort equation	Schedule equation	Reference
MM = 5.2(KDSI)**0.91	TDEV = 2.47(MM)**0.35	(WAL77)
MM = 4.9(KDSI)**0.98	TDEV = 3.04(MM)**0.36	(NEL78)
MM = 1.5(KDSI)**1.02	TDEV = 4.38(MM)**0.25	(FRE79)
MM = 2.4(KDSI)**1.05	TDEV = 2.50(MM)**0.38	(BOE81)
MM = 3.0(KDSI)**1.12	TDEV = 2.50(MM)**0.35	(BOE81)
MM = 3.6(KDSI)**1.20	TDEV = 2.50(MM)**0.32	(BOE81)
MM = 1.0(KDSI)**1.40	—	(JON77)
MM = 0.7(KDSI)**1.50	—	(HAL77)
MM = 28 (KDSI)**1.83	—	(SCH78)

the number of source instructions at an exponential rate slightly greater than 1. Other investigators have developed equations similar to Boehm's. Several different effort and development schedule estimators are presented in Table 3.2, which is adapted from Boehm (BOE81). As can be seen in Table 3.2, some investigators believe that the rate of increase in effort grows at an exponential rate slightly less than 1, but most use an exponent in the range of 1.05 to 1.83.

Using exponents of 0.91 and 1.83 (the extremes in Table 3.2) results in estimates of 1.88 and 3.5 more effort for a product that is twice as large, and factors of 8.1 and 67.6 for products that are 10 times as large as a known product. These estimates differ by factors of 1.86 (3.5/1.88) for products that are twice as large, and 8.3 (76.6/8.1) for products that are 10 times as large. Depending on the exponent used, we can easily be off by a factor of 2 in estimating effort for a product twice the size of a known product, and by a factor of 10 for a product 10 times the size of a known product, even if all other factors that influence cost remain constant.

Note that the development time estimators in Table 3.2 are in closer agreement than the effort estimators, but they too are only as good as our ability to estimate the number of delivered source instructions.

3.1.4 Available Time

Total project effort is sensitive to the calendar time available for project completion. Several investigators have studied the question of optimal development time, and most of them agree that software projects require more total effort if development time is compressed or expanded from the optimal time. The results of these studies are summarized in Figure 3.3, which is adapted from Boehm (BOE81).

The most striking feature of Figure 3.3 is the Putnam curve (PUT78). According to Putnam, project effort is inversely proportional to the fourth power of development time, $E = k/(Td**4)$. This curve indicates an extreme penalty for schedule compression and an extreme reward for expanding the project schedule. For example, doubling the development schedule for a 100 programmer-month project would reduce the total effort required to 100/2**4 = 6.25 programmer-

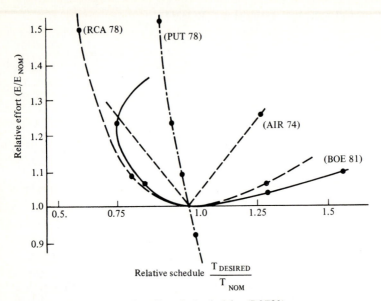

Figure 3.3 Relative effort for off-nominal schedules *(BOE81)*.

months. Carried to an absurdity, the formula predicts zero effort for infinite development time. In practice, the SLIM cost estimation model developed by Putnam uses linear programming techniques to restrict the range of the fourth-power curve to a relatively small region around the nominal development time. Nevertheless, many investigators think the Putnam curve is too sensitive, and that increasing development time beyond some optimal time increases, rather than decreases, total effort.

Putnam also states that the development schedule cannot be compressed below about 86 percent of the nominal schedule, regardless of the number of people or resources utilized. The inverse fourth-power equation predicts a required increase in staff by a factor of 1.82 for a schedule compression of .86.

The other curves in Figure 3.3 are in closer agreement, particularly concerning schedule compression. In a study of 63 software projects, Boehm found that only four had compression factors less than 75 percent of the development time predicted by his cost estimation model. On the basis of this study, Boehm states: "There is a limit beyond which a software project cannot reduce its schedule by buying more personnel and equipment. This limit occurs roughly at 75% of the nominal schedule."

3.1.5 Required Level of Reliability

Software reliability can be defined as the probability that a program will perform a required function under stated conditions for a stated period of time. Reliability can be expressed in terms of accuracy, robustness, completeness, and consistency of the source code (these terms are defined in Table 2.2). Reliability characteristics

Table 3.3 Development effort multipliers for software reliability (adapted from BOE81)

Category	Effect of failure	Effort multiplier
Very low	Slight inconvenience	0.75
Low	Losses easily recovered	0.88
Nominal	Moderately difficult to recover losses	1.00
High	High financial loss	1.15
Very high	Risk to human life	1.40

can be built into a software product, but there is a cost associated with the increased level of analysis, design, implementation, and verification and validation effort that must be exerted to ensure high reliability.

The desired level of reliability should be established during the planning phase by considering the cost of software failures. In some cases, product failure may cause only slight inconvenience to the user, while failure of other products may incur high financial loss or risk to human life.

Boehm describes five categories of reliability and recommends a development effort multiplier for each (BOE81). Boehm's reliability categories and the effort multiplier for each category are presented in Table 3.3. Note that the multipliers range from 0.75 for very low reliability to 1.4 for very high reliability. The effort ratio is thus 1.87 (1.4/0.75).

3.1.6 Level of Technology

The level of technology in a software development project is reflected by the programming language, the abstract machine (hardware plus software), the programming practices, and the software tools used. It is well known that the number of source instructions written per day is largely independent of the language used, and that program statements written in high-level languages such as FORTRAN and Pascal typically expand into several machine-level statements. Use of a high-level language instead of assembly language thus increases programmer productivity by a factor of 5 to 10. In addition, the type-checking rules and self-documenting aspects of high-level languages improve the reliability and modifiability of high-level-language programs. Modern programming languages such as Ada provide additional features to improve programmer productivity and software reliability. These features include strong type-checking, data abstraction, separate compilation, exception handling, interrupt handling, and concurrency mechanisms.

The abstract machine is the set of hardware and software facilities used during the development process. Familiarity with, the stability of, and ease of access to the abstract machine all influence programmer productivity, and hence the cost of a software project. Productivity will suffer if programmers must learn a new machine environment as part of the development process, or if the machine is being developed in parallel with the software, or if programmers have only restricted access to the machine.

Modern programming practices include use of systematic analysis and design techniques, structured design notations, walkthroughs and inspections, structured coding, systematic testing, and a program development library. Software tools range from elementary tools, such as assemblers and basic debugging aids, to compilers and linkage editors, to interactive text editors and data-base management systems, to program design language processors and requirements specification analyzers, to fully integrated development environments that include configuration management and automated verification tools.

Boehm provides effort multipliers for modern programming practices that range from 1.24 (no modern practices) to 0.82 (full use of modern practices), and effort multipliers for software tools that range from 1.24 (very basic tools) to 0.83 (advanced development tools). Thus, the use of modern practices and the use of modern development tools can each reduce programming effort to 0.67 (0.82/1.24) of the effort required using assembly language and primitive development tools. Use of both modern practices and modern development tools can, in Boehm's opinion, reduce development effort to 0.45 (0.67∗0.67) of that required using primitive tools and techniques.

3.2 SOFTWARE COST ESTIMATION TECHNIQUES

Within most organizations, software cost estimates are based on past performance. Historical data are used to identify cost factors and determine the relative importance of various factors within the environment of that organization. This, of course, means that cost and productivity data must be collected on current projects in order to estimate future ones.

Cost estimates can be made either top-down or bottom-up. Top-down estimation first focuses on system-level costs, such as the computing resources and personnel required to develop the system, as well as the costs of configuration management, quality assurance, system integration, training, and publications. Personnel costs are estimated by examining the cost of similar past projects.

Bottom-up cost estimation first estimates the cost to develop each module or subsystem. Those costs are combined to arrive at an overall estimate. Top-down estimation has the advantage of focusing on system-level costs, but may overlook various technical factors in some of the modules to be developed. Bottom-up estimation emphasizes the costs associated with developing individual system components, but may fail to account for system-level costs, such as configuration management and quality control. In practice, both top-down and bottom-up cost estimates should be developed, compared, and iterated to eliminate differences.

3.2.1 Expert Judgment

The most widely used cost estimation technique is expert judgment, which is an inherently top-down estimation technique. Expert judgment relies on the experience, background, and business sense of one or more key people in the organization.

An expert might arrive at a cost estimate in the following manner:

The system to be developed is a process control system similar to one that was developed last year in 10 months at a cost of $1 million. We did not get rich on the project, but we did make a respectable profit; therefore, no adjustment to the baseline project is required. The new system has similar control functions, but has 25 percent more activities to control; thus, we will increase our time and cost estimates by 25 percent. The previous system was the first of its type that we developed; however, we will use the same computer and external sensing/controlling devices, and many of the same people are available to develop the new system, so we can reduce our estimate by 20 percent. Furthermore, we can reuse much of the low-level code from the previous product, which reduces the time and cost estimates by 25 percent. The net effect of these considerations is a time and cost reduction of 20 percent, which results in an estimate of $800,000 and 8 months development time. We know that the customer has budgeted $1 million and 1 year delivery time for the system. Therefore, we add a small margin of safety and bid the system at $850,000 and 9 months development time.

The biggest advantage of expert judgment, namely, experience, can also be a liability. The expert may be confident that the project is similar to a previous one, but may have overlooked some factors that make the new project significantly different. Or, the expert making the estimate may not have experience with a project similar to the present one.

In order to compensate for these factors, groups of experts sometimes prepare a consensus estimate. This tends to minimize individual oversights and lack of familiarity with particular projects, and neutralizes personal biases and the (perhaps subconscious) desire to win the contract through an overly optimistic estimate. The major disadvantage of group estimation is the effect that interpersonal group dynamics may have on individuals in the group. Group members may be less than candid due to political considerations, the presence of authority figures in the group, or the dominance of an overly assertive group member. The Delphi technique can be used to overcome these disadvantages.

3.2.2 Delphi Cost Estimation

The Delphi technique was developed at the Rand Corporation in 1948 to gain expert consensus without introducing the adverse side effects of group meetings (HEL66). The Delphi technique can be adapted to software cost estimation in the following manner.

1. A coordinator provides each estimator with the *System Definition* document and a form for recording a cost estimate.
2. Estimators study the definition and complete their estimates anonymously. They may ask questions of the coordinator, but they do not discuss their estimates with one another.

3. The coordinator prepares and distributes a summary of the estimators' responses, and includes any unusual rationales noted by the estimators.
4. Estimators complete another estimate, again anonymously, using the results from the previous estimate. Estimators whose estimates differ sharply from the group may be asked, anonymously, to provide justification for their estimates.
5. The process is iterated for as many rounds as required. No group discussion is allowed during the entire process.

A Delphi cost estimation form is illustrated in Figure 3.4.
The following approach is a variation on the standard Delphi technique that increases communication while preserving anonymity:

1. The coordinator provides each estimator with a *System Definition* and an estimation form.
2. The estimators study the definition, and the coordinator calls a group meeting so that estimators can discuss estimation issues with the coordinator and one another.
3. Estimators complete their estimates anonymously.
4. The coordinator prepares a summary of the estimates, but does not record any rationales.
5. The coordinator calls a group meeting to focus on issues where the estimates vary widely.
6. Estimators complete another estimate, again anonymously. The process is iterated for as many rounds as necessary.

It is possible that several rounds of estimates will not lead to a consensus estimate. In this case, the coordinator must discuss the issues involved with each estimator to determine the reasons for the differences. The coordinator may have to gather additional information and present it to the estimators in order to resolve the differences in viewpoint.

Project: Operating system   Date: 6/6/84

Range of estimates from the 3d round

Your estimate

Median estimate

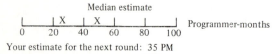

Your estimate for the next round: 35 PM

Rational for your estimate:

Looks like a standard process control operating system.
Our people have had lots of experience with such systems.
They should have no trouble with this one.
I am increasing my estimate to account for the new DMA
channel mentioned by one of the estimators.

Figure 3.4 A Delphi cost estimation form.

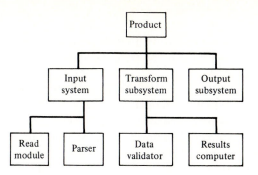

Figure 3.5a A product work breakdown structure.

3.2.3 Work Breakdown Structures

Expert judgment and group consensus are top-down estimation techniques. The work breakdown structure method is a bottom-up estimation tool. A work breakdown structure is a hierarchical chart that accounts for the individual parts of a system. A WBS chart can indicate either product hierarchy or process hierarchy.

Product hierarchy identifies the product components and indicates the manner in which the components are interconnected. A WBS chart of process hierarchy identifies the work activities and the relationships among those activities. Typical product and process WBS charts are illustrated in Figures 3.5a and b. Using the WBS technique, costs are estimated by assigning costs to each individual component in the chart and summing the costs.

Some planners use both product and process work breakdown structure charts for cost estimation. The primary advantages of the WBS technique are in identifying and accounting for various process and product factors, and in making explicit exactly which costs are included in the estimate.

Expert judgment, group consensus, and work breakdown structures are the most widely used cost estimation techniques. Many organizations use all three approaches and iterate on the estimates until differences have been resolved.

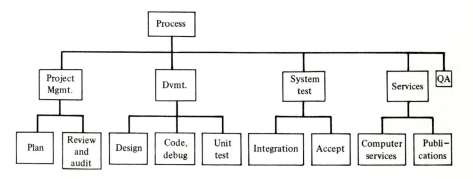

Figure 3.5b A process work breakdown structure.

3.2.4 Algorithmic Cost Models

Algorithmic cost estimators compute the estimated cost of a software system as the sum of the costs of the modules and subsystems that comprise the system. Algorithmic models are thus bottom-up estimators.

The Constructive Cost Model (COCOMO) is an algorithmic cost model described by Boehm (BOE81). COCOMO is briefly summarized here.

When using COCOMO, the equations presented in Section 3.1 are used to provide nominal estimates of programmer-months and development schedule for a program unit, based on the estimated number of Delivered Source Instructions (DSI) in the unit. Effort multipliers are then used to adjust the estimate for product attributes, computer attributes, personnel attributes, and project attributes. Table 3.4 summarizes the COCOMO effort multipliers and their ranges of values. The equations and effort multipliers were developed by examining data from 63 software development projects, and by use of the Delphi technique among a group of software experts.

The COCOMO equations incorporate a number of assumptions. For example, the nominal organic mode (applications programs) equations apply in the following types of situations:

Small to medium-size projects (2K to 32K DSI)
Familiar applications area
Stable, well-understood virtual machine
In-house development effort

Table 3.4 COCOMO effort multipliers

Multiplier	Range of values
Product attributes	
Required reliability	0.75 to 1.40
Data-base size	0.94 to 1.16
Product complexity	0.70 to 1.65
Computer attributes	
Execution time constraint	1.00 to 1.66
Main storage constraint	1.00 to 1.56
Virtual machine volatility	0.87 to 1.30
Computer turnaround time	0.87 to 1.15
Personnel attributes	
Analyst capability	1.46 to 0.71
Programmer capability	1.42 to 0.70
Applications experience	1.29 to 0.82
Virtual machine experience	1.21 to 0.90
Programming language experience	1.14 to 0.95
Project attributes	
Use of modern programming practices	1.24 to 0.82
Use of software tools	1.24 to 0.83
Required development schedule	1.23 to 1.10

Effort multipliers are used to modify these assumptions.
The following activities are covered by the estimates:

Covers design through acceptance testing
Includes cost of documentation and reviews
Includes cost of project manager and program librarian

The effort estimators exclude planning and analysis costs, installation and training costs, and the cost of secretaries, janitors, and computer operators. The DSI estimate includes job control statements and source statements, but excludes comments and unmodified utility routines. A DSI is considered to be one line or card image, and a programmer-month consists of 152 programmer-hours.

Other assumptions concerning the nature of software projects estimated by COCOMO include the following:

Careful definition and validation of requirements is performed by a small number
    of capable people.
The requirements remain stable throughout the project.
Careful definition and validation of the architectural design is performed by a small
    number of capable people.
Detailed design, coding, and unit testing are performed in parallel by groups of
    programmers working in teams.
Integration testing is based on early test planning.
Interface errors are mostly found by unit testing and by inspections and walk-
    throughs before integration testing.
Documentation is performed incrementally as part of the development process.

In other words, systematic techniques of software engineering are used throughout the development process.

The following example of algorithmic cost estimation using COCOMO is adapted from Boehm (BOE81):

The product to be developed is a 10-KDSI embedded mode software product for telecommunications processing on a commercially available microprocessor. The nominal effort equations for a 10-KDSI embedded mode product predict 44.4 programmer-months and 8.4 elapsed months for product development:

$$PM = 2.8*(10)**1.20 = 44.4$$

$$TDEV = 2.5*(44)**0.32 = 8.4$$

Effort multipliers are used to adjust the estimate for off-nominal aspects of the project. For instance, the software is expected to be highly complex, but this is balanced by the planned use of highly qualified analysts and programmers. The effort multipliers for this project are presented in Table 3.5.

The effort adjustment factor of 1.17 is the product of the effort multipliers. When applied to the nominal estimate, the effort adjustment factor produces an estimate of 51.9 programmer-months and 8.8 months development time. Assuming

Table 3.5 Effort multipliers for embedded telecommunications example

Multiplier	Rationale	Value
Reliability	Local use only. No serious recovery problems (nominal)	1.00
Database	20,000 bytes (low)	0.94
Complexity	Telecommunication processing (very high)	1.30
Timing	Will use 70% of processing time (high)	1.11
Storage	45K of 64K available (high)	1.06
Machine	Stable. Commercially available microprocessor (nominal)	1.00
Turnaround	Two hours average (nominal)	1.00
Analysts	Good senior people (high)	0.86
Programmers	Good senior people (high)	0.86
Experience	Three years in telecomm (nominal)	1.00
Experience	Six months on the micro (low)	1.10
Experience	Twelve months with the language (nominal)	1.00
Practices	More than 1 year experience with modern techniques (high)	0.91
Tools	Basic micro software (low)	1.10
Schedule	Nine months; 8.4 estimated (nominal)	1.00
Effort adjustment factor = 1.17		

that the programmers and analysts cost $6000 per person-month (a not unreasonable amount for fully burdened personnel cost), the total cost of project personnel will be

$$\text{DOLLARS} = (51.9 \text{ PM}) * (\$6000 \text{ per PM}) = \$311,400$$

COCOMO can also be used to investigate trade-offs in the development process by performing sensitivity analysis on the cost estimate. For example, less capable personnel might be used to implement the telecommunications processor at a cost savings of $1000 per person-month; however, the analyst and programmer capability multipliers must both be increased from 0.86 to 1.00 to reflect the change. Under these conditions, the effort adjustment factor becomes 1.58, and the DOLLARS amount becomes $350,760, which is a cost increase of $39,360. In addition, the estimated development schedule expands to 9.7 months. It is therefore better to use more highly qualified, and hence more expensive, personnel.

On the other hand, assume that we can expand the microprocessor memory from 46K to 96K for an additional $10,000. The additional memory will reduce the storage multiplier from 1.06 to 1.00, which results in a new cost adjustment factor of 1.10 and a new estimated cost of $293,000, for a net savings of $18,400. In addition, the effort reduction produces a slight reduction in the development time estimate. Purchasing the additional memory is thus a wise decision, not only for the cost savings during development, but also to provide a margin on main storage for product enhancements and modifications during the maintenance phase.

Table 3.6 lists the steps required to perform a cost estimate using COCOMO. The greatest advantage of COCOMO is that the model can be used to gain insight into the cost factors within an organization. Data can be collected and analyzed, new factors can be identified, and the effort multipliers can be adjusted as necessary to calibrate COCOMO to the local environment. Perhaps the greatest weakness of

Table 3.6 Cost estimation procedure using COCOMO

1. Identify all subsystems and modules in the product.
2. Estimate the size of each module and calculate the size of each subsystem and the total system.
3. Specify module-level effort multipliers for each module. The module-level multipliers are: product complexity, programmer capability, virtual machine experience, and programming language experience.
4. Compute the module effort and development time estimates for each module, using the nominal estimator equations and the module-level effort multipliers.
5. Specify the remaining 11 effort multipliers for each subsystem.
6. From steps 4 and 5, compute the estimated effort and development time for each subsystem.
7. From step 6, compute the total system effort and development time.
8. Perform a sensitivity analysis on the estimate to establish trade-off benefits.
9. Add other development costs, such as planning and analysis, that are not included in the estimate.
10. Compare the estimate with one developed by top-down Delphi estimation. Identify and rectify the differences in the estimates.

COCOMO is that use of a multiplicative effort adjustment factor assumes that the various effort multipliers are independent. In reality, varying one factor often implies that other factors should also be adjusted. Often, it is not clear how variations in one factor influence the other factors.

The version of COCOMO outlined here is Boehm's intermediate model. In his text, Boehm also presents a detailed model that accounts for differences in the effort multipliers by development phase. Although we have drawn heavily on Boehm's text in this discussion, our purpose is not to present an exhaustive discussion of COCOMO, but rather to indicate the factors that influence software cost and the manner in which COCOMO accounts for those factors.

One final note is the observation that most cost estimation models do not incorporate cost estimates for reuse of existing code. In one instance, the cost of reusing code was 20 percent of the cost of developing the equivalent amount of new code (ZEL83).

3.3 STAFFING-LEVEL ESTIMATION

The number of personnel required throughout a software development project is not constant. Typically, planning and analysis are performed by a small group of people, architectural design by a larger, but still small, group, and detailed design by a larger number of people. Implementation and system testing require the largest numbers of people. The early phase of maintenance may require numerous personnel, but the number should decrease in a short time. In the absence of major enhancement or adaptation, the number of personnel for maintenance should remain small.

In 1958, Norden observed that research and development projects follow a cycle of planning, design, prototype, development, and use, with the correspond-

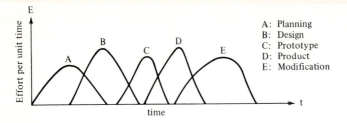

Figure 3.6 Cycles in a research and development project *(NOR58)*.

ing personnel utilization illustrated in Figure 3.6. He also observed that the sum of the areas under the curves in Figure 3.6 can be approximated by the Rayleigh equation, as illustrated in Figure 3.7 (NOR58). Any particular point on the Rayleigh curve represents the number of full-time equivalent personnel required at that instant in time. Note that the Rayleigh curve is specified by two parameters: *td*, the time at which the curve reaches its maximum value, and *K*, the total area under the curve, which represents the total effort required for the project.

In 1976, Putnam reported that the personnel level of effort required throughout the life cycle of a software product has a similar envelope. Putnam subsequently studied 50 Army software projects and 150 other projects to determine how the Rayleigh curve can be used to describe the software life cycle (PUT76, PUT78).

Among other things, Putnam observed that the time at which the Rayleigh curve reaches its maximum value, *td*, corresponds to the time of system testing and product release for many software products. The area under the Rayleigh curve in any interval represents the total effort expended in that interval. Approximately 40 percent of the area under the Rayleigh curve is to the left of *td* and 60 percent is to the right. This is a reasonable estimate of the distribution of effort between development and maintenance for many product life cycles. Putnam's interpretation of the Rayleigh curve is illustrated in Figure 3.8. Note that planning, requirements analysis, and functional design (external and architectural design) are not included in the project curve.

Boehm observes that the Rayleigh curve is a reasonably accurate estimator of

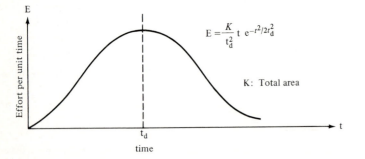

Figure 3.7 The Rayleigh curve of effort vs. time.

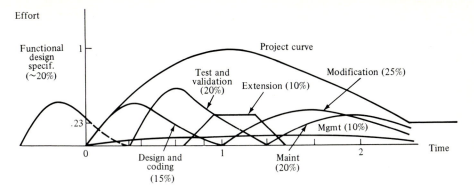

Figure 3.8 Putnam's interpretation of the Rayleigh Curve *(PUT76)*.

personnel requirements for the development cycle from architectural design through implementation and system testing if the portion of the curve between $0.3td$ and $1.7td$ is used (BOE81). The Rayleigh curve is then of the form

$$FSP = PM\left(\frac{0.15TDEV + 0.7t}{0.25(TDEV)^2}\right)e^{-\frac{(0.15TDEV + 0.7t)^2}{0.5(TDEV)^2}}$$

where PM is the estimated number of programmer-months for product development (excluding planning and analysis), and TDEV is the estimated development time. Given these two factors, the number of full-time software personnel, FSP, required at any particular time t, where t is in the range $0.3td$ to $1.7td$, can be computed. Note that td is still the time of peak staff requirements, but it is no longer interpreted as the elapsed development time. A plot of the personnel requirement as a function of time for a 32-KDSI, 91-PM, 14-month project is illustrated in Figure 3.9.

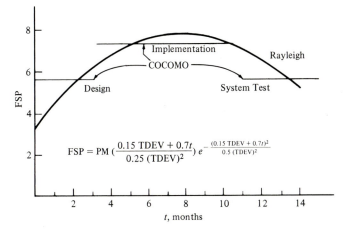

Figure 3.9 Rayleigh approximation to cocomo estimate *(32 KDSI, 91 PM, 14 mo project (BOE81)*.

Table 3.7 Distribution of effort for applications programs

Activity	Effort 32 KDSI	Effort 128 KDSI	Schedule 32 KDSI	Schedule 128 KDSI
Plans and requirements	6%	6%	12%	13%
Architectural design	16%	16%	19%	19%
Detailed design	24%	23%	combined values:	
Coding and unit test	38%	36%	55%	51%
System test	22%	25%	26%	30%

Table 3.8 Distribution of effort, schedule, and personnel

Activity	Effort 32 KDSI	Effort 128 KDSI	Schedule 32 KDSI	Schedule 128 KDSI	Personnel 32 KDSI	Personnel 128 KDSI
Plans and requirements	5 PM	24 MM	1.2 MO	3.1 MO	2.9 FSP	8 FSP
Architectural design	15 PM	63 MM	2.2 MO	4.6 MO	5.6 FSP	14 FSP
Detailed design	22 PM	90 MM	combined values:			
Implementation	34 PM	141 MM	7.7 MO	12.2 MO	7.3 FSP	19 FSP
System test	20 PM	90 MM	3.6 MO	7.2 MO	5.6 FSP	14 FSP

Boehm also presents tables that specify the distribution of effort and schedule in a software development project. For example, a 32-KDSI applications project has the estimated distribution of effort presented in Table 3.7.

The total number of programmer-months and total development time can be used to obtain an estimate of the actual number of programmer-months and elapsed time for each activity. An estimate of the number of full-time software personnel required in each phase of software development can be obtained by dividing the number of programmer-months required by the elapsed time available. Table 3.8 illustrates the distribution of effort, schedule, and required personnel for a 32-KDSI, 91-PM, 14-month project and a 128-KDSI, 292-PM, 24-month project.

Observe that system testing receives proportionally more time and effort on the larger project, and that programmer productivity on the 128-KDSI project, as measured in DSI/PM, drops to 93 percent of productivity on the 32-KDSI project. Figure 3.9 compares the Rayleigh distribution with the stepwise distribution for the 32-KDSI project.

3.4 ESTIMATING SOFTWARE MAINTENANCE COSTS

Software maintenance typically requires 40 to 60 percent, and in some cases as much as 90 percent, of the total life-cycle effort devoted to a software product. Maintenance activities include adding enhancements to the product, adapting the product to new processing environments, and correcting problems.

A widely used rule of thumb for the distribution of maintenance activities is 60 percent for enhancements, 20 percent for adaptation, and 20 percent for error correction. In a survey of 487 business data processing installations, Lientz and Swanson determined that the typical level of effort devoted to software maintenance was around 50 percent of total life-cycle effort, and that the distribution of maintenance activities was 51.3 percent for enhancement, 23.6 percent for adaptation, 21.7 percent for repair, and 3.4 percent for other (LIE80). These percentages are further broken down in Table 3.9.

The major concerns about maintenance during the planning phase of a software project are estimating the number of maintenance programmers that will be needed and specifying the facilities required for maintenance.

A widely used estimator of maintenance personnel is the number of source lines that can be maintained by an individual programmer. Lientz and Swanson determined that the typical maintenance programmer in a business data processing installation maintains 32K source instructions. For real-time and aerospace software, numbers in the range of 8K to 10K are more typical. Table 3.10 summarizes various figures that have appeared in the literature (BOE81).

An estimate of the number of full-time software personnel needed for software maintenance can be determined by dividing the estimated number of source instructions to be maintained by the estimated number of instructions that can be maintained by a maintenance programmer. For example, if a maintenance programmer can maintain 32 KDSI, then two maintenance programmers are required to maintain 64 KDSI:

$$FSPm = (64 \text{ KDSI})/(32 \text{ KDSI}/FSP) = 2 \text{ FSPm}$$

Boehm suggests that maintenance effort can be estimated by use of an activity ratio, which is the number of source instructions to be added and modified in any given time period divided by the total number of instructions:

$$ACT = (DSI_{added} + DSI_{modified})/DSI_{total}$$

Table 3.9 Maintenance effort distribution (from LIE80)

Activity	% Effort
Enhancement	51.3
Improved efficiency	4.0
Improved documentation	5.5
User enhancements	41.8
Adaptation	23.6
Input data, files	17.4
Hardware, operating system	6.2
Corrections	21.7
Emergency fixes	12.4
Scheduled fixes	9.3
Other	3.4

Table 3.10 Source instructions per maintenance programmer (adapted from BOE81)

Reference	Application area	KDSI/FSPm
WOL80	Aerospace	8
FER79	Aerospace	10
BOE81, 25th percentile	Numerous	10
DAL77	Real-time	10–30
GRI80	Real-time	12
ELL77	Business	20
GRA77	Business	20
BOE81, median	Numerous	25
LIE 80	Business	32
BOE81, 75th percentile	Numerous	36

The activity ratio is then multiplied by the number of programmer-months required for development in a given time period to determine the number of programmer-months required for maintenance in the corresponding time period:

$$PMm = ACT * MM_{dev}$$

A further enhancement is provided by an effort adjustment factor EAF, which recognizes that the effort multipliers for maintenance may be different from the effort multipliers used for development:

$$PMm = ACT * EAF * MM_{dev}$$

For example, heavy emphasis on reliability and the use of modern programming practices during development may reduce the amount of effort required for maintenance, while low emphasis on reliability and modern practices during development may increase the difficulty of maintenance.

3.5 SUMMARY

Software cost estimation is one of the most difficult and error-prone tasks in software engineering. Cost estimation techniques rely on historical data covering past performance by particular organizations on particular types of software projects. Thus, a cost estimate is only as good as our ability to extrapolate from past performance to future performance. Also, most cost estimates are in terms of estimated number of source instructions in the product to be developed. The cost estimate will be no better than our ability to estimate the number of source instructions in the product.

Expert judgment and algorithmic prediction are two fundamental approaches to cost estimation. In practice, more than one estimation technique should be used and the results compared and reconciled.

In this chapter, we have discussed the major factors that influence software cost, and the quantification scheme developed by Boehm was used to indicate the relative influence of various cost factors (BOE81). The Delphi technique of cost estimation by a group of experts was described, and the principal features of the Constructive Cost Model (COCOMO) were presented. A brief introduction to the SLIM model, which is based on the Rayleigh equation, was presented.

Estimation of staffing-level requirements using Rayleigh curves and COCOMO was described, and techniques for estimating software maintenance costs were discussed.

Detailed discussions of COCOMO, SLIM, and other cost models, such as the Walston-Felix model, the Doty model, and Price S, are discussed in (BAS80) and in the references to this chapter.

Software cost estimates are typically based on historical data. Thus, data must be collected during current projects in order to estimate effort and schedule for future ones. The collected data can also be used to indicate problem areas in the processes used to develop and maintain software products. Perhaps the most beneficial aspect of algorithmic cost estimation models is the attention that is focused on collection and analysis of project data.

REFERENCES

(AIR74) U.S. Air Force: *Proceeding, Government/Industry Software Sizing and Costing Workshop,* U.S. Air Force Electronic Systems Div., Bedford, MA, October 1974.

(BAS80) Basili, V.: *Tutorial on Models and Metrics for Software Management and Engineering,* IEEE Catalog No. EHO-167-7, 1980.

(BOE81) Boehm, B.: *Software Engineering Economics,* Prentice-Hall, Englewood Cliffs, NJ, 1981.

(BRO74) Brooks, F.: "The Mythical Man-Month," *Datamation,* December 1974.

(DAL77) Daly, E.: "Management of Software Engineering," *IEEE TSE,* vol. SE-3, no. 3, May 1977.

(ELL77) Elliott, I.: "Life-Cycle Planning for a Large Mix of Commercial Systems," *Proc. U.S. Army ISRAD Software Workshop,* August 1977.

(FER79) Ferens, D., and R. Harris: "Avionics Computer Software Operation and Support Cost Estimation," *Proc. NAECON79,* Dayton, Ohio, May 1979.

(FRE79) Freburger, K., and V. Basili: *The Software Engineering Laboratory: Relationship Equations,* Report TR764, University of Maryland, May 1979.

(GRA77) Graver, C., et al.: *Cost Reporting Elements and Activity Cost Tradeoffs for Defense System Software,* General Research Corporation, Santa Barbara, CA, March 1977.

(GRI80) Griffin, E.: "Real-Time Estimating," *Datamation,* June 1980.

(HAL77) Halstead, M.: *Elements of Software Science,* Elsevier, 1977.

(HEL66) Helmer, O.: *Social Technology,* Basic Books, 1966.

(JON77) Jones, T.: *Program Quality and Programmer Productivity,* IBM TR 02.764, January 1977.

(LIE80) Lientz, B., and E. Swanson: *Software Maintenance Management: A Study of the Maintenance of Computer Application Software in 487 Data Processing Organizations,* Addison-Wesley, Reading, MA, 1980.

(NEL78) Nelson, R.: *Software Data Collection and Analysis at RADC,* Rome Air Development Center, Rome, NY, 1978.

(NOR58) Norden, P.: "Curve Fitting for a Model of Applied Research and Development Scheduling," *IBM J. Rsch. Dev.,* vol. 2, no. 3, July 1958.

(PUT76) Putnam, L.: "A Macro-Estimating Methodology for Software Development," *Proc. IEEE COMPCON 76,* September 1976.

(PUT78) ———: "A General Empirical Solution to the Macro Software Sizing and Estimating Problem," *IEEE TSE,* vol. SE-4, no. 4, July 1978.

(RCA78) RCA PRICE SYSTEMS: *PRICE Software Model: Supplemental Information,* RCA, Cherry Hill, NJ, March 1978.

(SAC68) Sackman, H., et al.: "Exploratory Experimental Studies Comparing Online and Offline Programming Performance," *CACM,* vol. 11, no. 1, January 1968.

(SCH78) Schneider, V.: "Prediction of Software Effort and Project Duration: Four New Formulas," *ACM SIGPLAN Notices,* June 1978.

(WAL77) Walston, C., and C. Felix: "A Method of Programming Measurement and Estimation," *IBM Syst. J.,* vol. 16, no. 1, January 1977.

(WOL80) Wolverton, R.: *Airborne Systems Software Acquisition Engineering Guidebook: Software Cost Analysis and Estimating,* U.S. Air Force ASD/EN, Wright-Patterson AFB, OH, February 1980.

(ZEL83) Zelkowitz, M.: Private communication.

EXERCISES

3.1 Use the COCOMO equations to estimate the programmer-months and development time for your term project. Prepare a range of estimates based on probable product size.

3.2 Develop an effort adjustment factor for your estimates in Exercise 3.1. Apply the adjustment factor to obtain a new estimate.

What factors will enhance your team's productivity?

What factors will hurt productivity?

What can be done to improve those factors?

3.3 Keep records by activity phase of the actual amount of effort expended by your team throughout the semester. At the end of the semester, compare actual effort with predicted effort, using the actual size of your product. What factors caused the difference between estimated and actual effort?

3.4 Suppose you are planning for maintenance of a 15-KDSI utility program. During the next year you expect to add 2 KDSI and modify 3 KDSI. How many programmer-months will be required? How many programmers?

3.5. (*a*) Suppose you are planning to add 2 KDSI and modify 3 KDSI in a 150-KDSI utility program during the coming year. How many programmer-months and programmers will be required?

(*b*) Compare the estimates in part *a* with those in Exercise 3.4. What can you conclude about scaling of maintenance effort with product size?

The next three problems are concerned with the buy/build decision for software products.

3.6 Suppose that a 40-KDSI application program can be purchased for $500,000. Assuming that your in-house programmers cost $4000 per programmer-month (including overhead), would it be more cost-effective to buy the product or to build it? What additional costs are not included in COCOMO? What additional factors should be considered in making the buy/build decision?

3.7 Assume that the company providing the commercial product in Exercise 3.6 will furnish maintenance of their product at 15 percent annual change level for $75,000 per year. If in-house maintenance programmers cost $4000 per month, would it be better to buy or build when the total cost of the product and a 5-year maintenance contract are compared with the total cost of in-house building and maintenance for a 5-year period?

What other factors should be considered in making the buy/build maintenance decision?

3.8 Closer examination of in-house development and maintenance cost for the system described in Exercise 3.6 results in the following cost breakdown:

Activity	Cost
Analysis & design	$5000/PM
Programming	$4000/PM
System testing	$4500/PM
Maintenance	$4000/PM for the first year
	10% increase per year

Determine the cost to build the product and maintain it for 5 years.

3.9 It is conjectured that the effort multiplier for using software tools on the project previously described can be reduced from 1.2 to 0.9 by purchasing a sophisticated package of software development tools. The cost of the package and a training course for the programming team (including training time) is approximately $100,000. Assuming that the product will be developed in-house, would it be cost-effective to purchase the package?

What additional benefits might accrue from using the package of tools?

In what ways might use of the new tools be detrimental to the project?

FOUR

SOFTWARE REQUIREMENTS DEFINITION

INTRODUCTION

The analysis phase of software development involves project planning and software requirements definition. Planning was discussed in Chapters 2 and 3; the outcome of planning is recorded in the *System Definition*, the *Project Plan*, and the preliminary *User's Manual*. The *Software Requirements Specification* records the outcome of the software requirements definition activity.

The *System Definition, Project Plan,* and preliminary *User's Manual* are primarily concerned with the user and the external view of the software product. In contrast, the *Software Requirements Specification* is a technical specification of requirements for the software product. The goal of software requirements definition is to completely and consistently specify the technical requirements for the software product in a concise and unambiguous manner, using formal notations as appropriate. Depending on the size and complexity of the product, the software requirements document may consist of a few pages or it may be packaged in several volumes.

The *Software Requirements Specification* is based on the *System Definition*. High-level requirements specified during initial planning are elaborated and made more specific in order to characterize the features that the software product will incorporate. Ideally, the requirements specification will state the "what"of the software product without implying "how." Software design is concerned with specifying how the product will provide the required features.

In this chapter, the format and contents of a *Software Requirements Specification* are discussed, formal techniques for specifying functional properties of software are described, and some automated tools for requirements specification are presented.

The format and contents of a *Software Requirements Specification* document are discussed in the following section.

4.1 THE *SOFTWARE REQUIREMENTS SPECIFICATION*

The format of a requirements specification document is presented in Table 4.1. As illustrated there, Sections 1 and 2 of the requirements document present an overview of product features and summarize the processing environments for development, operation, and maintenance of the product. This information is an elaboration of the software product characteristics contained in the *System Definition* and the preliminary *User's Manual*.

Section 3 specifies the externally observable characteristics of the software product. Items in Section 3 include user displays and report formats, a summary of user commands and report options, data flow diagrams, and a data dictionary. Specifications for the user interface displays and reports are refinements of information contained in the *System Definition* and the preliminary *User's Manual*. High-level data flow diagrams and a data dictionary are derived at the time this section is written.

Data flow diagrams specify data sources and data sinks, data stores, transformations to be performed on the data, and the flow of data between sources, sinks, transformations, and stores. A data store is a conceptual data structure, in the sense that physical implementation details are suppressed; only the logical characteristics of data are emphasized on a data flow diagram.

Data flow diagrams can be depicted informally, as illustrated in Figure 4.1, or by using special notation as illustrated in Figure 4.2, where data sources and data sinks are depicted by shaded rectangles, transformations by ordinary rectangles, and data stores by open ended rectangles. The arcs in a data flow diagram specify

Table 4.1 Format of a software requirements specification

Section 1: Product Overview and Summary
Section 2: Development, Operating, and Maintenance Environments
Section 3: External Interfaces and Data Flow
Section 4: Functional Requirements
Section 5: Performance Requirements
Section 6: Exception Handling
Section 7: Early Subsets and Implementation Priorities
Section 8: Foreseeable Modifications and Enhancements
Section 9: Acceptance Criteria
Section 10: Design Hints and Guidelines
Section 11: Cross-Reference Index
Section 12: Glossary of Terms

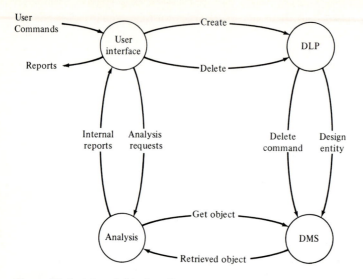

Figure 4.1 An informal data flow diagram.

data flow; they are labeled with the names of data items whose characteristics are specified in the data dictionary.

Like flowcharts, data flow diagrams can be used at any level of detail. They can be hierarchically decomposed by specifying the inner workings of the functional nodes using additional data flow diagrams. Unlike flowcharts, data flow diagrams are not concerned with decision structure or algorithmic details.

A data dictionary entry is illustrated in Table 4.2. Entries in a data dictionary include the name of the data item, and attributes such as the data flow diagrams where it is used, its purpose, where it is derived from, its subitems, and any notes that may be appropriate. Each named data item on each data flow diagram should

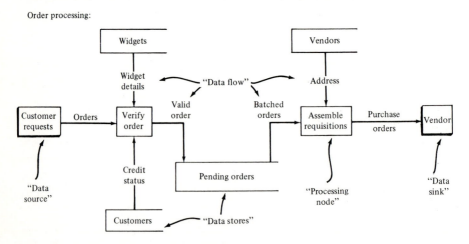

Figure 4.2 A formal data flow diagram *(GAN79)*.

Table 4.2 A Data dictionary entry

NAME:	Create
WHERE USED:	SDLP
PURPOSE:	Create passes a user-created design entity to the SLP processor for verification of syntax.
DERIVED FROM:	User Interface Processor
SUBITEMS:	Name Uses Procedures References
NOTES:	Create contains one complete user-created design entity.

appear in the data dictionary. The physical implementation details of data items are not of interest in the data dictionary (at this time).

Section 4 of a *Software Requirements Specification* specifies the functional requirements for the software product. Functional requirements are typically expressed in relational and state-oriented notations that specify relationships among inputs, actions, and outputs. Formal notations for specifying functional requirements are discussed in Section 4.3.

Performance characteristics such as response time for various activities, processing time for various processes, throughput, primary and secondary memory constraints, required telecommunication bandwidth, and special items such as extraordinary security constraints or unusual reliability requirements are specified in Section 5 of the requirements document. Performance characteristics must be stated in verifiable terms, and the methods to be used in verifying performance must also be specified. Although formal techniques for specifying the performance characteristics of software products are not well developed, it is nevertheless important that performance requirements be stated in a rigorous manner, so that logical reasoning can be applied to the statement of requirements.

Exception handling, including the actions to be taken and the messages to be displayed in response to undesired situations or events, is described in Section 6 of the *Software Requirements Specification*. A table of exception conditions and exception responses should be prepared. Categories of possible exceptions include temporary resource failure (e.g., temporary loss of a sensor or communications link); permanent resource failure (e.g., loss of a memory bank or processor); incorrect, inconsistent, or out-of-range input data, internal values, and parameters; violation of capacity limits (e.g., table overflow, array indices out of range, run-time stack overflow, heap overflow); and violations of restrictions on operators (e.g., division by zero, attempt to read past end of file). Ideally, the set of identified exception conditions should be sufficient to ensure that if none occur processing will proceed in the normal manner. In practice, it may not be possible to achieve this goal (HEN80).

Section 7 of the *Software Requirements Specification* specifies early subsets and implementation priorities for the system under development. As discussed in Section 2.3, software products are sometimes developed as a series of successive versions. The initial version may be a skeletal prototype that demonstrates basic user functions and provides a framework for evolution of the product. Each successive version can incorporate the capabilities of previous versions and provide additional processing functions. Successive versions of the product can be planned as useful products of limited capability. It is not unusual for a product to be planned in three versions: prototype, modest version, and enhanced version. The customer may desire early delivery of subset capabilities, and the successive versions can provide increasing levels of capabilities.

For the reasons mentioned in Section 2.2 (namely, that implementors should not decide the relative importance of various requirements), it is important to specify implementation priorities for various system capabilities. Essential features, desirable features, and "nice if" features must be identified to provide guidance to the designers and implementors; otherwise important decisions may be made at a later time without global information to guide the decision process.

Foreseeable modifications and enhancements that may be incorporated into the product following initial product release are specified in Section 8 of the product requirements. If the designers and implementors are aware of likely changes, they can design and build the product in a manner that will ease those changes. Foreseeable product modifications might occur as a result of anticipated changes in project budget or project mission, as a result of new hardware acquisition, or as a result of experience gained from an initial release of the product. In any event, it is important that known probable changes be identified and incorporated into the product requirements.

The software product acceptance criteria are specified in Section 9 of the requirements document. Acceptance criteria specify functional and performance tests that must be performed, and the standards to be applied to source code, internal documentation, and external documents such as the design specifications, the test plan, the user's manual, the principles of operation, and the installation and maintenance procedures. In addition, the desired functional and physical audits of source code, documents, and physical media are specified. It is important that the acceptance criteria verify the functional and performance requirements stated in Sections 4 and 5 of the product requirements.

Section 10 of the *Software Requirements Specification* contains design hints and guidelines. The requirements specification is primarily concerned with functional and performance aspects of a software product, and emphasis is placed on specifying product characteristics without implying how the product will provide those characteristics. The "how to" of product implementation is the topic of software design, and should be deferred to the design phase. Nevertheless, certain insights and understandings will be gained during planning and requirements definition. These thoughts should be recorded as hints and guidelines to the product designers, but not as rigid requirements for product design.

Section 11 relates product requirements to the sources of information used in deriving the requirements. A cross-reference directory should be provided to index specific paragraph numbers in the *Software Requirements Specification* to specific paragraphs in the *System Definition* and the preliminary *User's Manual,* and to other sources of information (people or documents). Knowing the sources of specific requirements permits verification and re-examination of requirements, constraints, and assumptions.

Section 12 of the *Software Requirements Specification* provides definitions of terms that may be unfamiliar to the customer and the product developers. In particular, care should be taken to define standard terms that are used in non-standard ways. Some software engineers make the glossary of terms the first, rather than last, section of the document.

Desirable properties. There are a number of desirable properties that a *Software Requirements Specification* should possess. In particular, a requirements document should be:

Correct
Complete
Consistent
Unambiguous
Functional
Verifiable
Traceable
Easily changed

An incorrect or incomplete set of requirements can result in a software product that satisfies its requirements but does not satisfy customer needs. An inconsistent specification states contradictory requirements in different parts of the document, while an ambiguous requirement is subject to different interpretations by different people.

Software requirements should be functional in nature; i.e., they should describe what is required without implying how the system will meet its requirements. This provides maximum flexibility for the product designers.

Requirements must be verifiable from two points of view; it must be possible to verify that the requirements satisfy the customer's needs, and it must be possible to verify that the subsequent work products satisfy the requirements. Due to the lack of formal verification techniques for software requirements, the most important verification tool currently available is rigorous, logical reasoning.

Finally, the requirements should be indexed, segmented, and cross-referenced to permit easy use and easy modification. Ideally, every software requirement should be traceable to specific customer statements and to specific statements in the *System Definition.* Changes will occur, and project success often depends on the ability to incorporate change without starting over. Dewey decimal notation is often used to index the sections and subsections of various documents in a software project. Cross-referencing can be accomplished by referring to the appropriate paragraph numbers in the appropriate documents.

The desirable properties of a *Software Requirements Specification* can be enhanced by use of formal notations and automated tools. These topics are discussed in the following sections.

4.2 FORMAL SPECIFICATION TECHNIQUES

Specifying the functional characteristics of a software product is one of the most important activities to be accomplished during requirements analysis. Formal notations have the advantage of being concise and unambiguous, they support formal reasoning about the functional specifications, and they provide a basis for verification of the resulting software product. Formal notations are not appropriate in all situations or for all types of systems. However, our experience indicates that there is usually too little formalism in software development, rather than too much; hence, our emphasis on formalisms.

Both relational and state-oriented notations are used to specify the functional characteristics of software. Relational notations are based on the concepts of entities and attributes. Entities are named elements in a system; the names are chosen to denote the nature of the elements (e.g., stack, queue, radar_pulse). Attributes are specified by applying functions and relations to the named entities. Attributes specify permitted operations on entities, relationships among entities, and data flow between entities.

The state of a system is the information required to summarize the status of system entities at any particular point in time; given the current state and the current stimuli, the next state can be determined. The execution history by which the current state was attained does not influence the next state; it is only dependent on the current state and current stimuli.

Relational notations include implicit equations, recurrence relations, algebraic axioms, and regular expressions. State-oriented notations include decision tables, event tables, transition tables, finite-state mechanisms, and Petri nets. All of these notations are formal, in the sense that they are concise and unambiguous. They are described in the following sections.

4.2.1 Relational Notations

Implicit equations. Implicit equations state the properties of a solution without stating a solution method. One might, for example, specify matrix inversion as

$$M \times M' = I \pm E \qquad (4.1)$$

In Equation (4.1), matrix inversion is specified such that the matrix product of the original matrix M and the inverse of M, M', yields the identity matrix I plus or minus the error matrix E, where E specifies allowable computational errors. Complete specification of matrix inversion must include items such as matrix size, type of data elements, and degree of sparseness. Given a complete functional specification for matrix inversion, design involves specifying a data structure, an algorithm for computing the inverse, and a packaging technique for the inversion module.

Implicit specification of a square root function, SQRT, can be stated as

$$(0 <= X <= Y) [ABS(SQRT(X)**2 - X) < E] \qquad (4.2)$$

Equation (4.2) states that for all (real?) values of X in the closed range 0 to Y, computing the square root of X, squaring it, and subtracting X results in an error value that is in some permissible error range.

Not all implicitly specified problems are guaranteed to have algorithmic solutions. For example, a variant of Fermat's last problem can be stated as follows:

$$(N > 2) [X**N + Y**N = Z**N] \qquad (4.3)$$

Fermat's problem involves finding values of integers X, Y, and Z such that, for arbitrarily chosen values of N, Equation (4.3) is satisfied. No solutions to this problem have been discovered for values of N greater than 2.

Recurrence relations. A recurrence relation consists of an initial part called the basis and one or more recursive parts. The recursive part(s) describe the desired value of a function in terms of other values of the function. For example, successive Fibonacci numbers are formed as the sum of the previous two Fibonacci numbers, where the first one is defined as 0, and the second as 1. The Fibonacci numbers can be defined by the recurrence

$$FI(0) = 0$$
$$FI(1) = 1$$
$$FI(N) = FI(N - 1) + FI(N - 2) \qquad \text{for all } N > 1$$

and Ackerman's function is defined as follows:

$$A(0,K) = K + 1 \qquad \text{for all } K > 0$$
$$A(J,0) = A(J - 1, 1) \qquad \text{for all } J > 0$$
$$A(J,K) = A(J - 1, A(J, K - 1)) \qquad \text{for all } J, K > 0$$

Recurrence relations are easily transformed into recursive programs; however, we do not intend to imply that every recursive specification should be implemented as a recursive program. This point is discussed in Chapter 6.

Algebraic axioms. Mathematical systems are defined by axioms. The axioms specify fundamental properties of a system and provide a basis for deriving additional properties that are implied by the axioms. These additional properties are called theorems. In order to establish a valid mathematical system, the set of axioms must be complete and consistent; i.e., it must be possible to prove desired results using the axioms, and it must not be possible to prove contradictory results. Elegance of definition is achieved if the axioms are independent (no axiom can be derived from the other axioms), but in practice independence of axioms is less important than completeness and consistency.

The axiomatic approach can be used to specify functional properties of software systems. As in mathematics, the intent is to specify the fundamental nature of a system by stating a few basic properties. This approach can be used to specify abstract data types (GUT77). A data type is characterized as a set of objects and a set of permissible operations on those objects. The term "abstract data type" (or "data abstraction") refers to the fact that permissible operations on the data objects are emphasized, while representation details of the data objects are suppressed.

In general, abstraction allows one to emphasize the important characteristics of a system while suppressing unimportant details. Thus, data abstraction emphasizes functional properties and suppresses representation details. Depending on the axioms provided, only some of many possible functional properties are specified.

Specification of an abstract data type using algebraic axioms involves defining the syntax of the operations and specifying axiomatic relationships among the operations. The syntactic definition specifies names, domains, and ranges of operations to be performed on the data objects, and the axioms specify interactions among operations. An example follows.

Axiomatic specification of the last-in first-out (LIFO) property of stack objects is specified in Figure 4.3. Observe that the type of data elements being manipulated, ITEM, is a parameter in the specification, and that the specification is representation independent. Operations NEW, PUSH, POP, TOP, and EMPTY are named to suggest their purposes, but the definition is not dependent on the particular names chosen.

Intuitive definitions of the stack operations are:

NEW creates a new stack.
PUSH adds a new item to the top of a stack.
TOP returns a copy of the top item.
POP removes the top item.
EMPTY tests for an empty stack.

Operation NEW yields a newly created stack. PUSH requires two arguments, a

SYNTAX:

OPERATION	DOMAIN	RANGE
NEW	( ) —>	STACK
PUSH	(STACK,ITEM) —>	STACK
POP	(STACK) —>	STACK
TOP	(STACK) —>	ITEM
EMPTY	(STACK) —>	BOOLEAN

AXIOMS:
(stk is of type STACK, itm is of type ITEM)
(1) EMPTY(NEW) = true
(2) EMPTY(PUSH(stk,itm)) = false
(3) POP(NEW) = error
(4) TOP(NEW) = error
(5) POP(PUSH(stk,itm)) = stk
(6) TOP(PUSH(stk,itm)) = itm

Figure 4.3 Algebraic specification of the LIFO property.

stack and an item; it produces a stack. POP requires a stack as its argument and yields a stack. TOP requires a stack and produces an item. EMPTY tests for an empty stack; it requires a stack and provides a Boolean value.

In the axiomatic definition of a stack presented in Figure 4.3, it is assumed that stacks do not overflow; thus PUSH always succeeds. Observe that nested entities provide the proper types as arguments for the entities in which they are nested. For example, in the axiom EMPTY(PUSH(stk,itm)) = false PUSH yields type STACK, which is the required argument type for EMPTY.

The axioms in Figure 4.3 can be stated in English as follows:

1. A new stack is empty.
2. A stack is not empty immediately after pushing an item onto it.
3. Attempting to pop a new stack results in an error.
4. There is no top item on a new stack.
5. Pushing an item onto a stack and immediately popping it off leaves the stack unchanged.
6. Pushing an item onto a stack and immediately requesting the top item returns the item just pushed onto the stack.

Thus, the axioms do not state anything that cannot be stated in English, but they do specify the fundamental characteristics of stacks in a precise and unambiguous manner. Furthermore, the axioms can be manipulated in a rigorous manner.

The intuitively defined entities NEW, PUSH, POP, TOP, and EMPTY are precisely specified in Figure 4.4 using a state-oriented approach; the notation is adapted from (ROB77). In Figure 4.4, an entity delimited by quotes [e.g., 'Valid_Stack(stk)'] denotes the state of the system immediately before the operation in which it is contained. An unquoted entity refers to the state of the system immediately following the containing operation. Observe that an exception condition has been specified for stack overflow in the definition of the PUSH function.

Using a state-oriented notation in conjunction with algebraic axioms allows precise specification of the entity names used in the axioms. This technique combines the advantages of the algebraic approach (precise specification of interactions among operations) and the finite-state approach (precise specification of the behavior of the individual operations).

The definitions in Figure 4.4 use primitive functions Valid_Stack and Number_Items. These functions perform the self-evident actions denoted by their names (checking that a given name denotes a valid stack and returning the number of items in a stack). Formal definitions for these functions can be given, but at some point the fundamental definitions in all formal systems must involve symbols whose meanings are intuitively understood. For instance, the set-theoretic approach in mathematics starts with the intuitive definition of a set as a collection of objects; it is assumed that the student understands the phrase "collection of objects." A major purpose of formal notations is to allow unambiguous specification of complex notions in terms of a few simple, well understood (intuitively understood) notions.

NEW

Purpose:	Create a new stack
Exceptions:	Memory_Full = true
Effects:	Valid_Stack(NEW) = true
	Number_Items(NEW) = 0

EMPTY(stk)

Purpose:	Test stk for empty property
Exceptions:	'Valid_Stack(stk)' = false
Effects:	if 'Number_Items(stk)' = 0 then true else false

PUSH(stk,item)

Purpose:	Place item on stk
Exceptions:	'Valid_Stack(stk)' = false
	'Number_Items(stk)' = MAX
Effects:	if 'Number_Items(stk)' = MAX then error
	else Number_Items(stk) = 'Number_Items(stk)' + 1

POP(stk)

Purpose:	Delete top item from stk
Exceptions:	'Valid_Stack(stk)' = false
	'Number_Items(stk)' = 0
Effects:	if 'Number_Items(stk)' = 0 then error else {stk = 'stk' - TOP(stk)
	Number_Items(stk) = 'Number_Items(stk)' - 1}

TOP(stk)

Purpose:	Return a copy of top item on stk
Exceptions:	'Valid_Stack(stk)' = false
	'Number_Items(stk)' = 0
Effect:	if 'Number_Items(stk)' = 0 then error
	else Number_Items(stk) = 'Number_Items(stk)'}

Figure 4.4 Definition of STACK function behavior.

Given a set of algebraic axioms, new operations can be defined in terms of existing ones. For example, REPLACE can be defined to have the property of replacing the top data item on a stack with a new item:

REPLACE(stk,itm) = if EMPTY(stk) then error else PUSH(POP(stk),itm)

The first-in first-out (FIFO) property of queues is specified in Figure 4.5. NEW creates a new queue, ADD adds an item to the rear of a queue, FRONT returns a copy of the front item in a queue without deleting it, REMOVE deletes the front item, and EMPTY tests for an empty queue. It is assumed that queues do not overflow; thus ADD always succeeds.

Observe the similarities and differences between the LIFO and FIFO properties as specified in Figures 4.3 and 4.5. Also observe that a certain symmetry exists among the relationships in each figure. The theory of algebraic specifications is stated in terms of "constructors," "modifiers," and "behaviors." In Figure 4.3 the constructors are NEW and PUSH. POP is a modifier, and TOP and EMPTY are behaviors. In Figure 4.5, NEW and ADD are constructors, REMOVE is a modifier, and FRONT and EMPTY are behaviors. In order to provide a "sufficiently

SYNTAX:

OPERATION	DOMAIN	RANGE
NEW	( ) —>	QUEUE
ADD	(QUEUE,ITEM) —>	QUEUE
FRONT	(QUEUE) —>	ITEM
REMOVE	(QUEUE) —>	QUEUE
EMPTY	(QUEUE) —>	BOOLEAN

AXIOMS:
(que is of type QUEUE, itm is of type ITEM)
(1) EMPTY(NEW) = true
(2) EMPTY(ADD(que,itm)) = false
(3) FRONT(NEW) = error
(4) REMOVE(NEW) = error
(5) FRONT(ADD(que,itm)) = if EMPTY(que) then itm else FRONT(que)
(6) REMOVE(ADD(que,itm)) = if EMPTY(que) then NEW else ADD(REMOVE(que),itm)

Figure 4.5 Algebraic specification of the FIFO property.

complete" set of axioms it is necessary to provide an axiom of the form

$$Modifier(Constructor(\ )) = ?$$

and

$$Behavior(Constructor(\ )) = ?$$

for each constructor, modifier, and behavior in the set. The examples in Figures 4.3 and 4.5 are sufficiently complete. Given a sufficiently complete set of algebraic axioms, one can always construct an equivalent finite state specification. The theory of algebraic specifications for abstract data types is further discussed by Guttag (GUT78).

The examples presented in Figures 4.3 and 4.5 should not be taken to mean that data abstraction techniques are limited to specification of simple abstractions such as stacks and queues. Abstract data types can be used to define complex hierarchies of entities, and modern programming languages such as CLU and Ada provide features to support implementation of abstract data types. Data abstraction is one of the most important developments in software engineering in recent years. We will return to the discussion of abstract data types in subsequent chapters of the text.

Algebraic axioms can be used in three distinct ways: as definitional tools (illustrated above); as foundations for deductive proofs of desired properties, and as frameworks for examining the completeness and consistency of functional requirements.

As an example of deductive reasoning about abstract data types, consider the definition of the stack operator REPLACE:

REPLACE(stk,itm) = if EMPTY(stk) then error else PUSH(POP(stk),itm)

Assuming that stk is not empty, the definitions provided in Figure 4.4 can be used to rigorously demonstrate that REPLACE has the effect of replacing the top item on a stack with a new item; i.e., REPLACE(stk*.itm1,itm2) = stk*.itm2, where stk* denotes all of the stack except the top item and stk*.itm denotes the entire stack.

$$
\begin{aligned}
\text{REPLACE(stk*.itm1,itm2)} &= \text{PUSH(POP(stk*.itm1),itm2)} \\
&= \text{PUSH(stk*.itm1-TOP(stk*.itm1),itm2)} \\
&= \text{PUSH(stk*.itm1-itm1,itm2)} \\
&= \text{PUSH(stk*,itm2)} \\
&= \text{stk*.itm2}
\end{aligned}
$$

A similar argument can be made to show that REPLACE does not change the number of items in a stack.

There are two types of completeness concerns for a requirement specification: external completeness and internal completeness. External completeness is a pragmatic consideration. A requirement specification is externally complete if all the desired properties are specified. For instance, in Figure 4.5 there is no specification for a SIZE function to return the current number of elements in a queue. If the application requires SIZE, the specification is incomplete. External completeness is ultimately a question of whether the customer's needs will be satisfied by a software product that incorporates all the stated specifications.

A requirement specification that is internally complete has no undefined entities in the specification. For example, use of the term TOP without defining its meaning would result in a specification for STACK that is internally incomplete.

Consistency involves the relationships among specifications. If, for example, the TOP operation for stacks is sometimes assumed to delete the top element of a stack and sometimes assumed to retain the top element, then TOP is used inconsistently. The formal definition of TOP in Figure 4.4 indicates that TOP does not change the stack configuration. Given a formal definition of TOP, inconsistent usage of TOP becomes incorrect usage in some of the inconsistent cases.

Symbolic execution techniques (described in Chapter 8) can be used to "execute" algebraic specifications. Symbolic execution systems can perform sequences of function applications and report the results obtained, or report error conditions encountered in attempting a sequence of operations. For example, applying the sequence q := NEW; ADD(q,5); REMOVE(ADD(q,3)); FRONT(ADD(q,4)); will return the value 3 and result in a queue that contains (3,4). The sequence q := NEW; ADD(q,5); REMOVE(q); REMOVE(q); will result in an underflow error and an empty queue.

Symbolic execution can be used to investigate completeness and consistency of algebraic specifications. The software engineer can exercise the specifications using a symbolic execution tool to understand how the specifications interact, and to discover incompleteness and inconsistencies. An alternative approach to testing of algebraic specifications is described in (GAN81).

If an axiomatic specification is complete and consistent, any implementation that satisfies the stated relationships among operations will embody the desired characteristics (e.g., the LIFO property). A complete and consistent set of functional specifications provides a complete and consistent set of functional test cases for an implementation of the software product; for instance, any implementation that provides a set of functions that satisfy the relations illustrated in Figure 4.3 exhibits the LIFO property. If the desired functional characteristics of a software system are completely and consistently specified, and if the implementation satisfies those specifications, there is no need for further testing or verification of the source code, except to verify performance, and to verify that the code does not produce additional, undesired side effects (such as launching a missile as an unspecified side effect of POP).

Regular expressions. Regular expressions can be used to specify the syntactic structure of symbol strings. Because many software products involve processing of symbol strings, regular expressions provide a powerful and widely used notation in software engineering. Every set of symbol strings specified by a regular expression defines a formal language. Regular expressions can thus be viewed as language generators.

The rules for forming regular expressions are quite simple:

1. Atoms: The basic symbols in the alphabet of interest form regular expressions.
2. Alternation: If R1 and R2 are regular expressions, then (R1│R2) is a regular expression.
3. Composition: If R1 and R2 are regular expressions, then (R1 R2) is a regular expression.
4. Closure: If R1 is a regular expression, then (R1)* is a regular expression.
5. Completeness: Nothing else is a regular expression.

An alphabet of basic symbols provides the atoms. The alphabet is made up of whatever symbols are of interest in the particular application. Alternation, (R1│R2), denotes the union of the languages (sets of symbol strings) specified by R1 and R2, and composition, (R1 R2), denotes the language formed by concatenating strings from R2 onto strings from R1. Closure, (R1)*, denotes the language formed by concatenating zero or more strings from R1 with zero or more strings from R1.

Observe that rules 2, 3, and 4 are recursive; i.e., they define regular expressions in terms of regular expressions. Rule 1 is the basis rule, and rule 5 completes the definition of regular expressions. Examples of regular expressions follow:

1. Given atoms a and b, then a denotes the set { a } and b denotes the set { b }.
2. Given atoms a and b, then (a│b) denotes the set { a, b }.
3. Given atoms a, b, and c, then ((a│b)│c) denotes the set { {a,b}, c}.
4. Given atoms a and b, then (a b) denotes the set { ab } containing one element ab.
5. Given atoms a, b, and c, then ((a b) c) denotes the set { abc } containing one element abc.

6. Given atom a, then (a)* denotes the set {e, a, aa, aaa, ...}, where e denotes the empty string.

Complex regular expressions can be formed by repeated application of recursive rules 2, 3, and 4:

1. (a (b|c)) denotes {ab, ac}.
2. (a|b)* denotes {e, a, b, aa, bb, ab, ba, aab, ...}.
3. ((a (b|c)))* denotes {e, ab, ac, abab, acac, abac, acab, ababac, ...}

Closure, (R1)*, denotes zero or more concatenations of elements from R1. A commonly used notation is (R1) + , which denotes one or more concatenations of elements in R1. The "*" and " + " notations are called the Kleene star and Kleene plus notations. They are named for their inventor.

Regular expressions can be given many different interpretations, and are thus useful in many different situations. For instance, ((a (b|c))) + might denote any of the following:

1. A data stream. If a, b, and c are input data symbols, then valid data streams must always start with an "a", followed by "b"s and "c"s in any order, but always interleaved by "a" and terminated by "b" or "c".
2. Message transmission. a, b, and c can be interpreted as message types such as resource request or release, job initiation request, or end of file. The regular expression then specifies legal sequences of messages.
3. Operation sequence. If a, b, and c represent procedures, then legal calling sequences are "a" followed by a call to "b" or "c" followed by zero or more returns to "a" followed by calls to "b" or "c". (The ambiguity of the preceding sentence illustrates the desirability of using formal notations.)
4. Resource flow. Symbols a, b, and c might denote system components such as a process or a user. The regular expression ((a (b|c))) + is associated with a resource such as a processor, a tape unit, a file, or a system table. The regular expression then states the a must get the resource first, then either b or c may have it after a releases it, and that a must always have the resource between allocations to b or c.

Hierarchical specifications can be constructed by assigning names to regular expressions and using the names in other regular expressions.

Regular expression notation can be extended to allow modeling of concurrency. By definition, the effect of concurrent execution of two software components, P1 and P2, is the same if the execution histories of P1 and P2 are interleaved. Interleaving of the regular expressions for P1 and P2 can be specified using an operation known as the "shuffle operator." The resulting expressions are called message transfer expressions, flow expressions, and event expressions (SHA75, RID79).

Path expressions are another useful notation based on regular expressions. They can be used to specify the sequencing of operations in concurrent systems (CAM74). The use of regular expressions for specifying software characteristics is nicely summarized in (SHA80).

Another important application of regular expressions is in defining user interface dialogues. A user command string might, for example, be of the form command name Name, followed by one or more white spaces, ws, followed by zero or more Options, followed by a Param_List. A Command might consist of zero or more Command_Strings terminated by a Delimiter. The syntax of Commands can thus be specified as follows:

Command = (Command_String)* Delimiter
Command_String = Name ws+ (Options ws+)* Param_List
Options = '-' Option (ws+ '-' Option)*
Param_List = Name (ws+ Name)*
Name = Letter (Letter | Digit)*
Delimiter = EOL
ws = ' '

In the specification of Command, symbols contained in single quotes are literals that can appear in commands. A complete specification for Command would include specifications for the syntax of Option, Letter, and Digit.

4.2.2 State-Oriented Notations

Decision tables. Decision tables provide a mechanism for recording complex decision logic. Decision tables are widely used in data processing applications and have an extensively developed literature (POO74). As illustrated in Table 4.3, a decision table is segmented into four quadrants: condition stub, condition entry,

Table 4.3 Basic elements of a decision table

	Decision rules			
	Rule 1	Rule 2	Rule 3	Rule 4
(Condition stub)		(Condition entries)		
(Action stub)		(Action entries)		

Table 4.4 Limited-entry decision table

	1	2	3	4
Credit limit is satisfactory	Y	N	N	N
Pay experience is favorable	—	Y	N	N
Special clearance is obtained	—	—	Y	N
Perform approve order	X	X	X	
Go to reject order				X

action stub, and action entry. The condition stub contains all of the conditions being examined. Condition entries are used to combine conditions into decision rules. The action stub describes the actions to be taken in response to decision rules, and the action entry quadrant relates decision rules to actions.

Table 4.4 illustrates the format of a limited-entry decision table (entries are limited to Y, N, -, and X). In a limited-entry decision table, Y denotes "yes," N denotes "no," - denotes "don't care," and X denotes "perform action." According to Table 4.4, orders are approved if the credit limit is not exceeded, or if the credit limit is exceeded but past experience is good, or if a special arrangement has been made. If none of these conditions hold, the order is rejected.

The (Y,N,-) entries in each column of the condition entry quadrant form a decision rule. If more than one decision rule has identical (Y,N,-) entries, the table is said to be ambiguous. Ambiguous pairs of decision rules that specify identical actions are said to be redundant, and those specifying different actions are contradictory. Contradictory rules permit specification of nondeterministic and concurrent actions. Table 4.5 illustrates redundant rules (R3 and R4) and contradictory rules (R2 and R3, and R2 and R4).

Table 4.5 An ambiguous decision table

	Decision rule			
	Rule 1	Rule 2	Rule 3	Rule 4
C1	Y	Y	Y	Y
C2	Y	N	N	N
C3	N	N	N	N
A1	X			
A2		X		
A3			X	X

Table 4.6 An incomplete and over-specified decision table

C1	Y		N
C2		Y	N
C3			Y
A1		X	
A2	X		
A3			X

A decision table is complete if every possible set of conditions has a corresponding action prescribed. There are $2**N$ combinations of conditions in a table that has N condition entries. Failure to specify an action for any one of the combinations results in an incomplete decision table. For example, in Table 4.6 the combination (N,N,N) for conditions C1, C2, and C3 has no action specified. Note also that the condition (Y,Y,N) specifies both actions A1 and A2. This multiply-specified action may be desired, or it may indicate a specification error.

Figure 4.6 illustrates the use of a Karnaugh map to check a decision table for completeness and multiply-specified actions. The specification is incomplete if there are any blank entries in the Karnaugh map. The specification is multiply-specified if there are any multiple entries in the Karnaugh map.

Event tables. Event tables specify actions to be taken when events occur under different sets of conditions. A two-dimensional event table relates actions to two variables; f(M, E) = A, where M denotes the current set of operating conditions, E is the event of interest, and A is the action to be taken. Tables of higher dimension can be used to incorporate more independent variables (HEN80).

Table 4.7 illustrates an event table where the actions to be taken are related to the current mode of operation and the events that may occur within modes. Thus, if the system is in start-up mode SU and event E13 occurs, action A16 is to be taken; f(SU, E13) = A16. Special notations can be invented to suit particular situations. For example, actions separated by semicolons (A14; A32) might denote A14 followed sequentially by A32, while actions separated by commas (A6, A2) might denote concurrent activation of A6 and A2. Similarly, a dash (-) might indicate no action required, while an X might indicate an impossible system configuration (e.g., E13 cannot occur in steady-state mode).

	C2	*C3*		
C1	*A1* *A2*	*A1* *A2*	*A2*	*A2*
	A1	*A1*	*A3*	

Figure 4.6 Karnaugh map corresponding to decision table 4.6.

Table 4.7 A two-dimensional event table

	Event				
Mode	E13	E37	E45	. . .	. . .
Start-up	A16	—	A14; A32		
Steady	X	A6, A2	—		
Shut-down	. . .	. . .	. . .		
Alarm	. . .	. . .	. . .		

Transition tables. Transition tables are used to specify changes in the state of a system as a function of driving forces. The state of a system summarizes the status of all entities in the system at a particular time. Given the current state and the current conditions, the next state results; if, when in state Si, condition Cj results in a transition to state Sk, we say f(Si, Cj) = Sk.

Table 4.8 illustrates the format of a simple transition table; in Table 4.8, given current state S1 and current input b, the system will go to state S0; i.e., f(S1, b) = S0. Table 4.9 illustrates a transition table that is augmented to indicate actions to be performed and outputs to be generated in the transition to the next state.

Transition diagrams are alternative representations for transition tables. In a transition diagram, states become nodes in a directed graph and transitions are represented as arcs between nodes. Arcs are labeled with conditions that cause transitions. Figure 4.7 illustrates the transition diagram corresponding to the transition table in Table 4.8. Transition diagrams and transition tables are representations for finite state automata. The theory of finite state automata is rich, complex, and highly developed (HOP79).

Decision tables, event tables, and transition tables are notations for specifying actions as functions of the conditions that initiate those actions. Decision tables specify actions in terms of complex decision logic, event tables relate actions to system conditions, and transition tables incorporate the concept of system state. The notations are of equivalent expressive power; a specification in one of the notations can be readily expressed in the other two. The best choice among tabular

Table 4.8 A simple transition table

	Current input	
Current state	a	b
S0	S0	S1
S1	S1	S0
	Next state	

Table 4.9 An augmented transition table

Present state	Input	Action	Output	Next state
S0	a b			S0 S1
S1	a b			S0 S1

forms for requirements specification depends on the particular situation being specified.

Finite state mechanisms. Data flow diagrams, regular expressions, and transition tables can be combined to provide a powerful finite state mechanism for functional specification of software systems (BAB80). Figure 4.8 depicts the data flow diagram for a software system consisting of a set of processes interconnected by data streams. Each of the data streams can be specified using a regular expression, and each of the processes can be described using a transition table.

Although our examples of regular expressions have been quite simple, one can describe highly complex data streams using regular expressions. For example, a data stream might be specified as

$$(X(((X \ Y))^* \,|\, Z) \,|\, ((((X \,|\, Y) \ Z)) + Y)).$$

In general, the descriptive power of a regular expression is limited to languages that can be recognized by finite state automata. Thus, a regular expression can be used to specify $\{x^m y^n \,|\, m, n > 0\}$, but not $\{x^n y^n \,|\, n > 0\}$.

Figure 4.9 specifies a system for which the incoming data stream consists of a start marker Ds, followed by zero or more D11 messages, followed by zero or more D12 messages, followed by an end-of-data marker De. The purpose of process "split" is to route D11 messages to file F6 and D12 messages to file F7. The transition table in Figure 4.9 specifies the action of "split." Process split starts in initial state S0 and waits for input Ds. Any other input in state S0 is ignored (alternatively, other inputs could result in error processing). Arrival of input Ds in state S0 triggers the opening of files F6 and F7 and transition to state S1. In S1, D11 messages are written to F6 until either a D12 message or a De message is received (note that a Ds De data stream with no D11 messages and no D12 messages is possible). On receipt of a D12 message, process split closes F6, writes the message D12 to F7 and goes to state S2. In state S2, split writes zero or more D12 messages to F7, then, on receipt of the end-of-data marker, De, closes F7 and returns to state S0 to await the next transmission (BAB80).

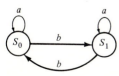

Figure 4.7 Transition diagram corresponding to Table 4.8.

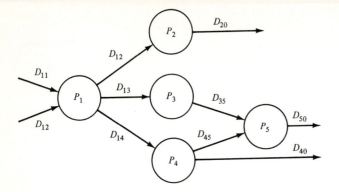

Figure 4.8 A network of data streams and processes.

One drawback of finite-state mechanisms is the so-called state explosion phenomenon. Complex systems may have large numbers of states and many combinations of input data. Specifying the behavior of a software system for all combinations of current state and current input can become unwieldy.

Hierarchical decomposition is one technique for controlling the complexity of a finite-state specification. Using hierarchical decomposition, higher level concepts are given names, the meaning and validity of which are established at a lower level. For example, D11 and D12 in Figure 4.9 might have complex internal structures. Establishing the validity of D11 or D12 might be accomplished by other lower-level finite-state mechanisms.

Petri nets. Petri nets were invented in the 1960s by Carl Petri at the University of Bonn, West Germany. Petri nets have been used to model a wide variety of

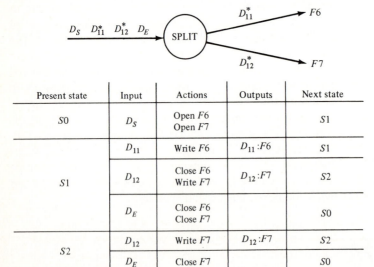

Present state	Input	Actions	Outputs	Next state
S0	D_S	Open $F6$ Open $F7$		S1
S1	D_{11}	Write $F6$	$D_{11}:F6$	S1
	D_{12}	Close $F6$ Write $F7$	$D_{12}:F7$	S2
	D_E	Close $F6$ Close $F7$		S0
S2	D_{12}	Write $F7$	$D_{12}:F7$	S2
	D_E	Close $F7$		S0

Figure 4.9 Specification of the "Split" process *(BAB80)*.

situations (PET77), (AGE79); they provide a graphical representation technique, and systematic methods have been developed for synthesizing and analyzing Petri nets. Petri nets were invented to overcome the limitations of finite state mechanisms in specifying parallelism.

In this section, we briefly describe the characteristics of Petri nets and give examples of using Petri nets to model various aspects of concurrent systems. Concurrent systems are designed to permit simultaneous execution of the software components, called tasks or processes, on multiple processors. Alternatively, execution of tasks can be interleaved on a single processor. Concurrent tasks must be synchronized to permit communication among tasks that operate at differing execution rates, to prevent simultaneous updating of shared data, and to prevent deadlock. Deadlock occurs when all tasks in the system are waiting for data or other resources that can only be supplied by tasks that are also waiting on other tasks. The fundamental problems of concurrency are thus synchronization, mutual exclusion, and deadlock.

A Petri net is represented as a bipartite directed graph. The two types of nodes in a Petri net are called places and transitions. Places are marked by tokens; a Petri net is characterized by an initial marking of places and a firing rule. A firing rule has two aspects: a transition is enabled if every input place has at least one token. An enabled transition can fire; when a transition fires, each input place of that transition loses one token, and each output place of that transition gains one token. A marked Petri net is formally defined as a quadruple, consisting of a set of places P, a set of transitions T, a set of arcs A, and a marking M. $C = (P,T,A,M)$, where

$$p = \{p1, p2, \ldots pm\}$$
$$T = \{t1, t2, \ldots tn\}$$
$$A \subset \{P \times T\} \cup \{T \times P\} = \{(pi, tj) \ldots (tk, pl) \ldots\}$$
$$M: P \longrightarrow I; \text{ i.e., } M(p1, p2, \ldots pm) = (i1, i2, \ldots im)$$

Marking M associates an integer number of tokens ik with each place pk.

When a transition fires, the marking of places p changes from $M(p)$ to $M'(p)$ as follows:

$$M'(p) = M(p) + 1 \text{ if } p \in O(t) \text{ and } p \notin I(t)$$
$$M'(p) = M(p) - 1 \text{ if } p \notin I(t) \ \& \ p \in O(t)$$
$$M'(p) = M(p) \text{ otherwise}$$

where $I(t)$ is the set of input places of transition t and $O(t)$ is the set of output places of transition t.

A transition t is enabled if $M(p) > 0$ for all $p \in I(t)$.

Figures 4.10, 4.11, and 4.12 illustrate several aspects of Petri nets. In Figure 4.10 the Petri net models the indicated computation; each transition in the net corresponds to a task activation and places are used to synchronize processing. Completion of t0 removes the initial token from p0 and places a token on p1, which enables the co-begin. Firing of the co-begin removes the token from p1 and places a token on each of p2, p3, and p4. This enables t1, t2, and t3; they can fire simultaneously or in any order. This corresponds to concurrent execution of tasks

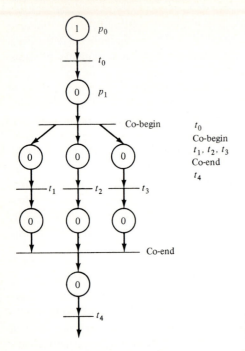

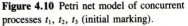

t_0
Co-begin
t_1, t_2, t_3
Co-end
t_4

Figure 4.10 Petri net model of concurrent processes t_1, t_2, t_3 (initial marking).

t1, t2, and t3. When each of tasks t1, t2, and t3 completes its processing, a token is placed on the corresponding output place, p5, p6, or p7. Co-end is not enabled until all three tasks complete their processing. Firing of co-end removes the tokens from p5, p6, and p7 and places a token on p8, thus enabling p4, which can then fire.

Figure 4.11 illustrates a deadlock situation. Both t1 and t2 are waiting for the other to fire and neither can proceed.

Conflict in Petri nets provides the basis for modeling of mutual exclusion. Conflict is illustrated in Figure 4.12; both t1 and t2 are enabled, but only one can fire. Firing one will disable the other.

As an example of mutual exclusion, a Petri net of the producer/consumer problem is illustrated in Figure 4.13. Here t1 is the producing process; t2 places a produced item in the buffer; t3 removes an item from the buffer; and t4 consumes

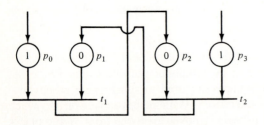

Figure 4.11 A deadlocked Petri net.

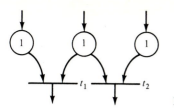

Figure 4.12 A conflict situation.

it. The number of tokens on place E indicates the current number of empty buffer positions. Initially, E has a number of tokens equal to the total number of buffer positions. The number of tokens on place F indicates the current number of filled buffer positions. Initially, F has zero tokens.

M prevents simultaneous insertion and removal of items from the buffer. Initially, M has one token, P1 has one token, P2 has no token, P3 has one token, P4 has no token, E has N tokens, and F has zero tokens.

In Figure 4.13, E, F, and M function as semaphores. E prevents buffer overflow, F prevents buffer underflow, and M prevents simultaneous reading and writing of the buffer. For purposes of comparison, Figure 4.14 presents the classical semaphore solution to the producer/consumer problem. Arcs in the net of Figure 4.13 have been labeled to indicate P and V operations on E, F, and M.

Various properties of Petri nets can be determined using analysis techniques based on the notion of net invariants. An invariant is a set of places whose total number of tokens remains constant, and which has no invariant subsets. In Figure 4.13, the invariants are {P1, P2}, {P3, P4}, {P5, P7}, and {P6}. Methods for calculating invariants are described in (PET77) and (AGE79). The net in Figure 4.13 is "bounded" because each place is in some invariant, and the net has N + 3 total tokens. The net is "conservative" because the invariants are disjoint and inclusive. Thus, N + 3 is a constant number of tokens. The Petri net in Figure 4.13 exhibits mutual exclusion between T2 and T3 because both are marked by P6, and

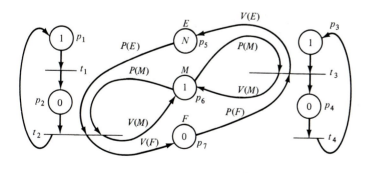

t_1: Produce

t_2: Place in buffer

t_3: Remove from buffer

t_4: Consume

Figure 4.13 Initial marking for the producer/consumer Petri Net.

```
SEMAPHORE      E, F, M;
INITIALLY      E : = N, F : = 0, M : = 1;
   LOOP: t₁ (Produce)                    LOOP:  P(F), P(M)
         P(E), P(M)                             t₃ (Remove from buffer)
         t₂ (Place in buffer)                   V(E), V(M)
         V(F), V(M)                             t₄ (Consume)
   END_LOOP                              END_LOOP
```

$P(K) \equiv$ if $K > 0$ then $K := K - 1$ else wait
$V(K) \equiv K := K + 1$;
      Initiate one waiting process

Figure 4.14 Semaphore solution to the producer/consumer problem.

{P6} is an invariant, having one token. Thus, T2 and T3 are in conflict and mutually exclusive. The buffer cannot underflow because {P5, P7} is an invariant, with N tokens. Thus, M(P5) + M(P7) = N at all times. If M(P5) = N, then the buffer is empty; i.e., M(P7) = N implies M(P5) = 0, and the buffer cannot overflow.

Deadlock is not possible in the net of Figure 4.13 (in a deadlocked net, no transitions can fire). Assume the net is deadlocked. Then, in particular, T2 cannot fire. Thus, M(P5) = 0, or M(P2) = 0. Assume that M(P2) = 0. If M(P2) = 0, then M(P1) = 1 and T1 can fire because {P1, P2} is an invariant having one token. Now assume that M(P5) = 0. This implies M(P7) = N because {P5, P7} is an invariant with N tokens. If M(P7) = N and M(P3) = 1, T3 can fire. If M(P3) = 0, then M(P4) = 1 because {P3, P4} is an invariant. If M(P4) = 1, then T4 can fire. If T2 cannot fire, we have proven that T1 or T3 or T4 can fire. Thus, the net in Figure 4.13 cannot deadlock.

Many of the analysis techniques for Petri nets depend on knowing the net invariants. See (PET77) and (AGE79) for methods for calculating invariants.

Bounded, conservative Petri nets are equivalent to finite-state automata. In a finite-state automaton representation of a Petri net, the state of the net is given by the marking configuration, and transitions leading to next states change the markings to reflect changes in the next state. The equivalence of bounded, conservative Petri nets to finite-state automata makes all the analysis tools for finite-state automata available for this class of Petri nets. Although bounded, conservative Petri nets are equivalent to finite-state automata, Petri nets provide a more convenient notation for specifying and analyzing concurrent systems; unbounded and non-conservative Petri nets provide more powerful mechanisms than do finite automata.

4.2.3 Summary

In summary, we have discussed several notations for specifying the functional characteristics of software products. The notations were categorized as relational and state-oriented. Relational notations discussed include implicit equations, recurrence relations, algebraic axioms, and regular expressions. Relational notations are particularly well suited for specifying functional requirements without implying any particular implementation scheme. This provides maximum flexibility for the software designer who develops the solution strategy.

Implicit equations are so named because they implicitly specify the desired characteristics of a software product. The desired functional behavior is embedded within relationships among system entities. Mathematical problems are often specified using implicit equations.

A recurrence relation specifies a desired outcome in terms of identical outcomes for simpler versions of the problem. In order to avoid circularity of definition, at least one outcome for a simple version of the problem is defined without reference to the recurrence. Recurrence relations are often used to specify signal processing and other similar time series operations. Although specifications in the form of recurrence relations suggest recursive implementations, it is often possible to develop more efficient algorithms using iteration.

Algebraic axioms are used to specify the properties of abstract data types. The syntax of the operators and the relationships among operators are specified. The operators are categorized as constructor, modifier, and selector functions, and their interactions are specified using functional notation. Algebraic axioms are formalizations of property lists; they specify the desired interactions that operators are to have. As with other relational notations, they provide no indication of how to implement the operators in order to achieve the desired effects. In practice, this is a mixed blessing.

Regular expressions are concise notations for defining both finite and infinite sets of symbol strings. The resulting sets of strings can be interpreted in many different ways, thus making regular expressions a versatile notation for specifying various properties of software products. Typical applications of regular expressions include specification of valid data streams, the syntax of user command languages, and legal sequences of events in a system.

State-oriented notations discussed include decision tables, event tables, transition tables, finite state mechanisms, and Petri nets. Decision tables are used to specify actions in terms of complex decision criteria. They are particularly useful when logical combinations of numerous conditions are used to specify the desired behaviors of a system.

An event table is useful for specifying system behavior when different stimuli result in different actions or outcomes for each of several different modes of operation.

Transition tables (and transition diagrams) can be used to specify the next desired state of a system, given the current state and current stimuli. Using techniques from automata theory, it can be shown that every regular expression has a corresponding transition table and vice versa. Transition tables and transition diagrams thus provide mechanisms for specifying the various states that a system must occupy when processing symbols from strings specified by the corresponding regular expressions.

Finite-state mechanisms utilize data flow diagrams in which the data streams are specified using regular expressions and the actions in the processing nodes are specified using transition tables. They are particularly useful for specifying high-level system behavior in response to various input stimuli.

Petri nets are state oriented notations for specifying parallelism of operations. They can be used to specify synchronization and mutual exclusion among concurrent operations. Petri nets were invented to overcome the limitations of finite state mechanisms for specifying parallelism. Certain restricted forms of Petri nets are equivalent to finite state automata.

This brief survey of relational and state-oriented notations is not exhaustive. Many similar notations are routinely used to specify functional requirements for software products. However, the survey does provide an overview of the kinds of formal notations that are available for use. Formal notations are concise and unambiguous, and in many cases they support formal analysis of completeness and consistency of the resulting specifications. Use of formal notations also allows formal reasoning about various characteristics of the product being specified.

4.3 LANGUAGES AND PROCESSORS FOR REQUIREMENTS SPECIFICATION

A number of special-purpose languages and processors have been developed to permit concise statement and automated analysis of requirements specifications for software. Some specification languages are graphical in nature, while others are textual; all are relational in nature. Some specification languages are manually applied, and others have automated processors. In this section we provide a brief overview of a few specification languages. These and other languages are well documented elsewhere (TSE77). Our purpose is to provide a brief introduction to requirements specification languages and processors.

4.3.1 PSL/PSA

The Problem Statement Language (PSL) was developed by Professor Daniel Teichrow at the University of Michigan (TEI77). The Problem Statement Analyzer (PSA) is the PSL processor. PSL and PSA were developed as components of the ISDOS project; the PSL/PSA system is sometimes referred to as the ISDOS system. PSL is based on a general model of systems. This model describes a system as a set of objects, where each object may have properties, and each property may have property values. Objects may be interconnected; the connections are called relationships. The general model is specialized to information systems by allowing only a limited number of predefined objects, properties, and relationships.

The objective of PSL is to permit expression of much of the information that commonly appears in a *Software Requirements Specification*. In PSL, system descriptions can be divided into eight major aspects:

1. System input/output flow
2. System structure
3. Data structure
4. Data derivation
5. System size and volume
6. System dynamics

7. System properties
8. Project management

PSL contains a number of types of objects and relationships to permit description of these eight aspects. The system input/output flow aspect deals with the interaction between a system and its environment. System structure is concerned with the hierarchies among objects in a system. The data structure aspect includes all the relationships that exist among data used and/or manipulated by a system as seen by the users of the system. The data derivation aspect of the system description specifies which data objects are involved in particular processes in the system. Data derivation describes data relationships that are internal to a system. The system size and volume aspect is concerned with the size of the system and those factors that influence the volume of processing required. The system dynamics aspect of a system description presents the manner in which the system "behaves" over time. The project management aspect requires that project-related information, as well as product-related information, be provided. This involves identification of the people involved, their responsibilities, schedules, cost estimates, etc.

The Problem Statement Analyzer (PSA) is an automated analyzer for processing requirements stated in PSL. The structure of PSA is illustrated in Figure 4.15. PSA operates on a data base of information collected from a PSL description. The PSA system can provide reports in four categories: data-base modification reports, reference reports, summary reports, and analysis reports.

Data-base modification reports list changes that have been made since the last report, together with diagnostic and warning messages; these reports provide a record of changes for error correction and recovery. Reference reports include the *Name List Report,* which lists all the objects in the data base with types and dates

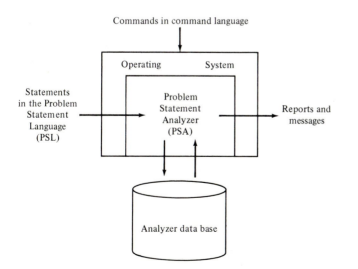

Figure 4.15 Structure of the problem statement analyzer.

PROCESS DESCRIPTION:	hourly-employee-processing
	this process performs those actions needed to interpret time cards to produce a pay statement for each hourly employee.;
GENERATES:	pay-statement, error-listing, hourly-employee-report;
RECEIVES:	time-card;
SUBPARTS ARE:	hourly-paycheck-validation, hourly-emp-update, h-report-entry-generation, hourly-paycheck-production;
PART OF:	payroll-processing;
DERIVES:	pay-statement
USING:	time-card, hourly-employee-record;
DERIVES:	hourly-employee-report
USING:	time-card, hourly-employee-record;
DERIVES:	error-listing
USING:	time-card, hourly-employee-record;

PROCEDURE:
1. compute gross pay from time card data.
2. compute tax from gross pay.
3. subtract tax from gross pay to obtain net pay.
4. update hourly employee record accordingly.
5. update department record accordingly.
6. generate paycheck.

note: if status code specifies that the employee did not work this week, no processing will be done for this employee;

HAPPENS:	number-of-payments TIMES-PER pay period;
TRIGGERED BY:	hourly-emp-processing-event;
TERMINATION-CAUSES:	new-employee-processing-event;
SECURITY-IS:	company-only;

Figure 4.16 Example of a PSL Formatted Problem Statement *(adapted from TEI77)*.

of last change. *The Formatted Problem Statement Report* shows properties and relationships for a particular object (see Figure 4.16). The *Dictionary Report* provides a data dictionary.

Summary reports present information collected from several relationships. The *Data Base Summary Report* provides project management information by listing the total number of objects of various types and how much has been said about them. The *Structure Report* shows complete and partial hierarchies, and the *External Picture Report* depicts data flows in graphical form.

Analysis reports include the *Contents Comparison Report*, which compares the similarity of inputs and outputs. The *Data Processing Interaction Report* can be used to detect gaps in information flow and unused data objects. The *Processing Chain Report* shows the dynamic behavior of the system.

PSL/PSA is a useful tool for documenting and communicating software requirements. Some users of PSL become disillusioned when they discover that PSL does not solve the "requirements problem," but rather provides analysis, formatting, and report generation of the stated requirements. Other users of PSL discover that PSL/PSA significantly changes the ways in which software is developed in their organization. Sometimes this is for the better, but sometimes for the worse.

These are common problems with all software tools. The fault is not with the tool, but rather with the incorrect perceptions and expectations of the users. Tools do not solve problems; people solve problems. Software tools support the problem solving that is done by humans; however, many people fail to recognize this fundamental fact. Good software tools that are properly used can significantly improve software quality and programmer productivity, but the value of a software tool can only be assessed in light of stated goals and intended usage of the tool.

As illustrated in Figure 4.16, PSL/PSA not only supports requirements analysis; it also supports design. This intermixing of analysis considerations and design considerations in PSL is not entirely beneficial. It is easy for the PSL user to fall into the trap of becoming too involved with design details before high-level requirements are completed. The tendency to become too involved in too many details too soon is a pervasive problem in software engineering, and PSL/PSA does little to correct this tendency.

PSL/PSA is sometimes criticized because it does not incorporate any specific problem-solving techniques. PSA does provide the capability to define new PSL constructs and new report formats, which allows the system to be tailored to specific problem domains and specific solution methods. PSL/PSA has been used in many different situations, ranging from commercial data processing applications to air defense systems.

4.3.2 RSL/REVS

The Requirements Statement Language (RSL) was developed by the TRW Defense and Space Systems Group to permit concise, unambiguous specification of requirements for real-time software systems (ALF77). The Requirements Engineering Validation System (REVS) processes and analyzes RSL statements; both RSL and REVS are components of the Software Requirements Engineering Methodology (SREM). Many of the concepts in RSL are based on PSL. For example, RSL has four primitive concepts: elements, which name objects; attributes, which describe the characteristics of elements; relationships, which describe binary relations between elements; and structures, which are composed of nodes and processing steps. "Data" is an example of an RSL language element. "Initial Value" is an attribute of the element Data, and Input specifies a relationship between a data item and a processing step.

The fundamental characteristic of RSL is the flow-oriented approach used to describe real-time systems. RSL models the stimulus-response nature of process-control systems; each flow originates with a stimulus and continues to the final response. Specifying requirements in this fashion makes explicit the sequences of processing steps required. A processing step may be accomplished by several different software components, and a software component may incorporate several processing steps. In fact, a sequence of processing steps may involve hardware, software, and people components.

The flow approach also provides for direct testability of requirements. A system can be tested to determine that responses are as specified under various stimuli, and performance characteristics and validation conditions can be associated with particular points in the processing sequence.

Flows are specified in RSL as requirements networks (R-NETS). R-NETS have both graphical and textual representations, as illustrated in Figure 4.17a and b. R-NETS can be used to specify parallel (order-independent) operations using the AND node (&). Fan-in at the end of an AND structure is a synchronization point; all parallel paths must be completed before any subsequent processes are initiated.

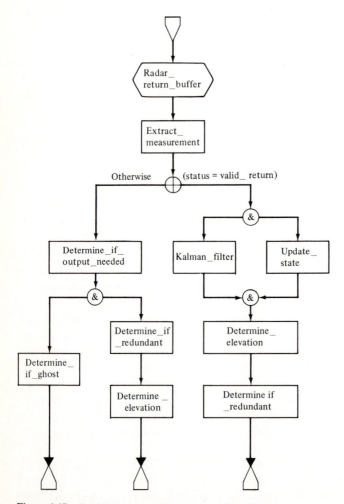

Figure 4.17a Graphical representation of an R-NET *(BEL77).*

```
R_NET: PROCESS_RADAR_RETURN
  STRUCTURE:
    INPUT_INTERFACE_RADAR_RETURN_BUFFER
    EXTRACT_MEASUREMENT
    DO (STATUS = VALIDRETURN)
      DO UPDATE_STATE AND KALMAN_FILTER END
      DETERMINE ELEVATION
      DETERMINE_IF_REDUNDANT
      TERMINATE
    OTHERWISE
      DETERMINE_IF_OUTPUT_NEEDED
      DO DETERMINE_IF_REDUNDANT
        DETERMINE_ELEVATION
        TERMINATE
      AND DETERMINE_IF_GHOST
      TERMINATE
      END
    END
  END
```

Figure 4.17b Textual representation of an R-NET *(adapted from BEL77)*.

The OR node (+) has a condition associated with each path. Each OR node must have an Otherwise path that is processed if none of the conditions are true. If more than one condition is true, the first path, as indicated by either implicit or explicit ordering, is processed. The third structure type is the For_Each, which contains only one path. The path is processed once for each element in a specified set of system entities. Iteration over the set is not implied to be in any particular order.

RSL incorporates a number of predefined element types, relationships, attributes, and structures. Pre-defined elements include Alpha, Data, and R_NET. An Alpha specifies the functional characteristics of a processing step in an R-NET. Alphas are described in terms of other elements such as Inputs, Outputs, and Descriptions.

Similarly, a Data Element specifies data elements at the conceptual level, using relationships such as Input_To and Output_From, attributes such as Initial Value and Includes, and elements such as Description. Figure 4.18 illustrates two Alphas, one Data, and one Originating_Requirement.

In addition to the predefined elements, types, relationships, and attributes in RSL, new elements, relationships, and attributes can be added to the language using Define. Figure 4.19 illustrates the definition of two new elements: Input_Interface and Message and the definition of their relationship, Passes. A complete definition would include relationships to associate particular items of Data with Messages. After the new items have been defined, they can be used to specify other attributes of the system.

The Requirements Engineering and Validation System (REVS) operates on RSL statements. REVS consists of three major components:

1. A translator for RSL
2. A centralized data base, the Abstract System Semantic Model (ASSM)
3. A set of automated tools for processing information in ASSM

ALPHA: EXTRACT_MEASUREMENT.
  INPUTS: CORRELATED_RETURN
  OUTPUTS: VALID_RETURN, MEASUREMENT.
  DESCRIPTION: "DOES RANGE SELECTION PER CISS REFERENCE 2-7."

ALPHA: DETERMINE_IF_REDUNDANT.
  INPUTS: CORRELATED_RETURN
  OUTPUTS: REDUNDANT_IMAGE.
  DESCRIPTION: "THE IMAGE OF THE RADAR RETURN IS ANALYZED TO
        DETERMINE IF IT IS REDUNDANT WITH ANOTHER IMAGE."

DATA: MEASUREMENT.
  INCLUDES: RANGE_MARK_TIME, AMPLITUDE,
      RANGE_VARIANCE, RD_VARIANCE,
      R_AND_RD_CORRELATION.
  OUTPUT FROM: ALPHA EXTRACT_MEASUREMENT.
  DESCRIPTION: "THIS IS THE ESSENCE OF THE INFORMATION IN THE RETURN."

ORIGINATION_REQUIREMENT:
  DPSPR_3.2.2.A_FUNCTIONAL.
  DESCRIPTION: "ACTION: SEND RADAR ORDER INFORMATION: INFORMATION:
      RADAR ORDER, IMAGE(REDUNDANT)."
  TRACES TO: ALPHA COMMAND_PULSES
      ALPHA DETERMINE_IF_REDUNDANT
      MESSAGE RADAR_ORDER_MESSAGE
      DATA REDUNDANT_IMAGE
      ENTITY_CLASS IMAGE

Figure 4.18 Examples of ALPHA, DATA, and ORIGINATING_REQUIREMENT *(adapted from BEL77).*

DEFINE ELEMENT_TYPE: INPUT_INTERFACE
      (*A port between the data processing system and the
      rest of the system which accepts data from another
      part of the system*).

DEFINE ELEMENT_TYPE: MESSAGE
      (*An aggregation of DATA and FILES that PASS through
      an interface as a logical unit.*).

DEFINE RELATIONSHIP: PASSES
      (*An INPUT_INTERFACE "PASSES" a logical aggregation
      of data called a MESSAGE from the outside system into
      the data processing system*).

COMPLEMENTARY RELATIONSHIP: PASSED_BY.

SUBJECT: INPUT_INTERFACE.

OBJECT: MESSAGE.

Figure 4.19 Examples of the DEFINE attribute from RSL *(adapted from BEL77).*

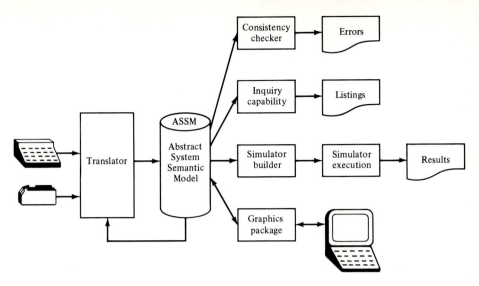

Figure 4.20 Structure of the REVS processor *(BEL77)*.

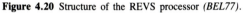

A schematic diagram of REVS is presented in Figure 4.20. ASSM is a relational data base similar in concept to the PSL/PSA data base. Automated tools for processing information in the ASSM include an interactive graphics package to aid in specifying flow paths, static checkers that check for completeness and consistency of the information used throughout the system, and an automated simulation package that generates and executes simulation models of the system. In addition to the standard displays and reports, REVS provides a capability for defining specific analyses and reports that may be needed on particular projects.

REVS is a large, complex software tool. Use of the REVS system is cost-effective only for specification of large, complex real-time systems. Of course, the RSL notation can be manually applied to specify real-time system characteristics.

4.3.3 Structured Analysis and Design Technique (SADT)*

SADT was developed by D. T. Ross and colleagues at Softech, Inc. (ROS77). SADT incorporates a graphical language and a set of methods and management guidelines for using the language. The SADT language is called the Language of Structured Analysis (SA). The SA language and the procedures for using it are similar to the engineering blueprint systems used in civil and mechanical engineering.

An SADT model consists of an ordered set of SA diagrams. Each diagram is drawn on a single page, and each diagram must contain three to six nodes plus interconnecting arcs. Two basic types of SA diagrams are the activity diagram (actigram) and the data diagram (datagram). On an actigram the nodes denote

---

* SADT is a trademark of Softech, Inc.

activities and the arcs specify data flow between activities. Actigrams are thus the SA version of data flow diagrams (not to be confused with datagrams). Datagrams specify data objects in the nodes and activities on the arcs. Actigrams and datagrams are thus duals. In practice, activity diagrams are used more frequently than data diagrams; however, data diagrams are important for at least two reasons: to indicate all activities affected by a given data object, and to check the completeness and consistency of an SADT model by constructing data diagrams from a set of activity diagrams.

Figure 4.21a and b illustrates the formats of actigram and datagram nodes. It is important to note that four distinct types of arcs can be attached to each node. Arcs coming into the left side of a node carry inputs and arcs leaving the right side of a node convey outputs. Arcs entering the top of a node convey control and arcs entering the bottom specify mechanism. The concepts of input, output, control, and mechanism bound the context of each node in an SA diagram.

Outputs provide input and control for other nodes. Outputs from some nodes are the system outputs to the external environment. Every output must connect to other nodes or to the external environment. Similarly, input and control must come from the output of other nodes or from the external environment. Input, control, and output may be connected to nodes on other pages in a set of diagrams. Connecting lines to other diagrams are indicated by a composite diagram/line number.

In an activity diagram the inputs and outputs are data flows and the mechanisms are processors (mechanical or human). Control is data that is used, but not modified, by the activity. In a data diagram the input is the activity that creates the data object and the output is the activity that uses the data object. Mechanisms in data diagrams are the devices used to store the representations of data objects. Control in a datagram controls the conditions under which the node will be activated. In both actigrams and datagrams controls are provided by the external environment and by the outputs of other nodes.

Figure 4.22a illustrates some structural characteristics of SA diagrams, and Figure 4.22b illustrates an activity diagram for the activity of performing requirements analysis. In Figure 4.22a, I1 is the external input to the diagram and C1 is

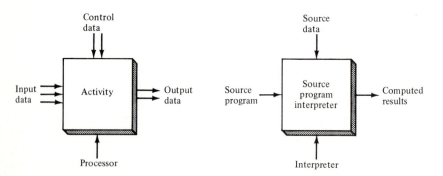

Figure 4.21a Activity diagram components.

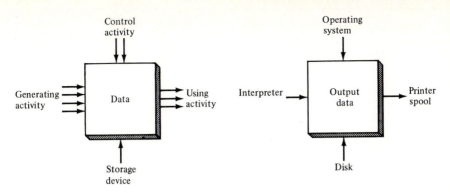

Figure 4.21b Data diagram components.

an external control. The output of activity A11 is input to activities A12 and A14, and control for activity A13. Activities A12 and A14 can proceed in parallel, but activity A13 is controlled by the output of A12 and must wait for that output. The output of activity A13 feeds back to control activity A11. Outputs from the diagram are O1 and O2. Mechanisms are indicated by M1 through M4. The diagram is an expanded view of node A1, which is illustrated in the lower left corner of the figure. Note that the input, control, and outputs of node A1 are the external input, control, and outputs of the expanded diagram for A1.

As illustrated in Figure 4.22a, each node in an SA diagram can be expanded into other diagrams that are titled and numbered to indicate the hierarchical relationships among diagrams. External inputs, outputs, controls, and mechanisms for a diagram that is a decomposition of a node in another diagram are restricted

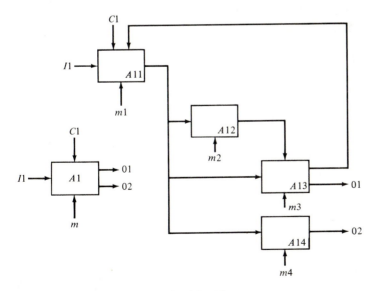

Figure 4.22a An expanded view of activity A1.

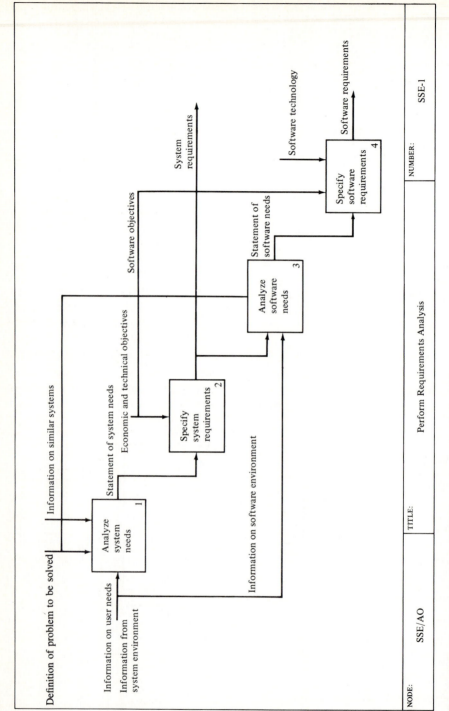

Figure 4.22b An activity diagram depicting the requirements analysis activity.

124

to the inputs, outputs, controls, and mechanisms of the node being decomposed. Furthermore, all the arcs incident on the node in the parent diagram must be depicted in the expanded diagram.

Figure 4.22b illustrates the versatility of SA diagrams. They are not limited to specification of software requirements, but can be used to specify a wide range of human problem solving activities. Note that the diagram carries a node name, title, and number for ease of identification.

The SA language has a large number of features for indicating aspects such as bounded context, necessity, dominance, relevance, exclusion, interfaces to parent diagrams, unique decomposition, shared decomposition, and cooperation (ROS77). A primary goal for the language is to provide a medium in which a wide variety of complex situations can be specified using decomposition and structural relationships.

An SADT model of a system is composed of a set of SA diagrams, and each set has a cover sheet reminiscent of the cover sheets for engineering blueprints. A cover sheet is illustrated in Figure 4.23.

Management techniques for developing an SADT model include author-reader cycles for reviewing the diagrams, and a project librarian who assigns document numbers and controls the flow of documents. Various fields of the cover sheet illustrated in Figure 4.23 support the activities of the librarian and permit tracking of reviews by readers and updates by authors.

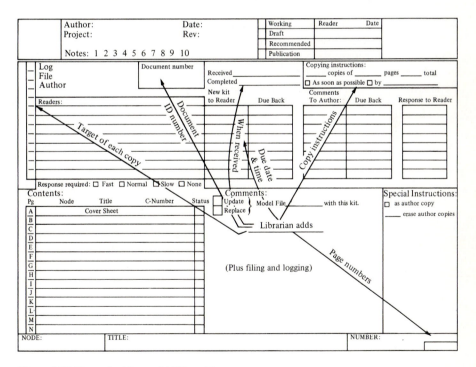

Figure 4.23 Cover sheet for an SADT model.

The SADT methodology provides a notation and a set of techniques for understanding and recording complex requirements in a clear and concise manner. Major strengths of SADT include the top-down methodology inherent in decomposing high-level nodes into subordinate diagrams, the distinction between input, output, control, and mechanism for each node, the duality of activity and datagrams, and the management techniques for developing, reviewing, and coordinating an SADT model. SADT can be applied to all types of systems; it is not limited to software applications. On the other hand, one would probably use SADT only on large, complex projects.

4.3.4 Structured System Analysis (SSA)

Two similar versions of Structured System Analysis (SSA) have been described by Gane and Sarson (GAN79) and by DeMarco (DEM78). The present discussion is based on the Gane and Sarson version. The DeMarco version is similar, but does not incorporate the data-base concepts of Gane and Sarson. SSA is used primarily in traditional data processing environments. Like SADT, SSA uses a graphical language to build models of systems. Unlike SADT, SSA incorporates data-base concepts; however, SSA does not provide the variety of structural mechanisms available in SADT. There are four basic features in SSA: data flow diagrams, data dictionaries, procedure logic representations, and data store structuring techniques.

SSA data flow diagrams are similar to SADT actigrams, but they do not indicate mechanism and control, and an additional notation is used to show data stores. An SSA data flow diagram is illustrated in Figure 4.24. As discussed in connection with Figure 4.2, open-ended rectangles indicate data stores, labels on the arcs denote data items, shaded rectangles depict sources and sinks for data, and the remaining rectangles indicate processing steps.

Order processing:

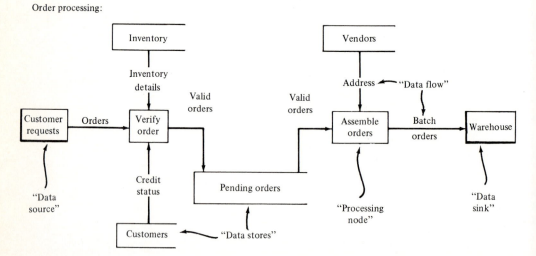

Figure 4.24 A data flow diagram *(adapted from (GAN79))*.

A data dictionary is used to define and record data elements, and processing logic representations, such as decision tables and structured English, are used to specify algorithmic processing details. Processing logic representations are used to precisely specify processing sequences in terms that are understandable to customers and developers. A typical data dictionary entry is presented in Figure 4.25, and a processing logic representation is illustrated in Figure 4.26.

As illustrated in Figure 4.26, an SSA specification can be refined to the level of detailed design. As with PSL, there is danger that programmers using SSA will proceed to the detailed design level for some processing nodes before the data flow

DATA FLOW: ORDER

COMPOSITION:

      CUSTOMER_IDENTITY
      ORDER_DATE
      ITEM_ORDERED +
            CATALOG_NUMBER
            ITEM_NAME
            UNIT PRICE
            QUANTITY
            TOTAL_COST

DATA STORE: CUSTOMER_IDENTITY

COMPOSITION:

    NAME
        FIRST
        MIDDLE
        LAST

    PHONE
        AREA_CODE
        NUMBER
        EXTENSION (Optional)

    SHIP_TO_ADDRESS
        STREET
        CITY
        STATE-ZIP

    BILL_TO_ADDRESS (Same as above if empty)
        STREET
        CITY
        STATE-ZIP

DATA STORE: ORDER_DATE

COMPOSITION:

        TIME
        DAY
        MONTH
        YEAR

NOTE: The " + " Notation Denotes One or More Occurrences of the ITEM_ORDERED Field

Figure 4.25 Data dictionary entries in SSA.

INITIALIZE the program (open files, initialize counters and tables)
READ the first order record
WHILE there are more order records DO
 WHILE there are more item_ordered fields in the order record DO
  EXTRACT the next item_ordered
  SEARCH the order_table for the extracted item
  IF the extracted item is found THEN
   INCREMENT the extracted item's occurrence count
  ELSE
   INSERT the extracted item into the order_table and
   INCREMENT the occurrence count
  ENDIF
  INCREMENT the items_processed counter
 ENDWHILE at the end of the order record
ENDWHILE when all order records have been processed
WRITE the order_table and the items_processed counter
TO the batch_order file
CLOSE files
TERMINATE the program

Figure 4.26 An SSA Processing Logic representation.

diagram and data dictionary are completed. This may be advisable for certain critical nodes, but as a general rule it is better to defer detailed design considerations until analysis is complete.

An important feature of SSA, as presented by Gane and Sarson, is the use of a relational model to specify data flows and data stores. Relations are composed from the fields of data records. The fields are called the domains of the relation. If a record has N fields, the corresponding relation is called an N-tuple. For example, the ORDER record in Figure 4.25 can be represented by the 7-tuple:

ORDER("CUSTOMER_IDENTITY,ORDER_DATE,CATALOG_NUMBER,"
ITEM_NAME,UNIT_PRICE,QUANTITY,TOTAL_COST)

This relation is in "first normal form" because there are no repeating groups in the relation. The ORDER record in Figure 4.25 was converted to first normal form by associating CUSTOMER_IDENTITY and ORDER_DATE with each individual item ordered. The first three domains of the relation are quoted to indicate that they form the key for unique identification of each order.

The simplest form of relation is "third normal form," which is obtained by transforming first normal form to second normal form, and second normal form to third normal form. In order to obtain the second normal form of a relation, first normal form must be transformed so that all non-key domains are fully functionally dependent on the key. In this example, ITEM_NAME and UNIT_PRICE depend only on the CATALOG_NUMBER portion of the key; they are not fully dependent on the entire key. On the other hand, the QUANTITY cannot be determined without knowing the entire key. Thus, QUANTITY is fully functionally dependent on the key, but ITEM_NAME and UNIT_PRICE are not.

The partial dependence of ITEM_NAME and UNIT-PRICE can be eliminated by placing the domains that describe the ordered item in a separate relation. This results in the following second normal form:

ORDER("CUSTOMER_IDENTITY,ORDER_DATE,CATALOG_NUMBER,"
QUANTITY,TOTAL_COST)

ITEM("CATALOG_NUMBER,"ITEM_NAME,UNIT_PRICE)

To obtain third normal form from second normal form, we must ensure that every non-key domain is functionally independent of all other non-key domains. In this example, TOTAL_COST can be computed from QUANTITY and UNIT_PRICE. Therefore, TOTAL_COST is eliminated to produce two relations that are both in third normal form:

ORDER("CUSTOMER_IDENTITY,ORDER_DATE,CATALOG_NUMBER,"
QUANTITY)

ITEM("CATALOG_NUMBER,"ITEM_NAME,UNIT_PRICE)

This is the simplest, and thus most desirable, form of normalization.

The unwieldy three-domain key in the ORDER relation can be eliminated by adding a new key domain called ORDER_NUMBER to produce the relation

ORDER("ORDER_NUMBER,"CUSTOMER_IDENTITY,ORDER_DATE,
CATALOG_NUMBER,QUANTITY)

This has the advantage of simplifying access to orders, but it also requires that the order number be known before an order relation can be accessed.

4.3.5 Gist

Gist is a formal specification language developed at the USC/Information Sciences Institute by R. Balzar and colleagues (BAL81). Gist is a textual language based on a relational model of objects and attributes. A Gist specification is a formal description of valid behaviors of a system. A specification is composed of three parts:

1. A specification of object types and relationships between these types. This determines a set of possible states.
2. A specification of actions and demons which define transitions between possible states.
3. A specification of constraints on states and state transitions.

The valid behaviors of a system are those transition sequences that do not violate any constraints.

Preparing a Gist specification involves several steps:

1. Identify a collection of object types to describe the objects manipulated by the process. Types are typically described by concrete nouns that convey meaningful information.

2. Identify individual objects (values) within types. These individuals are not variables in the programming language sense; they may be used to describe constraints or to describe dynamic aspects of a process. Often, a specification will have no individual objects.
3. Identify relationships to specify the ways in which objects can be related to one another. The nature of relationships is highly dependent on the process being specified. Typical relationships include "connects to," "is part of," and "derived from."
4. Identify types and relationships that can be defined (possibly by recursive definition) in terms of other types and relations. These situations provide the basis for derivation rules. Derivation rules permit expansion of the specification vocabulary.
5. Identify static constraints on the types and relationships. Static constraints identify processing states that should never arise. Static constraints occur because of the physical reality being modeled, and because the derived process may restrict potential states.
6. Identify actions that can change the state of the process in some way. For each action, the specification should state the types of objects on which the action can operate, any precondition on such objects that restricts the situations in which the action can be performed, and a statement of how the action changes the process state.
7. Identify dynamic constraints. They consist of conditions that restrict allowable changes in the process state. Typical dynamic constraints include restrictions prohibiting changes in certain relationships between objects following their creation, and restrictions on the nature of changes in relations.
8. Identify active participants in the process being specified, and group them into classes, such that common actions are formed by the participants in a class.

Figure 4.27 illustrates the use of types, relations, constraints, and actions in a Gist specification. The specification identifies types ship, cargo, and tonnage. Ships include individuals such as the U.S.S. Constitution and the H.M.S. Queen Mary. Cargoes are grain and fuel. Tonnage is a natural number; natnum is a predefined

```
type SHIP includes (USS_CONST, HMS_QM2);
type CARGO definition (GRAIN, FUEL);
type TONNAGE definition natnum;

relation CONTAINS (SHIP, CARGO, TONNAGE)
   where always prohibited (SHIP, FUEL, GRAIN) ||
                         CONTAINS(SHIP, FUEL, $)
                         CONTAINS(SHIP, GRAIN, $);

action LOADSHIP(SHIP, CARGO, INCR: TONNAGE)
   precondition SHIP: DOCK: HANDLES = CARGO,
   definition if CONTAINS(SHIP, CARGO, $)
                      then update TONNAGE
end
```

Figure 4.27 A Gist specification
(adapted from (BAL81)).

type in Gist. The relation "CONTAINS" in Figure 4.27 states that ships contain cargoes of specified tonnage; for example, CONTAINS(USS_CONST, GRAIN, 50) means that the U.S.S. Constitution contains 50 tons of grain. CONTAINS is restricted to prohibit simultaneous cargoes of grain and fuel. Action "LOADSHIP" describes the change in process state that occurs when a cargo is added to a ship. The precondition states that the ship must be docked at a pier that handles the specified cargo.

The Initial Operating Capability (IOC) is a prototype testing facility for software specifications written in Gist. The purpose of IOC is to validate functional specifications by "executing" them on real test data. IOC consists of an evaluator capable of executing specifications expressed in a subset of Gist, and programs that permit entering, editing, and displaying of Gist specifications. In addition, IOC permits state initialization, displaying of states, and interactive breakpointing and tracing of test case evaluation.

Gist has a well-defined, but rather complex, syntax. Learning the syntax of Gist is similar to learning the syntax of a new programming language. Learning to use Gist (or RSL or SADT or …) is complicated by the fact that one is not only learning a new notation, but also learning a new way of thinking about systems and learning new techniques for specifying functional behavior.

In this section, we have discussed five notations for requirements specification. Two of them (SADT and SSA) do not have automated processors. Nevertheless, they incorporate techniques that are quite useful for analyzing and documenting the requirements for software products. Primary application areas for the notations and tools discussed in this section are summarized as follows:

PSL/PSA: Originally developed for data processing applications. Widely used in other applications.

RSL/REVS: Real-time process control systems.

SADT: Interconnection structure of any large, complex system. Not restricted to software systems.

SSA: Gane and Sarson version used in data processing applications that have data-base requirements. DeMarco version suited to data flow analysis of software systems.

GIST: Object-oriented specification and design. Refinement of specifications into source code.

4.4 SUMMARY

Software requirements definition is concerned with preparation of the *Software Requirements Specification*. The format and contents of the *Software Requirements Specification* have been discussed, and relational and state oriented notations for specifying the functional characteristics of a software product were presented.

Several notations and automated tools for software requirements were described. Some of the notations (SADT and SSA) do not have automated processors, but are nevertheless useful techniques. Most of the automated tools for requirements definition are in fact analysis and design tools; they incorporate notations for describing structure and processing details. In our opinion, this is a weakness in a requirements definition tool. Requirements definition is (or should be) concerned with the "what" of the software product. Premature concern with the "how" of software implementation can sidetrack the unwary software engineer into inappropriate levels of detail too early in the development process. Involvement in too much detail too soon is one of the most prevalent problems in software engineering.

Automated tools for software requirements definition must be used with caution to prevent requirements definition from becoming entangled with software design. On the other hand, automated requirements tools can produce various types of formatted reports, and they can often provide diagnostic messages based on automated analysis of completeness and consistency of the requirements definition. Like all tools, software requirements tools can be misused by unsophisticated users.

REFERENCES

(AGE79) Agerwala, T.: "Putting Petri Nets to Work," *COMPUTER,* vol. 12, no. 12, December 1979.

(ALF77) Alford, M.: "A Requirements Engineering Methodology for Real-Time Processing Requirements," *Trans. Software Eng.,* vol. SE-3, no. 1, January 1977.

(BAB80) Babb, R. and L. Tripp: "Toward Tangible Realizations of Software Systems," Proc. 13th Hawaii Intl. Conf. on System Sciences, January 1980.

(BAL81) Balzer, R.: Gist Final Report, Information Sciences Institute, University of Southern California, February 1981.

(BEL77) Bell, T., et al.: "An Extendable Approach to Computer-Aided Software Requirements Engineering," *Trans. Software Eng.,* vol. SE-3, no. 1, January 1977.

(BOE73) Boehm, B., et al.: *Characteristics of Software Quality,* TRW Publication TRW-SS-73-09, TRW, Redondo Beach, Calif., 1973.

(DEM78) DeMarco, T.: *Structured Analysis and System Specification,* Yourdon Press, New York, 1978.

(GAN79) Gane, C., and T. Sarson: *Structured Systems Analysis: Tools and Techniques,* Prentice-Hall, Englewood Cliffs, N.J., 1979.

(GAN81) Gannon, J., et al.: "Data Abstraction Implementation, Specification, and Testing," *ACM TOPLAS,* vol. 3, no. 3, July 1981.

(GUT77) Guttag, J.: "Abstract Data Types and the Development of Data Structures," *Comm. ACM,* vol. 20, no. 6, June 1977.

(GUT78) Guttag, J. and J. Horning: "The Algebraic Specification of Abstract Data Types," *Acta Informatica,* vol. 10, no. 1, 1978.

(HEA72) Heaps, H.: *An Introduction to Computer Languages,* Prentice-Hall, Englewood Cliffs, N.J., 1972.

(HEN80) Heninger, K.: "Specifying Software Requirements for Complex Systems: New Techniques and Their Application," *IEEE Trans. Software Eng.,* vol. SE-6, no. 1, January 1980.

(HOP79) Hopcroft, J. and J. Ullman: *Introduction to Automata Theory, Languages, and Computation,* Addison-Wesley, Reading, Mass., 1979.

(PET77) Peterson, J.: "Petri Nets," *ACM Computing Surveys,* vol. 9, no. 3, September 1977.

(POO74) Pooch, U.: "Translation of Decision Tables," *ACM Computing Surveys,* vol. 6, no. 2, June 1974.

(RID79) Riddle, W.: "An Approach to Software System Behavior Descriptions," *Computer Languages,* vol. 4, no. 1, 1979.

(ROB77) Robinson, L., et al.: "A Formal Methodology for the Design of Operating System Software," in *Current Trends in Programming Methodology,* vol. I, R. Yeh (ed.), Prentice-Hall, Englewood Cliffs, N.J., 1977.

(ROS77) Ross, D.: "Structured Analysis (SA): A Language for Communicating Ideas," *Trans. Software Eng.,* vol. SE-3, no. 1, January 1977.

(SHA78) Shaw, A.: "Software Descriptions with Flow Expressions," *IEEE TSE,* vol. SE-4, no. 3, May, 1978.

(SHA80) Shaw, A.: "Software Specification Languages Based on Regular Expressions," in *Software Development Tools,* W. Riddle and R. Fairley (eds.), Springer-Verlag, Berlin, 1980.

(TEI77) Teichrow, D., and E. Hershey: "PSL/PSA: A Computer Aided Technique for Structured Documentation and Analysis of Information Processing Systems," *Trans. Software Eng.,* vol. SE-3, no. 1, January 1977.

(TEI80) Teitelman, W.: *Interlisp Reference Manual,* Xerox Palo Alto Research Center, October 1978.

(TSE77) Special Issue on Requirements Analysis, *IEEE Trans. Software Eng.,* vol. SE-3, no. 1, January 1977.

(WEI71) Weinberg, G.: *The Psychology of Computer Programming,* Van Nostrand Reinhold, New York, 1971.

EXERCISES

4.1 Obtain, from an organization of your choice, a *Software Requirement Specification.* Assess the strengths and weaknesses of the document in terms of the suggested format and contents described in Section 4.1.

4.2 *(a)* Use the recursive definition of Fibonacci numbers from Section 4.2.1 to calculate FI(5).

    (b) Use the recursive definition of binomial coefficients given in Section 4.2.1 to calculate B(3,2).

    (c) Write an iterative routine to calculate FI(n). Present convincing arguments that your routine satisfies the recursive definition of Fibonacci numbers.

4.3 (HEA72) A recursive definition of polynomial evaluation for polynomials of the form

$$P(N,A,X) = A(0)*X**N + A(1)*X**(N-1) + ...A(N-1)*X + A(N)$$

is

$$P(0,A,X) = A(0)$$
$$P(J,A,X) = X*P(J-1,A,X) + A(J) \text{ for } 1 < = J < = N$$

    (a) Write a recursive procedure to evaluate polynomials based on the recursive specification.

    (b) Write an iterative procedure to evaluate polynomials based on the recursive specification.

    (c) Present a convincing argument to show that your iterative routine and your recursive routine both satisfy the specification.

    (d) Compare the iterative and recursive routines for simplicity and clarity, for utilization of memory, and for execution time.

4.4 Give English-language descriptions of the queue axioms presented in Figure 4.5.

4.5 Add a queue operator, SIZE, that requires a queue name as its argument and returns the number of elements in the queue.

    (a) Define the syntax of SIZE.

    (b) Provide algebraic axioms to specify the interactions of SIZE with other queue operators.

4.6 Provide formal definitions for the queue operators NEW, ADD, FRONT, REMOVE, EMPTY, and SIZE similar to the definitions in Figure 4.4.

4.7 Given the following definition of the ROTATE operator for queues:

ROTATE(que) = if EMPTY(que) or SIZE(que) = MAX then error
else REMOVE(ADD(que,FRONT(que)))

(*a*) Describe the effect of ROTATE in English.
(*b*) Using the definitions from Exercise 4.6, prove that ROTATE behaves as specified in part a.
(*c*) Using the definitions from Exercise 4.6, prove that

SIZE(que) = SIZE(ROTATE(que))

4.8 Provide algebraic axioms to specify operations on character strings.
(*a*) Specify the operations NEW, INSERT, DELETE, APPEND, CONCAT, and LENGTH in English.
(*b*) Specify the syntax of the operators.
(*c*) Specify algebraic axioms for the operators.
(*d*) Present convincing arguments that your axioms are complete and consistent.
(*e*) Specify a minimal, independent set of string operators from which the other operators can be defined.

4.9 Formally define each of the operators in Exercise 4.8 using the notation of Figure 4.4.

4.10 (*a*) Use the operators in Exercise 4.8 to define a new string operator, REPLACE(str1,str2,str3), that replaces str1 in str2 with str3.
(*b*) Use the formal definitions in Exercise 4.9 to prove that your definition of REPLACE is correct.

4.11 Use the definitions of regular expressions to prove the following statements by showing that both sides of a statement specify the same set of symbol strings. The precedence of operators is (*, +), concatenation, |, highest to lowest.
(*a*) a a* = a +
(*b*) a|ab* = ab*
(*c*) x (a|b)*|y (a|b)* = (x|y) (a|b)*
(*d*) (a|b)* = (b|a)*
(*e*) (a b)* = (b a)*

4.12 Obtain a copy of the guidelines for federal income tax deductions.
(*a*) Write the guidelines in decision table format.
(*b*) Use the decision table to prove that the guidelines are completely and consistently specified.

4.13 Use a decision table to specify the rules for a board game such as checkers, dominoes, or Othello.

4.14 Event tables are particularly useful for specifying exception handling. Rows are labeled with status information and columns with exception events. Table entries specify exception handling actions to be performed in response to a raised exception condition. For instance, a status entry might be "performing matrix inversion," and a corresponding exception event might be "zero divisor." The table entry would specify the corrective actions to be taken.
(*a*) Use an event table to specify events, exception conditions, and exception handling for the process of reading real data values into a matrix and computing the eigenvalues of the matrix.
(*b*) Use an event table to specify modes, exception conditions, and exception handling in a text editor.
(*c*) Use an event table to specify events, exception conditions, and exception handling for a microprocessor control system on an automobile.

4.15 Construct a transition table and a transition diagram to specify the operation of a bank teller machine.

4.16 Construct a transition table and a transition diagram to specify the moves in a board game.

4.17 Construct a transition table and a transition diagram to specify a microprocessor control system for an automobile.

4.18 For every regular expression, a transition diagram (transition table) can be constructed to specify processing of symbol strings specified by the regular expression. The transition diagram has an initial state So and one or more final states corresponding to acceptance of legal symbol strings. For example, the regular expression a(b|c)* has the following transition diagram (final states are indicated by concentric circles):

(*a*) State rules for constructing transition diagram segments for the following regular expressions:

$$a \quad (a\ b) \quad (a\ |\ b) \quad (a)* \quad (a)+$$

(*b*) Use your rules from part a to construct transition diagrams for the following regular expressions:

$$(a\ (b\ |\ c)+\ )$$
$$(a\ (b\ |\ c)\ +\ )\ |\ (c\ (a\ |\ b)*\ d)$$

4.19 A transition diagram (transition table) is completely specified if there is a transition for every possible combination of state and input symbol; otherwise the diagram is incomplete. An incompletely specified transition diagram (transition table) can be completely specified by adding a trap state T, which is entered for otherwise unspecified transitions. Once in the trap state, the system remains there forever. For example, a completely specified transition diagram for a (b|c)* is:

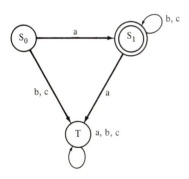

(*a*) Convert your incompletely specified transition diagrams in Exercise 4.18 to complete specifications. Use both transition diagrams and transition tables to express the specification. What actions might be appropriate in the trap state?

(*b*) Convert the transition diagrams of Exercises 4.18 and 4.19 to transition tables.

4.20 (*a*) Construct a Petri net for the following program segment:

```
A : =  1;
B : =  2;
C : =  A*A;
D : =  A + B;
E : =  C*D;
```

(*b*) Which computations can occur concurrently? Which must be done sequentially?

4.21 (*a*) In an organization of your choice, determine whether automated tools are used for requirements analysis.

(*b*) If automated tools are used, what are the good and bad experiences of the tools' users?

(*c*) If automated tools are not used, why not? Is there any plan to experiment with automated tools? Why or why not?

4.22 Obtain user's manuals and other documentation for one or more automated tools for requirements analysis.

(*a*) What types of analysis and documentation support are provided by the tools?

(*b*) Does the tool appear to be difficult to learn and to use?

(*c*) Is the tool an analysis tool or an analysis and design tool?

(*d*) Who are the users of the tool? What are their experiences?

(*e*) What machine resources are required to use the tool?

(*f*) Under what conditions would you recommend using the tool?

FIVE

SOFTWARE DESIGN

INTRODUCTION

According to Webster, the process of design involves "conceiving and planning out in the mind" and "making a drawing, pattern, or sketch of." In software design, there are three distinct types of activities: external design, architectural design, and detailed design. Architectural and detailed design are collectively referred to as internal design.

External design of software involves conceiving, planning out, and specifying the externally observable characteristics of a software product. These characteristics include user displays and report formats, external data sources and data sinks, and the functional characteristics, performance requirements, and high level process structure for the product. External design begins during the analysis phase and continues into the design phase. In practice, it is not possible to perform requirements definition without doing some preliminary design. Requirements definition is concerned with specifying the external, functional, and performance requirements for a system, as well as exception handling and the other items listed in Table 4.1. External design is concerned with refining those requirements and establishing the high level structural view of the system. Thus, the distinction between requirements definition and external design is not sharp, but is rather a gradual shift in emphasis from detailed "what" to high-level "how."

Internal design involves conceiving, planning out, and specifying the internal structure and processing details of the software product. The goals of internal design are to specify internal structure and processing details, to record design decisions and indicate why certain alternatives and trade-offs were chosen, to elaborate the test plan, and to provide a blueprint for implementation, testing, and maintenance activities. The work products of internal design include a specification of architectural structure, the details of algorithms and data structures, and the test plan.

Architectural design is concerned with refining the conceptual view of the system, identifying internal processing functions, decomposing high-level functions into subfunctions, defining internal data streams and data stores, and establishing relationships and interconnections among functions, data streams, and data stores. Issues of concern during detailed design include specification of algorithms that implement the functions, concrete data structures that implement the data stores, the actual interconnections among functions and data structures, and the packaging scheme for the system.

The test plan describes the objectives of testing, the test completion criteria, the integration plan (strategy, schedule, responsible individuals), particular tools and techniques to be used, and the actual test cases and expected results. Functional tests and performance tests are developed during requirements analysis and are refined during the design phase. Tests that examine the internal structure of the software product and tests that attempt to break the system (stress tests) are developed during detailed design and implementation. Software testing techniques are discussed in Chapter 8.

External design and architectural design typically span the period from Software Requirements Review to Preliminary Design Review. Detailed design spans the period from Preliminary Design Review to Critical Design Review. The situation is illustrated in Figure 5.1.

In this chapter, we discuss fundamental design concepts for software, modules and modularization criteria, notations for software design, architectural design techniques, detailed design considerations, design considerations for distributed and real-time systems, design guidelines, and test plans.

5.1 FUNDAMENTAL DESIGN CONCEPTS

Every intellectual discipline is characterized by fundamental concepts and specific techniques. Techniques are the manifestations of the concepts as they apply to particular situations. Techniques come and go with changes in technology, intel-

Phases:	Analysis	Design	Implementation
Activities:	Planning Requirements definition	External Architectural Detailed	Coding Debugging Testing
Reviews:	SRR	PDR	CDR

Figure 5.1 Timing of the Software Requirements Review (SRR), the Preliminary Design Review (PDR), and the Critical Design Review (CDR).

lectual fads, economic conditions, and social concerns. By definition, fundamental principles remain the same throughout. They provide the underlying basis for development and evaluation of techniques. Fundamental concepts of software design include abstraction, structure, information hiding, modularity, concurrency, verification, and design aesthetics.

5.1.1 Abstraction

Abstraction is the intellectual tool that allows us to deal with concepts apart from particular instances of those concepts. During requirements definition and design, abstraction permits separation of the conceptual aspects of a system from the (yet to be specified) implementation details. We can, for example, specify the FIFO property of a queue or the LIFO property of a stack without concern for the representation scheme to be used in implementing the stack or queue. Similarly, we can specify the functional characteristics of the routines that manipulate data structures (e.g., NEW, PUSH, POP, TOP, EMPTY) without concern for the algorithmic details of the routines.

During software design, abstraction allows us to organize and channel our thought processes by postponing structural considerations and detailed algorithmic considerations until the functional characteristics, data streams, and data stores have been established. Structural considerations are then addressed prior to consideration of algorithmic details. This approach reduces the amount of complexity that must be dealt with at any particular point in the design process.

Architectural design specifications are models of software in which the functional and structural attributes of the system are emphasized. During detailed design, the architectural structure is refined into implementation details. Design is thus a process of proceeding from abstract considerations to concrete representations. This contrasts to the use of abstraction in science and mathematics, where fundamental principles are abstracted from a collection of concrete situations. Instead, the software designer proceeds from abstractions of entities that don't yet exist to the physical realizations of those entities.

Three widely used abstraction mechanisms in software design are functional abstraction, data abstraction, and control abstraction. These mechanisms allow us to control the complexity of the design process by systematically proceeding from the abstract to the concrete. Functional abstraction involves the use of parameterized subprograms. The ability to parameterize a subprogram and to bind different parameter values on different invocations of the subprogram is a powerful abstraction mechanism. Functional abstraction can be generalized to collections of subprograms, herein called "groups" (packages in Ada, clusters in CLU). Within a group, certain routines have the "visible" property, which allows them to be used by routines in other groups. Routines without the visible property are hidden from other groups and can only be used within the containing group. A group thus provides a functional abstraction in which the visible routines communicate with other groups and the hidden routines exist to support the visible ones.

Data abstraction involves specifying a data type or a data object by specifying legal operations on objects; representation and manipulation details are suppressed. Thus, the type "stack" can be specified abstractly as a LIFO mechanism in which the routines NEW, PUSH, POP, TOP, and EMPTY interact as specified in Figures 4.3 and 4.4. Several modern programming languages, including CLU and Ada, provide abstract data types. In those languages, objects of type "stack", for instance, can be created and manipulated by the operations specified in the type definition. The term "data encapsulation" is used to denote a single instance of a data object defined in terms of the operations that can be performed on it; the term "abstract data type" is used to denote declaration of a data type (such as stack) from which numerous instances can be created.

Abstract data types are abstract in the sense that representation details of the data items and implementation details of the functions that manipulate the data items are hidden within the group that implements the abstract type. Other groups that use the abstraction do not have access to the internal details of abstract objects. Objects of abstract type are thus known only by the functions that can be performed on them. During architectural design, the visible functions that operate on abstract objects are specified. Specification of representation details for data objects and algorithmic details for the functions are postponed until detailed design. Figure 5.2 illustrates the visible part and the private part of an Ada package for a stack abstraction. The function names in Figure 5.2 satisfy the algebraic axioms and formal specifications presented in Figures 4.3 and 4.4. Instances of stacks can be created as indicated in Figure 5.2. Further details concerning abstract data types in Ada are presented in Chapter 7.

It should not be inferred from our simple examples that data abstraction is only useful to specify simple data items such as stacks and queues. The contents of a graphics display screen or a run-time activation record for a block-structured programming language might, for example, be an object of abstract type that is

```
package STACK_TYPE is
   type STACK is limited private;
procedure PUSH(I: in INTEGER; S: in out STACK);
procedure POP(I: out INTEGER; S: in out STACK);
function EMPTY(S: in STACK) return BOOLEAN;
function FULL(S: in STACK) return BOOLEAN;
   STKFULL, STKEMPTY: exception;
private
   type STACK is
      record
         INDEX: INTEGER range 0..100 := 0;
         STORE: array(1..100) of INTEGER;
      end record;
end STACK_TYPE;
STACK1, STACK2: STACK;
:::::
PUSH(X,STACK1);
POP(Y,STACK2);
B := EMPTY(STACK1);
:::::
```

Figure 5.2 Specification and use of abstract data type STACK.

defined in terms of permitted operations on that object. An abstract data type can be defined in terms of other abstract types. This permits design of hierarchical data types. Of course, primitive data types must be provided to avoid circularity of definition.

Control abstraction is the third commonly used abstraction mechanism in software design. Control abstraction is used to state a desired effect without stating the exact mechanism of control. IF statements and WHILE statements in modern programming languages are abstractions of machine code implementations that involve conditional jump instructions. A statement of the form

"for all I in S sort files I"

leaves unspecified the sorting technique, the nature of S, the nature of the files, and how "for all I in S" is to be handled.

Another example of control abstraction is the monitor construct, which is a control abstraction for concurrent programming; implementation details of the operator are hidden inside the construct. At the architectural design level, control abstraction permits specification of sequential subprograms, exception handlers, and coroutines and concurrent program units without concern for the exact details of implementation.

5.1.2 Information Hiding

Information hiding is a fundamental design concept for software. The principle of information hiding was formulated by Parnas (PAR71). When a software system is designed using the information hiding approach, each module in the system hides the internal details of its processing activities and modules communicate only through well-defined interfaces. Our previous examples of functional, data, and control abstraction exhibit information hiding characteristics.

According to Parnas, design should begin with a list of difficult design decisions and design decisions that are likely to change. Each module is designed to hide such a decision from the other modules. Because these design decisions transcend execution time, design modules may not correspond to processing steps in the implementation of the system.

In addition to hiding of difficult and changeable design decisions, other candidates for information hiding include:

1. A data structure, its internal linkage, and the implementation details of the procedures that manipulate it (this is the principle of data abstraction)
2. The format of control blocks such as those for queues in an operating system (a "control-block" module)
3. Character codes, ordering of character sets, and other implementation details
4. Shifting, masking, and other machine dependent details

Information hiding can be used as the principal design technique for architectural design of a system, or as a modularization criterion in conjunction with other design techniques. Examples of information hiding used as a design technique can be found in (PAR72a) and (PAR72b).

5.1.3 Structure

Structure is a fundamental characteristic of computer software. The use of structuring permits decomposition of a large system into smaller, more manageable units with well-defined relationships to the other units in the system.

The most general form of system structure is the network. A computing network can be represented as a directed graph, consisting of nodes and arcs. The nodes can represent processing elements that transform data and the arcs can be used to represent data links between nodes. Alternatively, the nodes can represent data stores and the arcs data transformation.

In simplest form, a network might specify data flow and processing steps within a single subprogram, or the data flow among a collection of sequential subprograms. The most complex form of computing network is a distributed computing system in which each node represents a geographically distinct processor with private memory.

The structure inside a complex processing node might consist of concurrent processes executing in parallel and communicating through some combination of shared variables and synchronous and asynchronous message passing. Inside each process, one might find functional abstraction groups, data abstraction groups, and control abstraction groups. Each group might consist of a visible specification part and a hidden body. The visible portion would provide attributes such as procedure interfaces, data types, and data objects available for use by other groups. The body of a processing group is typically a hierarchical collection of subprograms and static data areas that implement the attributes specified in the visible specification part of the group.

The entire network might be a complex abstraction that provides an information utility and in turn forms a node in a more complex structure of people and machines. The process network view of software structure is illustrated in Figure 5.3.

The relationship "uses" and the complementary relationship "is used by" provide the basis for hierarchical ordering of abstractions in a software system. The "uses" relationship can be represented as a directed graph, where the notation A → B means "A uses B" or "B is used by A."

Hierarchical ordering of abstractions is established by the following rule:

> If A and B are distinct entities, and if A uses B,
> then B is not permitted to use A or any entity
> that makes use of A.

A hierarchical ordering relation can be represented as an acyclic, directed graph with a distinguished node that represents the root entity. The root uses other entities, but is not used by any entity. Subsidiary nodes in the hierarchical structure

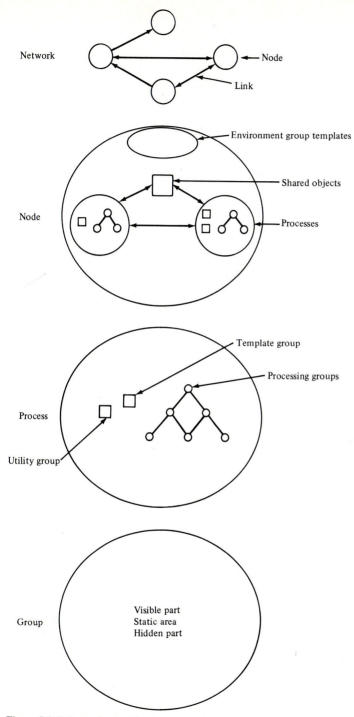

Figure 5.3 Software System Structure.

represent subordinate entities that are used by their superordinates and in turn make use of their subordinates.

Hierarchical structures may or may not form tree structures. Figure 5.4*a* and *b* illustrate a directed, acyclic graph and a tree structure respectively. Note that in a tree there is a unique path from the root to each node. In an acyclic, directed graph there may be more than one path from the root to a node.

The diagrams illustrated in Figure 5.4*a* and *b* are called structure charts. They are not flowcharts because there is no indication of the processing sequence, and no indication of the conditions under which *A* might use *B*.

In cases where the structure chart depicts the structure of subroutines in a system, the data passed between routines can be indicated on the arcs connecting routines, as illustrated in Figure 5.4, or in an associated table, as illustrated in Figure 5.7.

Directly recursive routines (those that invoke themselves) can be indicated on a structure chart by placing closed arcs on the nodes for those routines. Indirectly recursive routines ($A \rightarrow B \rightarrow C \rightarrow A$) violate the hierarchical structuring rule, and should generally be avoided. Allowable exceptions include mutually recursive routines and coroutines ($A \longleftrightarrow B$).

The hierarchical structures illustrated in Figure 5.4a and b are desirable because they reduce the complexity of interactions among software components. As illustrated in Figure 5.5, there are $N(N - 1)/2$ interconnections of N nodes in a connected graph, but only $N - 1$ interconnections of N nodes connected in a tree structure. Observe that $N - 1$ is the minimum number of connections for N nodes.

A hierarchical structure isolates software components and promotes ease of understanding, implementation, debugging, testing, integration, and modification of a system. In addition, programmers can be assigned, either individually or in teams, to implement the various subsystems in a hierarchical structure. In this

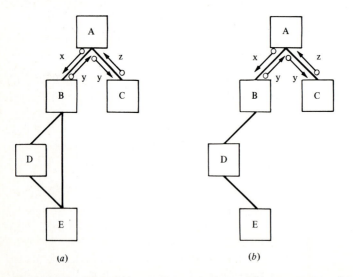

(*a*)   (*b*)

Figure 5.4 Examples of (a) a graph structure chart and (b) a tree structure chart.

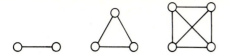

Figure 5.5a Illustrating $N(N-1)/2$ links among N nodes in a connected graph.

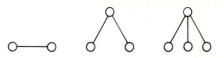
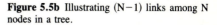

Figure 5.5b Illustrating $(N-1)$ links among N nodes in a tree.

sense, the structure of the product prescribes the structure of the implementation team. It has been suggested that the structure of software products tends to resemble the structure of the teams that develop them. Perhaps the emphasis should be inverted: The organizational structure of teams that develop software systems should resemble the desired structure of the software being developed.

In hierarchical systems, there are usually one or more groups of routines designated as utility groups. These groups typically contain lowest level routines (routines that do not use other routines) that are used throughout the hierarchy. Typical utilities include math library functions, I/O routines, plotting packages, and other general-purpose software.

Several different criteria are available to guide hierarchical decomposition of a software system. These include decomposition into processing steps and sub-steps, decomposition to reinforce information hiding, coupling and cohesion, data encapsulation, and/or problem modeling. These and other decomposition criteria are discussed in Section 5.2.

5.1.4 Modularity

There are many definitions of the term "module." They range from "a module is a FORTRAN subroutine" to "a module is an Ada package" to "a module is a work assignment for an individual programmer." All of these definitions are correct, in the sense that modular systems incorporate collections of abstractions in which each functional abstraction, each data abstraction, and each control abstraction handles a local aspect of the problem being solved. Modular systems consist of well-defined, manageable units with well-defined interfaces among the units. Desirable properties of a modular system include:

1. Each processing abstraction is a well-defined subsystem that is potentially useful in other applications.
2. Each function in each abstraction has a single, well defined purpose.
3. Each function manipulates no more than one major data structure.
4. Functions share global data selectively. It is easy to identify all routines that share a major data structure.
5. Functions that manipulate instances of abstract data types are encapsulated with the data structure being manipulated.

Modularity enhances design clarity, which in turn eases implementation, de-bugging, testing, documenting, and maintenance of the software product. Modularization criteria are discussed in Section 5.2.

5.1.5 Concurrency

Software systems can be categorized as sequential or concurrent. In a sequential system, only one portion of the system is active at any given time. Concurrent systems have independent processes that can be activated simultaneously if multiple processors are available. On a single processor, concurrent processes can be interleaved in execution time. This permits implementation of time-shared, multi-programmed, and real-time systems.

Problems unique to concurrent systems include deadlock, mutual exclusion, and synchronization of processes. Deadlock is an undesirable situation that occurs when all processes in a computing system are waiting for other processes to complete some actions so that each can proceed. Mutual exclusion is necessary to ensure that multiple processes do not attempt to update the same components of the shared processing state at the same time. Synchronization is required so that concurrent processes operating at differing execution speeds can communicate at the appropriate points in their execution histories.

In the past only those software engineers involved with operating systems, data-base systems, and real-time applications needed to be concerned with concurrency issues. But as hardware becomes more sophisticated, and as computing systems become more complex, it becomes increasingly necessary for every software engineer to understand the issues and techniques of concurrent software design. Concurrency is a fundamental principle of software design because parallelism in software introduces added complexity and additional degrees of freedom into the design process. Design considerations for concurrent systems are discussed in Section 5.6.

5.1.6 Verification

Verification is a fundamental concept in software design. Design is the bridge between customer requirements and an implementation that satisfies those requirements. A design is verifiable if it can be demonstrated that the design will result in an implementation that satisfies the customer's requirements. This is typically done in two steps: (1) verification that the software requirements definition satisfies the customer's needs (verification of the requirements); and (2) verification that the design satisfies the requirements definition (verification of the design).

We re-emphasized that the test plan is a product of the design process. The test plan must be coupled to specifications that are testable. In control theory, one speaks of system states as being observable and controllable. In software design, one must ensure that the system is structured so that the internal states can be observed, tested, and the results related to the requirements.

5.1.7 Aesthetics

Aesthetic considerations are fundamental to design, whether in art or technology. Simplicity, elegance, and clarity of purpose distinguish products of outstanding quality from mediocre products. When we speak of mathematical elegance or structural beauty, we are speaking of those properties that go beyond mere satisfaction of the requirements. It is reported that a Supreme Court Justice, in ruling on a pornography case, stated: "I can't define it, but I know it when I see it." It is difficult to list objective criteria for evaluating the aesthetic factors in a software product, but an aesthetically pleasing product is easily recognized.

5.2 MODULES AND MODULARIZATION CRITERIA

Architectural design has the goal of producing well-structured, modular software systems. In this section of the text, we consider a software module to be a named entity having the following characteristics:

1. Modules contain instructions, processing logic, and data structures.
2. Modules can be separately compiled and stored in a library.
3. Modules can be included in a program.
4. Module segments can be used by invoking a name and some parameters.
5. Modules can use other modules.

Examples of modules include procedures, subroutines, and functions; functional groups of related procedures, subroutines, and functions; data abstraction groups; utility groups; and concurrent processes. Modularization allows the designer to decompose a system into functional units, to impose hierarchical ordering on function usage, to implement data abstractions, and to develop independently useful subsystems. In addition, modularization can be used to isolate machine dependencies, to improve the performance of a software product, or to ease debugging, testing, integration, tuning, and modification of the system.

There are numerous criteria that can be used to guide the modularization of a system. Depending on the criteria used, different system structures may result. Modularization criteria include the conventional criterion, in which each module and its submodules correspond to a processing step in the execution sequence; the information hiding criterion, in which each module hides a difficult or changeable design decision from the other modules; the data abstraction criterion, in which each module hides the representation details of a major data structure behind functions that access and modify the data structure; levels of abstraction, in which modules and collections of modules provide a hierarchical set of increasingly complex services; coupling-cohesion, in which a system is structured to maximize the cohesion of elements in each module and to minimize the coupling between modules; and problem modeling, in which the modular structure of the system matches the structure of the problem being solved. There are two versions of problem modeling: either the data structures match the problem structure and the visible functions manipulate the data structures, or the modules form a network of communicating processes where each process corresponds to a problem entity.

In practice, a software system can be modularized using a single design criterion or aspects of several criteria. In any case, structures of higher quality (easier to understand, easier to implement, easier to modify) are produced when the designer uses well-defined modularization criteria to guide the design process.

5.2.1 Coupling and Cohesion

A fundamental goal of software design is to structure the software product so that the number and complexity of interconnections between modules is minimized. An appealing set of heuristics for achieving this goal involves the concepts of coupling and cohesion.

Coupling and cohesion were first described by Stevens, Constantine, and Myers as part of the "structured design" approach to software design discussed in Section 5.4 (STE74). The strength of coupling between two modules is influenced by the complexity of the interface, the type of connection, and the type of communication. Obvious relationships result in less complexity than obscure or inferred ones. For example, interfaces established by common control blocks, common data blocks, common overlay regions of memory, common I/O devices, and/or global variable names are more complex (more tightly coupled) than interfaces established by parameter lists passed between modules.

Modification of a common data block or control block may require modification of all routines that are coupled to that block. If modules communicate only by parameters, and if the interfaces between modules remain fixed, the internal details of modules can be modified without having to modify the routines that use the modified modules.

Connections established by referring to other module names are more loosely coupled than connections established by referring to the internal elements of other modules. In the latter case, the entire content of a referenced module may have to be taken into account when updating the module that refers to it.

Communication between modules involves passing of data, passing elements of control (such as flags, switches, labels, and procedure names), and modification of one module's code by another module. The degree of coupling is lowest for data communication, higher for control communication, and highest for modules that modify other modules.

Coupling between modules can be ranked on a scale of strongest (least desirable) to weakest (most desirable) as follows:

1. Content coupling
2. Common coupling
3. Control coupling
4. Stamp coupling
5. Data coupling

Content coupling occurs when one module modifies local data values or instructions in another module. Content coupling can occur in assembly language programs. In common coupling, modules are bound together by global data structures. For instance, common coupling results when all routines in a FORTRAN program reference a single common data block. Control coupling involves passing control flags (as parameters or globals) between modules so that one module controls the sequence of processing steps in another module.

Stamp coupling is similar to common coupling, except that global data items are shared selectively among routines that require the data. Named common blocks in FORTRAN and packages in Ada support stamp coupling. Stamp coupling is more desirable than common coupling because fewer modules will have to be modified if a shared data structure is modified.

Data coupling involves the use of parameter lists to pass data items between routines. The most desirable form of coupling between modules is a combination of stamp and data coupling.

The internal cohesion of a module is measured in terms of the strength of binding of elements within the module. Cohesion of elements occurs on the scale of weakest (least desirable) to strongest (most desirable) in the following order:

1. Coincidental cohesion
2. Logical cohesion
3. Temporal cohesion
4. Communication cohesion
5. Sequential cohesion
6. Functional cohesion
7. Informational cohesion

Coincidental cohesion occurs when the elements within a module have no apparent relationship to one another. This results when a large, monolithic program is "modularized" by arbitrarily segmenting the program into several small modules, or when a module is created from a group of unrelated instructions that appear several times in other modules.

Logical cohesion implies some relationship among the elements of the module; as, for example, in a module that performs all input and output operations, or in a module that edits all data. A logically bound module often combines several related functions in a complex and interrelated fashion. This results in passing of control parameters, and in shared and tricky code that is difficult to understand and modify. Math library routines often exhibit logical cohesion. Logically cohesive modules usually require further decomposition. For example, a logically cohesive module to process records might be decomposed into four modules to process master records, process update records, process addition records, and process deletion records.

Modules with temporal cohesion exhibit many of the same disadvantages as logically bound modules. However, they are higher on the scale of binding because all elements are executed at one time, and no parameters or logic are required to determine which elements to execute. A typical example of temporal cohesion is a module that performs program initialization.

The elements of a module possessing communicational cohesion refer to the same set of input and/or output data. For example, "Print and Punch the Output

File" is communicationally bound. Communicational binding is higher on the binding scale than temporal binding because the elements are executed at one time and also refer to the same data.

Sequential cohesion of elements occurs when the output of one element is the input for the next element. For example, "Read Next Transaction and Update Master File" is sequentially bound. Sequential cohesion is high on the binding scale because the module structure usually bears a close resemblance to the problem structure. However, a sequentially bound module can contain several functions or part of a function, since the procedural processes in a program may be distinct from the functioning of the program.

Functional cohesion is a strong, and hence desirable, type of binding of elements in a module because all elements are related to the performance of a single function. Examples of functionally bound modules are "Compute Square Root," "Obtain Random Number," and "Write Record to Output File."

Informational cohesion of elements in a module occurs when the module contains a complex data structure and several routines to manipulate the data structure. Each routine in the module exhibits functional binding. Informational cohesion is the concrete realization of data abstraction. Informational cohesion is similar to communicational cohesion in that both refer to a single data entity. However, they differ in that communicational cohesion implies that all code in the module is executed on each invocation of the module. Informational cohesion requires that only one functionally cohesive segment of the module be executed on each invocation of the module.

The cohesion of a module can be determined by writing a brief statement of purpose for the module and examining the statement. The following tests are suggested by Constantine:

1. If the sentence has to be a compound sentence containing a comma or containing more than one verb, the module is probably performing more than one function; therefore, it probably has sequential or communicational binding.
2. If the sentence contains words relating to time, such as "first," "next," "then," "after," "when," "start," then the module probably has sequential or temporal binding.
3. If the predicate of the sentence does not contain a single, specific object following the verb, the module is probably logically bound. For example, "Edit All Data" has logical binding; "Edit Source Data" may have functional binding.
4. Words such as "Initialize" and "Clean Up" imply temporal binding.

Functionally bound modules can always be described by a simple statement of purpose; however, there is a potential problem in deciding how far to decompose a module that appears to be functionally bound. For instance, one might argue that the communicational cohesion apparent in "print and punch the output file" can be masked by changing the description to "manipulate output file." There are two problems with the latter description. First, the term "manipulate" is very vague.

Specific terms must be used in the functional description. Second, examination of what is meant by "manipulate" indicates that manipulate contains subfunctions that could be used alone (e.g., "print" and "punch"). A module is sufficiently decomposed when it contains no subfunctions that are potentially useful in other contexts.

In summary, the goal of modularizing a software system using the coupling-cohesion criteria is to produce systems that have stamp and data coupling between the modules, and functional or informational cohesion of elements within each module.

In practice, there may be additional considerations (some are discussed in the following section) that prevent strict attainment of the coupling-cohesion modularization goals. Also, it may be difficult to decide exactly which levels of coupling or cohesion are exhibited by various segments of a system. We view the various levels as being suggestive rather than strictly quantitative; they should be interpreted as guidelines. Nevertheless, the concepts of coupling and cohesion provide a valuable intellectual framework for thinking about software modules and software modularity.

5.2.2 Other Modularization Criteria

Additional criteria for deciding which functions to place in which modules of a software system include: hiding difficult and changeable design decisions; limiting the physical size of modules; structuring the system to improve observability and testability; isolating machine dependencies to a few routines; easing likely changes; providing general-purpose utility functions; developing an acceptable overlay structure in a machine with limited memory capacity; minimizing page faults in a virtual memory machine; and reducing the call-return overhead of excessive subroutine calls. For each software product, the designer must weigh these factors and develop a consistent set of modularization criteria to guide the design process.

Efficiency of the resulting implementation is a concern that frequently arises when decomposing a system into modules. A large number of small modules having data coupling and functional cohesion implies a large execution time overhead for establishing run-time linkages between the modules.

The preferred technique for optimizing the efficiency of a system is to first design and implement the system in a highly modular fashion. System performance is then measured, and bottlenecks are removed by reconfiguring and recombining modules, and by hand coding certain critical linkages and critical routines in assembly language if necessary. In these situations, the modular source code should be retained as documentation for the assembly language routines.

The soundness of this technique is based on two observations. First, most software systems spend a large portion of processing time in a small portion of the code; typically 80 percent or more of execution time is spent in 20 percent or less of the code. Furthermore, the region of code where the majority of time is spent is usually not predictable until the program is implemented and actual performance is measured. Second, it is relatively easy to reconfigure and recombine small modules into larger units if necessary for better performance; however, failure to initially decompose a system far enough may prevent identification of a function that could be used in other contexts. We repeat our previous advice: When in doubt, err in the direction of decomposing too finely.

5.3 DESIGN NOTATIONS

In software design, as in mathematics, the representation schemes used are of fundamental importance. Good notation can clarify the interrelationships and inter-actions of interest, while poor notation can complicate and interfere with good design practice. At least three levels of design specifications exist: external design specifications, which describe the external characteristics of a software system; architectural design specifications, which describe the structure of the system; and detailed design specifications, which describe control flow, data representation, and other algorithmic details within the modules.

Some design representations are appropriate for use on more than one level of design, while others are appropriate for only one level. Because the boundary between requirements analysis and external design is not well defined, some of the notations described in Chapter 4 are also useful for external design.

Notations used to specify the external characteristics, architectural structure, and processing details of a software system include data flow diagrams, structure charts, HIPO diagrams, procedure specifications, pseudocode, structured English, and structured flowcharts. These notations are discussed in subsequent sections of this chapter.

5.3.1 Data Flow Diagrams

Data flow diagrams ("bubble charts") are directed graphs in which the nodes specify processing activities and the arcs specify data items transmitted between processing nodes. Like flowcharts, data flow diagrams can be used at any desired level of abstraction. A data flow diagram might represent data flow between individual statements or blocks of statements in a routine, data flow between sequential routines, data flow between concurrent processes, or data flow in a distributed computing system where each node represents a geographically remote processing unit. Unlike flowcharts, data flow diagrams do not indicate decision logic or conditions under which various processing nodes in the diagram might be activated.

Data flow diagrams can be expressed using informal notation, as illustrated in Figure 5.6a, or special symbols can be used to denote processing nodes, data sources, data sinks, and data stores, as illustrated in Figure 5.6b.

Data flow diagrams are excellent mechanisms for communicating with custom-ers during requirements analysis; they are also widely used for representation of external and top-level internal design specifications. In the latter situations, data flow diagrams are quite valuable for establishing naming conventions and names of system components such as subsystems, files, and data links.

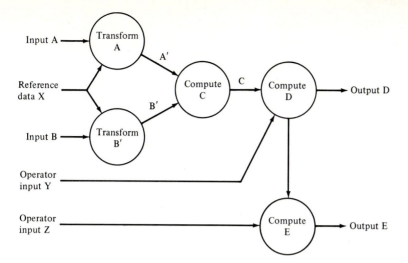

Figure 5.6a An informal data flow diagram or "bubble chart."

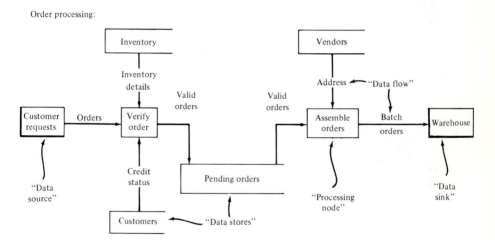

Figure 5.6b A formal data flow diagram *(adapted from GAN79)*.

5.3.2 Structure Charts

Structure charts are used during architectural design to document hierarchical structure, parameters, and interconnections in a system. A structure chart differs from a flowchart in two ways: a structure chart has no decision boxes, and the sequential ordering of tasks inherent in a flowchart can be suppressed in a structure chart.

The structure of a hierarchical system can be specified using a structure chart as illustrated in Figure 5.7. The chart can be augmented with module-by-module

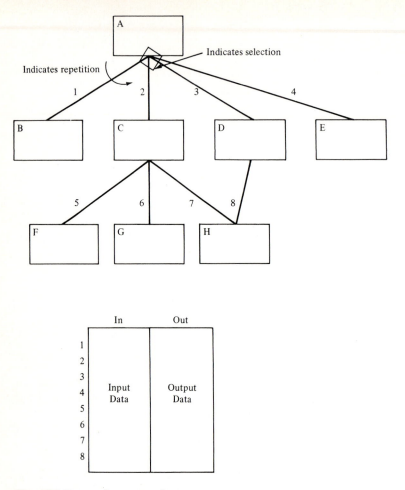

Figure 5.7 Format of a structure chart.

specification of the input and output parameters, as well as the input and output parameter attributes. During architectural design the parameter attributes are abstract; they are refined into concrete representations during detailed design.

5.3.3 HIPO Diagrams

HIPO diagrams (Hierarchy-Process-Input-Output) were developed at IBM as design representation schemes for top-down software development, and as external documentation aids for released products.

A set of HIPO diagrams contains a visual table of contents, a set of overview diagrams, and a set of detail diagrams. The visual table of contents is a directory to the set of diagrams in the package; it consists of a tree-structured (or graph-structured) directory, a summary of the contents of each overview diagram, and a

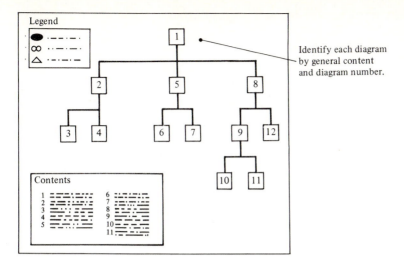

Figure 5.8a Visual table of contents for a HIPO package.

legend of symbol definitions (see Figure 5.8). The visual table of contents is a stylized structure chart.

Overview diagrams specify the functional processes in a system. Each overview diagram describes the inputs, processing steps, and outputs for the function being specified. An overview diagram can point to several subordinate detail diagrams, as required. Detail diagrams have the same format as overview diagrams. The format is illustrated in Figure 5.9.

5.3.4 Procedure Templates

The format of a procedure interface specification is illustrated in Figure 5.10. In the early stages of architectural design, only the information in level 1 need be supplied. As design progresses, the information on levels 2, 3, and 4 can be included in successive steps.

The term "side effect" in Figure 5.10 means any effect a procedure can exert on the processing environment that is not evident from the procedure name and parameters. Modifications to global variables, reading or writing a file, opening or closing a file, or calling a procedure that in turn exhibits side effects are all examples of side effects.

It is recommended that only the information on level 1 in Figure 5.10 be provided during initial architectural design, because detailed specification of side effects, exception handling, processing algorithms, and concrete data representations will sidetrack the designer into inappropriate levels of detail too soon.

During detailed design, the processing algorithms and data structures can be specified using structured flowcharts, pseudocode, or structured English. The syntax utilized to specify procedure interfaces during detailed design may, in fact, be

156

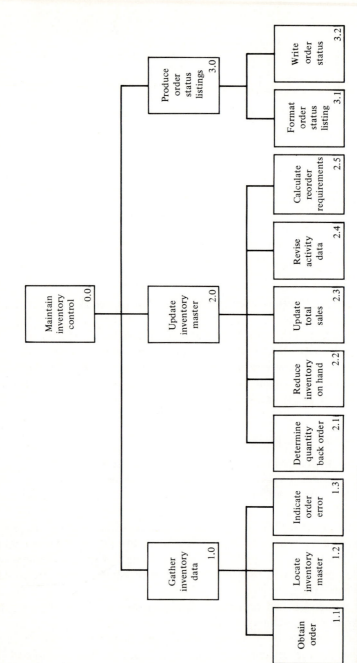

Figure 5.8b HIPO table of contents (*JON76*).

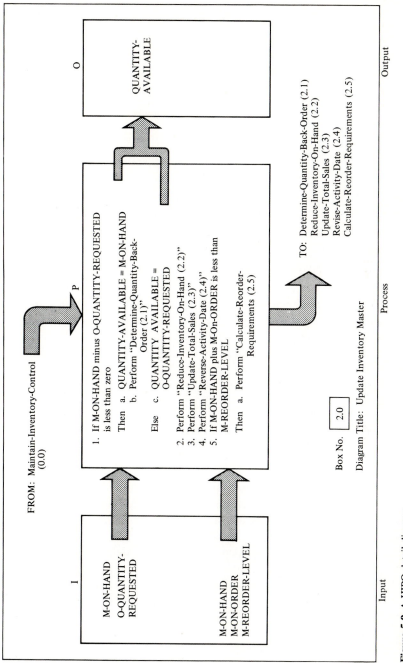

I

M-ON-HAND
O-QUANTITY-
REQUESTED

M-ON-HAND
M-ON-ORDER
M-REORDER-LEVEL

FROM: Maintain-Inventory-Control
(0.0)

P

1. If M-ON-HAND minus O-QUANTITY-REQUESTED
   is less than zero

   Then a. QUANTITY-AVAILABLE = M-ON-HAND
         b. Perform "Determine-Quantity-Back-
            Order (2.1)"

   Else c. QUANTITY AVAILABLE =
           O-QUANTITY-REQUESTED

2. Perform "Reduce-Inventory-On-Hand (2.2)"
3. Perform "Update-Total-Sales (2.3)"
4. Perform "Reverse-Activity-Date (2.4)"
5. If M-ON-HAND plus M-On-ORDER is less than
   M-REORDER-LEVEL

   Then a. Perform "Calculate-Reorder-
           Requirements (2.5)

Box No.  2.0

Diagram Title: Update Inventory Master

O

QUANTITY-
AVAILABLE

TO: Determine-Quantity-Back-Order (2.1)
    Reduce-Inventory-On-Hand (2.2)
    Update-Total-Sales (2.3)
    Revise-Activity-Date (2.4)
    Calculate-Reorder-Requirements (2.5)

Input   Process   Output

Figure 5.9 A HIPO detail diagram.

PROCEDURE NAME:
PART OF: (subsystem name & number)
CALLED BY: LEVEL 1
PURPOSE:
DESIGNER/DATE(s):
_____

PARAMETERS: (names, modes, attributes, purposes)
INPUT ASSERTION: (preconditions)   LEVEL 2
OUTPUT ASSERTION: (postconditions)
GLOBALS: (names, modes, attributes, purposes, shared with)
SIDE EFFECTS:
_____

LOCAL DATA STRUCTURES: (names, attributes, purposes)
EXCEPTIONS: (conditions, responses)   LEVEL 3
TIMING CONSTRAINTS:
OTHER LIMITATIONS:
_____

PROCEDURE BODY: (pseudocode, structured English,   LEVEL 4
            structured flowchart, decision table)

Figure 5.10 Format of a procedure template.

the syntax of the implementation language. In this case, the procedure interface and pseudocode procedure body can be expanded directly into source code during product implementation.

Procedure interface specifications are effective notations for architectural design when used in combination with structure charts and data flow diagrams. They also provide a natural transition from architectural to detailed design, and from detailed design to implementation.

5.3.5 Pseudocode

Pseudocode notation can be used in both the architectural and detailed design phases. Like flowcharts, pseudocode can be used at any desired level of abstraction. Using pseudocode, the designer describes system characteristics using short, concise, English language phrases that are structured by key words such as If-Then-Else, While-Do, and End. Key words and indentation describe the flow of control, while the English phrases describe processing actions. Using the top-down design strategy, each English phrase is expanded into more detailed pseudocode until the design specification reaches the level of detail of the implementation language.

Pseudocode can replace flowcharts and reduce the amount of external documentation required to describe a system. The use of pseudocode for detailed design specification is illustrated in Figure 5.11.

5.3.6 Structured Flowcharts

Flowcharts are the traditional means for specifying and documenting algorithmic details in a software system. Flowcharts incorporate rectangular boxes for actions,

```
INITIALIZE tables and counters; OPEN files
READ the first text record
WHILE there are more text records DO
   WHILE there are more words in the text record DO
      EXTRACT the next word
      SEARCH word_table for the extracted word
      IF the extracted word is found THEN
         INCREMENT the extracted word's occurrence count
      ELSE
         INSERT the extracted word into the word_table
      ENDIF
      INCREMENT the words_processed counter
   ENDWHILE at the end of the text record
ENDWHILE when all text records have been processed
PRINT the word_table and the words_processed counter
CLOSE files
TERMINATE the program
```

Figure 5.11 An example of a pseudo-code design specification.

diamond shaped boxes for decisions, directed arcs for specifying interconnections between boxes, and a variety of specially shaped symbols to denote input, output, data stores, etc.

Structured flowcharts differ from traditional flowcharts in that structured flowcharts are restricted to compositions of certain basic forms. This makes the resulting flowchart the graphical equivalent of a structured pseudocode description. A typical set of basic forms and the pseudocode equivalents are illustrated in Figure 5.12.

The basic forms are characterized by single entry into and single exit from the form. Thus, forms can be nested within forms to any arbitrary depth, and in any arbitrary fashion, so long as the single entry, single exit property is preserved. A composite structured flowchart and the pseudocode equivalent are illustrated in Figure 5.13.

Because structured flowcharts are logically equivalent to pseudocode, they have the same expressive power as pseudocode; both can be used to express any conceivable algorithm. However, structured flowcharts may be preferred in situations where clarity of control flow is to be emphasized.

The single entry, single exit property allows hierarchical nesting of structured flowchart constructs to document a design in top-down fashion, starting with top level structure and proceeding through detailed design. Structured flowcharts emphasize flow of control mechanisms due to the graphical nature of the visual image. They are thus appropriate when decision mechanisms and sequencing of control flow are to be emphasized. On the other hand, flowcharts make it easy to violate the single entry, single exit property, and they are not machine-readable or machine-modifiable, as is pseudocode.

One can envision a graphics package that provides the option of working with either pseudocode or structured flowcharts. Alternatively, a design tool might accept pseudocode as input and produce structured flowcharts as output.

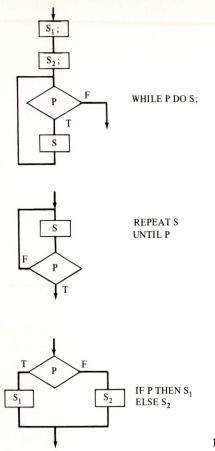

WHILE P DO S;

REPEAT S
UNTIL P

IF P THEN S_1
ELSE S_2

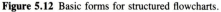

Figure 5.12 Basic forms for structured flowcharts.

5.3.7 Structured English

Structured English can be used to provide a step-by-step specification for an algorithm. Like pseudocode, structured English can be used at any desired level of detail. Structured English is often used to specify cookbook recipes:

1. Preheat oven to 350 degrees F.
2. Mix eggs, milk, and vanilla.
3. Add flour and baking soda.
4. Pour into a greased baking dish.
5. Cook until done.

An example of using structured English for software specification is provided in Figure 5.9, where it is used to specify the processing part of the HIPO diagram.

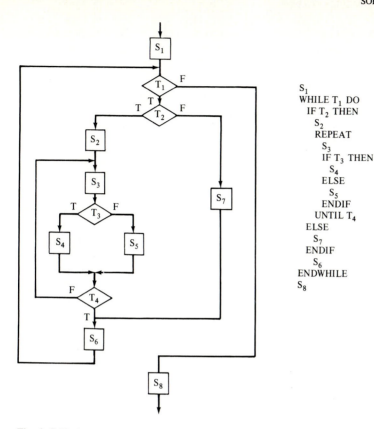

```
S1
WHILE T1 DO
   IF T2 THEN
      S2
      REPEAT
         S3
         IF T3 THEN
            S4
         ELSE
            S5
         ENDIF
      UNTIL T4
   ELSE
      S7
   ENDIF
   S6
ENDWHILE
S8
```

Figure 5.13 A structured flowchart and pseudocode equivalent.

5.3.8 Decision Tables

Decision tables can be used to specify complex decision logic in a high-level software specification, as was discussed in Chapter 4. They are also useful for specifying algorithmic logic during detailed design. At this level of usage, decision tables can be specified and translated into source code logic. Several preprocessor packages are available to translate decision tables into COBOL.

5.4 DESIGN TECHNIQUES

The design process involves developing a conceptual view of the system, establishing system structure, identifying data streams and data stores, decomposing high-level functions into subfunctions, establishing relationships and interconnections among components, developing concrete data representations, and specifying algorithmic details.

Developing a conceptual view of a software system involves determining the type of system to be built. The system may be a data-base system, a graphics system, a telecommunications system, a process control system, or a data processing system; or the system may combine aspects of different system types (e.g., a combined database, graphics, and real time system). In each of these application areas there are certain viewpoints, terminology, tools, and notations suitable to that class of applications. It is essential that the software design team have a strong conceptual understanding of the nature of the system to be constructed and be familiar with the tools and techniques in the appropriate application areas. It is not uncommon for a design team to be composed of one or more specialists from each appropriate area.

A data store is a conceptual data structure. During external and architectural design, one may identify the need for a stack, queue, or file, for example, but the exact implementation details of the data structure should be deferred until detailed design. Detailed design decisions should be delayed as long as possible. Early binding of design decisions, particularly in regard to representation details for data structures, can result in a system structure that is difficult to modify during subsequent development and maintenance activities. During external and architectural design, data structures should be defined as data abstractions, with emphasis placed on the desired operations and not on implementation details.

Data streams and data stores can be specified using data flow diagrams, data dictionaries, and data abstraction techniques. External data streams are identified during software requirements analysis and external design; internal data streams and data stores are developed during architectural design. Decomposition of high-level functions can be initiated from data flow diagrams and often involves use of structure diagrams, HIPO diagrams, and procedure specifications.

During the past few years, several techniques have been developed for software design. These techniques include stepwise refinement, levels of abstraction, structured design, integrated top-down development, and the Jackson design method. Although these techniques are often called "design methodologies" they are in fact viewpoints and guidelines for the design process. Software design is a creative activity. As with all creative processes, a framework and a viewpoint are essential. These are provided by the various design techniques mentioned above.

Design techniques are typically based on the "top-down" and/or "bottom-up" design strategies. Using the top-down approach, attention is first focused on global aspects of the overall system. As the design progresses, the system is decomposed into subsystems and more consideration is given to specific issues. Backtracking is fundamental to top-down design. As design decisions are decomposed to more elementary levels, it may become apparent that a high-level decision has led to inefficient or awkward decomposition of lower-level functions. Thus, a high-level decision may have to be reconsidered and the system restructured accordingly. In order to minimize backtracking, many designers advocate a mixed strategy that is predominately top-down, but involves specifying the lowest-level modules first. The primary advantage of the top-down strategy is that attention is first directed to the customer's needs, user interfaces, and the overall nature of the problem being solved.

In the bottom-up approach to software design, the designer first attempts to identify a set of primitive objects, actions, and relationships that will provide a basis for problem solution. Higher-level concepts are then formulated in terms of the primitives. The bottom-up strategy requires the designer to combine features provided by the implementation language into more sophisticated entities. These entities are combined in turn until a set of functions, data structures, and interconnections has been constructed to solve the problem using elements available in the actual programming environment. Bottom-up design may also require redesign and design backtracking. The success of bottom-up design depends on identifying the "proper" set of primitive ideas sufficient to implement the system.

Bottom-up design and implementation permits assessment of subsystem performance during system evolution. When using top-down methods, performance evaluation must be deferred until the entire system is assembled. On the other hand, top-down design and implementation permits early demonstration of functional capabilities at the user level; dummy routines (program stubs) can be used to simulate the lower, unimplemented levels of the system.

In practice, design of a software system is seldom, if ever, accomplished in pure top-down or pure bottom-up fashion. A predominately top-down strategy is most successful when a well-defined environment exists for software development, as, for example, when writing a compiler for use with a stable operating system, or when writing an application program in a well-defined compiler environment. When the environment is ill-defined, as in the development of system software for a new machine, the design strategy must, of necessity, be mixed or predominately bottom-up.

Several design techniques are described in the following sections. We do not intend to provide detailed discussions of these techniques. Our aim is rather to introduce the viewpoints and fundamental concepts of the techniques. Detailed information concerning each technique can be found in the cited references.

5.4.1 Stepwise Refinement

Stepwise refinement is a top-down technique for decomposing a system from high-level specifications into more elementary levels. Stepwise refinement is also known as "stepwise program development" and "successive refinement." As originally described by Wirth (WIR71), stepwise refinement involves the following activities:

1. Decomposing design decisions to elementary levels.
2. Isolating design aspects that are not truly interdependent.
3. Postponing decisions concerning representation details as long as possible.
4. Carefully demonstrating that each successive step in the refinement process is a faithful expansion of previous steps.

Incremental addition of detail at each step in the refinement process postpones design decisions as long as possible and allows the designer to argue convincingly that the resulting software product is consistent with the design specifications.

Stepwise refinement begins with the specifications derived during requirements analysis and external design. The problem is first decomposed into a few major processing steps that will demonstrably solve the problem. The process is then repeated for each part of the system until it is decomposed in sufficient detail so that implementation in an executable programming language is straightforward.

An explicit representation technique is not prescribed in stepwise refinement. However, use of structure charts, procedure specifications, and pseudocode is consistent with successive refinement. The early stages of refinement are typically stated in an informal pseudocode that becomes more precise as the refinement proceeds. The resulting design is quite close to, and may actually incorporate, statements from the implementation language.

Successive refinement can be used to perform detailed design of the individual modules in a software product. The following example, adapted from Wirth (WIR73), illustrates detailed design by the method of successive refinement. A routine is required to write the first N prime numbers into file F. N is a formal parameter in the routine, and F is globally known.

The initial version of the routine might be:

```
Initial version:  procedure PRIME(N: integer);
                       var I,X: integer;
                   begin rewrite(F); X := 1;
                     for I := 1 to N do
                     begin X := "next prime number";
                         write(F,X)
                     end;
                   end {PRIME};
```

The next step is to refine the statement X : = "next prime number";. By introducing a Boolean variable, PRIM, the statement can be expressed as

```
Refinement 1:  repeat X := X + 1;
                   PRIM := "X is a prime number"
               until PRIM;
```

All prime numbers except the first (which is 2) are odd. We can treat 2 as a special case and increment X by 2 in the repeat loop.

```
Refinement 2:  begin rewrite(F); X :=1;
                   if N >= 1 then write(F,2);
                   for I := 2 to N do
                   begin
                       repeat X := X + 2;
```

```
        PRIM := "X is a prime number"
      until PRIM;
      write(F,X)
    end
  end;
```

The next refinement involves determining whether X is a prime number. X is prime if it is divisible only by 1 and itself with zero remainder.

```
Refinement 3:  repeat X := X + 2; K :=2;
               repeat
               K := K  +  1;
                 PRIM := "X is not divisible by K"
               until not(PRIM) or (K = X-1)
               until PRIM;
```

The remainder function, mod, can be used to determine whether X is divisible by K:

```
Refinement 4:  PRIM := (X mod K) = 0;
```

Our procedure now has the following structure:

```
        procedure PRIME(N: integer);
         var I,X,K: integer;
          PRIM: boolean;
        begin rewrite(F); X := 1;
         if N >= 1 then write(F,2);
         for I := 2 to N do
           begin
            repeat X := X + 2; K :=2;
             repeat K := K  +  1;
               PRIM := (X mod K) = 0;
             until not(PRIM) or (K = X-1);
            until PRIM;
            write(F,X)
           end
        end ;
```

The procedure for computing the first N prime numbers and writing them in file F is complete. It is demonstrably correct because each refinement follows logically from the previous version. It is complete because each pseudocode statement has been refined into executable source code. However, the efficiency of the program can be vastly improved in several ways. For example, it is not necessary to check X for divisibility by every number K between 3 and X - 1. Recall that every nonprime number can be expressed as the product of prime factors. If X is divisible by a nonprime number K, it is also divisible by the prime factors of K. Thus, we can keep the prime numbers already calculated in an array P, and only check X for divisibility by the elements of P. This results in

```
Refinement 5:  X := 1; P[1] := 2; LIM := 1;
               for I := 2 to N do
               begin
                 repeat X := X + 2; K := 2; PRIM := true;
                 while PRIM and (K < LIM) do
                 begin
                   PRIM := (X mod P[K]) <> 0;
                   K := K + 1;
                 end;
                 until PRIM;
                 P[I] := X; LIM := LIM + 1;
               end;
```

In his text, Wirth intermixes refinement of the design and refinement for efficiency considerations. Our approach is to first develop an obviously correct program and then modify it to improve efficiency. We have shown only one of the ways in which efficiency of the prime number program can be improved; the interested reader is referred to Wirth's text (WIR73).

The major benefits of stepwise refinement as a design technique are:

1. Top-down decomposition
2. Incremental addition of detail
3. Postponement of design decisions
4. Continual verification of consistency (formally or informally)

Using stepwise refinement, a problem is segmented into small, manageable pieces, and the amount of detail that must be dealt with at any particular time is minimized. In this manner, the designer's thought processes are channelled to the proper concerns at the proper time. It must be observed, however, that successive refinement is not so much a design technique as a general approach to problem solving. Success with the method is highly dependent on having a clear conceptual understanding of the desired solution, and on the ability of the designer.

5.4.2 Levels of Abstraction

Levels of abstraction was originally described by Dijkstra as a bottom-up design technique in which an operating system was designed as a layering of hierarchical levels starting at level 0 (processor allocation, real-time clock interrupts) and building up to the level of processing independent user programs (DIJ68). In Dijkstra's system (the T.H.E. system), each level of abstraction is composed of a group of related functions, some of which are externally visible (can be invoked by functions on higher levels of abstraction) and some of which are internal to the level. Internal functions are hidden from other levels; they can only be invoked by functions on the same level. The internal functions are used to perform tasks common to the work being performed on that level of abstraction. Of course, functions on higher levels cannot be used by functions on lower levels; function usage establishes the levels of abstraction.

Each level of abstraction performs a set of services for the functions on the next higher level of abstraction. Thus, a file manipulation system might be layered as a set of routines to manipulate fields (bit vectors on level 0), a set of routines to manipulate records (sets of fields on level 1), and a set of routines to manipulate files (sets of records on level 2).

Each level of abstraction has exclusive use of certain resources (I/O devices, data structures) that other levels are not permitted to access. Higher-level functions can invoke functions on lower levels, but lower-level functions cannot invoke or in any way make use of higher-level functions. This latter restriction is important because lower levels are then self-sufficient for supporting other abstractions. The lower levels can be used without change as the lower-level routines in other applications, or in adaptations and modifications to an existing system. In addition, the strict hierarchical ordering of routines facilitates "intellectual manageability" of a complex software system. The levels of abstraction utilized in the T.H.E. operating system are listed in Table 5.1.

5.4.3 Structured Design

Structured design was developed by Constantine as a top-down technique for architectural design of software systems (STE74). The basic approach in structured design is systematic conversion of data flow diagrams into structure charts. Design heuristics such as coupling and cohesion are used to guide the design process (see Section 5.2).

As discussed in Section 5.2, coupling measures the degree to which two distinct modules are bound together, and cohesion is a measure of the relationship of elements within a module to one another. A well-designed system exhibits a low degree of coupling between modules and a high degree of cohesion among elements in each module. These concepts are discussed more extensively in section 5.2.

Table 5.1 Levels of abstraction in the T.H.E. operating system

Level 0:	Processor allocation clock interrupt handling
Level 1:	Memory segment controller
Level 2:	Console message interpreter
Level 3:	I/O buffering
Level 4:	User programs
Level 5:	Operator

The first step in structured design is review and refinement of the data flow diagram(s) developed during requirements definition and external design. The second step is to determine whether the system is transform-centered or transaction-driven, and to derive a high-level structure chart based on this determination. In a transform-centered system, the data flow diagram contains Input, Processing, and Output segments that are converted into Input, Processing, and Output subsystems in the structure chart. Boundaries between the three major subsystems in a transform-centered system are identified by determining the point of most abstract input data and the point of most abstract output data on the data flow diagram. The situation is illustrated in Figure 5.14.

The point of most abstract input data is the point in the data flow diagram where the input stream can no longer be identified. Similarly, the point of most abstract output data is the point in the data flow diagram where components of the output data stream can first be identified. Identification of these boundaries is somewhat subjective, but Constantine reports that with practice, designers become consistent in identifying them.

The third step in structured design is decomposition of each subsystem using guidelines such as coupling, cohesion, information hiding, levels of abstraction, data abstraction, and the other decomposition criteria discussed in Section 5.2.

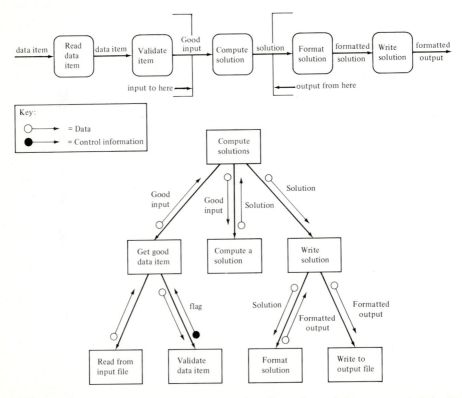

Figure 5.14 Conversion of a transform-centered data flow diagram into an input, process, output structure chart.

According to Constantine, a hierarchical tree structure is the solution form that usually results in the lowest cost implementation (where cost refers to the cost of designing, coding, testing, modifying, and maintaining the system).

Decomposition of processing functions into modules should be continued until each module contains no subset of elements that can be used alone, and until each module is small enough that its entire implementation can be grasped at once. Weinberg suggests that 30 implementation language statements is the upper limit that can be assimilated on a first reading of a module (WEI71). In the initial design phase, one should subdivide too finely when in doubt, because small modules can be easily recombined at a later time. Functions that are useful in several places may not be identified if the subdivision is too coarse. Architectural design typically involves numerous iterations and revisions before an appropriate structure is obtained.

As discussed in Section 5.2, a data dictionary can be used in conjunction with a structure chart to specify data attributes, relationships among data items, and data sharing among modules in the system.

In addition to coupling, cohesion, data abstraction, information hiding, and other decomposition criteria, the concepts of "scope of effect" and "scope of control" can be used to determine the relative positions of modules in a hierarchical framework. The "scope of control" of a module is that module plus all modules that are subordinate to it in the structure chart. In Figure 5.15, the scope of control of module B is B, D, and E. The "scope of effect" of a decision is the set of all modules that contain code that is executed based on the outcome of that decision. In general, systems are more loosely coupled when the scope of effect of a decision is within the scope of control of the module containing the decision. The following example illustrates the situation.

In Figure 5.15, suppose execution of some code in module B depends on the outcome of a decision, X, in module E. Either E will return a control flag to B or the decision process will have to be repeated in B. The former approach requires additional code to implement the flag and results in control coupling between B and E. The latter approach requires duplication of some of E's code (decision process X) in module B. Duplication of code is inefficient and causes difficulties in coordinating changes to both copies if the decision process should change. The situation

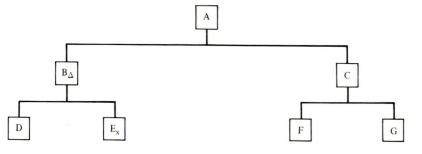

Figure 5.15 A hierarchical structure chart.

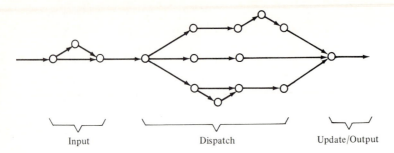

| Input | Dispatch | Update/Output |

Figure 5.16 Transaction-driven data flow diagram.

can be remedied by modifying the system so that the scope of effect of decision X is within its scope of control. Moving the decision process upward into B or moving the code in B affected by the decision into E (or into a routine subordinate to E) will produce the desired effect.

Detailed design of the individual modules in a system can be accomplished using the successive refinement technique (discussed in Section 5.4.1), and by using detailed design notations such as HIPO diagrams, procedure templates, pseudocode, and/or structured English.

A transform-centered system is characterized by similar processing steps for each data item processed by the Input, Process, and Output subsystems. In a transaction-driven system, one of several possible paths through the data flow diagram is traversed by each transaction. The path traversed is typically determined by user input commands. Transaction-driven systems have data flow diagrams of the form illustrated in Figure 5.16, which is converted into a structure chart having Input, Controller, Dispatcher, and Update/Output subsystems as illustrated in Figure 5.17. Often, the subsystems in a transaction-driven system will be transform-centered with Input-Process-Output structure. Figure 5.18 illustrates a top-level transaction-driven data flow diagram and structure chart for an automated bank teller machine.

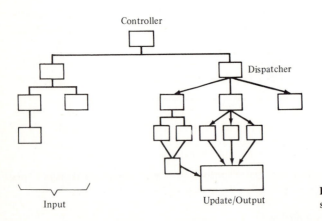

Controller

Dispatcher

Input   Update/Output

Figure 5.17 Transaction-driven structure chart.

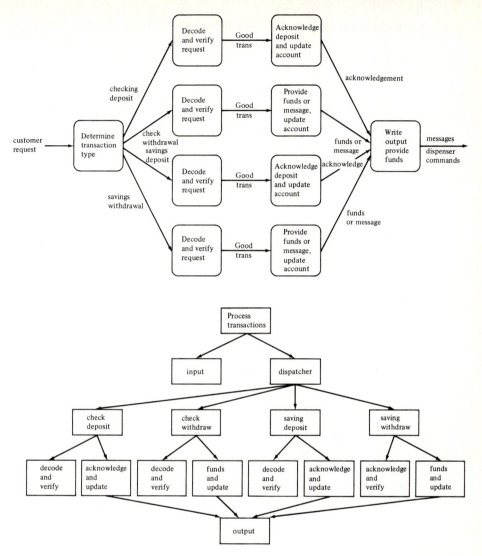

Figure 5.18 First-level data flow diagram and structure chart for a transaction-driven automated bank teller (*GAN79*).

Steps for decomposing a transaction-driven system are similar to those described for a transform-centered system. The major difference is that a transaction-driven system usually manipulates and updates master files of information (account files, reservation files, inventory files, etc.). Master file processing often involves concurrent processing and mutual exclusion of processes from files.

In summary, the primary benefits of structured design are:

1. The use of data flow diagrams focuses attention on the problem structure. This follows naturally from requirements analysis and external design.

2. The method of translating data flow diagrams into structure charts provides a method for initiating architectural design in a systematic manner.
3. Data dictionaries can be used in conjunction with structure charts to specify data attributes and data relationships.
4. Design heuristics such as coupling and cohesion, and scope of effect and scope of control provide criteria for systematic development of architectural structure and for comparison of alternative design structures.
5. Detailed design techniques and notations such as successive refinement, HIPO diagrams, procedure specification forms, and pseudocode can be used to perform detailed design of the individual modules.

The primary strength of structured design is provision of a systematic method for converting data flow diagrams into top-level structure charts. However, the method does not provide much guidance for decomposing top-level structure charts into detailed structures.

The primary disadvantage of structured design is that the technique produces systems that are structured as sequences of processing steps. Decomposing a system into processing steps is inconsistent with the design criterion of information hiding. Disregard for information hiding and separation of concerns may result in a system that is difficult to modify.

Additional information concerning the tools and techniques of structured design can be found in texts by Yourdan and Constantine (YOU79), Page-Jones (PAG80), Stevens (STE81), Myers (MYE78), and the original paper by Stevens, Myers, and Constantine (STE74).

5.4.4 Integrated Top-Down Development

Integrated top-down development integrates design, implementation, and testing. Using integrated top-down development, design proceeds top-down from the highest-level routines; they have the primary function of coordinating and sequencing the lower-level routines. Lower-level routines may be implementations of elementary functions (those that call no other routines), or they may in turn invoke more primitive routines. There is thus a hierarchical structure to a top-down system in which routines can invoke lower-level routines but cannot invoke routines on a higher level.

The integration of design, implementation, and testing is illustrated by the following example. It is assumed that the design of a system has proceeded to the point illustrated in Figure 5.19. The purpose of procedure MAIN is to coordinate and sequence the GET, PROCESS, and PUT routines. These three routines can communicate only through MAIN; similarly, SUB1 and SUB2 (which support PROCESS), can communicate only through PROCESS.

The implementation and testing strategy for the example might be as illustrated in Figure 5.19. The stubs referred to in Figure 5.19 are dummy routines written to simulate subfunctions that are invoked higher-level functions. As coding and testing progresses, the stubs are expanded into full functional units that may in turn require lower-level stubs to support them.

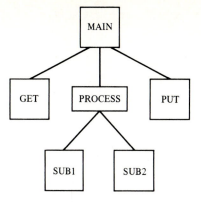

STRATEGY:
```
DESIGN     MAIN
CODE       MAIN
STUBS FOR GET, PROCESS, PUT
TEST       MAIN
DESIGN     GET
CODE       GET
TEST MAIN GET
DESIGN     PROCESS
CODE       PROCESS
STUBS FOR SUB1, SUB2
TEST MAIN GET, PROCESS
DESIGN     PUT
CODE       PUT
TEST MAIN, GET, PROCESS, PUT
DESIGN     SUB1
CODE       SUB1
TEST MAIN, GET, PROCESS, PUT, SUB1
DESIGN     SUB2
CODE       SUB2
TEST MAIN, GET, PROCESS, PUT, SUB1, SUB2
```

Figure 5.19 Integrated top-down development strategy.

Stubs can fulfill a number of useful purposes prior to expansion into full functionality. They can provide output messages, test input parameters, deliver simulated output parameters, and simulate timing requirements and resource utilization. Use of program stubs in top-down development provides an operational prototype of the system as development progresses.

Some designers restrict data communication between modules to the parameter lists, while other designers allow global variables that are common to two or more modules. A reasonable compromise is to communicate data between levels via parameter lists and to permit access to common global data by modules on the same level of hierarchy. This approach is particularly attractive when each hierarchical level is identified as a level of abstraction in the system. Each level of abstraction provides supporting functions for the next higher level in the hierarchy, and is supported by the levels below it.

The integrated top-down design technique provides an orderly and systematic framework for software development. Design and coding are integrated because expansion of a stub will typically require creation of new stubs to support it. Test cases are developed systematically, and each routine is tested in the actual operating environment. A further advantage of the integrated top-down approach is distribution of system integration across the project; the interfaces are established, coded, and tested as the design progresses.

The primary disadvantage of the integrated top-down approach is that early high-level design decisions may have to be reconsidered when the design progresses to lower levels. This may require design backtracking and considerable rewriting of code. These are other disadvantages to integrated top-down development: the system may be a very expensive test harness for newly added procedures; it may not be possible to find high-level test data to exercise newly added procedures in the desired manner; and, in certain instances such as interrupt handlers and I/O drivers, procedure stubs may not be suitable. It may be necessary to first write and test some low-level procedures before proceeding with top-down development.

Despite these disadvantages, the ability to demonstrate early prototypes of the system using program stubs, and the distribution of system integration throughout the project schedule make top-down development an attractive approach. Many systems are developed in a predominately top-down manner, with bottom-up development used on some of the subsystems.

5.4.5 Jackson Structured Programming

Jackson Structured Programming was developed by Michael Jackson as a systematic technique for mapping the structure of a problem into a program structure to solve the problem (JAC75). The mapping is accomplished in three steps:

1. The problem is modeled by specifying the input and output data structures using tree structured diagrams.
2. The input-output model is converted into a structural model for the program by identifying points of correspondence between nodes in the input and output trees.
3. The structural model of the program is expanded into a detailed design model that contains the operations needed to solve the problem.

Input and output structures are specified using a graphical notation to specify data hierarchy, sequences of data, repetition of data items, and alternate data items. Specification of data item A is illustrated in Figure 5.20. According to this notation, item A consists of a B followed by a C followed by a D (reading left to right on the same level). B and D have no substructures. C consists of either an E or an F (denoted by "o"). E consists of zero or more occurrences of G (denoted by "*"), and F consists of an H followed by an I. This notation is the graphical equivalent of regular expressions (HUG79). The formats of input and output data structures are thus specified using graphical representations of regular grammars.

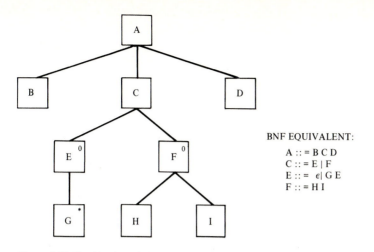

Figure 5.20 Specification of object A using Jackson Structured Programming notation.

The second step of the Jackson method involves converting the input and output structures into a structural model of the program. This is accomplished by identifying points of commonality in the input and output structures and combining the two structures into a program structure that maps inputs into outputs. Labels on data items in the resulting structure are converted to process names that perform the required processing of the data items.

The third step expands the structural model of the program into a detailed design model containing the operations needed to solve the problem. This step is performed in three substeps:

1. A list of operations required to perform the processing steps is developed.
2. The operations are associated with the program structure.
3. Program structure and operations are expressed in a notation called schematic logic, which is stylized pseudocode. Control flow for selection and iteration are specified in this step.

The following example illustrates the basic concepts of the Jackson method. An input file consists of a collection of inventory records sorted by part number. Each record contains a part number and the number of units of that item issued or received in one transaction. An output report is to be produced that contains a heading and a net movement line for each part number in the input file. Because the input file is sorted by part number, all issues and receipts of a given part number are in a contiguous portion of the file called a part group. Each record in a part group is called a movement record.

The input and output structures are illustrated in Figure 5.21. The input file consists of zero or more part groups. Each part group consists of zero or more movement records. A movement record is either an issue record or a receipt record. The output report consists of a heading followed by a body (reading left to right on the same level). The body consists of zero or more net movement lines.

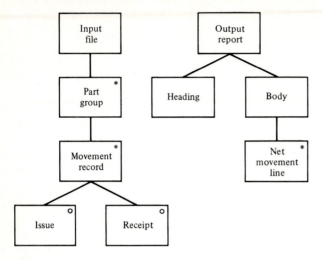

Figure 5.21 Input and output structures for an inventory problem.

The correspondence between input and output structures is illustrated in Figure 5.22. The input file corresponds to the output report, and each part group in the input file corresponds to a net movement line in the output report. The program structure is derived by superimposing the input file structure on the output report structure and overlaying the corresponding nodes in the two graphs. The resulting program structure is illustrated in Figure 5.23.

The program consists of a number of processing steps. There is a processing step to write the report heading, followed by a step to write the report body. The body consists of repetitive invocation of PTGP & line (part group and line), one invocation per part group in the input file. PTGP & line contains a processing step

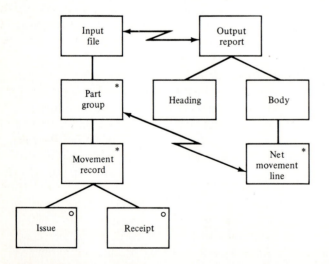

Figure 5.22 Correspondence between input and output structure for an inventory problem.

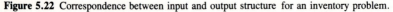

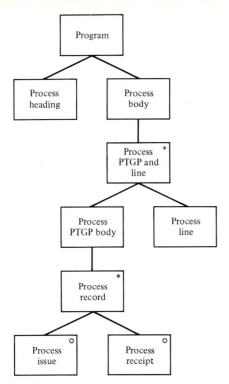

Figure 5.23 Program structure for an inventory problem.

for a part group followed by a step to print the net movement line for that part group.

The part group body consists of a processing step that is invoked once for each part record in the part group. Each invocation of process record processes an issue or a receipt.

Detailed design involves developing a list of operations needed in the program, associating the operations with program structure, and translating the annotated structure diagram into schematic logic (pseudocode). These steps are illustrated in Figures 5.24, 5.25, and 5.26.

Difficulties encountered in applying the Jackson method include structure

1. OPEN FILES
2. CLOSE FILES
3. STOP RUN
4. READ A RECORD INTO PART_NUM, MOVMNT
5. WRITE HEADING
6. WRITE NET_MOVEMENT LINE
7. SET NET_MOVMNT TO ZERO
8. ADD MOVMNT TO NET_MOVMNT
9. SUBTRACT MOVMNT FROM NET_MOVMNT

Figure 5.24 Operations needed in the inventory program.

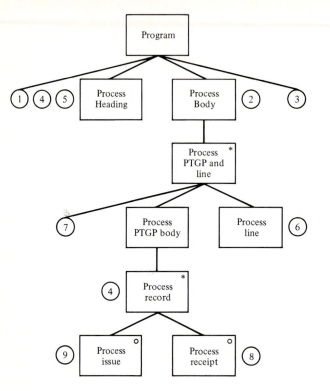

Figure 5.25 Association of operations with program structure.

clashes and the need for look-ahead. Structure clashes occur when points of commonality between input and output data structures cannot be identified. Structure clashes can be resolved by a technique called program inversion. Using program inversion, a consumer routine calls on a producer routine to deliver the next required data item. The producer delivers values to the consumer on a demand basis, and, to the consumer, it appears as if the values are being produced from a sequential file of values. Implementation of program inversion can be accomplished using a coroutine structure for the producer and consumer.

The need for look-ahead arises when processing of a data item depends on some characteristics of yet-to-be-processed data. This situation can occur, for example, when a set of data records is to be treated as bad data if any record in the set is bad; otherwise, each record is processed as good data. Look-ahead problems can be resolved by a technique called backtracking, which involves saving the program state at the beginning of each processing sequence that may be incorrect. If it is determined that a processing sequence is incorrect, the program state is reset to the state prior to entry of that processing sequence and an alternative processing sequence is invoked.

More recently, Michael Jackson has developed a method for software design called the Jackson Design Method (JAC83). This approach involves modeling the real world phenomenon of interest as a network of sequential processes that com-

```
BEGIN PROGRAM
  OPEN FILES
  READ PART-NUM, MOVMNT
  WRITE HEADING
  ITERATE WHILE NOT(END-OF-FILE)
    SET NET-MOVMNT TO ZERO
    ITERATE WHILE SAME-PART-NUMBER
      IF (MOVMNT = ISSUE) THEN
        SUBTRACT MOVMT FROM NET-MOVMNT
      ELSE IF (MOVMNT = RECEIPT) THEN
        ADD MOVMNT TO NET-MOVNMT
      END IF
      READ PART-NUM, MOVMNT
    END WHILE
    WRITE NET-MOVEMENT LINE
  END WHILE
  CLOSE FILES
  STOP
END PROGRAM
```

Figure 5.26 Schemtic logic representation of an inventory program.

municate using serial data streams. Detailed design of the processes can be accomplished using Jackson Structured Programming, as described above. Because the process model may result in excessive numbers of processes, it may be necessary to perform transformations on the model to reduce the number of processes. Transformations are performed during detailed design and implementation to produce a system that can be implemented on conventional machine architectures.

This discussion has provided only a brief introduction to the basic concepts and viewpoints of the Jackson methods. A comprehensive treatment of Jackson structured programming is provided in (JAC75). Jackson's newer work on the Jackson Design Method is described in (JAC83). Jackson Structured Programming is widely used and is quite effective in situations where input and output data structures can be defined in a precise manner. It appears to be most effective in data processing applications. The utility of the Jackson Design Method is yet to be determined; more experience with the method is required.

5.4.6 Summary of Design Techniques

The preceding discussion does not constitute an exhaustive survey of software design techniques. It is clear, however, that all the techniques described are concerned with fundamental issues such as abstraction, structure, modularity, and design verification. It is also clear that there are many different ways to view and express these concepts. The following comments reflect an admittedly subjective evaluation of the various techniques.

Stepwise refinement provides a general framework for problem solving by placing emphasis on the importance of proceeding from general concerns to specific details in small incremental steps. The greatest strength of successive refinement is the attention focused on verifying that each successive step in the refinement process is a faithful expansion of previous steps. The greatest weakness of successive refinement is the foresight required to accomplish top-down decomposition.

Depending on the skill of the designer and the nature of the system being designed, the need for backtracking and redesign may become apparent only when the lowest (and last) levels of the system are being designed. Successive refinement is, however, a valuable technique for detailed design of the individual modules in a software system.

Levels of abstraction involves bottom-up definition of increasingly more powerful hierarchies of abstract machines, in which the functions and services provided by any given level define the machine tailored to the needs of the next higher level. The greatest strengths of levels of abstraction are the strict hierarchical ordering imposed between levels, the hiding of internal functions within levels, and the sharing of global data only within levels. This makes lower levels in the hierarchy self-sufficient for supporting abstractions up to that level, which eases adaptation and modification of the system. The greatest weakness of levels of abstraction is the lack of criteria to guide the placement of functions within the hierarchy. Often it is not clear which features should be incorporated into which virtual machines. Successful use of levels of abstraction is strongly dependent on the skill of the designer and the nature of the application.

Structured design is an architectural design technique that involves conversion of data flow diagrams into structure charts. The structure charts are then refined using modularization criteria such as cohesion of functionality within modules and coupling between modules. The greatest strengths of structured design are provided by the systematic transition from data flow diagrams to structure charts; the emphasis placed on interfaces when using structure charts, and the use of coupling, cohesion, and other modularization criteria. The greatest weakness of structured design is that the use of data flow diagrams and structure charts decomposes a system into a sequence of processing steps. According to Parnas, who developed the concept of information hiding, decomposing a system into a sequence of processing steps is usually inconsistent with information hiding.

Integrated top-down development integrates design, implementation, and testing. Development proceeds from the highest-level routines to lower-level routines. Integrated top-down development incorporates stubs to simulate lower-level subsystems and routines. In this manner, a large portion of the code may be implemented before other modules have been designed. Advantages of integrated top-down development include the ability to experiment with successive prototypes as the system evolves, and the gradual integration of subsystems. The main disadvantage of integrated top-down development is the necessity for design backtracking and the potential for considerable rewriting of code. Also, the evolving system may become too large to be an efficient test harness for new modules being integrated into the system, and it may not be possible to simulate some of the low-level routines using stubs. Some bottom-up implementation and testing may be required.

Jackson Structured Programming transforms input and output data structures into a program structure that will map the input files to the output files. The greatest strength of the Jackson method is the almost mechanical process of creating a program structure from the data structures. The primary weaknesses of the method are the problems of structure clash and backtracking, and the limited amount of

Table 5.2 Design techniques classified by application area

	Stepwise refinement	Levels of abstraction	Integrated top-down development	Structured design	Jackson Structured Programming
Scientific applications	*		+	*	+
Data processing applications	+		+	+	*
Operating systems		*			
Utility programs	*		+	*	
Real-time systems		*			

* = Recommended
+ = Useful

creativity possible within the framework of the method (some would argue that this is a strength of the method).

Table 5.2 indicates some application areas for which the various design techniques are well suited.

5.5 DETAILED DESIGN CONSIDERATIONS

Detailed design is concerned with specifying algorithmic details, concrete data representations, interconnections among functions and data structures, and packaging of the software product. Detailed design is strongly influenced by the implementation language, but it is not the same as implementation; detailed design is more concerned with semantic issues and less concerned with syntactic details than is implementation.

The starting point for detailed design is an architectural structure for which algorithmic details and concrete data representations are to be provided. While there is a strong temptation to proceed directly from architectural structure to implementation, there are a number of advantages to be gained in the intermediate level of detail provided by detailed design.

Implementation addresses issues of programming language syntax, coding style, internal documentation, and insertion of testing and debugging probes into the code. The difficulties encountered during implementation are almost always due to the fact that the implementor is simultaneously performing analysis, design, and coding activities while attempting to express the final result in an implementation language. Detailed design permits design of algorithms and data representations at a higher level of abstraction and notation than the implementation language provides.

Detailed design separates the activity of low-level design from implementation, just as the analysis and design activities isolate consideration of what is desired from the structure that will achieve the desired result. An adequate detailed design specification minimizes the number of surprises during product implementation.

Detailed design activities inevitably expose flaws in the architectural structure, and the ensuing modifications will be eased by having fewer details to manipulate than would be present in the implementation language. Detailed design also provides a vehicle for design inspections, structured walkthroughs, and the Critical Design Review. Notations for detailed design include HIPO diagrams, pseudocode, structured English, structured flowcharts, data structure diagrams, and physical layouts for data representations. The detailed design representation may utilize key words from the implementation language to specify control flow, and declaration statements from the implementation language to specify data representation.

Product packaging is an important aspect of detailed design. Packaging is concerned with the manner in which global data items are selectively shared among program units, specification of static data areas, packaging of program units as functions and subroutines, specification of parameter passing mechanisms, file structures and file access techniques, and the structure of compilation units and load modules.

Detailed design should be carried to a level where each statement in the design notation will result in a few (less than 10) statements in the implementation language. Given the architectural and detailed design specifications, any programmer familiar with the implementation language should be able to implement the software product.

5.6 REAL-TIME AND DISTRIBUTED SYSTEM DESIGN

Many of the popular design "methodologies" were developed as design techniques for applications programs, operating systems, and utility programs (compilers, editors, loaders, etc.). These methods support concepts such as hierarchical decomposition, modularity, information hiding, and data abstraction. These design concepts are important for real-time and distributed systems, but they do not explicitly incorporate methods to deal with performance characteristics or problems of network configuration and communication protocols. In this section we discuss some of the problems encountered in designing real-time and distributed systems.

According to Franta, a distributed system consists of a collection of nearly autonomous processors that communicate to achieve a coherent computing system (FRA81). Each processor possesses a private memory, and processors communicate through an interconnection network.

Major issues to be addressed in designing a distributed system include specifying the topology of the communication network, establishing rules for accessing the shared communication channel, allocating application processing functions to processing nodes in the network, and establishing rules for process communication and synchronization. The design of distributed systems is further complicated by the need to allocate network functionality between hardware and software components of the network.

For example, trade-offs of costs and complexity between hardware and software components of network interconnection devices are not obvious. Message traffic between nodes must be analyzed to establish the necessary communication rates. Reliability issues such as coping with loss of a communication link or loss of a processing node must be considered. Mechanisms for message flow control (e.g., what to do if the receiving node queue is full), error control in response to failures of redundancy checks in arriving messages, systems status monitoring, and network diagnostic techniques must be considered.

In particular, mechanisms for addressing processes in remote nodes, queue management in the network interconnection devices, message flow control between nodes, allocation of the communication network to various nodes, messages parity error checks, and system status monitoring must all be specified.

By definition, real-time systems must provide specified amounts of computation within fixed time intervals. Real-time systems typically sense and control external devices, respond to external events, and share processing time between multiple tasks. Processing demands are both cyclic and event-driven in nature. Event-driven activities may occur in bursts, thus requiring a high ratio of peak to average processing. Real-time systems often form distributed networks; local processors may be associated with sensing devices and actuators.

A real-time network for process control may consist of several minicomputers and microcomputers connected to one or more large processors. Each small processor may be connected to a cluster of real-time devices. In this manner, processing power can be placed at "natural" sites in the system, and data can be processed at the point of reception rather than at a central node, thus reducing communication bandwidth needs. Decomposition criteria for distributed real-time systems include the need to maintain process simplicity and to minimize interprocess communication bandwidths by communicating simple processed messages rather than raw data.

Process control systems often utilize communication networks having fixed, static topology and known capacity requirements. In contrast, more elaborate real-time systems provide dynamic reconfiguration of the network topology and support unpredictable load demands.

Many process control systems are designed with only two levels of abstraction, which comprise basic system functions and application programs. It is not clear whether a two-level hierarchy is the result of process control system characteristics or process control designer characteristics.

The SREM system discussed in Section 4.3 was developed to support analysis of real-time system requirements. Important features of SREM for specifying real-time systems include the flow-oriented approach of stimulus-response and the ability to associate performance characteristics and validation conditions with particular points in the processing sequence. SREM includes a simulation package to permit evaluation of performance characteristics for various system configurations.

Several notations have been developed to support analysis and design of real-time and distributed systems. They include RSL, SDLP, NPN, communication ports, and the notation developed by Kramer and Cunningham (ALF77), (FAI84), (BOE79), (MAO80), (KRA78). Most of these notations are state-oriented because a real-time system can be thought of as possessing a (perhaps large) number of processing states, with the transitions between states triggered by external stimuli. Petri nets (Section 4.3) are a fundamental state-oriented notation that can be used to specify requirements and high level design of real-time and distributed systems. Petri nets were developed because traditional finite state mechanisms are not adequate for specifying parallel and concurrent system properties.

In summary, the traditional considerations of hierarchy, information hiding, and modularity are important concepts for the design of real-time systems. However, these concepts are typically applied to the individual components of a real-time system. Higher-level issues of networking, performance, and reliability must be analyzed and designed before the component nodes or processes are developed.

5.7 TEST PLANS

The test plan is an important, but often overlooked, product of software design. A test plan prescribes various kinds of activities that will be performed to demonstrate that the software product meets its requirements.

The test plan specifies the objectives of testing (e.g., to achieve error-free operation under stated conditions for a stated period of time), the test completion criteria (to achieve a specified rate of error exposure, to achieve a specified percent of logical path coverage), the system integration plan (strategy, schedule, responsible individuals), methods to be used on particular modules (walkthroughs, inspections, static analysis, dynamic tests, formal verification), and the particular test cases to be used.

There are four types of tests that a software product must satisfy: functional tests, performance tests, stress tests, and structural tests. Functional tests and performance tests are based on the requirements specifications; they are designed to demonstrate that the system satisfies its requirements. Therefore, the test plan can be only as good as the requirements, which in turn must be phrased in quantified, testable terms.

Functional test cases specify typical operating conditions, typical input values, and typical expected results. Functional tests should also be designed to test boundary conditions just inside and just beyond the boundaries (e.g., square root of negative numbers, inversion of one-by-one matrices, etc.). Also, special values, such as files and arrays containing identical values, the identity matrix, the zero matrix, etc., should be tested. Assumed initial values and system defaults should be tested, and inputs having assumed ordering relations should be tested with data that have both correct and incorrect ordering.

Performance tests should be designed to verify response time (under various loads), execution time, throughput, primary and secondary memory utilization, and traffic rates on data channels and communication links. Performance tests will often indicate processing bottlenecks to be addressed during system testing and tuning.

Each functional test and performance test should specify the machine configuration, assumptions concerning the system status for the test case, the requirements being tested, the test inputs, and the expected results. It is particularly important that the expected results of each test be specified prior to system implementation and actual testing. Otherwise, it is easy to rationalize an incorrect result.

Stress tests are designed to overload a system in various ways, such as attempting to sign on more than the maximum allowed number of terminals, processing more than the allowed number of identifiers or static levels, or disconnecting a communication link. The purposes of stress testing are to determine the limitations of the system and, when the system fails, to determine the manner in which the failure is manifest. Stress tests can provide valuable insight concerning the strengths and weaknesses of a system. Stress tests are derived from the requirements, the design, and the hunches and intuitions of the designers.

Structural tests are concerned with examining the internal processing logic of a software system. The particular routines called and the logical paths traversed through the routines are the objects of interest. The goal of structural testing is to traverse a specified number of paths through each routine in the system to establish thoroughness of testing.

The recommended approach is to perform the functional, performance, and stress tests on the implemented system, and to augment these tests with additional structure tests to achieve the desired level of test coverage. Thus, structural tests cannot be designed until the system is implemented and subjected to the predefined test plan. Structural testing and test coverage criteria are discussed in Chapter 8.

5.8 MILESTONES, WALKTHROUGHS, AND INSPECTIONS

One of the most important aspects of a systematic approach to software development is the resulting visibility of the evolving product. The system becomes explicit, tangible, and accessible. Products of analysis and design to be examined during system development include specifications for the externally observable characteristics of the system, the evolving *User's Manual,* architectural design specifications, detailed design specifications, and the test plan.

Development of these intermediate work products provides the opportunity to establish milestones and to conduct inspections and reviews. These activities in turn expose errors, provide increased project communication, keep the project on schedule, and permit verification that the design satisfies the requirements.

The two major milestones during software design are the Preliminary Design Review (PDR) and the Critical Design Review (CDR). The PDR is typically held near the end of architectural design and prior to detailed design. CDR occurs at the end of detailed design and prior to implementation.

Depending on the size and complexity of the product being developed, the PDR and CDR may be large, formal affairs involving several people, or they may consist of an informal meeting between a programmer and the project leader. In any case, a formal sign-off should occur to indicate that the milestone has been achieved.

The major goal of a PDR is to demonstrate that the externally observable characteristics and architectural structure of the product will satisfy the customer's requirements. Functional characteristics, performance attributes, external interfaces, user dialogues, report formats, exception conditions and exception handling, product subsets, and future enhancements to the product should all be reviewed during the PDR.

The appropriate level of product detail for a PDR includes the information contained in levels 1 and 2 of the procedure specification forms illustrated in Figure 5.10.

One of two outcomes is likely for a PDR: the PDR may expose enough serious problems that a subsequent PDR is scheduled; or the PDR may expose only minor errors that can be corrected and reviewed at CDR.

The CDR is held at the end of detailed design and prior to implementation. Among other things, CDR provides a final management decision point to build or cancel the system. The CDR is in essence a repeat of the PDR, but with the benefit of additional design effort. The team conducting a CDR may or may not examine the additional level of detail contained in the detailed design specification. In many cases, only critical modules are subjected to detailed review. As usual, a sign-off is required to indicate that the milestone has been achieved.

The involvement of customers in design reviews is a sensitive and difficult issue. The product designers may benefit from increased customer involvement. On the other hand, the customer may use the design reviews to interject changes to the requirements that necessitate significant design changes. Conventional wisdom says to involve the customer to the greatest extent possible. Experience indicates that too much customer involvement can hinder progress.

5.8.1 Walkthroughs and Inspections

A structured walkthrough is an in-depth, technical review of some aspect of a software system. Walkthroughs can be used at any time, during any phase of a software project. Thus, all or any part of the software requirements, the architectural design specifications, the detailed design specifications, the test plan, the code, supporting documents, or a proposed maintenance modification can be reviewed at any stage of evolution.

A walkthrough team consists of four to six people. The person whose material is being reviewed is responsible for providing copies of the review material to members of the walkthrough team in advance of the walkthrough session, and team members are responsible for reviewing the material prior to the session. During the walkthrough the reviewee "walks through" the material while the reviewers look for errors, request clarifications, and explore problem areas in the material under review.

It is important to emphasize that the material is reviewed, and not the reviewee. Thus, everyone's work should be reviewed in turn, and high-level managers should not attend walkthrough sessions. The focus of a walkthrough is on detection of errors and not on corrective actions. A designated secretary for the session records action items to be pursued by the reviewee following the review session. The reviewee is responsible for follow-up and for informing the reviewers of corrective actions taken. More detailed information concerning the format and conduct of walkthrough sessions is provided in Chapter 8.

Design inspections are conducted by teams of trained inspectors who work from checklists of items to examine. Special forms are used to record problems encountered. A typical design inspection team consists of a moderator/secretary, a designer, an implementor, and a tester. The designer, implementor, and tester may or may not be the people responsible for actual design, implementation, and testing of the product being inspected. Team members are trained for their specific roles and typically conduct two 2-hour sessions per day.

In one experiment, 67 percent of the errors found in a software product during product development were found using design and code inspection prior to unit testing (FAG76). Another experimenter reported 70 percent error removal using inspections (JON77). Many software developers report similar results. Formal design and code inspections are thus an effective mechanism for error detection and removal. Inspections are discussed in greater detail in Chapter 8.

5.9 DESIGN GUIDELINES

There is no magic formula or recipe for software design. Design is a creative process that can be guided and directed, but it can never be reduced to an algorithmic procedure. The design of a real-time system is a much different activity than the design of a data processing application. The following guidelines do not constitute a "design methodology," but rather provide some guidance for organizing the activities of software design.

1. Review the requirements specification. In particular, study the desired functional characteristics and performance attributes of the system.
2. Review and expand the external interfaces, user dialogues, and report formats developed during requirements analysis.
3. Review and refine the data flow diagrams developed during requirements analysis and external design. Identify internal data stores and elaborate the processing functions.
4. Identify functional abstractions and data abstractions. Record them using a design notation.
5. Define the visible interfaces for each functional abstraction and each data abstraction. Record them using a design notation.
6. Define the modularization criteria to be used in establishing system structure.
7. Apply the techniques of your particular design method to establish system structure. For example, derive the input and output data structures and convert the data structures into a processing structure, as in Jackson Structured Programming; or convert the data flow diagrams into structure charts, as in structured design; or derive a system structure that maximizes information hiding, or a structure that enhances the overlay capabilities or real-time response rate, etc.
8. Iterate steps 4 through 7, and, as necessary, steps 1 through 7 until a suitable structure is achieved.
9. Verify that the resulting system structure satisfies the requirements.
10. Develop interface specifications for the procedures in each module.
11. Conduct the Preliminary Design Review. The level of detail should be inclusive to levels 1 and 2 of the procedure templates in Figure 5.10.
12. Develop concrete data representations for the data stores and data abstractions.

13. Expand the procedure templates of Figure 5.10 to include the information in level 3.
14. Specify algorithmic details for the body of each procedure in the system, using successive refinement, HIPO diagrams, pseudocode, structured English, and/or structured flowcharts. Develop concrete data representations and inter-connections between data structures and algorithms.
15. Conduct the Critical Design Review.
16. Redesign as necessary.

The major difficulties in software design are caused by inadequate require-ments, failure to consider alternative design strategies, and the temptation to pro-vide too much detail too soon. A great deal of iteration among the various design steps is to be expected as understanding of the problem and various possibilities for solutions improve. The use of systematic design notations will greatly enhance your thought processes and improve your ability to think about, communicate, and verify the design.

5.10 SUMMARY

Design is the bridge between software requirements and an implementation that satisfies those requirements. The software design bridge is built in three stages: external design, architectural design, and detailed design. External design is the transitional step from requirements definition (detailed "what") to system architec-ture (high-level "how"). The goal of architectural design is to specify a system structure that satisfies the requirements, the external design specifications, and the implementation constraints. Detailed design provides the algorithmic details, data representations, and packaging for the software product.

In this chapter, we have discussed fundamental design concepts including abstraction, information hiding, structure, modularity, concurrency, verification, and design aesthetics. Modularization criteria include coupling and cohesion, data abstraction, information hiding, and other factors discussed in Section 5.2.

Design notations discussed in this chapter include data flow diagrams, structure charts, HIPO diagrams, procedure templates, pseudocode, structured flowcharts, structured English, and Jackson structure diagrams.

Several design techniques were introduced, including stepwise refinement, levels of abstraction, structured design, integrated top-down development, and Jackson Structured Programming. The viewpoints and basic concepts of the meth-ods were presented, and the various approaches were compared and contrasted. The cited references provide additional information concerning the methods. The se-mester project gives students the opportunity to study one or more of the methods in detail.

The need for detailed design was discussed, and the notations and activities of detailed design were described. Notations such as pseudocode, structured flowcharts, structured English, data structure diagrams, and data representation diagrams can be used in conjunction with stepwise refinement to accomplish detailed design of the modules. Packaging concerns for the software product were discussed, and it was observed that detailed design is complete when any programmer familiar with the implementation language can implement the system from the architectural and detailed design specifications.

Design considerations for real-time and distributed systems were presented, test plans were discussed, and the use of walkthroughs and design inspections was examined. More details concerning test plans, walkthroughs, and inspections are provided in Chapter 8. Finally, guidelines for the design process were presented.

Design is a creative activity, in both art and technology. Systematic notations and disciplined approaches are as necessary for the design of a software system as for the design of a poem or a painting. However, it is not to be expected that adoption of a particular tool or technique will solve the software design problem any more than adoption of a particular method will solve the poetry problem. The design problem is the problem-solving problem of building systems to satisfy human needs. Systematic methods, tools, and techniques are necessary for software design, and it is certainly true that better tools and techniques, and better use of existing tools and techniques, will improve the process of software design, but it is also true that tools and techniques are not panaceas. There is no substitute for creativity, intelligence, and hard work applied within a systematic framework.

REFERENCES

(ALF77) Alford, M.: "A Requirements Engineering Methodology for Real-Time Processing Requirements," *Trans. Software Eng.,* vol. SE-3, no. 1, January 1977.
(BOE79) Boebert, W., et al.: "NPN: A Finite-State Specification Technique for Distributed Software," *Conf. Proc. Specifications of Reliable Software,* IEEE Cat. No. 79 CH1401-9C, 1979.
(DIJ68) Dijkstra, E.: "The Structure of the 'THE'-Multiprogramming System," *Comm. ACM,* vol. 11, no. 6, May 1968.
(FAG76) Fagan, M.: "Design and Code Inspections to Reduce Errors in Program Development," *IBM Systems Journal,* vol. 15, no. 3, 1976.
(FAI84) Fairley, R.: "A Model of Software Structure," Proc. 17th Hawaii Intl. Conf. on System Sciences, Western Periodicals, 1984.
(FRA81) Franta, W., et al.: "Real-Time Distributed Computing Systems," in *Advances in Computers,* vol. 20, Academic Press, New York, 1981.
(HUG79) Hughes, J.: "A Formalization and Explication of the Michael Jackson Method of Program Design," *Software-Practice and Experience,* vol. 9, p. 191-202, 1979.
(JAC75) Jackson, M.: *Principles of Program Design,* Academic Press, 1975.
(JAC83) Jackson, M.: *System Design,* Prentice-Hall International, Englewood Cliffs, N.J., 1983.
(JON77) Jones, T. C.: *Program Quality and Programmer Productivity,* IBM Technical Report TR02.764, January 1977.
(KRA78) Kramer, J., and R. Cunningham: "Towards a Notation for the Functional Design of Distributed Processing Systems," *Proc. Intl. Conf. on Parallel Processing,* 1978.
(MAO80) Mao, T., and R. Yeh: "Communication Port: A Language Concept for Concurrent Programming," *Trans. Software Eng.,* vol. SE-6, no. 2, February 1980.
(MYE78) Myers, G.: *Composite/Structured Design,* Van Nostrand Reinhold, 1978.
(NAU63) Naur, P. (ed): "Revised Report on the Algorithmic Language ALGOL60," *Comm. ACM,* vol. 6, no. 1, January 1963.

(PAG80) Page-Jones, M.: *The Practical Guide to Structured System Design,* Yourdon Press, 1980.
(PAR71) Parnas, D.: "Information Distribution Aspects of Design Methodology," *IFIP Congress Proceedings,* Ljubljana, Yugoslavia, 1971.
(PAR72a) Parnas, D.: "A Technique for Software Module Specification with Examples," *Comm. ACM,* vol. 15, no. 5, May 1972.
(PAR72b) Parnas, D.: "On the Criteria to be Used in Decomposing Systems into Modules," *Comm. ACM,* vol. 15, no. 12, December 1972.
(STE81) Stevens, W.: *Using Structured Design: How to Make Programs Simple, Changeable, Flexible, and Reusable,* Wiley-Interscience, New York, 1981.
(STE74) Stevens, W., G. Myers, and L. Constantine: : "Structured Design," *IBM Systems Journal,* vol. 13, no. 2, 1974.
(WEI71) Weinberg, G.: *The Psychology of Computer Programming,* Van Nostrand Reinhold, New York, 1971.
(WIR71) Wirth, N.: "Program Development by Stepwise Refinement," *Comm. ACM,* vol. 14, no. 4, April 1971.
(WIR76) Wirth, N.: *Algorithms + Data Structures = Programs,* Prentice-Hall, Englewood Cliffs, N.J., 1976.
(YOU79) Yourdon, E. and L. Constantine: *Structured Design: Fundamentals of A Discipline of Computer Program and Systems Design,* Prentice-Hall, Englewood Cliffs, N.J., 1979.

EXERCISES

5.1 Describe the following concepts. Provide examples from the software field and from other fields:
(a) abstraction
(b) hierarchy
(c) modularity
(d) verification
(e) design aesthetics

5.2 Select a software product of your choice (or your instructor's choice) and evaluate it for:
(a) information hiding
(b) levels of abstraction
(c) coupling and cohesion
(d) data sharing/data locality

5.3 (a) Explain the difference between external design, architectural design, and detailed design.
(b) What notations are appropriate in each design phase?
(c) Explain how the transitions are made from requirements analysis to external design, from external design to architectural design, and from architectural design to detailed design.

5.4 Develop a high level data flow diagram and a structure chart for each of the following systems. Which systems are transform centered? Which are transaction driven?
(a) A compiler
(b) Job processing in a multiprogrammed operating system
(c) An inventory control program
(d) An airline reservation system
(e) A process control system

5.5 Describe the systems in Exercise 5.4 using levels of abstraction. What functions and data structures are on each level? What criteria did you use to determine the placement of functions and data structures in the levels?

5.6 Experiment with data dictionaries, decision tables, Jackson structure notation, HIPO diagrams, procedure specification forms, pseudocode, structured flowcharts, and structured English to specify portions of the detailed design of your term project. Which notations do you prefer? Why?

5.7 Try using procedure stubs and integrated top-down development on a portion (all?) of your term project. What difficulties do you foresee?

5.8 Use the technique of stepwise refinement to develop algorithms for:

(*a*) Solving a system of linear equations

(*b*) Converting the character string representation of floating point numbers into internal representation

(*c*) The Dutch National Flag problem (DIJ76)

(*d*) The eight queens problem (WIR71)

5.9 Document the algorithms developed in Exercise 5.8 using

(*a*) Pseudocode

(*b*) Structured flowcharts

(*c*) Structured English

(*d*) HIPO diagrams

5.10 (*a*) Use the Jackson notation to specify the structure of an input data file that contains payroll information (employee name, hours worked, pay rate, deductions, etc.).

(*b*) Use the Jackson notation to specify the structure of an output report that contains pay information for each employee (name, hours worked, overtime hours, gross amount, net amount, etc.)

(*c*) Identify points of commonality on the diagrams from parts a and b. Convert the resulting composite diagram into a structure chart for a program.

5.11 Read some papers on design walkthroughs (YOU79) and design inspections (FAG76).

(*a*) How are they similar and how do they differ?

(*b*) What are the relative advantages and disadvantages of walkthroughs and inspections?

(*c*) Why would you use a walkthrough rather than an inspection?

(*d*) Why would you use an inspection rather than a walkthrough?

5.12 Develop design inspection checklists for use by the analyst, the designer, the implementor, and the tester roles in an inspection team. What issues are important to each of these roles?

5.13 Use the design inspection checklists developed in Exercise 5.12 to inspect the design specifications for your term project.

5.14 Conduct an in-class walkthrough of the architectural design and a portion of the detailed design of your term project.

SIX

IMPLEMENTATION ISSUES

INTRODUCTION

The implementation phase of software development is concerned with translating design specifications into source code. The primary goal of implementation is to write source code and internal documentation so that conformance of the code to its specifications can be easily verified, and so that debugging, testing, and modification are eased (recall the distribution of effort in Figure 1.2). This goal can be achieved by making the source code as clear and straightforward as possible. Simplicity, clarity, and elegance are the hallmarks of good programs; obscurity, cleverness, and complexity are indications of inadequate design and misdirected thinking.

Source-code clarity is enhanced by structured coding techniques, by good coding style, by appropriate supporting documents, by good internal comments, and by the features provided in modern programming languages. In this chapter, structured coding techniques, coding style, program unit notebooks, and internal documentation of source code are discussed. Modern programming languages are discussed in the next chapter.

Production of high-quality software requires that the programming team have a designated leader, a well-defined organizational structure, and a thorough understanding of the duties and responsibilities of each team member. Programming team structures are discussed in Chapter 2. Written job descriptions and management by objectives are also discussed in Chapter 2.

The implementation team should be provided with a well-defined set of software requirements, an architectural design specification, and a detailed design description. Also, each team member must understand the objectives of implementation. In a well-known experiment, Weinberg gave five programmers five different implementation goals for the same program: minimize the memory re-

Outcome / Major objective	Minimum memory	Clarity of		Minimum number of statements	Minimum Dvmt. time
		Output	Program		
Minimize primary memory	1	4	4	2	5
Maximize output readability	5	1	1–2	5	2–3
Maximize source text readability	3	2	1–2	3	4
Minimize number of statements	2	5	3	1	2–3
Minimize development time	4	3	5	4	1

1: Best
5: Worst

Figure 6.1 Outcome of a programming experiment *(WEI71)*.

quired, maximize output readability, maximize source text readability, minimize the number of source statements, and minimize development time (WEI71). The results of that experiment are summarized in Figure 6.1. It is clear that each programmer achieved the desired objective and ranked high on related objectives. For example, the programmer who minimized memory ranked second in minimizing the number of source statements (and vice versa). The programmer who maximized output readability ranked second in source-code readability (and vice versa). Most programmers will strive to achieve the stated objectives, provided those objectives are well understood.

6.1 STRUCTURED CODING TECHNIQUES

The goal of structured coding is to linearize control flow through a computer program so that the execution sequence follows the sequence in which the code is written. The dynamic structure of a program as it executes then resembles the static structure of the written text. This enhances readability of code, which eases understanding, debugging, testing, documentation, and modification of programs. It also facilitates formal verification of programs. Linear flow of control can be achieved by restricting the set of allowed program constructs to single entry, single exit formats; however, strict adherence to nested, single entry, single exit constructs leads to questions concerning efficiency, questions about "reasonable" violations of single entry, single exit, and questions about the proper role of the goto statement in structured coding. These issues are discussed in the following subsections.

6.1.1 Single Entry, Single Exit Constructs

In 1966, Bohm and Jacopini published a paper in which they demonstrated that sequencing, selection among alternative actions, and iteration is a sufficient set of constructs for describing the control flow of every conceivable algorithm (BOH66). They argued that every Turing machine program can be written in this manner. Because the Turing machine is the fundamental model of computation, it follows that every algorithm (every Turing machine program) can be written using sequencing, selection, and iteration.

A modified version of the Bohm-Jacopini theorem can be stated as follows:

> Any single entry, single exit program segment that has all statements on some path from the entry to the exit can be specified using only sequencing, selection, and iteration.

A sufficient set of single entry, single exit constructs for specifying control flow in algorithms is

Sequencing: S1; S2; S3;
Selection: if B then S1 else S2;
Iteration: while B do S;

The single entry, single exit nature of these constructs is illustrated in Figure 6.2. The single entry, single exit property permits nesting of constructs within one another in any desired fashion; each statement Si might be an assignment statement, a procedure call, an if_then_else, or a while_do. Statements of the latter forms may in turn contain nested statements. The most important aspect of the single entry, single exit property is that linearity of control flow is retained, even with arbitrarily deep nesting of constructs.

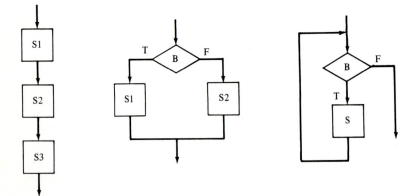

Figure 6.2 A sufficient set of constructs for structured coding.

Additional single entry, single exit constructs are widely used in practice. For example, Pascal provides the control-flow constructs illustrated in Figure 6.3. Each construct in Figure 6.3 can be expressed in terms of sequencing, if_then_else, and while_do: "if B then S" as "if B then S else null"; "case" as a sequence of nested if_then_else; and "repeat" as the sequence

> S1;
>
> while (not B) do S1;

A "for" loop can be expressed as a sequence of the form

> S0;
>
> while B loop
>
> S1;
>
> S2;
>
> end loop;

where S0 initializes the loop variable, B tests the limit, and S2 increments (or decrements) the loop variable; S1 is the loop body.

It should not be surprising that the constructs illustrated in Figure 6.3 can be expressed in terms of sequence, if_then_else, and while_do. This is assured by the Bohm-Jacopini theorem. A different sufficient set of constructs for structured coding is sequencing, the case statement for selection, and repeat_until for iteration; all of the constructs in Figure 6.3 can be expressed in terms of sequence, case, and repeat constructs. The total set of constructs provided by Pascal and other modern programming languages offers increased notational convenience, increased readability, and, in some cases, increased efficiency. They are not necessary; sequencing and conditional branching are the only necessary control flow mechanisms because the Bohm-Jacopini requirements of selection and iteration can be implemented using conditional branching.

The set of structured constructs selected for use in any particular application is primarily a matter of notational convenience; however, the selected constructs should be conceptually simple and widely applicable in practice.

6.1.2 Efficiency Considerations

A recurring criticism of strict adherence to single entry, single exit constructs is that they result in inefficient use of memory space and execution time. The need for auxiliary variables, repeated segments of code, and excessive subprogram calls are often cited. The following material illustrates these situations. A strategy for using single entry, single exit constructs and coping with efficiency considerations is then presented.

The following example illustrates the need for auxiliary variables in a search loop on a linked list:

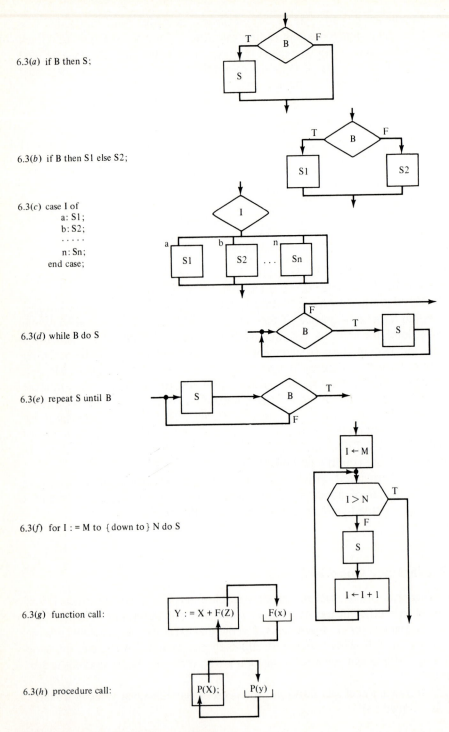

6.3(a) if B then S;

6.3(b) if B then S1 else S2;

6.3(c) case I of
        a: S1;
        b: S2;
        . . . . .
        n: Sn;
     end case;

6.3(d) while B do S

6.3(e) repeat S until B

6.3(f) for I : = M to {down to} N do S

6.3(g) function call:

6.3(h) procedure call:

Figure 6.3 Control flow constructs in Pascal.

196

```
P := L;
while (P /= null) and (P.val /= X) loop
P := P.LINK;
end loop;
if (P /= null) then
  -- code for X in list
else
  -- code for X not in list
end if;
```

The purpose of the loop is to search a linked list L for value X. The list structure is illustrated in Figure 6.4.

On loop exit, P will contain the address of the memory cell that contains X, provided X is in the list (in this case, loop exit occurs on P.VAL = X). If X is not in the list, the outcome depends on the program language being used, and often on the local implementation of the language. Many language translators evaluate all relational expressions in a boolean expression before performing the boolean operation. In the example, if X is not in the list, P is assigned the null value (P := P.LINK) when the end of the list is encountered. Control is then transferred to the start of the loop, and the loop test evaluates the relational expressions (P = null) and (P.VAL = X) before applying the AND operation; in this situation P.VAL is undefined because P is null.

Some language translators avoid this problem by evaluating relational expressions in left-to-right fashion. If the leftmost operand in an AND is false, the entire AND must be false. Therefore, the rightmost operand need not be evaluated. If the language translator evaluates relationals in left-to-right fashion, the example will execute correctly; otherwise, an exception will occur.

The Ada programming language provides and_then and or_else boolean operators for these situations. These operators are called "short-circuit conditions."

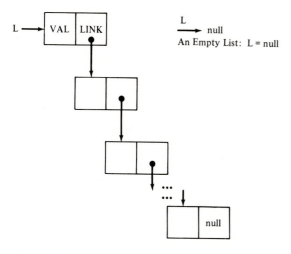

Figure 6.4 A linked list, L.

Using short-circuit conditions, the example can be rewritten as

```
while (P /= null) and then (P.VAL /= X) loop
    P := P.LINK;
end loop;
```

If a language standard does not specify the way in which boolean expressions are to be evaluated (as in the case of Pascal), different translators will handle the situation according to the viewpoints of different language implementors (efficiency arguments favor evaluation of all operands before evaluating booleans).

An "obvious" solution to the above problem is to use a goto statement for premature loop exit and to handle alternative actions on loop exit:

```
             while (P /= null) loop
                 if (P.VAL = X) then go to L1;
                 P := P.LINK;
             end loop;
<< L1 >>     if (P /=null) then
                 -- code for X in list;
             else
                 -- code for X not in list;
             end if;
```

Figure 6.5 illustrates three alternative "structured" solutions for the search loop. Each solution requires an auxiliary variable to achieve the same effect as the goto solution. Solution *a* uses an auxiliary pointer variable, Q, to record the location of X in the list. On exit, Q will point to the last occurrence of X in the list, provided X is in the list. Otherwise, Q will be null on exit. Solution *a* is incorrect if the first of multiple occurrences of X is desired and inefficient if the first occurrence of X is acceptable because the entire list must be traversed even though X may be found in the first or second node of a very long list. If the last occurrence of X is desired, then solution *a* is correct. The first occurrence of X can be found by modifying the loop test in Figure 6.5a as follows:

```
while (P /= null) and (Q = null) loop
```

Solution *b* uses a boolean variable (a flag) to trigger loop exit when the first occurrence of X is located. If X is in the list, FOUND will be true on loop exit, and P will point to the location of the first X. If X is not in the list, B will be false, and P will be null on exit. Solution *c* assumes that the total number of nodes in the list, N, is known and uses an integer counter I to count the number of nodes visited. On exit, P will point to the first occurrence of an X in the list; otherwise, P will be null on exit.

In summary, solutions *a* and *c* find the last X in the list, and solution *b* finds the first X in the list. Solution *a* can be modified as indicated to find the first X in

```
P := L;
Q := null;
while (P /= null) loop
  if (P.VAL = X) then Q := P;
  P := P.LINK;
end loop;
if (Q /= null) then
  -- code for X in list
else
  -- code for X not in list
end if;
```

Figure 6.5a Auxiliary pointer variable solution.

```
P:=L;
FOUND := false;
while (P /= null) and (not FOUND) loop
  if (P.VAL = X) then FOUND := true;
  else P := P.LINK;
end loop;
if (P /= null) then
  -- code for X in list
else
  -- code for X not in list
end if;
```

Figure 6.5b Auxiliary flag variable solution.

```
P := L;
I := 1;
while (I <= N) loop
  if (P. VAL /= X) then
    P := P.LINK;
    I := I + 1;
end loop;
if (P /= null) then
  -- code for X in list
else
  -- code for X not in list
end if;
```

Figure 6.5c Node-count solution.

Figure 6.5 Three linked list search algorithms

the list. Solution *c* is not desirable because it is inconvenient to maintain the total node count N in dynamic list processing.

Finally, we observe that the problems encountered in this example can be avoided by a slight change in the data structure. Adding a header node L to the list, as illustrated in Figure 6.6, permits the following search algorithm:

```
P := L;
while (P.LINK /= null) and (P.VAL /= X) loop
  P := P.LINK;
end loop;
if (P.VAL = X) then
  -- code for X in list L
else
  -- code for X not in list L
end if;
```

Observe that the loop test has been changed to test P.LINK /= null, rather than

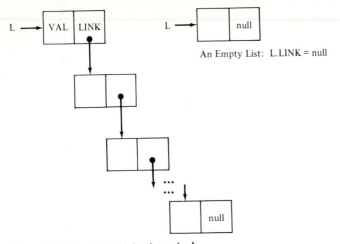

Figure 6.6 Linked list with header node, L.

P /= null. An empty list is denoted by L.LINK = null. The search algorithm requires that the value field of the header node, L.VAL, not equal X for any permissible X. If the list is empty, P.LINK is null on loop entry, and control will fall through the loop. In this case, P equals L on loop exit. If an X is in the list, P will point to the location of the first X on loop exit. Otherwise, P will point to the last node on the list on loop exit, which may or may not contain X.

This modification illustrates three important points about structured coding: First, and most important, structured coding practices give no guidance in the design and method of access to data representations. Structured coding is a technique for linearizing control flow. Often, careful thought about data representation and data access techniques will ease awkward situations when they arise. Second, the modified example finds the first X in the list. Perhaps the second or the Nth or the last X is required, and this will require a different search algorithm. Third, it may not be possible to design a data structure that will satisfy all requirements in an optimal manner. The data structure illustrated in Figure 6.4 (without a header node) may be required for other purposes, thus requiring one of the search algorithms in Figure 6.5.

Another major concern about efficiency in structured coding is the need to repeat segments of code, or alternatively, to place a code segment in a subprogram and call it repeatedly (thus increasing overhead cost for subprogram linkage). Otherwise, the single entry, single exit rule must be violated. Figure 6.7 illustrates four versions of a code segment. Version *a* adheres to the three basic constructs, with repeated code segments (or repeated subprogram calls). Version *b* uses an if_then construct to reduce the number of repeated code segments, and versions *c* and *d* use goto statements to completely eliminate repeated code segments. Observe that version *c* has multiple entry points into code segments A and B, and that version *d* has multiple entry points into code segment A.

```
if P then A; B;
    else B;
end if;
while Q loop
 A; B;
end loop;
```

Figure 6.7a if_then_else solution.

```
if P then A; end if;
B;
while Q loop
 A; B;
end loop;
```

Figure 6.7b if_then solution.

```
if P then << L1 >> A;
    go to L2;
  else << L2 >> B;
end if;
if Q then go to L1;
```

Figure 6.7c goto solution.

```
if P then << L1 >> A; end if;
B;
if Q then go to L1;
```

Figure 6.7d Alternative goto solution.

Figure 6.7 Four representations for an algorithm.

It is sometimes true (for example, on microprocessors with limited memory and real-time processing constraints) that efficiency considerations will require a code segment to be implemented as in Figure 6.7d. In order to address efficiency considerations when using single entry, single exit constructs, the following strategy is advised: First, implement the algorithm using single entry, single exit constructs, as in Figure 6.7b. Place the repeated code segments in subprograms and invoke them as needed, or repeat them in-line, perhaps using an Include or macro facility. When the system or a major subsystem becomes operational, measure the percentage of execution time spent in various regions of the code (typically, a large percentage of execution time is spent in a small region of the code). Identify a few code segments that are candidates for performance enhancement. Within those code segments, it may be necessary to convolute the code as in Figure 6.7d. If this is done, use both internal and external documentation to explain why the code is written in this manner. Within the internal documentation, include an equivalent structured form of the code, such as Figure 6.7b to aid understanding of an otherwise obscure code segment. In this manner, critical regions of code can be collapsed together for efficiency purposes, and the remaining code (typically the majority of the code) will retain a clear and understandable structure.

6.1.3 Violations of Single Entry, Single Exit

The goal of structured coding is to improve the clarity and readability of source programs. Clarity is greatly enhanced by use of single entry, single exit constructs. There are, however, commonly occurring situations which warrant violation of strict adherence to single entry, single exit and yet are consistent with the goal of improved clarity. Three commonly occurring situations are multiple loop exits,

```
      DO 10 I = 1,N
      :::::
      IF (COND1) GO TO 20
      :::::
      IF (COND2) GO TO 30
      :::::
10    CONTINUE
20    -- CODE FOR COND1 EXIT
      GO TO 40
30    -- CODE FOR COND2 EXIT
40    CONTINUE
```

Figure 6.8 Multiple loop exits in FORTRAN IV.

```
for I in 1..MAX loop
  ::::::
  exit when COND1;
  ::::::
  exit when COND2;
  ::::::
end loop;
if (COND1) then
  —code for COND1 exit
elsif (COND2) then
  —code for COND1 exit
end if;
  —code for normal exit
```

Figure 6.9 Multiple loop exits in Ada.

error handling, and data encapsulation. Multiple loop exits are discussed subsequently. Use of gotos for error handling is illustrated in Figure 6.10 in conjunction with the discussion of data encapsulation techniques.

It is not unusual to have several different conditions for termination of a loop. The best procedure for dealing with multiple loop exits is to redesign the algorithm so that multiple loop exits are not required. If this is not possible (one should not reach this conclusion too quickly), one technique for achieving multiple loop exits is to introduce a boolean flag variable for each condition and test the flags on each iteration of the loop, in the manner of Figure 6.4b. There are three difficulties with this approach: first, the need for additional variables; second, the additional tests required on loop exit to determine which condition caused the exit; and third, the requirement, in many cases, that the loop body be terminated immediately on occurrence of a given condition and not at the start of the next iteration, as would occur on testing a loop flag.

A reasonable solution, expressed in FORTRAN IV, is illustrated in Figure 6.8. Although gotos are used to achieve multiple loop exits and to isolate alternative actions on exit, the spirit of clarity and locality is maintained; control is transferred only to the vicinity of the loop exit.

Multiple loop exits in the Ada programming language are illustrated in Figure 6.9. An Ada exit statement transfers control to the statement immediately following the end of the containing loop when the associated condition becomes true. In Figure 6.9, if statements following the loop are used to determine the reason for loop termination. In Ada, loops can be given names, and exit statements of the form

$$\text{if CONDITION then exit LOOP2;}$$

can be used to achieve exit from nested loops, or from an inner loop to an outer loop. Again, we caution that one should not be too hasty to create multiple loop exits. Algorithms can often be redesigned to eliminate the need for multiple exits.

6.1.4 Data Encapsulation

Data encapsulation involves packaging of a data structure and its access routines in a single module. The data structure is manipulated only by the access routines, and other routines use the data structure by calling the appropriate access routine. A data structure is thus defined by the operations that can be performed on it. Routines that use the structure need not know the details of data representation or data manipulation. In this manner, encapsulated data structures provide abstract objects in the same way that mathematical library routines provide abstract operations.

Data encapsulation should not be confused with abstract data types nor with data abstraction. An abstract data type is a user-defined template that can be used to create numerous instances of encapsulated data objects, in the same way that the integer type can be used to create numerous instances of integer objects. Data encapsulation refers to a single instance of an abstract data object. Data abstraction is used to describe a design principle that incorporates both data encapsulation and abstract data types.

In primitive programming languages such as FORTRAN, data encapsulation can be implemented in a manner that violates single entry, single exit and yet maintains linearity and locality of control flow. An example is presented in the following discussion.

An encapsulated stack of integers, implemented in FORTRAN IV, is illustrated in Figure 6.10. The example is presented in FORTRAN to illustrate that modern concepts can often be implemented in primitive programming languages by using disciplined programming style. Subroutine INTSTK has three entry points, five RETURN statements, and two GOTO statements. Yet, we maintain that the routine is well structured. INTSTK is called to initialize the array index. Entry points PUSH and POP are invoked to place items on, and retrieve items from, the stack array. On impending stack overflow (INDEX.GE.100) or impending stack underflow (INDEX.LE.0) a GOTO statement is used to transfer control to error-handling code that sets the error flag appropriately and returns control to the calling routine. It is the calling routine's responsibility to test the error flag and proceed accordingly.

To be strictly correct, STACK and INDEX should be placed in a COMMON block to make them static objects. Although most FORTRAN IV implementations allocate memory statically, there is no requirement to do so in the language standard; only COMMON blocks are guaranteed to be static. Placing the STACK array and INDEX pointer in a COMMON block would make them globally accessible, and this would violate the principle of information hiding used in the encapsulation. However, we would rely on programmer discipline to leave the COMMON block untouched by other routines, no matter how tempting or convenient.

The FORTRAN example in Figure 6.10 illustrates five basic features that must be provided by a data encapsulation facility:

1. Multiple entry and return points

```
SUBROUTINE INTSTK(ITEM,ERRFLG)
C
C   ITEM IS THE STACK VALUE
C   ERRFLG IS THE ERROR FLAG
C   ERRFLG RETURN 0 IS NORMAL
C   ERRFLG RETURN 1 IS STACK FULL
C   ERRFLG RETURN -1 IS STACK EMPTY
C
            INTEGER ITEM, ERRFLG, INDEX, STACK(100)
C   INDEX IS THE STACK POINTER
C   STACK IS THE ARRAY REPRESENTATION
C   INITIALIZATION CODE FOLLOWS
            INDEX = 0
            RETURN
C   PUSH SECTION FOLLOWS
            ENTRY PUSH
              IF (INDEX.GE.100) GO TO 10
              ERRFLG = 0
              INDEX = INDEX + 1
              STACK(INDEX) = ITEM
            RETURN
C   POP SECTION FOLLOWS
            ENTRY POP
              IF (INDEX.LE.0) GO TO 20
              ERRFLG = 0
              ITEM = STACK(INDEX)
              INDEX = INDEX - 1
            RETURN
C   ERROR HANDLERS
   10       ERRFLG = 1
            RETURN
   20       ERRFLG = - 1
            RETURN
            END
```

Figure 6.10 Stack encapsulation in FORTRAN IV.

2. Local hidden source code and data representations
3. Static data objects
4. An initialization section
5. Exception handling

6.1.5 The Goto Statement

The goto statement provides unconditional transfer of control and thus allows violation of the single entry, single exit condition of structured coding. We have presented several examples where goto statements were used to achieve a desired result in a manner that violates single entry, single exit and yet maintained locality and linearity of control flow.

The goto statement also can be used to simulate single entry, single exit constructs in primitive programming languages. Figure 6.11 illustrates use of the

```
if B then S1 else S2;        IF(.NOT.(B)) GO TO 10
                             S1
                             GO TO 20
                         10  S2
                         20  CONTINUE
```

Figure 6.11a Simulation of if_then_else in FORTRAN IV.

```
while B do S                 10  IF(.NOT.(B)) GO TO 20
                                 S
                                 GO TO 10
                             20  CONTINUE
```

Figure 6.11b Simulation of while_do in FORTRAN IV.

Figure 6.11 Simulation of structured control flow in FORTRAN IV.

goto statement in FORTRAN IV to simulate if_then_else and while_do. As before, we use FORTRAN to illustrate that structured coding is possible in primitive programming languages through use of disciplined programming style. Preprocessors and macro processors are available to automatically translate structured constructs into FORTRAN IV, COBOL, and various assembly languages (KER76).

As illustrated in the previous discussion, the goto statement can be used in a positive manner. The goto statement is available in Pascal, Ada, and most other modern programming languages. Wirth provides the following advice concerning the goto statement (WIR74):

> A goto statement should be reserved for unusual or uncommon situations where the natural structure of an algorithm has to be broken. A good rule is to avoid the use of jumps to express regular iteration or conditional execution of statements, for such jumps destroy the reflection of the structure of the computation in the textual (static) structure of the program. Moreover, the lack of correspondence between textual and computational (static and dynamic) structure is extremely detrimental to the clarity of the program and makes the task of verification much more difficult.

Although the goto statement can often be used with positive effect on program clarity, it is an extremely low-level construct (analogous to a machine-level jump operation), and is easily misused. A serious problem in using goto statements is the insidious mind set that results from thinking in terms of gotos. For instance, code for a four-way selection might be implemented using gotos in the following manner:

```
if (Condition 1) then go to L1;
if (Condition 2) then go to L2;
if (Condition 3) then go to L3;
goto L4;
L1: -- Code for Condition 1
goto L5
```

```
L2: -- Code for Condition 2
       goto L5
L3: -- Code for Condition 3
       goto L5
L4: -- Code for all other conditions
L5: Continue
```

In primitive programming languages, this goto version may be the best structure that can be achieved.

A preferable structure is the more compact form:

```
if (Condition 1) then
        -- Code for Condition 1;
elsif (Condition 2) then
        -- Code for Condition 2;
elsif (Condition 3) then
        -- Code for Condition 3;
else
        -- Code for Condition 4;
end if;
```

If one is accustomed to programming with gotos, the clearer and more compact solution that results from nested else_if constructs may not come to mind as readily as the goto version, even though else_if is available in the implementation language.

In summary, the goto statement can be a valuable mechanism when used in a disciplined and stylistic manner. As a general rule, forward gotos to exit local constructs and to transfer control to local error-handling code are acceptable. Goto statements that transfer control to remote regions of the code, or that jump in and out of code segments in clever ways, destroy the linearity and locality of control flow. They are to be avoided.

6.1.6 Recursion

A recursive subprogram is one that calls itself, either directly or indirectly; recursion is a powerful and elegant programming technique. When properly used, recursive subprograms are easy to understand, and are just as efficient as, if not more efficient than, iterative implementations of inherently recursive algorithms. The goals of clarity and efficiency are thus served by appropriate use of recursion.

Recursive algorithms arise naturally in conjunction with recursive data structures (e.g., linked lists, trees) when the exact topology and number of elements in the structure are not known, and in other situations that require backtracking algorithms. For example, an algorithm for in-order traversal of binary trees can be expressed recursively as

```
procedure IN_ORDER(T:POINTER) is
begin
 if (T /= null) then
  IN_ORDER(T.LEFT);
  P(T);
  IN_ORDER(T.RIGHT);
 end if;
end IN_ORDER;
```

In this example, P(T) is a procedure that is invoked to process nodes of the tree as they are encountered in IN_ORDER fashion.

The distinguishing characteristic of recursive subprograms is use of a system-provided stack to hold values of local variables, parameters, and return points during recursive calls. A FORTRAN system that uses static memory allocation cannot support recursive subprograms because a stack is required to record successive return addresses on successive invocations prior to returns. Recursive invocation of a routine under static memory management would result in overwriting of the original return address for the routine. Recursion can be simulated in statically allocated languages such as FORTRAN, but a great deal of code must be supplied by the programmer to manipulate an explicitly declared stack data structure. The required effort is usually not cost-effective.

Recursion is used inappropriately to implement algorithms that are inherently iterative; such algorithms do not require a stack or any other backtracking mechanism. Examples of inappropriate use of recursion include routines to compute factorials and Fibonacci numbers:

```
function FACTORIAL(N: NATURAL) return NATURAL is
begin
  return(if N = 0 then 1 else N * FACTORIAL(N-1));
end FACTORIAL;

procedure FIBONACCI(N: NATURAL) return NATURAL is
begin
  return(if (N = 0) then 0
    elsif(N = 1) then 1
  else FIBONACCI(N-2) + FIBONACCI(N-1));
end FIBONACCI;
```

These routines are often used in introductory programming texts to illustrate recursive implementation of recursive specifications:

```
FACTORIAL(0) = 1
FACTORIAL(N) = N * FACTORIAL(N-1) for all N > 0
```

and

FIBONACCI(0) = 0   FIBONACCI(1) = 1
FIBONACCI(N) = FIBONACCI(N-1) + FIBONACCI(N-2) for all N > 1

Recursion is a powerful specification technique, and in appropriate circumstances a powerful implementation technique. However, a recursive specification does not necessarily imply a recursive implementation. Functional specifications state what is required, not how to achieve it. The algorithmic form of a recursive specification is often best expressed in an iterative manner. Straightforward iterative algorithms for factorial and Fibonacci follow:

```
function FACTORIAL(N: NATURAL) return NATURAL is
   FAC: NATURAL := 1;
begin
for I in 2..N loop
   FAC := FAC * I;
end loop;
return(FAC);
end FACTORIAL;
```

```
function FIBONACCI(N: NATURAL) return NATURAL is
FIB,UPDATE,TEMP: NATURAL;
 begin
if N = 0 then return(0); endif;
if N = 1 then return(1); endif;
   FIB := 1; UPDATE := 1;
   for I in 3..N loop
      TEMP := FIB;
      FIB := FIB + UPDATE;
      UPDATE := TEMP;
end loop;
   return(FIB);
end FIBONACCI;
```

Recursive implementations of factorial and Fibonacci numbers are inappropriate because there is no inherent need for recursion as there is in tree traversal and other backtracking algorithms. One might argue that the recursive implementation of Fibonacci is easier to understand than the iterative version, and this might be sufficient justification for using a recursive version of an inherently iterative algorithm.

On the other hand, an iterative implementation of an inherently recursive algorithm will result in a user-maintained stack to simulate recursion or clever manipulation of pointers in the data structure to set up backtracking links. This is sometimes less efficient and is always less understandable than a recursive implementation.

We note in passing that some features of the Ada programming language have been used to improve the quality of the factorial function illustrated above. We have assumed that type NATURAL is a user-defined data type whose objects are the nonnegative integers (user-defined data types are discussed in Section 7.3). It is illegal for objects of type NATURAL to take on negative values. The run-time system will check this condition, and it is thus not necessary for the program to check negative values of N on entry to the routine.

Local variable FAC is initialized to 1 in the declaration statement. If the value of N passed in is 0 or 1, control will fall through the for loop, and the proper value (1) will be associated with the function name via the return statement. If N is not 1, FAC is properly initialized for the loop.

On subsequent entries to the routine, FAC will be reinitialized to 1, ensuring correct functioning of the routine. Note that FAC is initialized dynamically at run time, rather than statically at compile time. This is analogous to initializing a variable using an assignment statement in FORTRAN rather than using the DATA statement, which causes static initialization.

6.2 CODING STYLE

Style is the consistent pattern of choices made among alternative ways of achieving a desired effect. A person's "life style" is manifest in one's choice of spouse, friends, clothing, food, automobiles, religious affiliation, and so forth. In computer programming, coding style is manifest in the patterns used by a programmer to express a desired action or outcome. Programmers who work together soon come to recognize the coding styles of their colleagues.

During the past few years, a great deal of attention has been focused on coding style (KER74). It has been recognized that good coding style can overcome many of the deficiencies of a primitive programming language, while poor style can defeat the intent of an excellent language. The goal of good coding style is to provide easily understood, straightforward, elegant code.

There is no single set of rules that can be applied in every situation; however, there are general guidelines that are widely applicable. A number of those guidelines are listed in Tables 6.1 and 6.2, which present dos and don'ts of good coding style. The guidelines are examined in the following discussion.

Use a few standard control constructs. The previous discussion of single entry, single exit constructs indicates that there is no standard set of constructs for structured coding. Nesting of statement sequences, selection among alternatives, and a mechanism for iteration are sufficient. If implementation is to be done in a primitive programming language such as FORTRAN, COBOL, or Basic, structured constructs can be achieved by using conditional and unconditional branching in stylistic patterns to achieve the effects of if_then_else, while_do, repeat_until, case, etc. Preprocessors are sometimes used to translate structured constructs into primitive languages. In assembly language, a macro facility is often used to define templates for structured constructs and to expand structured constructs into stylistic patterns of assembler code.

Table 6.1 Dos of good coding style

Use a few standard, agreed-upon control constructs

Use gotos in a disciplined way

Introduce user-defined data types to model entities in the problem domain

Hide data structures behind access functions

Isolate machine dependencies in a few routines

Provide standard documentation prologues for each subprogram and/or compilation unit

Carefully examine routines having fewer than 5 or more than 25 executable statements

Use indentation, parentheses, black spaces, blank lines and borders around comment blocks to enhance readability

---

If the implementation language does not provide structured coding constructs, a few stylistic patterns should be used by the programmers who implement the system. This will make coding style more uniform among various programmers, with the result that programs will be easier to read, easier to understand, and easier to modify.

Use gotos in a disciplined manner. In primitive programming languages, the goto statement can be used in conjunction with the if statement to achieve the format and effect of structured coding constructs. As illustrated in Section 6.1, the goto statement is also valuable in achieving multiple and premature loop exits, and for transferring control to error handling code. In all these cases, the goto is used in a stylistic, disciplined manner to achieve a desired result. In particular, the acceptable uses of the goto statement are almost always forward transfers of control within a local region of code. Using a goto to achieve backward transfer of control or to perform a forward jump to a remote region of a program is seldom warranted.

The Ada programming language provides numerous structured constructs, exit statements for loop termination, and exception handling mechanisms. These facilities reduce the need for goto statements; however, the goto is provided in Ada and most other modern programming languages. The purpose of the goto statement in modern languages is to permit construction of stylistic patterns that are not provided by the language; the goto statement is not provided to encourage violation of structured coding practices. The goto statement, coupled with the if statement, permits user definition of needed control flow mechanisms in the same way that user-defined data types permit user definition of unavailable data representations. Both goto statements and user-defined data types should be used to further the goals of simplicity, clarity, and elegance of programs.

Introduce user-defined data types to model entities in the problem domain. Ada and other modern programming languages provide user-defined data types. Use of distinct data types makes it possible for humans and computer systems to distinguish between entities from the problem domain. For example, enumeration data types can be used to enumerate the elements of an indexing sequence; subtypes can be used to place constraints on objects of a given type; and derived types permit segregation of objects that have similar representations. Each of these concepts is illustrated here and discussed in detail in Chapter 7. The enumeration type declaration

    type COLOR = (RED,GREEN,YELLOW,BLUE);

permits array indices and loop variables of the form

    for I in GREEN..BLUE loop
     X(I) := 0;
    end loop;
    X(RED) := 0;

Subtypes of the form

    type SMALL_INTEGER is INTEGER (1..10);

place range constraints on objects of type SMALL_INTEGER, and derived types of the form

    type TEMP_IN_DEG_KELVIN is FLOAT;
    type VELOCITY_IN_FPS is FLOAT;

permit differentiation between temperature objects and velocity objects.

In primitive programming languages there are a limited number of predefined data types (logical, integer, real, complex, double precision, and array in FORTRAN IV), and no mechanism for user-defined types. All entities in the problem domain must be mapped into objects of predefined type. Integers are typically used for indexing, and the programmer must maintain a mental correspondence between integer values and index values (e.g., color values). Range constraints must be explicitly tested in the program, or worse, ignored. Different entities in the problem domain are mapped into the same data type in FORTRAN IV. For example, velocity objects and temperature objects both map into objects of type REAL. No protection is provided against inadvertent mixing of velocity objects and temperature objects, or worse, between objects of type velocity_in_feet_per_second and type velocity_in_miles_per_hour. User-defined data types that segment the problem domain in a logical manner can greatly improve the clarity and readability of a source program. Under strong type-checking rules, user-defined data types also provide increased data security.

Programs written in languages that do not support user-defined data types cannot be made as clear or as secure as programs written in a modern language; however, naming conventions for object declarations can be adopted to improve the quality of source code. For example, all velocity objects might use V as the first character of velocity identifiers, and all temperature identifiers might begin with T.

A source code preprocessor could be used to determine adherence to naming conventions.

Hide data structures behind access functions. Isolate machine dependencies in a few routines. These guidelines are manifestations of the principle of information hiding. In a software system designed using information hiding, each module makes visible only those features required by other modules. All other aspects of the modules are hidden from external view. Hiding data structures behind access functions is the approach taken in data encapsulation, wherein a data structure and its access routines are encapsulated in a single module (see Figure 6.9).

In languages having global scope (assembly language, BASIC, COBOL), disciplined programming style can be used to ensure that major data structures are manipulated in only a few regions of the source code. All other code segments that use a data structure should do so by invoking the appropriate access code. This approach improves the modularity of a source program, and new access functions can be provided as needed. Changes in the details of data representation require only local changes to, and only local recompilation of, access code. If the specification part of an access routine is changed, all routines that call the modified access routine must be modified and recompiled, but the modification required is very simple: only the call statements to the access routines, and perhaps the ways in which the calling parameters are used, need be modified. Call statements needing modification can be identified using a call graph listing.

Similar reasoning applies to the isolation of machine dependencies in a few separate routines. If the nature of data representation need be changed, or if the program is moved to a different machine, details of machine dependencies are localized and can be modified accordingly.

Provide standard documentation prologues for each subprogram and/or compilation unit. A documentation prologue contains information about a subprogram or compilation unit that is not obvious from reading the source text of the subprogram or compilation unit. The exact form and content of a prologue depends on the nature of the implementation language. A routine written in Ada is more self descriptive than one written in assembly language, and will require less information in the documentation prologue. For instance, the prologue of an assembly language routine should describe the ways in which various machine registers and parameter areas are used by the routine. In Ada, the use of IN, OUT, and IN OUT parameter modes, when used in conjunction with user-defined data types for formal parameter specification, makes this aspect of Ada routines self- documenting:

procedure CALC(X in VEL_IN_FPS; Y in out TEMP_IN_DEG_KELVIN);

In FORTRAN routines, the documentation prologue should describe the input/output modes and problem domain characteristics of formal parameters. Similarly, exception handling should be documented in the prologues of FOR-

TRAN and assembly language routines; exception-handling code in Ada and PL/1 is largely self-documenting.

Information to be provided through a combination of the documentation prologue and the self-documenting features of the implementation language are listed in Table 6.3 (see Section 6.4.3). Use of a preprogrammed editor can reduce the tedium of providing this information for every routine and/or compilation unit. If, as suggested in Section 5.5, this information is developed in top-down fashion during detailed design, it can be incorporated directly into the implementation of the routine.

Carefully examine routines having fewer than 5 or more than 25 statements. A subprogram consists of a specification part, a documentation prologue, declarations, executable statements, and, in some languages, exception handlers. The executable portion of a subprogram should implement a well-defined function that can be described by a simple sentence having an active verb (see the modularization criteria in Section 5.2). Experience indicates that, in many situations, routines that have 5 to 25 executable statements satisfy these criteria. A subprogram that has more than 25 executable statements probably contains one or more well-defined subfunctions that can be packaged as distinct subprograms and invoked when needed. Also, it has been suggested that 30 executable statements is the upper limit of comprehension for a single reading of a subprogram written in a procedural programming language (WEI71).

A subprogram that has fewer than five statements is usually too small to provide a well-defined function; it is usually preferable to insert five or fewer statements in-line as needed rather than to invoke a subprogram. Efficiency should not be the overriding concern during initial implementation of a system, but linkage overhead is a significant portion of a five statement subprogram, and common sense should prevail in all cases.

Obvious exceptions to these guidelines exist: absolute value and mod routines of fewer than 5 lines can be quite useful, and routines such as optimization algorithms, for example, are often much larger than 25 lines; however, a routine having fewer than 5 or more than 25 executable statements should be closely examined for in-line placement in the calling routines (less than 5 statements), and identification of well-defined subfunctions that can be placed in separate routines and called as needed (more than 25 statements). Often, the well-defined subfunctions that are placed in separate routines provide stand-alone utilities that can be used in other contexts.

Use indentation, parentheses, blank spaces, blank lines, and borders around blocks of comments to enhance readability. As illustrated in Figure 6.12a and b, a pleasing format of presentation greatly enhances the readability of a source program. Formatting of source text can be done manually by the programmer, or by a "pretty print" routine that automatically indents code to emphasize the syn-

```
while B1 loop if B2 then S1; else
for I in 1..N loop COUNT(I) := 0; end loop;
end if; end loop;
```

Figure 6.12a Poor source-code formatting.

```
while B1 loop
  if B2 then S1;
  else
    for I in 1..N loop
      COUNT(I) := 0;
    end loop;
  end if;
end loop;
```

Figure 6.12b Good source-code formatting.

Figure 6.12 Two examples of source-code formatting.

tactic structure of the programming language (MOH78). A formatting routine can also insert blank lines and borders around comment statements. If formatting of source text is done by the programmers, standard conventions should be agreed to and adhered to by all programmers. If formatting is done by a program, all source code should be processed by the formatter before it is retained in a permanent file.

When using primitive programming languages, source text formatting is sometimes accomplished in conjunction with preprocessing or macro expansion of structured coding constructs. Translators for modern programming languages sometimes provide a pretty-print option as part of the parsing operation. If none of these options are available, a special-purpose formatting program can be written. In any case, a source text formatting program is a valuable tool.

Table 6.2 lists several don't guidelines for good coding style.

Don't be too clever. This point is illustrated by the following segment of code written in FORTRAN IV (KER74):

```
        DO 10 I = 1,N
        DO 10 J = 1,N
10  A(I,J) = (I/J)*(J/I)
```

Not only is the code segment obscure, it is also inefficient. Before continuing, pause for a moment to determine what is accomplished by this code segment.

The following code segment achieves the same result in a clearer and more efficient manner.

```
        DO 20 I = 1,N
        DO 10 J = 1,N
        A (I,J) = 0.0
10      CONTINUE
        A (I,I) = 1.0
20      CONTINUE
```

Table 6.2 Don'ts of good coding style

Don't be too clever

Avoid null Then statements

Avoid Then_If statements

Don't nest too deeply

Avoid obscure side effects

Don't suboptimize

Carefully examine routines having more than five formal parameters

Don't use an identifier for multiple purposes

The second version of this algorithm makes obvious the initialization of matrix A using N extra assignment statements (one extra assignment per matrix row). However, the first version requires an integer multiply operation, two integer division operations, and a floating-point conversion for each of the (N squared) elements in the matrix; thus, the second version is not only much clearer but also far more efficient than the first version.

Avoid null then statements. A null then statement is of the form

$$\text{if B then ;}$$
$$\text{else S;}$$

which is equivalent to

$$\text{if (not B) then S;}$$

While one would probably not write a null then in such an obvious manner, the following pattern is sometimes observed in primitive programming languages such as FORTRAN and assembly language:

```
      IF (A.GT.B) GOTO 30
      GOTO 25
30    S
25    CONTINUE
```

Avoid then_if statements. A then_if statement is of the form

```
if (A > B) then
   if (X > Y) then
      A := X;
   else
      A := B;
   end if;
else
   A := B;
end if;
```

Then_if statements tend to obscure the conditions under which various actions are performed. A then_if statement can always be rewritten in the more obvious else_if forms, as in the following Ada segment:

```
if (A  <  B) then
    A := B;
elsif (X > Y) then
    B := Y;
else
    A := X;
end if;
```

Don't nest too deeply. The major advantage of single entry, single exit constructs is the ability to nest constructs within one another to any desired depth while maintaining linearity of control flow. If the nesting becomes too deep, as in

```
while B1 loop
    if B2 then
        repeat S1
            while B3 loop
                if B4 then S2
```

it becomes difficult to determine the conditions under which statement S2 will be executed; the clarity of the code is obscured. Excessive nesting is also an indication of fuzzy thinking and poor design. As a general guideline, nesting of program constructs to depths greater than three or four levels should be avoided. In addition, procedures should only be nested one level deep within one another. Again, we observe that these are only general guidelines and should not be taken as rigid standards.

Avoid obscure side effects. A side effect of a subprogram invocation is any change to the computational state that occurs as a result of calling the invoked routine. Side effects include modification of parameters passed by reference or by value-result, modification of global variables, I/O operations, and other items listed in Section 6.4.3. An obscure side effect is one that is not obvious from the invocation of the called routine. An invocation of the form

```
GET(X);
```

that reads a value from a default input file and stores the value in location X exerts an obvious, self-documenting side effect. If, in addition, the GET routine sorts a file, rewinds a tape, and launches a guided missile, it exerts obscure side effects.

Most programming languages do not provide any special notation to describe the side effects of called routines. In the statement

```
SORT(X,Y,Z);
```

the transmission modes of X, Y, and Z, and the global variables modified by SORT can only be determined by examining the SORT routine. The SIDE_EFFECTS section of the documentation prologue for SORT is thus essential for understanding the effect of a call to SORT(X,Y,Z). For greater ease of understanding, and especially in cases where the source text of SORT is not available, including the SIDE_EFFECTS section of a called routine's documentation prologue in the calling routine's prologue is highly desirable.

Don't suboptimize. Suboptimization occurs when one devotes inordinate effort to refining a situation that has little effect on the overall outcome. There are two aspects to suboptimization of software. First, it is usually not possible to determine what portion of the code will occupy the majority of execution time until execution characteristics of the running program are measured. Second, unless one has intimate knowledge of the language translator, operating system, and hardware, it usually is not clear how various situations will be handled by the system. Thus, the programmer may waste time and effort worrying about situations that are handled in nonintuitive ways by the system, and that have little effect on overall performance. One should, of course, choose the optimal approach when it is obvious. One should not, however, agonize over minor decisions.

Carefully examine routines having more than five formal parameters. Parameters and global variables are the mechanisms used to communicate data values among routines. Parameters bind different arguments to a routine on different invocations of the routine, and global variables communicate arguments whose bindings do not change between calls to the routine. Parameters and global variables should be few in number. Long, involved parameter lists result in excessively complex routines that are difficult to understand and difficult to use; they result from inadequate decomposition of a software system. Global variables should be shared among routines on a selective, as needed basis. The manner in which data are communicated among routines is a major criterion for guiding and assessing the quality of detailed design (see Section 5.5).

Selection of the number five as the suggested upper bound on the number of parameters in a subprogram is not an entirely arbitrary choice. It is well known that human beings can deal with approximately seven items or concepts at one time (MIL56). Ease of understanding a subprogram call, or the body of a subprogram definition, is a sensitive function of the number of parameters and global variables used in the routine, as well as of the purposes for which they are used.

Fewer parameters and fewer global variables improve the clarity and simplicity of subprograms. In this regard, five is a very lenient upper bound. In practice, we prefer no more than three or four formal parameters and the smallest possible number of global variables (none being optimal); however, we recognize that the realities of computer programming often require global variables and several parameters in a routine.

Don't use an identifier for multiple purposes. Programmers sometimes use one identifier to denote several different entities. The rationale is memory efficiency: Three variables will require three or more memory cells, whereas one variable used in three different ways requires only one-third as many memory cells. There are several things wrong with this practice. First, each identifier in a program should be given a descriptive name that suggests its purpose. This is not possible if the identifier is used for multiple purposes. Second, the use of a single identifier for multiple purposes indicates multiple regions of code that have low cohesion (see Section 5.2). Third, using an identifier for multiple purposes is a dangerous practice because it makes the source code very sensitive to future modifications. Finally, use of an identifier for multiple purposes can be extremely confusing to the reader of a program.

The one acceptable exception to this practice occurs in Ada, where loop variables are implicitly declared and have the scope of the loop body. In this situation, no harm comes from using I or J repeatedly as the loop variable in different loops. Because of the scope rules, multiple uses of I are actually uses of distinct memory cells, all named I.

If a system is so tightly constrained in memory space that single identifiers must be used for multiple purposes, the system should be segmented into several smaller routines with an overlay structure. If this violates execution time restrictions, the system should be redesigned.

6.3 STANDARDS AND GUIDELINES

Coding standards are specifications for a preferred coding style. Given a choice of ways to achieve an effect, a preferred way is specified. Coding standards are often viewed by programmers as mechanisms to constrain and devalue the programmer's creative problem solving skills. This argument is usually advanced by programmers who do not understand the spirit or intent of good coding style. Creativity always occurs within a basic framework of standards. Artists follow the basic tenets of structure and composition, poets adhere to the rhyme and meter of language, and musicians use fundamental chord progressions. Without a framework of standards to guide and channel an activity, creativity becomes meaningless chaos.

Thus, it is desirable that all programmers on a software project adopt similar coding styles so that code of uniform quality is produced. This does not mean that all programmers must think alike, or that they must slavishly implement all algorithms in exactly the same manner. Indeed, the individual style of each programmer on a project is identifiable even when rigid adherence to standards of programming style is observed.

We prefer to use the term "programming guidelines" rather than "programming standards."

A programming standard might specify items such as

1. Goto statements will not be used.
2. The nesting depth of program constructs will not exceed five levels.
3. Subroutine length will not exceed 30 lines.

A guideline rephrases these specifications in the following manner:

1. The use of goto statements should be avoided in normal circumstances.
2. The nesting depth of program constructs should be five or less in normal circumstances.
3. The number of executable statements in a subprogram should not exceed 30 in normal circumstances.
4. Departure from normal circumstances requires approval by the project leader.

Some people categorize standards as those features that are machine checkable (backward gotos, proper indentation, size of routines) and guidelines as those aspects that must be verified by human beings (use of meaningful identifier names, adherence to specific modularization criteria, etc.).

Several conditions are necessary to obtain voluntary adherence to programming guidelines, and to ensure that the guidelines are in fact followed. First, programmers must understand the value of programming guidelines. Second, programmers must have the opportunity to participate in establishing the guidelines. Third, the guidelines must be subject to review and revision when they become burdensome. Fourth, there must be a mechanism for allowing violations of the guidelines in special circumstances. Fifth, automated tools must be used to check adherence to the guidelines.

As a general rule, it is not possible to manually inspect code for adherence to programming guidelines. If automated checks are not performed, the guidelines will be worthless. Under the conditions outlined above, programming guidelines can be developed and evolved to enhance the quality of software. With proper tact and diplomacy, programmers will view programming guidelines as positive aspects of the work environment.

6.4 DOCUMENTATION GUIDELINES

Computer software includes the source code for a system and all the supporting documents generated during analysis, design, implementation, testing, and maintenance of the system. Internal documentation includes standard prologues for compilation units and subprograms, the self documenting aspects of the source code, and the internal comments embedded in the source code. Program unit notebooks provide mechanisms for organizing the work activities and documentation efforts of individual programmers. This section describes some aspects of supporting documents, the use of program unit notebooks, and some guidelines for internal documentation of source code.

6.4.1 Supporting Documents

Requirements specifications, design documents, test plans, user's manuals, installation instructions, and maintenance reports are examples of supporting documents. These documents are the products that result from systematic development and maintenance of computer software. Tools, techniques, and notations for generating and maintaining these documents are discussed throughout this text.

A systematic approach to software development assures that supporting documents evolve in an orderly manner, and that the documents are available when needed. In the ad hoc approach to software development, preparation of supporting documents is usually deferred until system implementation is completed. Because of time constraints and lack of motivation, documents generated in this manner are usually inadequate to support testing, training, modification, and maintenance activities.

Supporting documents of substandard quality, that are not available when needed, are a strong indication of problems with the processes being used to develop and maintain software. These documents should evolve as a natural by-product of the development process. Customer needs and constraints are recorded in the requirements specification; the requirements provide the framework for architectural design; detailed design evolves from architectural design; source code is developed from the architectural and detailed designs. Test plans, user's manuals, training programs, installation instructions, and maintenance procedures evolve throughout the development cycle (recall Figure 2.3). The quality, quantity, timeliness, and utility of the supporting documents are primary measures of the health and well being of a software project.

6.4.2 Program Unit Notebooks

A program unit is a unit of source code that is developed and/or maintained by one person; that person is responsible for the unit. In a well-designed system a program unit is a subprogram or group of subprograms that provide a well-defined function or form a well defined subsystem. A program unit is also small enough, and modular enough, that it can be thoroughly tested in isolation by the programmer who develops or modifies it. Program unit notebooks are used by individual programmers to organize their work activities, and to maintain the documentation for their program units.

A program unit notebook (also referred to as a "unit development folder") consists of a cover sheet and several sections. The cover sheet is the table of contents and the sign-off sheet for the various milestones associated with the program unit. Figure 6.13 illustrates the cover sheet of a program unit notebook. Maintaining the notebook is the responsibility of the programmer currently assigned to the program unit. The notebook stays with the program unit throughout the lifetime of the unit, and passes from programmer to programmer as responsibility for the unit shifts.

UNIT NAME: _____ PROGRAMMER: _____
ROUTINES INCLUDED: _____

SECTION	CONTENTS	DUE DATE	COMPLETED DATE	REVIEWER/DATE
1	RQMTS.			
2	ARCH. DESIGN			
3	DETAIL DESIGN			
4	TEST PLAN			
5	SOURCE CODE			
6	TEST RESULTS			
7	CHANGE REQUESTS			
8	NOTES			

RELEASE APPROVAL: _____ DATE: _____

Figure 6.13 Cover sheet for a program unit notebook.

The sections in a program unit notebook correspond to the various phases of the unit's life cycle. The cover sheet is used to record projected and actual milestone dates, and the sign-off by a reviewer indicates satisfactory completion of a life cycle phase. Reviewers are usually team leaders or project managers who have responsibility for the total system or a significant subsystem. The collection of cover sheets for all program units in a system provides a detailed summary of the current status of the project at any given point in time. This serves to improve project visibility and to highlight problem areas.

The requirements section of a program unit notebook contains only the specifications that relate to that particular program unit. Both the initial version, as agreed to by the customer, and copies of subsequent modifications to the requirements are maintained in the notebook.

The architectural and detailed design sections of the notebook contain working papers and the final design specifications. Working papers should be organized to indicate why various alternatives were chosen and others rejected. This information can be valuable to guide subsequent modifications.

The unit test plan contains a description of the approach to be used in unit testing, the testing configuration, the actual test cases, the expected outcomes for each test case, and the unit testing completion criteria. The unit test plan evolves in conjunction with design and implementation of the unit.

The section containing unit source code contains a listing of the current version of the unit and listings of significant previous versions. It is not expected that all syntactic and debugging runs will be retained, but listing of earlier versions that existed prior to significant modifications should be retained, particularly in the maintenance phase of the life cycle.

The test results section contains results from the test runs and an analysis of those results in terms of expected results. Again, not all debugging runs will be retained, but significant test runs (both successful and unsuccessful) should be retained.

Problem reports are filed after the system comes under configuration control. At some point in the life cycle (usually during acceptance testing, or at product release) a system comes under configuration control, and any subsequent changes must be reviewed and approved by a change control board (see Chapter 9). Problem reports are the mechanism typically used to initiate a change. The problem report may describe an error situation or a desired modification. A copy of each problem report and its disposition should be retained in the program unit notebooks of affected program units. Over time, the problem reports will show the history of the units. In some cases, review of the problem reports will reveal recurring problems in certain units or collections of units. It is sometimes advisable to rewrite troublesome units rather than to continue repairing them.

6.4.3 Internal Documentation

Internal documentation consists of a standard prologue for each program unit and compilation unit, the self-documenting aspects of the source code, and the internal comments embedded in the executable portion of the code. A typical format for prologues is illustrated in Table 6.3.

As discussed previously, the syntax of the programming language used to implement the system may incorporate some of the information specified in Table 6.3. In Ada, for instance, each routine must specify the transmission mode for

Table 6.3 Typical format of subprogram and compilation unit prologues

Name of author:
Date of compilation:
Function(s) performed:
Algorithms used:
Author/date/purpose of modifications:
Parameters and modes:
Input assertion:
Output assertion:
Global variables:
Side effects:
Major data structures:
Calling routines:
Called routines:
Timing constraints:
Exception handling:
Assumptions:

Table 6.4 Commenting conventions

1. Minimize the need for embedded comments by using:
   Standard prologues
   Structured programming constructs
   Good coding style
   Descriptive names from the problem domain for user-defined data types, variables, formal
   parameters, enumeration literals, subprograms, files, etc.
   Self-documenting features of the implementation language, such as user-defined exceptions,
   user-defined data types, data encapsulation, etc.
2. Attach comments to blocks of code that:
   Perform major data manipulations
   Simulate structured control constructs using goto statements
   Perform exception handling
3. Use problem domain terminology in the comments.
4. Use blank lines, borders, and indentation to highlight comments.
5. Place comments to the far right to document changes and revisions.
6. Don't use long, involved comments to document obscure, complex code. Rewrite the code.
7. Always be sure that comments and code agree with one another, and with the requirements and
   design specifications.

formal parameters, and user defined data types can be named to denote problem domain attributes of the parameters. In FORTRAN, on the other hand, the mode of parameter transmission is always by reference or value-result, and parameters can be only of predefined types; thus, the problem domain characteristics and the transmission modes of parameters (the modes used in the routine) should be documented in the prologues of FORTRAN routines.

Most programming languages do not require information concerning the transmission mode of actual parameters to be provided in a calling routine. This information should be provided in the prologue of the calling routine, along with a description of nonobvious side effects caused by each called routine.

Because Ada and PL/1 provide self-documenting exception handling mechanisms, the exception handling portion of the prologue in an Ada or PL/1 routine will be more concise than the corresponding information in an assembly language routine. More primitive implementation languages will require more extensive prologues. Standard prologues should be designed for each programming language and for each project in order to accommodate the implementation language and the needs of the project.

In some cases, a compilation unit will correspond to an individual subprogram. In other cases, a compilation unit may contain several routines, or an entire subsystem. When a compilation unit contains several routines, it may be possible to limit the redundancy of information in prologues by factoring out some components of the information in the subprogram prologues and placing them in the compilation unit prologue. For example, in an Ada package, much of the prologue may be common among all subprograms in the package, thus reducing the need to repeat similar information in each subprogram. Again, we emphasize that the exact format and content of prologues must be specified for each implementation language and each project. When software design and implementation proceed in top-down fashion, most of the information in the prologues will be specified before implementation begins.

Use of standard prologues, structured programming constructs, good coding style, and meaningful (problem domain) identifier names to denote user-defined data types, variables, enumeration literals, parameters, and subprograms can vastly improve the readability of source code and minimize the need for internal comments in the executable portion of a subprogram. Some basic guidelines for internal commenting are presented in Table 6.4.

6.5 SUMMARY

A primary goal of software implementation is production of source code that is easy to read and understand. Clarity of source code eases debugging, testing, and modification, and these activities consume a large portion of most software budgets.

In this chapter, structured coding techniques, coding style, standards and guidelines, program unit notebooks, and internal documentation of source code have been discussed. The essential aspect of structured coding is linearity of control flow. Linearity is assured by use of single entry, single exit program constructs, but practical considerations such as premature loop exits, exception handling, and data encapsulation often require departure from single entry, single exit. Several examples were presented to illustrate "structured" violations of single entry, single exit that maintain locality of control flow. The proper role of recursion in structured programming was also discussed.

Coding style is manifest in the patterns of choices made among alternative ways of expressing an algorithm. Consistent coding style among different programmers enhances project communication and eases debugging, testing, and modification of the source code. Several guidelines for good coding style were presented, and references for further study were provided. Dos and don'ts of good coding style were illustrated by examples.

Standards and guidelines were discussed, and several conditions were stated to assure adherence to programming guidelines. Under the proper conditions, most programmers will view standards and guidelines as positive aspects of the work environment.

The desirability of developing supporting documents such as requirements specifications, design documentation, test plans, and user's manuals in parallel with product evolution was discussed. Supporting documents of substandard quality that are not available when needed are a strong indication of problems in the software development process. The quality, quantity, timeliness, and utility of supporting documents are primary indicators of the health and well-being of a software project.

Program unit notebooks are used to organize work activities and to maintain documents and documentation for individual program units. A program unit is a unit of source code that is developed or maintained by an individual programmer. The notebook stays with the program unit throughout its lifetime as it passes from programmer to programmer. The format and content of program unit notebooks and the role played by program unit notebooks in software development and maintenance were discussed.

Internal documentation of source code consists of the self-documenting aspects of the implementation language, a standard prologue for each subprogram and compilation unit, and the internal comments embedded in the executable portions of the source code. Information to be provided by the prologue and the self documenting aspects of the implementation language was illustrated, and guidelines for embedded comments were presented.

Most of the difficulties encountered in implementing a software product are due to inadequate analysis and design. A systematic approach to software development eases the implementation task and allows programmers to concentrate on improving the clarity, simplicity, and elegance of their programs. Such programs are easier to debug, test, and modify than are the complex and obscure programs that result from using ad hoc programming techniques.

REFERENCES

(BOH66) Bohm, C., and G. Jacopini: "Flow Diagrams, Turing Machines, and Languages with only Two Formation Rules," *Comm. ACM,* vol. 9, no. 5, May 1966.

(KER74) Kernighan, B., and P. Plauger: *The Elements of Programming Style,* McGraw-Hill, New York, 1974.

(KER76) Kernighan, B., and P. Plauger: *Software Tools,* Addison- Wesley, Reading, Mass., 1976.

(MIL56) Miller, G.: "The Magic Number Seven, Plus or Minus Two: Some Limits on Our Capability for Processing Information," *Psych. Review,* March 1956.

(MOH78) Mohilner, P.: "Prettyprinting Pascal Programs," *SIGPLAN NOTICES,* vol. 13, no. 7, July 1978.

(WEI71) Weinberg, G.: *The Psychology of Computer Programming,* Van Nostrand Reinhold, New York, 1971.

(WIR74) Wirth, N., and K. Jensen: *Pascal User Manual and Report,* Springer-Verlag, Berlin, 1974.

EXERCISES

6.1 Describe the relationship between structured coding and systematic design. In what ways do systematic design and structured coding reinforce one another?

6.2 (*a*) Give reasons to justify restricting the size of subprograms to between 5 and 25 executable statements.

(*b*) Give reasons to justify subprograms of less than 5 statements and subprograms of more than 25 statements.

6.3 Design and run an experiment to determine the execution time overhead for subprogram calls in your favorite programming language.

(*a*) Does the overhead vary with the number, types, or modes of the parameters?

(*b*) Does the overhead vary between sequential and recursive calls?

(*c*) Describe situations where the overhead of subprogram calls is an important factor in program quality.

6.4 (*a*) Give some reasons for using global variables rather than parameters.

(*b*) Describe several potential problems created by use of global variables.

(*c*) In what situations would you definitely not use globals?

6.5 The following example illustrates a routine with side effects:

```
procedure MAIN is
  G: INTEGER := 1;
  function SENSITIVE(X: INTEGER) return INTEGER is
  begin
    SENSITIVE := X + G;
      G := G + 1;
    return;
  end SENSITIVE;
  -- body of MAIN
  WRITE(SENSITIVE(0));
  WRITE(SENSITIVE(0));
  WRITE(SENSITIVE(0));
  end MAIN;
```

(*a*) What sequence of values is printed by the three calls to SENSITIVE?

(*b*) How does the test (G = SENSITIVE(G)) differ from   (SENSITIVE(G) = G)?

(*c*) What other difficulties might be created by side effects such as these?

(*d*) Describe some situations where use of side effects such as those exhibited by this routine might be justified.

6.6 (*a*) Describe several possible programming tricks in your favorite programming language. (A programming trick is a programming technique that produces nonobvious results. See Exercise 6.5 for an example.)

(*b*) In what circumstances are your programming tricks justified?

(*c*) Suggest alternative, straightforward ways of achieving the same effects.

(*d*) Describe effective techniques for documenting the programming tricks described in part a.

6.7 Flag variables are used to communicate processing conditions from one routine to another. For example, a SQRT routine might have a boolean parameter to indicate correct/incorrect operation:

procedure SQRT(X: in float, Y: out float, OK: in out BOOLEAN) is separate;

SQRT might be called as follows:

```
SQRT(A,C,B);
if B then WRITELN('the SQRT of',A,' is',C);
else WRITELN('failure of SQRT for argument',A);
```

(*a*) Explain the problems created by using flags.

(*b*) One technique for eliminating flag variables is to pass an error-handling routine as a parameter. How do the techniques of flags and error-handling routines differ?

(*c*) Describe some other techniques for error handling. What are the trade-offs between the techniques? Which techniques result in programs that are easy to understand and modify?

6.8 Which statement is easier to read:

$$A := (B*C) + (((3**D)/(-3))*X) + (Y*4);$$

or

$$A := B*C-3**D/3*X + Y*4;$$

Suppose you are developing a programming style guideline for your organization. How many operators should be allowed in an expression? How many levels of nested parentheses should be allowed in an expression?

6.9 (*a*) Develop a set of guidelines for insertion of error checking code in a computer program (checks for validity of input data, potential overflow, etc.).

(*b*) How extensive should error checking be?

(*c*) Discuss trade-offs between error checking and execution time/memory space overhead. How can the overhead be reduced or eliminated?

6.10 Suppose you have developed a routine to solve quadratic equations. You are going to place the routine in a library for use by other programmers.

(*a*) Write the documentation prologue for the routine.

(*b*) Write the external user documentation.

(*c*) What error-checking code will you add to the routine?

(*d*) How will you communicate errors to the calling routines?

(*e*) How will various solutions be communicated to the calling routine (real roots, complex roots, linear form, etc.)?

CHAPTER SEVEN

MODERN PROGRAMMING LANGUAGE FEATURES

INTRODUCTION

Programming languages are the notational mechanisms used to implement software products. Features available in the implementation language exert a strong influence on the architectural structure and algorithmic details of software. A Lisp-based software product will naturally be designed and implemented using list data structures and recursive functions, while a FORTRAN-based product will use arrays, iteration, COMMON blocks, and subroutines.

Modern programming languages provide a variety of features to support development and maintenance of software products. These features include strong type checking, separate compilation, user-defined data types, data encapsulation, data abstraction, generics, flexible scope rules, user-defined exception handling, and concurrency mechanisms. This chapter discusses these concepts, using features of FORTRAN, Pascal, Ada, and PL/1 for purposes of illustration.

Pascal was the first modern programming language; however it does not support all the mechanisms itemized above. Pascal, developed around 1970 by Niklaus Wirth, is a descendant of Algol60 (NAU63, WIR74). The two primary design goals for Pascal were that it be a suitable tool for teaching structured programming, and that it be easily and efficiently implementable on a variety of machine architectures. Major features of Pascal include structured constructs for specifying the execution sequence of a program, the data structuring facilities, and the type checking rules.

Pascal (as originally defined) has many deficiencies as a programming language for implementing software products. For instance, static data areas are not provided, variable dimensioning of arrays is not allowed, there is no provision for separate compilation of modules, there is no exception handling mechanism, the case statement does not provide an "otherwise" clause, and the string handling and

I/O facilities are weak. In addition, there are loopholes in the type checking rules. Various implementations of Pascal provide additional features to overcome some of the deficiencies, and an international standard for Pascal has been proposed. However, standard Pascal does not overcome all the deficiencies mentioned above (ADD80).

Some criticism of Pascal is warranted, but much is misdirected. In general, it is unfair to criticize a programming language for shortcomings in areas not addressed in the stated goals of the language designer. Pascal was not designed to support production and maintenance of large-scale software systems; it was designed to be a pedagogical tool. In spite of its deficiencies for software products, Pascal is used in a wide variety of applications and has spawned numerous research activities during the past decade. The widespread interest in Pascal is evidence of the gross inadequacy of earlier programming notations.

The Ada programming language is a recent descendant of Pascal. Ada incorporates many concepts from Pascal and other modern languages, such as Euclid, Lis, Mesa, Modula, Sue, Algol 68, Simula, Alphard, and Clu. Following an intensive design competition sponsored by the U.S. Department of Defense, the Green language, developed by J. Ichbiah and colleagues of the CII-Honeywell-Bull group in France, was selected to be the Ada programming language (ADA83). Ada is named for Lady Ada Lovelace, who was an associate of Charles Babbage during the 1800s. She is widely acknowledged to have been the world's first computer programmer.

The Ada* language was developed under sponsorship of the U.S. Department of Defense to support development of software for "embedded" computer systems. An embedded computer system is a component of a larger system and provides computation, communication, and control functions for that system. Embedded systems are often implemented using microprocessors and often incorporate concurrency and interrupt-driven real-time processing.

Ada not only incorporates special features for embedded systems (external interrupt handling, access to data representation details, low-level I/O), but also provides many advanced features to support programming in a wide variety of applications. Features such as data encapsulation, exception handling, and a concurrency mechanism make Ada a language of interest to a much wider community than the embedded systems area for which it was developed.

Ada has been criticized for being too large and too complex, and has been described as the predictable result of design by committee. On the other hand, the application area for which Ada was designed is the realm of large, complex, real-time systems. Perhaps a complex language is required for this complex application. Critics of Ada have the responsibility to study the characteristics of the intended application area and propose alternatives that account for those characteristics. In this manner, the technology of software engineering will evolve.

In any case, our purpose is neither to defend nor to praise Ada. The purpose of this chapter is to discuss and illustrate various modern language features that can

---

* Ada is a registered trademark of the U.S. Government, Ada Joint Program Office.

be used to improve software quality and increase programmer productivity. The features described here are useful as isolated concepts, but they become truly impressive in combination with one another. For example, strong type checking improves the quality of a program by catching errors in the declaration and use of data entities through a combination of compile time, load time, and execution time checks. However, many programmers feel that the rules of data usage under strong type checking inhibit the flexibility that is possible in languages without strong type checking (e.g., PL/1). In Ada and other modern programming languages, mechanisms such as explicit type conversion, subprogram overloading, operator overloading, user-defined data types, data abstraction, generic routines, and flexible scope rules provide the required programming flexibility within the framework of strong type checking. Thus, security and flexibility are both provided.

Major advances in the technology of software engineering will occur when notations and tools become available to support development and maintenance of reusable, "off the shelf" software components. Software engineering will remain a craft, and will not become a true technological discipline, until we are able to develop modular, building-block software. Modern programming languages such as Ada have the goal of providing the necessary tools for development of reusable software components through features such as those discussed in this chapter.

Type checking rules, separate compilation, user-defined data types, data abstraction, generics, scope rules, exception handling, and concurrency mechanisms are discussed in the following sections.

7.1 TYPE CHECKING

A data type specifies a set of data objects and a set of permitted operations on objects of that type. Thus, objects of type "integer" comprise an implementation-dependent range of integer values and a set of relational and arithmetic operators on literals and variables of integer type.

The purpose of data typing is to permit classification of objects according to intended usage, to allow the language translator to select storage representations for objects of different types, and, in the case of strongly typed languages, to detect and prevent operations among objects of different types.

Type checking refers to the restrictions and limitations imposed on the ways in which data items can be manipulated by the program. Different languages impose different restrictions, reflecting the differing philosophies of various language designers. At least five levels of type checking can be distinguished:

> Level 0: Typeless
> Level 1: Automatic Type Coercion
> Level 2: Mixed Mode
> Level 3: Pseudo-Strong Type Checking
> Level 4: Strong Type Checking

Each level is discussed in turn.

7.1.1 Typeless Languages

Some programming languages (BASIC, COBOL, APL, Lisp, Snobol) have no declaration statements. In BASIC, all data are stored in numeric format and relational and arithmetic operators are defined for numbers; there is no distinction between integers and reals as in FORTRAN. COBOL stores data in character and packed decimal formats. Numeric computations are performed using packed decimal arithmetic. Conversions between character and packed decimal representations are performed as necessary. The fundamental data structure in APL is the one-dimensional vector array. Array elements can be numbers, characters, and other arrays. The Lisp data structure is the linked list. In pure Lisp, list components (atoms) are numbers and letters. Character strings and patterns are the fundamental data types in Snobol. Numeric operations require conversion between data representations. Typeless languages are tailored to specific application areas and are usually of limited utility in other applications. For example, pure Lisp is not suited to numeric applications, nor is BASIC suitable for list processing.

7.1.2 Automatic Type Coercion

Automatic type coercion is utilized in the PL/1 programming language. PL/1 provides a variety of data types; the programmer declares the desired attributes of data objects, and the compiler chooses a representation that best matches those attributes. The approach to type checking in PL/1 is to automatically convert operands of incompatible type, thus allowing most operations to occur between operands of most different types. For example, in some PL/1 implementations, logical data objects have the numeric equivalents of zero for true and one for false (other implementations adopt the opposite convention). Thus a statement of the form

$$\text{if B then X = C; else X = D;}$$

can be written as

$$X = (1\text{-}B)*C + B*D;$$

In this example, a true value of B (numeric zero) implies $X = C$ and, if B is false (numeric one), $X = D$. The concatenation operator in some PL/1 implementations is "|". Given two integer variables Y and Z, an assignment of the form

$$X = Y \mid Z;$$

will result in conversion of Y and Z to character string format, concatenation of the character string representations of Y and Z, and conversion of the resulting character string to the type of X. If X, Y, and Z are integer variables, and $Y = 52$, $Z = 37$, the result of $X = Y$; might be $X = 5237$. (To determine the exact result, one would have to account for leading blanks in the character string representations of Y and Z, and the conversion of those blanks into zeros. Thus, the actual result is dependent on the exact type attributes of Y and Z.) For $Y = 52$ and $Z = -37$, an illegal conversion error will be raised when conversion of the character string

"52-37" to integer format is attempted. The PL/1 programmers' guide provides tables that specify the various conversions among data types for various operators. In general, the type conversions of PL/1 are quite complex.

Automatic type coercion provides maximum flexibility for the programmer, and maximum surprise when a programming error is made. There is no security of data manipulation. Errors in data typing and errors in operations among items of differing data types (such as $X = Y \mid Z$ for integers X, Y, and Z when $X = Y + Z$ was intended) are often difficult to locate when using a language that provides automatic type coercion.

7.1.3 Mixed Mode

FORTRAN permits mixed-mode operations between similar data types. Conversion is handled automatically by the language translator. The difference between automatic type coercion and mixed mode conversion is a matter of degree and not of kind. The conversions allowed in FORTRAN seldom result in surprising and unpredictable results, as in PL/1. In FORTRAN, an assignment statement of the form

$$I = J + X$$

where I and J are integers and X is real, will result in two conversions. J will be converted to real format, and floating-point addition will be performed between J and X. The result will then be converted to integer format for assignment to I. Similarly, a statement of the form

$$R = X + S$$

where R and S are complex and X is real will result in conversion of X to a complex representation with 0.0 as the imaginary part. The philosophy in FORTRAN is to convert the number of lesser precision to the representation of higher precision in mixed-mode calculations. Dissimilar data items cannot be mixed in FORTRAN. The statement

$$I = L + J$$

where I and J are integers and L is of logical type is not permitted in FORTRAN (but it is permitted in Pl/1). Major errors in data usage within expressions are thus detected in FORTRAN.

The major weakness of FORTRAN type checking is the lack of checking of the interfaces between program units (subprogram interfaces are not checked in PL/1 either). In FORTRAN, a program unit is a main program, a subprogram, a function subprogram, or a COMMON block. Each program unit is compiled independent of other program units. An external reference table is associated with each compiled program unit. These tables are used by the loader to link together the various units of the program, which include user-supplied units, library units, and run-time support units. However, no information is passed to the loader to permit checking of agreement in number and types of parameters between a calling unit and a called unit, or to check correct alignment of different instances of a COMMON block. These interface errors are among the most subtle and difficult to locate in an evolving software product.

7.1.4 Strong Type Checking

In a strongly typed programming language, operations are permitted only between objects of equivalent type. Enforcement of strong type checking requires a rule for determining equivalence of types. Type checking is accomplished using compile time checks on the operators and operands, and load time checks on the interfaces between compilation units. Run-time checks may be required to verify dynamic properties such as subrange constraints, proper use of variant records, and proper bounds on array subscripts.

Rules for determining type equivalence can be classified as name equivalence rules and structural equivalence rules. Under name equivalence, each type definition introduces a distinct type. Strong type checking under name equivalence prohibits operations between objects of identical structure, but distinct type names. In the following example, variables A and B are of different types, while C and D may be of the same type (but different from both A and B) under name equivalence:

A: array (1..10) of integer;
B: array (1..10) of integer;
C,D: array (1..10) of integer;

Operations between variables A and B (or A and C, A and D, B and C, B and D) are forbidden under name equivalence, while operations between C and D may or may not be allowed, depending on the language. In Ada, C and D are of differing types in the example above. The example illustrates anonymous type definition; the type definitions have no names, but are incorporated directly into the declarations of variables. In most cases, types are defined and given names in separate type declarations. Objects are then declared by type name, as in

type INT_ARRAY is array (1..10) of integer;
E,F: INT_ARRAY;

Thus, the term "name equivalence": Two objects are of the same type if they have the same type name. In Ada, E and F are of the same type.

Structural equivalence requires that equivalent types have identical structural properties. In the previous example, variables A, B, C, and D are of equivalent type under structural equivalence, and operations among them are allowed. For composite types (records, arrays, files), several different structural equivalencing rules can be envisioned. For example, two composite types might be structurally equivalent if they have the same number of components and the components differ only in name but have the same type names on a pairwise basis; or two composite types might be structurally equivalent if they have the same number of components and the components have different type names but the component types are structurally equivalent on a pairwise basis.

There are two problems with structural type equivalence. First, establishing structural equivalence of composite types can be a tedious, time consuming task for the human reader and for the language translator. Second, structural equivalence may accidentally permit undesired interactions among objects that happen to be structurally equivalent, but which denote different concepts in the problem domain. Figure 7.1 illustrates two records of identical structure but of vastly different meaning; structural equivalence would permit (incorrect) combination of employee data and automobile data, while name equivalence would prevent it.

In Ada, type declarations can be checked statically; however, subtypes are used to specify dynamic properties such as subranges of integers, record variants, and array bounds. Ada subtype properties must be checked at run time. Thus, Ada is strongly typed, and careful distinction is made between static properties and dynamic properties of the data types.

Ada utilizes name equivalence; every type definition introduces a distinct type. Given the strict rules of type compatibility under name equivalence, the realities of computer programming require that explicit mechanisms be provided to allow the necessary flexibility in operations between objects of differing types. In Ada, these mechanisms include explicit type conversion, subprogram overloading, operator overloading, and unchecked conversions. Explicit type conversion and unchecked conversions are discussed in conjunction with derived types. Subprogram overloading and operator overloading are described in the following discussion.

The need for subprogram overloading in a strongly typed language is motivated by the following considerations: Strong type checking requires that actual parameters in a subprogram call and formal parameters in a subprogram definition agree in type and number. I/O routines, such as GET and PUT, which are called with differing types of arguments, or math library functions such as MAX, which returns the largest of a varying number of numeric arguments, or, in general, any routine that accepts differing numbers and/or types of parameters would appear to be illegal in a strongly typed language. Subprogram overloading provides the needed capability.

Using subprogram overloading, several different routines having the same name, but differing in the ordering, number, and/or types of parameters (and the result type for a function) can be written. Calls to routines with the same name are resolved by the characteristics of the parameters and the returned value. Thus, a set of overloaded I/O routines might permit the following calls:

```
type EMPLOYEE is
record
  SENIORITY: INTEGER;
  SALARY:  REAL;
end record;

type AUTOMOBILE is
record
  YEAR:  INTEGER;
  MILES: REAL;
end record;
```

Figure 7.1 Two records of similar structure but different meaning.

PUT (28):   – – Integer Parameter
PUT (13.5):   – – Real Parameter
PUT ("No Ambiguity Here"):   – – String Parameter

Several different PUT routines can be provided, and the appropriate one invoked on the basis of parameter type. In Ada, both system-defined and user-defined routines can be overloaded.

Operator overloading, like subprogram overloading, permits association of different meanings with a symbol; the meaning of an operator is determined by the number and types of operands. In this manner, the " + " operator is used to denote several different operations:

+ 3   – – Unary +
3 + 4   – – Integer Add
3.5 + 4.2   – – Floating Point Add

In a strongly typed language, strict rules are enforced on legal combinations of operators and operands. For example, suppose Ada did not allow predefined mixed-mode arithmetic. Neither (3.5 + 4) nor (4 + 3.5) would be permitted. This restriction can be overridden by user-defined overloading of the " + " operator as illustrated in Figure 7.2.

In Ada, the following operators can be overloaded by user definition: logical operators, relational operators, unary operators (+ , -), adding operators (+ , -), multiplying operators (*, /), and exponentiation. Overloading of relational operators does not affect basic comparisons in the language, such as testing for membership in a range or evaluation of branching conditions in an if statement or a while loop. The equality operator can be overloaded, but only under extremely restricted conditions.

It should be observed that operator overloading is not the same as PL/1 type coercion. In PL/1, type coercion is automatically accomplished according to obscure and complex rules in the compiler. In Ada, the programmer explicitly defines the effects of operator overloading. This allows explicit programmer control over the diversity and complexity of operator meaning. Nevertheless, operator overloading, like many features available in modern programming languages, should be used with restraint and caution. In the extreme case, operator overloading definitions rivaling the complexity of PL/1 conversion rules could be predefined and stored in a library. This could produce unintended results from erroneous intermixing of operands of differing types.

```
function " + " (X: INTEGER; Y: REAL) return REAL;
begin
  return(REAL(X) + Y);
end " + ";

function " + " (X: REAL; Y: INTEGER) return REAL;
begin
  return(X + REAL(Y));
end " + ";
```

Figure 7.2 Overloading of " + " to permit mixed-mode arithmetic.

It is also possible to overload subprogram names and operators to yield non-intuitive results. GET might be defined to do an output operation on character strings, and " + " to do addition of integers, but multiplication of reals. To quote the designers of Ada:

> We believe that the language designer should not forbid an otherwise useful facility, on the grounds that it could be misused in isolated cases. (ICH79)

7.1.5 Pseudo-Strong Type Checking

Strong type checking allows operations only between data objects of equivalent type. Pseudo-strong type checking is strong type checking with loopholes. Pascal exemplifies pseudo-strong type checking; although type checking is strong in principle, there are significant loopholes in the Pascal type checking mechanisms.

Pascal, as originally defined, exhibits type-checking loopholes at translation time, at load time, and at execution time. Type checking of the parameters of functions and procedures passed as parameters to other functions and procedures could be checked at translation time, but Pascal does not require that these parameters be specified. Thus, correctness of procedure parameters cannot be checked. Pascal does not define a separate compilation mechanism. However, many implementations of Pascal provide independent compilation in the mold of FORTRAN; there is no checking at load time for agreement in the types and numbers of parameters to independently compiled routines. At run time, a variant record can dynamically acquire different variants at different points in the program. Most Pascal implementations do not provide run-time checks to ensure that the proper variant is in effect in various regions of a program.

7.2 SEPARATE COMPILATION

The ability to develop modules and subsystems, to compile and store them in libraries, and to have the loader automatically retrieve library units and link them into the object code of a system provides a powerful abstraction mechanism. Precompiled modules can be used as functional components of a system, and separate compilation allows different programmers to simultaneously develop or modify different modules in a system.

The designers of FORTRAN recognized the importance of independent compilation as early as the 1950s. The major weaknesses of independent compilation in FORTRAN IV are the failure to check alignment of variables in COMMON blocks, and failure to check agreement between the number and types of parameters in subprogram calls and subprogram definitions.

Ada supports the concept of separate compilation. Under separate compilation, type checking across the boundaries of separate compilation units must be as secure as type checking within a compilation unit. To accomplish separate compilation, Ada translators produce tables of external reference information for each compilation unit. Using these tables, the loader checks the correctness of interfaces between load modules. In this manner, the benefits of independent compilation are obtained, and the integrity of the interfaces between compilation units is ensured. The tables passed to the loader also provide the capability to incrementally recompile program modules affected by a change in another module. Thus, only a few routines in a large system might be recompiled as a result of a modification to the specification part of a given routine.

7.3 USER-DEFINED DATA TYPES

The set of data types provided by a programming language largely determines the applications for which the language is suited. FORTRAN IV provides integer, real, logical, complex, double-precision, Hollerith, and array types, while pure Lisp provides lists of atoms (letters and numbers), and Snobol provides character strings and patterns.

Modern programming languages (Pascal and its descendants) provide a variety of predefined data types, including integer, floating-point, boolean, character, string, pointer, record, array, and file. Not all languages provide all types. Instead, a few types may be predefined and mechanisms provided so that the user can define other types in terms of existing types. For instance, character strings might be defined by the user as variable-length arrays of characters.

There are two fundamental reasons for providing user-defined data types: to allow specification of often-needed types in terms of existing types (e.g., character strings as variable-length arrays of characters); and to allow mapping of concepts from the problem domain into the implementation language. In FORTRAN, for example, objects denoting temperature in Kelvin degrees and objects denoting velocity in feet per second are both encoded as objects of type REAL. Erroneous operations between temperature objects and velocity objects will be allowed by the FORTRAN system.

In languages that provide user-defined data types, objects that have different problem domain characteristics and identical representations can be declared to be different types. User-defined data types thus can be used to segment and model the problem domain. This can vastly improve the clarity and security of a computer program. Improved clarity and security ease the tasks of debugging, testing, documenting, and modifying a program. Proper utilization of user-defined data types is a strong indication of good program quality.

Erroneous operations among objects of differing user-defined types are prohibited due to strong typing constraints. Mechanisms such as explicit type conversion, subprogram overloading, and operator overloading permit operations among objects of different types; however, the programmer must explicitly define these operations in order to achieve the desired result. Subprogram and operator overloading facilities allow the programmer to define new operations on user-defined data types.

Ada provides several mechanisms that allow the programmer to define new data types. They include subtypes, derived types, enumeration types, record types, access types, data abstractions, and generic types.

7.3.1 Subtypes

A subtype places constraints on the set of possible values for an object of a given type, but does not change the set of permitted operations. In Ada there are four kinds of subtype constraints: range constraints, index constraints, accuracy constraints, and discriminant constraints. A subtype with range constraints inherits the set of operations of the parent type, but the allowed set of values is restricted to a subset of the parent values. In this manner, a small integer might be restricted to values in the range of 1 to 10:

subtype SMALL_INTEGER is integer (1..10);

and type LETTER might be a subset of the characters:

subtype LETTER is char (A..Z);

Index constraints are used to specify the ranges of array indices. Accuracy constraints are used to specify the precision of fixed-point and floating-point data objects, and discriminant constraints are used to specify allowable discriminant values for record objects. In Ada, a subtype declaration does not introduce a new type. Thus, operations between objects of parent type and a subtype are permitted as long as the resulting values satisfy the appropriate constraints. Run-time checks are required to determine that objects satisfy their subtype constraints, and violation of a constraint raises the CONSTRAINT_ERROR exception condition.

7.3.2 Derived Types

A derived-type facility can be used to declare new types for distinct objects in the problem domain that have similar representations in the solution domain. A derived type is a distinct type with all the characteristics of the base type, but intermixing of user-defined objects with objects of the base type and other distinct user-defined objects is prevented by the name equivalence type-checking rule. In the following example:

```
type ACCEL_IN_FPS is new float;
type POSITIVE_VELOCITY is new float (0.0..float'last);
```

Objects of type ACCEL_IN_FPS have all the characteristics (permitted values, operators, constants) of the predefined floating-point objects, while objects of type POSITIVE_VELOCITY have all the characteristics of type float, but the values are restricted to nonnegative floating-point numbers. The notation float'last denotes the largest positive floating-point number available in the local implementation.

Objects of type float, ACCEL_IN_FPS, and POSITIVE_VELOCITY cannot be combined under the name equivalence rule unless explicit type conversion or unchecked conversion is used. Explicit type conversion of objects can be accomplished as follows:

```
X: ACCEL_IN_FPS;
Y: POS_VELOCITY;
: : :
X := 32.2 * ACCEL_IN_FPS(Y);
Y := POSITIVE_VELOCITY(X)/32.2;
```

Note that the constant, 32.2, the multiplication operator, *, and the division operator, /, are inherited from the floating-point parent type.

In the Ada language, there are some restrictions on the use of explicit type conversion to ensure that the internal representation remains valid for converted objects. Conversion among objects of arbitrarily differing types can be accomplished using unchecked type conversion. An unchecked type conversion is achieved by using the built-in function UNCHECKED_CONVERSION. In the example:

```
B := UNCHECKED_CONVERSION(A);
```

the bit pattern defining source object A becomes the value of target object B. It is the programmer's responsibility to assure that unchecked conversions maintain the properties of objects of the target type. Programs that violate these properties by means of unchecked conversions are erroneous.

7.3.3 Enumeration Types

An enumeration type is defined by listing (enumerating) the set of values for objects of that type, as in

```
type COLOR is (RED,GREEN,BLUE,YELLOW);
```

or

```
type VOWEL is ('A', 'E', 'I', 'O', 'U');
```

Enumerated values are denoted by identifiers and character literals. They have the ordering relation specified in the enumeration; the position number of the first listed value is zero, and each successive value has a position number one greater than that of its predecessor.

In Ada, enumeration types and integer types, as well as subtypes and derived types of enumeration types and integer types, are referred to as discrete types. Objects of discrete type can be used for indexing and iteration, as in

```
COUNT: array (COLOR) of INTEGER;
   HUE: COLOR;
COUNT(RED) := 3;
for HUE in GREEN..YELLOW loop
  COUNT(HUE) := 0;
end loop;
HUE := GREEN;
```

As illustrated in the example (HUE := GREEN;), enumeration literals can be assigned to variables of the corresponding type. Internally, the language translator

```
type EMPLOYEE is
   record
                NAME: STRING(1..60);
             E_NUMBER: integer range 111111..999999;
          DEPARTMENT: integer range 01..87;
            JOB_TITLE: STRING(1..20);
      HOURLY_WAGES: float range 3.50..25.00;
         BIRTH_DATE: record
                   DAY: integer range 1..31;
                MONTH: (JAN,FEB,MAR,APR,MAY,JUN,JUL,AUG,SEP,
                           OCT,NOV,DEC);
                  YEAR: integer range 1900..1970;
            end record;
                  SEX: (MALE,FEMALE);
end record;
```

Figure 7.3 Ada type definition for personnel data records.

maps enumerated literals onto position numbers 0 through (N - 1), where N is the number of literals in the type definition. This permits relational and membership operators on objects of enumerated type, in addition to indexing and iteration. Input and output of enumeration literals is allowed in Ada, but not in Pascal.

In older programming languages, programmers are forced to use integers for indexing and to maintain a correspondence in their minds between integer indices and concepts in the problem domain. The use of enumerated types to model the problem domain greatly enhances program clarity. Strong type checking guards against accidental confusion of concepts.

7.3.4 Record Types

A record is a composite data object. The components of a record are named and can be of different types. Records can thus be tailored to the needs of a particular application. Figure 7.3 illustrates a type definition for personnel records, expressed in Ada. A set of record objects might be the components of a file or an array, so that the set of all personnel records can be referred to and manipulated as a single entity.

In most modern programming languages, records can be further tailored by use of discriminants and variants. Discriminants can be used to parameterize a record type, as in the following example:

```
type BUFFER (SIZE: INTEGER range 1..1024) is
record
    KEY: integer range 1..4096;
    VALUE: STRING (1..SIZE);
end record;
```

Declaration of objects of type BUFFER must include a value for the SIZE discriminant, as in

LINE: BUFFER(81);
MESSAGE: BUFFER(512);

The first of these declarations results in a record named BUFFER that has a VALUE field containing a string of 1 to 81 characters. Similarly, the second declaration produces an entity called MESSAGE having a VALUE field of 1 to 512 characters.

A record type can have a variant part, which specifies alternative lists of components, depending on the corresponding value of the associated discriminant. The following example illustrates the use of variant record types:

```
type DEVICE is (PRINTER, DISK, DRUM);
type STATE is (OPEN, CLOSED);
type PERIPHERAL(UNIT: DEVICE) is
record
  STATUS: STATE;
    case UNIT is
      when PRINTER =>
        LINE_COUNT: integer range 1..PAGE_SIZE;
      when OTHERS =>
    CYLINDER: CYLINDER_INDEX
      TRACK: TRACK_NUMBER;
    end case;
end record;
```

In this example, field STATUS can take on the values OPEN and CLOSED, and DEVICE can have the values PRINTER, DISK, and DRUM. Subtypes and variables of type PERIPHERAL can be declared as follows:

subtype DISK_UNIT is PERIPHERAL(DISK);

or

WRITER: PERIPHERAL(PRINTER);

In the example, the "when OTHERS" clause denotes all values of the discriminant type that are not specified in other choices (i.e., DISK and DRUM). Thus, the subtype declaration for the DISK_UNIT will have STATUS, CYLINDER, and TRACK fields, and WRITER will be an entity having STATUS and LINE_COUNT fields.

7.3.5 Pointer Types

Pointers are objects that provide access to other objects. Objects designated by pointers are allocated dynamically during execution of a program. When a dynamic object is created, the value of the associated pointer designates (points to) the newly created object. In some programming languages (e.g., PL/1), a single pointer can be used to gain access to objects of different types. Strong type checking is then impossible. In order to permit strong type checking of dynamic objects, most modern programming languages use the Pascal technique of associating unique pointer types with distinct object types.

User-defined dynamic data structures of any desired topology can be specified by associating pointer types with record types, and by embedding pointers within records to provide access to other records. The ability to specify an arbitrary topology and to dynamically allocate objects makes these structures useful when a directed graph of relationships among data items is needed, or when the required number of elements in a data structure varies dynamically, or when rapid access to particular data objects is required. Linked lists and binary trees are common examples of dynamic data structures.

In Ada, pointer types are called access types. An access type for a linked list of integers can be defined as follows:

```
type LINK is access INT_NODE;
type INT_NODE is
record
    ITEM:integer;
    NEXT:LINK;
end record;
```

The following statements declare HEAD to be an object of type LINK. An item of type INT_NODE is then created by the "new" construct and pointed to by access variable HEAD:

```
HEAD: LINK;
HEAD := new INT_NODE(0,null);
```

HEAD points to the newly created node, which has a value of zero stored in field HEAD.ITEM and a null value stored in field HEAD.NEXT. The statement

```
HEAD.NEXT := new INT_NODE (1,null);
```

allocates a second node of type INT_NODE, initializes it to values (1,null), and stores its address in HEAD.NEXT, thus linking it to the HEAD node. Observe that the nodes in the dynamic data structure are not named: they can be accessed only by pointers (typically by following a chain of pointers). The nodes in a dynamic data structure are said to be anonymous entities because they have no names.

Some programming languages (e.g., PL/1, Pascal) permit explicit programmer controlled deallocation of dynamic objects. This can result in dangling references, wherein a pointer has access to a deallocated object (garbage). In Pascal this effect can be expressed as follows:

```
X := new(INT_NODE);
Y := X;
dispose(X);
```

Assuming that X and Y are pointer variables and INT_NODE is a pointer type, the code segment will create an object of the type associated with INT_NODE and assign its address to variable X. Y is given the same value as X in the assignment statement, so that Y also points to the newly created node. The dispose command marks the node as unused and returns it to the dynamic storage pool (the "heap"). However, Y still contains the address of the node.

Subsequently, the memory cells pointed to by Y may be reallocated to another type of entity, as in Z := new(NODE2);. Because Y still points to this memory region, access can be gained, using Y, to a different type of entity than the type associated with Y. Explicit deallocation using the dispose command thus prevents strong type checking. The alternative used in strongly typed programming languages, such as Ada, is to prevent user-controlled deallocation of dynamic objects, and to let the run-time system automatically deallocate objects when they become inaccessible. Objects become inaccessible when there are no longer any pointers to them. The process of automatic deallocation is called garbage collection.

Depending on the particular implementation, Ada systems may or may not provide garbage collection. If the implementation does provide garbage collection, it is possible to inhibit collection on objects of any particular type. The following statement will result in allocation of storage areas of 1024 bytes for each object of type LINK, and inhibit garbage collection on those areas:

$$\text{for LINK'SIZE use } 1024 * \text{BYTE};$$

In this manner, time-critical processes can utilize access types (typically for efficiency of access to objects), and need not be interrupted at unpredictable, and perhaps critical, points in execution time by the garbage collector routine. It is the programmer's responsibility to ensure that the capacities of the statically allocated areas are not exceeded by the running program.

7.4 DATA ABSTRACTION

The concept of data abstraction incorporates both data encapsulation and abstract data types. Both mechanisms define composite data objects in terms of the operations that can be performed on them, and the details of data representation and data manipulation are suppressed by the mechanisms. In this manner, a stack can be characterized by operations such as PUSH, POP, EMPTY_TEST, and FULL_TEST. Similarly, a queue can be characterized by operations such INSERT and REMOVE, and a list by operations such as APPEND, REMOVE, SEARCH, and INSERT. Program units that make use of a stack, queue, or list do not know (or need care) how the stack, list, or queue is implemented, and need not know the details of the manipulating functions.

Data encapsulation differs from abstract data types in that encapsulation provides only one instance of an entity. An abstract data type is a template from which multiple instances can be created, in the same sense that the floating-point type is a template for the creation of multiple floating-point objects.

Data abstraction provides a powerful mechanism for writing well-structured, easily modified programs. The internal details of data representation and data manipulation can be changed at will and, provided the interfaces of the manipulating procedures remain the same, other components of the program will be unaffected by the change, except perhaps for changes in performance characteristics and capacity limits. Using a data abstraction facility, data entities can be defined in terms of predefined types, user-defined types, and other data abstractions, thus permitting systematic development of hierarchical abstractions.

Simple examples of data abstraction, such as stacks, queues, and lists, are often used as examples in textbooks. It should not be inferred from this that data abstraction is only useful in these instances. Data abstraction is a powerful mechanism, of comparable expressive power to the use of subprograms for functional abstraction.

An interactive display screen, for example, might be defined as a collection of display windows, where each window has certain permitted abstract operations and specified relationships to other windows. Or, the financial records of a company might be defined in terms of assets and liabilities. Assets might include cash, equipment, accounts receivable, and inventory. Liabilities might include accounts payable, amounts owed on facilities, notes payable, etc. Each of these items in turn might be defined as a data abstraction in terms of the operations to be performed on them.

7.4.1 Data Encapsulation

Data encapsulation provides only one instance of an entity. Data encapsulation of a FORTRAN stack entity is illustrated in Figure 6.10; data encapsulation in Ada is discussed and illustrated below.

Packages are the mechanism for both data encapsulation and abstract data types in Ada (packages are versatile constructs; data abstraction is only one way in which Ada packages can be used). In the most general case, a package consists of a specification part and a package body. The specification part contains the visible segment and private segment of the package. Interface specifications for the data manipulating routines are given in the visible part. Details of data representation and the data manipulating routines are specified in the package body, and are hidden from the users of the package. The private segment of the specification part is optional; it is not used in data encapsulation. Figure 7.4 illustrates data encapsulation of a single stack entity; Figure 7.4 is the Ada counterpart of Figure 6.10.

The error flag and error handlers in Figure 6.10 have been replaced by exception variables STKFULL and STKEMPTY in Figure 7.4. No exception handlers are provided in Figure 7.4. If an error is raised in the package body, the routine raising the condition will be terminated and the identical exception will be raised in the calling routine. Exception handling in Ada is discussed more fully in Section 7.6.

7.4.2 Abstract Data Types

An abstract data type facility allows the programmer to declare templates for the visible part and the representation and manipulation details of abstract data types.

```
package STACK is
  procedure PUSH(I: in INTEGER);
  procedure POP(I: out INTEGER);
  function EMPTY return BOOLEAN;
  function FULL return BOOLEAN;
  STKFULL, STKEMPTY: exception;
end
package body STACK is
    SIZE: constant := 100;
  INDEX: INTEGER range 0..SIZE := 0;
  STORE: array (1..SIZE) of INTEGER;
begin
  procedure PUSH(I: in INTEGER) is
  begin
   if FULL then raise STKFULL;
   INDEX := INDEX + 1;
   STORE(INDEX) := I;
  end PUSH;
  procedure POP(I: out INTEGER) is
  begin
   if EMPTY then raise STKEMPTY;
   I := STORE(INDEX);
   INDEX := INDEX - 1;
  end POP;
  function EMPTY return BOOLEAN is
  begin
   return (INDEX = 0);
  end EMPTY
  function FULL return BOOLEAN is
  begin
   return (INDEX = SIZE);
  end FULL;
end STACK;
```

Figure 7.4 STACK encapsulation in Ada.

Multiple objects can be created from the templates using declaration statements. Figure 7.5a and b illustrates the visible portion, the private part, and the package body for an integer stack data abstraction expressed in Ada. In Figure 7.5a, type STACK is declared to be "limited private." This prevents access to internal details of objects of type STACK by the routines that use STACK objects; the only operations that can be performed on objects of type STACK are those given in the visible part of the package: PUSH, POP, EMPTY, and FULL. In the absence of the "limited" keyword, the additional operations of comparison for equality and assignment to other variables of the same type are allowed by routines that create and use STACK objects. Thus, "limited" prevents equality tests and assignment; "private" prevents access to the representation details of STACK objects.

Implementation details for the functions and procedures specified in the visible portion are provided in the package body. In addition, hidden functions and procedures can be specified in the package body. Hidden program units cannot be

```
package STACK_TYPE is
   type STACK is limited private;
   procedure PUSH(I: in INTEGER; S: in out STACK);
   procedure POP(I: out INTEGER; S: in out STACK);
   function EMPTY(S: in STACK) return BOOLEAN;
   function FULL(S: in STACK) return BOOLEAN;
   STKFULL, STKEMPTY: exception;
private
   type STACK is
     record
        SIZE: constant := 100;
      INDEX: INTEGER range 0..SIZE := 0;
      STORE: array (1..SIZE) of INTEGER;
   end record;
end STACK_TYPE;
```

Figure 7.5a Package specification for abstract data type STACK_TYPE.

```
package body STACK_TYPE is
   procedure PUSH(I: in INTEGER; S: in out STACK) is
   begin
    if FULL then raise STKFULL;
    S.INDEX := S.INDEX + 1;
    S.STORE(S.INDEX) := I;
   end PUSH;
   procedure POP(I: out INTEGER; S: in out STACK) is
   begin
    if EMPTY then raise STKEMPTY;
    I := S.STACK(S.INDEX);
    S.INDEX := S.INDEX-1;
   end POP;
   function EMPTY(S: in STACK) return BOOLEAN is
   begin
     return (S.INDEX = 0);
   end EMPTY;
   function FULL(S: in STACK) return BOOLEAN;
   begin
     return (S.INDEX = S.SIZE);
   end FULL;
end STACK_TYPE;
```

Figure 7.5b Package body for abstract data type STACK_TYPE.

invoked from outside the package; they exist to support the implementation of visible units. Data objects declared at the package level are statically allocated. It is, of course, essential that data objects remain intact between invocations of program units within the package.

Package bodies can be compiled separately from package specifications. The programmer who uses a package might never see (and need not see) the source code for the package body. Similarly, the routines that use packages never "see" package bodies. This is one reason the private part of a package appears in the package specification rather than the package body. Even though the private part is in the package specification, details within the private part cannot be used by other parts of the program, but only by the compiler to allocate objects declared in the private part.

In order to use an abstract data type, objects of that type must be declared, as in

STACK1,STACK2: STACK;

Entities specified in the visible part of the package can be denoted by selected components (dot notation). For the package illustrated in Figure 7.5, the following statements might be used to distinguish operations on STACK1 from similar operations on STACK2:

if (not FULL(STACK1)) then PUSH(X,STACK1);
if (not EMPTY(STACK2)) then POP(X,STACK2);

7.4.3 Generic Facility

A generic facility permits textual parameterization of a program unit (in Ada, procedures, functions, packages, and tasks are program units). The parameters in a generic clause are replaced at translation time using macro expansion. In this discussion, we will concentrate on type parameterization of packages; however, the generic facility is a powerful general-purpose tool that can be used in many different contexts. Figure 7.6a and b illustrates the specification part and a segment of the body of a generic package for a stack abstraction.

The generic clause

generic
SIZE: NATURAL
type ELEM is private

specifies SIZE and ELEM as generic parameters. NATURAL is the predefined nonnegative integer type.

Every occurrence of SIZE and ELEM in the package (specification part, private part, and body) will be replaced with actual parameters at translation time. Generic program units thus define templates for actual program units. Parameter substitution must occur in order for instances of actual program units to be created from templates. This translation time process is referred to as instantiation. The following statements will be interpreted at translation time, and three instances of the generic package in Figure 7.6 will be created:

package INT_STACK is new GENERIC_STACK(100,INTEGER);
package BOOL_STACK is new GENERIC_STACK(50,BOOLEAN);
package ARRAY_STACK is new GENERIC_STACK(10, array(1..10) of REAL);

The first instance given above produces the package illustrated in Figure 7.5.

```
generic
SIZE: NATURAL;
type ELEM is private;
package GENERIC_STACK is
  type STACK is limited private;
  procedure PUSH(I: in ELEM; S: in out STACK);
  procedure POP(I: out ELEM; S: in out STACK);
  function EMPTY(S: in STACK) return BOOLEAN;
  function FULL (S: in STACK) return BOOLEAN;
  STKFULL, STKEMPTY: exception;
private
  type STACK is
    record
  INDEX: INTEGER range 0..SIZE := 0;
  STORE: array (0..SIZE) of ELEM;
    end record;
end GENERIC_STACK;
```

Figure 7.6a Specification part of a generic package.

```
package body GENERIC_STACK is
  procedure PUSH(I: in ELEM; S: in out STACK) is
  begin
    if FULL then raise STKFULL;
    S.INDEX := S.INDEX + 1;
    S.STORE(S.INDEX) := I;
  end PUSH;
  procedure POP(I: out ELEM; S: in out STACK) is
  begin
    if EMPTY then raise STKEMPTY;
    I := S.STACK(S.INDEX);
    S.INDEX := S.INDEX - 1;
  end POP;
  function EMPTY(S: in STACK) return BOOLEAN is
  begin
    return (S.INDEX = 0);
  end EMPTY;
  function FULL(S: in STACK) return BOOLEAN;
  begin
    return (S.INDEX = S.SIZE);
  end FULL;
end STACK_TYPE;
```

Figure 7.6b A generic package body.

Objects can be declared (i.e., INT_STK1: INT_STACK.STACK;) and manipulated, as in PUSH(X,INT_STK1); or POP(Y,INT_STK1).

Subprogram overloading occurs in cases where more than one stack object is visible, as in

INT_STK: INT_STACK.STACK;
BOOL_STK: BOOL_STACK.STACK;

A call to PUSH(Y,INT_STK) is resolved by the second argument.

The generic facility and subprogram overloading make it possible to define generic program units, store them in a library, create several instances of the program units, and use them, all within the framework of strong type checking. Thus, several instances of I/O routines might be created from a generic I/O package in the following manner:

```
package INT_IO is new IO(INTEGER);
package REAL_IO is new IO(FLOAT);
Package STRING_IO is new IO(STRING);
```

Generic clauses are a natural extension of subprogram parameterization. In general, a generic facility, such as that provided by Ada, permits factorization of common properties of program units. This results in a single copy of a program unit, which in turn promotes modularity and can result in greater efficiency for the translator, while supporting strong type checking.

To summarize, we have discussed strong type checking, user-defined data types, and the interactions between those concepts. An often-repeated criticism of strong type checking is that it inhibits the programmer's freedom to manipulate data objects. We have demonstrated, by way of the Ada programming language, that strong type checking need not interfere with flexible data manipulation. The mechanisms provided in Ada not only provide strong type checking of user-defined objects, but reenforce clarity and modularity of the resulting programs.

7.5 SCOPING RULES

A declaration associates an identifier with a program entity, such as a variable, a type, a subprogram, a formal parameter, or a record component. The region of source text over which a declaration has an effect is called the scope of the declaration. The scoping rules of a programming language dictate the manner in which identifiers can be defined and used by the programmer.

Scoping rules used in various programming languages include global scope, FORTRAN scope, nested scope, and restricted scope. Global scope is provided in BASIC and COBOL. All identifiers are known in all regions of a program. In FORTRAN, identifiers are known throughout the containing program unit, but are not known outside the unit unless they appear in a COMMON statement or as actual parameters in a subprogram invocation. Named COMMON blocks permit sharing of data among program units on a selective basis, and parameters permit communication of different data objects to program units on different invocations of those units. Ada packages can also be used to achieve the effect of named common blocks.

Nested scope was introduced in Algol60 and is utilized in Pascal and its descendants (including Ada). Variants of nested scope are used in most modern programming languages. In a nested scope programming language, program units can be nested within other units. Names declared on outer levels are available for use within nested units, unless those names are redeclared in a nested unit. The situation is illustrated in Figure 7.7.

Nested scope promotes modularity by providing natural groupings of related entities and by permitting distinction between global and local identifiers. In addition, nested scope is readily implemented using a stack-based run-time system. On the other hand, nesting is not consistent with information hiding and locality considerations. In order for a data object X to be shared between routines B and C in Figure 7.7, X must be declared at the next outer level, which also makes it accessible to routine A. This encourages indiscriminate access to global identifiers. Also, inadvertent declaration within a nested unit of an identifier that is already declared on an outer level may accidentally make the outer (global) instance of the name inaccessible within the nested unit. Nested scope programs are thus vulnerable to modification errors, because overlapping scopes are not allowed.

Several variations on nested scope have been adopted in order to retain the advantages of nesting while overcoming the disadvantages. An extreme approach is that taken in the Euclid language (LAM77). In Euclid, an import directive is required to make externally declared names visible within nested procedures. The disadvantage of this approach is that long lists of import names may result.

The Ada programming language utilizes nested scope. An identifier that becomes hidden by nested declaration of the same identifier can be made visible using dot notation for component selection. The name of the outer unit is used as a prefix to the identifier name, as illustrated in Figure 7.8. In many cases, global identifiers that are in conflict with local identifiers will be subprogram names that are made

	PROCEDURE	VISIBLE IDENTIFIERS
procedure MAIN is X,Y: REAL;	MAIN	X & Y

procedure A is
    Y,Z: REAL;
    ::::::
  end A;
	A	global X
		local Y & Z

procedure B is
    Z,W: REAL;
    ::::::
  end B;
	B	global X & Y
		local Z & W

procedure C is
    W,X: REAL;
    ::::::
  end C;
    ::::::
end MAIN;
	C	global Y
		local W & X

Figure 7.7 Illustrating nested block structure.

```
procedure MAIN is
  X,Y: REAL;

  procedure A is
    Y: REAL;
  begin
    MAIN.Y := X + Y;    -- X is MAIN.X, Y is A.Y
```

Figure **7.8** Illustrating selected components in Ada.

visible by subprogram overloading rules. Entities declared in the visible part of a package can be denoted by selected components. They can also be made visible by a use clause, as in

> use IO_PACKAGE;

An identifier made visible by a use clause can never hide another identifier. In case of conflict, the package entities are made visible using selected components. This prevents inadvertent use of a conflicting entity introduced in a use clause.

7.6 EXCEPTION HANDLING

An exception is an event that suspends normal execution of a program. Exception events include, for example, values out of range, violation of capacity limits, application of operators to illegal data values, and attempts to process unavailable data. An exception condition is raised when an exception event occurs. An exception handler constitutes the actions executed in response to a raised exception. Control is transferred to an exception handler when the corresponding exception condition is raised. In many programming languages, exception handlers are part of the run-time support system, and language users have no mechanism for controlling exception handling. The lack of user-defined exception handling mechanisms in higher-level programming languages is a major reason that programs are written in assembly language.

PL/1 and Ada both provide user-controlled exception handling. In both languages the user can specify exception handlers for several predefined exception conditions. If the user does not specify an exception handler for a predefined exception condition, a system-defined exception handler is invoked. In both languages, the user can also define new exception conditions and associated exception handlers. The two languages differ, however, in the way exceptions are handled.

7.6.1 Exception Handling in PL/1

PL/1 incorporates a resumption model of exception handling, while Ada provides a termination model. The resumption model (PL/1) permits resumption of program execution at the point of interruption, following execution of the associated excep-

```
ALPHA:  PROCEDURE( );
     ON ENDFILE(INPUT)
         RETURN;

     ON OVERFLOW BEGIN
             /* OVERFLOW EXCEPTION HANDLING CODE */     END;
     ::::::::::::
     ::::::::::::
END ALPHA;
```

Figure 7.9 Specification of exception handling in PL/1.

tion handler. If a return statement is the last statement in a resumption model exception handler, the containing program unit is terminated, and control returns to the calling unit. In the termination model (Ada), control is always returned to the calling unit following execution of the exception handler.

Specification of exception handling in a PL/1 procedure is illustrated in Figure 7.9. Exception handlers in PL/1 are called ON statements, and exception conditions are called ON conditions. In Figure 7.9, raising the ENDFILE condition for file INPUT in procedure ALPHA will transfer control to the ON ENDFILE code segment. Execution of the ON unit terminates procedure ALPHA and transfers control to the calling routine by executing the RETURN statement.

Overflow of a floating-point computation in procedure ALPHA in Figure 7.9 will transfer control to the associated ON statement. Following execution of the ON unit in the ON OVERFLOW statement, control will return to the statement immediately following the point where the exception condition occurred, provided there are no explicit transfers of control in the ON unit (e. g., GOTO, RETURN).

An ON unit can specify arbitrarily complex processes, including creation of local variables, subprogram calls, and use of I/O and data files. An ON unit may be null, as in

ON OVERFLOW;

In this case, no actions occur on floating-point overflow, except to transfer control to the statement immediately following the statement that caused the overflow condition. Some of the ON conditions provided in PL/1 are listed in Table 7.2.

7.6.2 Exception Handling in Ada

In the termination model of exception handling (Ada), the program unit in which an exception occurs is automatically terminated following execution of an exception handler; the exception handler is viewed as replacing the remaining body of the program unit. If no exception handler is provided for a given exception condition (either user-defined or predefined), the program unit is terminated, and the same exception is raised in the calling unit. This permits propagation of an exception to any desired calling level.

In Ada, the scope of an exception condition can be a block or the body of a

Table 7.2 Some PL/1 ON Conditions

CHECK (identifier list)
SIZE
SUBSCRIPTRANGE
STRINGRANGE
OVERFLOW
UNDERFLOW
ZERODIVIDE
CONVERSION
FIXEDOVERFLOW
AREA
FINISH
ERROR
ENDFILE(X)
ENDPAGE(X)
TRANSMIT(X)
UNDEFINEDFILE(X)
NAME(X)
KEY(X)
RECORD(X)
CONDITION(X)

subprogram, package, or task. Associations of exceptions with blocks allows flexible control over the scope of an exception condition. This is a primary use of blocks in Ada because a block can be introduced at any point in the program text as desired by the programmer. The following discussion is limited to exception handling in subprograms.

Exception handling in an Ada subprogram is illustrated in Figure 7.10. SINGULAR is declared to be a user-defined exception. Exception handlers are specified in the exception segment of the procedure. The user is responsible for specifying conditions under which user-defined exceptions are to be raised, as in

if (COND1) then raise SINGULAR;

or

if (COND2) then raise SINGULAR;

```
procedure P(  ) is
  -- optional declarations
  SINGULAR: exception;
  -- executable statements
  if (COND) then raise SINGULAR;
  -- executable statements
exception
  when SINGULAR =>
      -- exception-handling statements for SINGULAR condition
  when NUMERIC_ERROR =>
      -- user-supplied exception handler for NUMERIC_ERROR
      raise;
end P;
```

Figure 7.10 Specification of exception handling in Ada.

Table 7.3 Predefined exceptions in Ada

CONSTRAINT_ERROR
NUMERIC_ERROR
PROGRAM_ERROR
STORAGE_ERROR
TASKING_ERROR

In the absence of a user supplied exception handler, the run-time support system is responsible for handling predefined exceptions such as NUMERIC_ERROR. Predefined exception conditions in Ada are summarized in Table 7.3.

In Ada, an exception is propagated to the calling routine under two conditions: if there is no exception handler for a user-defined exception condition, or if a raise statement appears in an invoked exception handler. A propagated exception raises the same exception condition in the calling routine, unless the invoked exception handler in the called routine contains a statement of the form "raise SOME_OTHER_COND" which raises SOME_OTHER_COND in the calling routine. A propagated exception can be handled in the calling routine, or it may be propagated to that routine's caller. Propagation can be continued back to the system level. If an exception is handled locally, a calling routine cannot tell (and presumably has no need to know) whether the called routine terminated under normal conditions or under exception conditions.

When an exception is propagated, one option for the calling routine is to correct the condition and re-invoke the called routine. This possibility is illustrated in Figure 7.11.

In Ada, a pragma is an instruction to the translator. The INCLUDE pragma in

```
procedure RESTART_INSERT(ITEM: in ELEMENT) is
    pragma include FIX_UP;
    TABLE_FULL: exception;
    -- nested procedure INSERT
    procedure INSERT(ITEM: in ELEMENT) is
    begin
        -- test for full table
        if NO_SPACE then
            raise TABLE_FULL;
        end if;
        -- normal actions of INSERT
    end INSERT;
    -- start of executable code for RESTART_INSERT
    INSERT(ITEM);
    -- exception handler for TABLE_FULL
exception
    when TABLE_FULL =>
        FIX_UP(TABLE);
        INSERT(ITEM);
end RESTART_INSERT;
```

Figure 7.11 Fix-up and restart in Ada.

Figure 7.11 instructs the translator to retrieve a file named FIX_UP and include the file at that point in the program text. In this example the FIX_UP file contains a procedure called FIX_UP. A user-defined exception named TABLE_FULL is declared. TABLE_FULL is raised when NO_SPACE becomes true in nested procedure INSERT. Because there is no exception handler specified for the TABLE_FULL exception, procedure INSERT is terminated, and TABLE_FULL is raised in calling procedure RESTART_INSERT.

The exception handler for TABLE_FULL in RESTART_INSERT calls the FIX_UP routine (which may allocate more space for TABLE or allocate a new TABLE and copy the old TABLE into it). The TABLE_FULL exception handler then reinvokes INSERT. Presumably FIX_UP could fail, raising its own exception, e.g., OUT_OF_SPACE, which might be propagated through RESTART_INSERT to some higher-level calling routine where alternative actions can be taken when there is no more space for TABLE. An exception condition raised in FIX_UP might be allowed to propagate back to the system level, resulting in termination of the program that contained RESTART_INSERT.

The resumption model of exception handling (PL/1) subsumes the termination model (Ada). Resumption appears to be the more flexible and, therefore, more desirable approach to exception handling. According to the designers of Ada, the termination model was chosen because the resumption model violates program modularity, makes code optimization difficult (if not impossible), and makes formal verification of programs nearly impossible (ICH79).

The following example illustrates a well-known problem with the resumption model of exception handling:

$$X := P + Q;$$
$$Y := X - Q;$$

In the absence of overflow, the value of Y will be P following execution of the indicated statements. This will not be true if overflow occurs in the evaluation of $P + Q$ and if the exception handler provides a default value for X before resuming with the statement $Y := X - Q$; thus, one cannot assert (or assume) that Y always has the value P following execution of these two statements under the resumption model of exception handling. Using the termination model, as in Ada, execution will never reach the statement $Y := X - Q$; on overflow because the routine will return to its caller. Thus, it is safe to assert that when (if) control reaches this point, Y will have the value P.

The Ada philosophy of exception handling is to regard an exception as a terminating condition. As illustrated in Figure 7.11, the exception handler may restart the same sequence of actions under different conditions, but it will do so by a different invocation of the program unit, and not by a simple resumption. Also, recall that exception variables and exception handlers can be introduced locally using begin_end blocks within procedures. If an exception arises within a local block, only that block will be terminated and not the entire procedure. In this way the effect of exception propagation can be localized to small segments of code.

7.7 CONCURRENCY MECHANISMS

Two or more segments of a program can be executing concurrently if the effect of executing the segments is independent of the order in which they are executed. We refer to these program segments as tasks or processes. On multiple-processor machines, independent code segments can be executed simultaneously to achieve increased processing efficiency. On a single-processor machine, the execution of independent code segments can be interleaved to achieve processing efficiency: One task may be able to execute while another is waiting for an external event to occur or waiting for completion of an I/O operation.

The trend toward multiple-processor machines and the increasingly sophisticated applications of computers has resulted in higher-level language constructs for specifying concurrent tasks. Two fundamental problems in concurrent programming are synchronization of tasks so that information can be transferred between tasks, and prevention of simultaneous updating of data that are accessible to more than one task. These problems are referred to as the synchronization problem and the mutual exclusion problem.

There are three fundamental approaches to concurrent programming: shared variables, asynchronous message passing, and synchronous message passing. Each of these mechanisms is discussed in turn.

7.7.1 Shared Variables

In the shared variable approach to concurrency, multiple processes have access to a common region of memory. The simplest form of shared variable communication is the "test and set" approach. When two tasks are to synchronize, the first task to reach its synchronization point will test and then set a shared memory cell to indicate that it is waiting for the second task. When the second task reaches its synchronization point, it tests the shared cell and determines that the first task is waiting. Having synchronized, the two tasks can exchange information, reset the shared memory cell, and proceed concurrently until the next synchronization point is reached. Test and set also can be used to prevent one task from accessing shared data while another task is updating that data. Shared variable techniques include semaphores, critical regions, and monitors. The semaphore approach is discussed below.

The semaphore mechanism was first described by Dijkstra (DIJ68). A boolean semaphore S has two permitted values: true and false (busy and free). Two operations are defined for boolean semaphores:

P(S):   If S is true (busy), the task issuing P(S) is suspended. If S is false (free) it is set to true (busy) and the task issuing P(S) proceeds.

V(S):   S is set to false (free). If there are tasks suspended by P(S) operations, one of them is allowed to proceed.

Semaphores can be used for mutual exclusion by placing code that has access to shared data inside matching P and V operations:

```
TASK A                  TASK B
  P(S)                    P(S)
  -- Access shared data   -- Access shared data
  V(S)                    V(S)
```

Semaphores can also be used to synchronize tasks for information exchange between tasks. Assuming that S has been set to true (busy) and that task A always reaches its synchronization point before task B, the following statements might be used:

```
TASK A                      TASK B
  P(S)  -- Wait for B           -- Code to Place A's data in
                               -- shared memory
                          V(S) -- Release A and continue

-- Code to process data in
-- shared memory after B
-- releases the memory
```

Integer semaphores allow S to have a limited number of integer values. This is useful to permit access to a resource by a limited number of tasks or to provide access to a limited number of copies of a resource. An integer semaphore can be defined as follows:

P(S):   If S = 0 then the task issuing P(S) is suspended.

   else if S > 0 then S becomes S - 1 and the task issuing P(S) is allowed to continue.

   else error

V(S):   If S = 0 then S becomes S + 1 and one waiting task is allowed to proceed (the waiting task will reexecute its P(S) operation to decrement S).

   else if S > 0 then S becomes S + 1 (there are no waiting tasks)

   else error

Integer semaphores can be programmed using boolean semaphores. In practice they are only slightly more useful than boolean semaphores.

Semaphores are low-level concurrency mechanisms. In most applications they are hard to write, hard to understand, hard to verify, and hard to modify. Typical problems with semaphores include (ICH79):

1. A jump that bypasses a P operation can result in unprotected access to data.
2. A jump that bypasses a V operation can result in deadlock.

3. It is not possible to wait for one of several semaphores to become free.
4. Semaphores are often visible to tasks that need not have access to them.

Monitors and critical regions were invented to overcome some of the problems of semaphores.

7.7.2 Asynchronous Message Passing

Asynchronous message passing involves association of buffers with concurrent tasks. A sending task places information in a receiving task buffer. Items are removed from the buffer by the receiver as needed. Removal of items may be on a first-in first-out basis, or according to a priority scheme. A sending task synchronizes with the receiving task when it encounters a full buffer in the receiver; typically the sender is suspended until the receiver retrieves an item from the full buffer. More generally, the sending task may execute alternative actions while waiting for the receiver to retrieve an item. A receiving task synchronizes with the sending task when it attempts to retrieve information from an empty buffer. The receiver must suspend processing or execute alternative actions until the sender places an item in the buffer.

Figure 7.12 illustrates an asynchronous solution to the producer/consumer problem using semaphores. The producing task is the sender, and the consuming task is the receiver (see Figure 4.13 for the Petri Net corresponding to Figure 7.12). The semaphore approach (in general, any shared variable approach) to asynchronous message passing is unsuitable for distributed systems where tasks execute on distinct machines, because there is no shared memory. In such situations, the sender must wait for acknowledgement that the message has been placed in the receiver's buffer.

7.7.3 Synchronous Message Passing

The method of synchronization used in synchronous message passing is known as a rendezvous. Both symmetric and asymmetric rendezvous are possible. Sym-

```
SEMAPHORE: E,F,M;
INITIALLY: E :=N; F :=0; M :=1;

loop                              loop
  -- produce item                  P(F); P(M);
  P(E); P(M);                      -- remove item from buffer
  -- place item in buffer          V(E); V(M);
  V(F); V(M);                      -- consume item
end loop;                        end loop;
NOTE: E is the number-of-empty-cells semaphore
      F is the number-of-full-cells semaphore
      M is the mutual-exclusion semaphore
```

Figure 7.12 Semaphore solution to asynchronous producer/consumer.

metric rendezvous, as exemplified in CSP, requires each process to know the name of the other process involved in the rendezvous (HOA78). In CSP, communication between tasks can be viewed as synchronized input and output between the tasks. A symmetric rendezvous occurs in the following manner.

The first task to reach its input or output statement waits for the other task. When the second task reaches its complementary output or input statement, both tasks execute the I/O statements in synchronization, with the output from one task being the input to the other task. Following completion of synchronized I/O, the tasks proceed concurrently. Each task names the other in its I/O statement, and the source and destination of information transfer must be compatible. Because a rendezvous in CSP requires two-way symmetry of task names, it is impossible to write a library task that can provide resources and services to multiple unforeseen users. Asymmetric rendezvous overcomes this problem, but, as a result, sacrifices the mathematical elegance of formal reasoning possible for CSP programs.

An asymmetric rendezvous is similar to a procedure call in that the invoked task need not know the names of its users. Asymmetric rendezvous is also similar to a procedure call in that information can be transferred between tasks using parameter lists and global variables. Asymmetric rendezvous is the concurrency mechanism used in Ada.

Tasks are the mechanism for expressing concurrent processing in Ada. Ada tasks are similar to Ada packages in that a task consists of a specification part and a body. Ada tasks are illustrated in Figures 7.13 and 7.14. The specification part contains entry declarations and representation specifications. Entry declarations

```
task SHARED_ARRAY is
 -- INDEX and ELEM are global types
 entry READ(N: in INDEX; E: out ELEM);
 entry WRITE(N: in INDEX; E: in ELEM);
end;

task body SHARED_ARRAY is
 -- declarative part
 TABLE: array (INDEX) of ELEM :=(INDEX => 0);
begin
 -- executable statements
 loop
  select
   accept READ(N: in INDEX; E: out ELEM) do
    E := TABLE(N);
   end READ;
  or
   accept WRITE(N: in INDEX; E: in ELEM) do
    TABLE(N) := E;
   end WRITE;
  end select;
 end loop;
 -- optional exception handlers are placed here
end SHARED_ARRAY;
```

Figure 7.13 An Ada task specification and body.

```
task BUFFER is
  entry READ(C: out CHAR);
  entry WRITE(C: in CHAR);
end;
task body BUFFER is
  -- declarative part
  QUEUE_SIZE: constant INTEGER := 100;
  QUEUE:  array(1..QUEUE_SIZE) of CHAR;
  COUNT:  INTEGER range 0..QUEUE_SIZE := 0;
  IN_INDEX, OUT_INDEX: INTEGER range 1..QUEUE_SIZE := 1;
begin
  loop
    select
       when (COUNT  <  QUEUE_SIZE) =>
       -- producer writes
         accept WRITE(C: in CHAR) do
           QUEUE(IN_INDEX) := C;
         end;
           -- concurrently executed code
           IN_INDEX := IN_INDEX mod QUEUE_SIZE + 1;
           COUNT := COUNT + 1;
       or
       when (COUNT  >  0) =>
          -- consumer reads
          accept READ(C: out CHAR) do
            C := QUEUE(OUT_INDEX);
          end;
             -- concurrently executed code
             OUT_INDEX := OUT_INDEX mod QUEUE_SIZE + 1;
             COUNT := COUNT - 1;
       end select;
    end loop;
    -- exception handlers are placed here
end BUFFER;
```

Figure 7.14 Rendezvous solution to producer/consumer in Ada.

specify the names and parameter lists of entry points (synchronization points) in the task body. Representation specifications are discussed later.

As illustrated in Figures 7.13 and 7.14, a task body consists of an optional declarative part, a sequence of executable statements, and optional exception handlers. The sequence of executable statements contains "accept" statements that correspond to the entry declarations in the specification part. A task is initiated when a thread of control enters the scope of the task. There are no special statements for task initiation.

A task entry can be called by another task, as in

$$SHARED\_ARRAY.READ(I,X);$$

or

$$SHARED\_ARRAY.WRITE(J,Y);$$

If the calling task issues an entry call before the corresponding accept statement is reached in the task being called, execution of the calling task is suspended. If the called task reaches an accept statement prior to call of that entry, execution of the task is suspended until a call occurs. When an entry is called and the corresponding accept statement is reached, the sequence of statements associated with the accept statement is executed. Parameters can be passed back and forth between the tasks and shared global variables can be. The calling task remains suspended until the end of the accept statement is reached. The calling task and the called task then continue concurrent execution.

If several tasks call the same entry before a corresponding accept statement is reached, the calls are queued. There is one queue associated with each entry, and each execution of an accept statement removes one call from the corresponding queue. Calls are processed in order of arrival. A task in a entry queue is suspended until it is removed and the accept statement is processed. The rendezvous mechanism thus provides synchronization, communication, and mutual exclusion between concurrent tasks.

The task illustrated in Figure 7.13 provides shared read/write access to an array of objects of type ELEM. The array is indexed by objects of type INDEX. The task body consists of a nonterminating loop, which contains an entry point for READ calls and an entry point for WRITE calls. If several tasks have called READ and WRITE, both entry queues may be nonempty. In this case, the select statement will cause one of READ or WRITE to accept and process a rendezvous with the first waiting task on its entry queue. Selection between READ accept and WRITE accept is performed in a random, arbitrary manner; however, only one task can read or write the shared array at any given time. If one entry queue is empty and the other nonempty, the first task in the nonempty queue will be selected for rendezvous. If both entry queues are empty, the task waits for a call to READ or WRITE. The task illustrated in Figure 7.13 thus provides protected access to a shared array by multiple calling tasks.

The task illustrated in Figure 7.14 implements the producer/consumer algorithm on an array of characters that is processed as a circular queue. The array has two indices: IN_INDEX denotes the index of the next input character, and OUT_INDEX denotes the index of the next output character. The producing task might contain statements of the form

```
loop
   -- Produce Next Character
   BUFFER.WRITE(CHAR);
   exit when CHAR = END_OF_TRANSMISSION;
end loop;
```

and the consuming task might contain the statements

```
loop
   BUFFER.READ(CHAR);
   exit when CHAR = END_OF_TRANSMISSION;
   -- Consume CHAR;
end loop;
```

The exit statements are for loop exit; they transfer control to the statement immediately following end loop when the stated condition becomes true.

The buffer task illustrated in Figure 7.14 has two entry points: READ and WRITE. The task body contains declarations for the queue data structure and associated variables. The executable statements are similar in form to those of the previous example (Figure 7.13), with the notable difference being the "when" clauses. If the condition associated with a when clause is true, the corresponding accept entry is said to be open. If the condition is false, the entry is closed. A closed entry cannot be selected for rendezvous. Calls to a closed entry are placed on the corresponding entry queue, and the calling task is suspended. When the "when" clause becomes true, the associated accept entry is opened and becomes a candidate for rendezvous selection.

This discussion of Ada tasking is not intended to be exhaustive, but rather is intended to illustrate some aspects of concurrent processing using asynchronous rendezvous. Many other features of Ada tasking (conditional entry calls, timed entry calls, delay statements, priorities, aborts, etc.) are described in the *Ada Reference Manual* (ADA83).

One final aspect of Ada tasking will be mentioned. In Ada, external interrupts are viewed as task entries. The occurrence of an external interrupt acts as an entry call issued by a task with higher priority than that of any user-defined task. Address specifications given in the specification part of the task associate interrupt addresses with entry points. If control information is supplied by an interrupt, it is passed to an associated interrupt handler using "in" parameters. Figure 7.15 illustrates the form of an INTERRUPT_HANDLER task. In this example, hexadecimal locations 40 and 41 are the interrupt locations associated with SENSOR1 and SENSOR2. In

```
task INTERRUPT_HANDLER is
   entry SENSOR1(S: in STATUS);
   entry SENSOR2(S: in STATUS);
   for SENSOR1 use at 16#40#;
   for SENSOR2 use at 16#41#;
end;
task body INTERRUPT_HANDLER is
   -- optional declarative part
begin
   loop
      select
         accept SENSOR1(S: in STATUS) do
            -- interrupt actions for SENSOR1
         end;
      or
            accept SENSOR2(S: in STATUS) do
               -- interrupt actions for SENSOR2
         end;
      end select;
   end loop;
   -- optional exception handlers
end INTERRUPT_HANDLER;
```

Figure 7.15 External interrupt handler task in Ada.

some implementations, the priority of interrupts may be specified by the address specification associated with the interrupt entry.

7.8 SUMMARY

Programming languages are the notational vehicles used to implement software products. Features available in the implementation language exert a strong influence on the architectural structure and algorithmic details of programs written in the language.

In this chapter, type-checking rules, separate compilation, user-defined data types, data encapsulation, data abstraction, generics, scoping rules, exception handling, and concurrency mechanisms were discussed. FORTRAN IV, Pascal, Ada, and PL/1 were used to illustrate various concepts.

The deficiencies of Pascal for development of large software products were described, and the differing philosophies of type checking and exception handling in PL/1 and Ada were contrasted.

The goal of this chapter has been to illustrate various modern programming language features that can be used to improve the quality of source code. Strong type checking prevents erroneous use of data objects and reduces the surprise factor of incorrect data usage. Separate compilation allows one to incorporate pre-compiled library units with the same security of data usage that exists within a compilation unit.

User-defined data types permit creation of data types that model entities in the problem domain. Under the name equivalence type-checking rule, objects that have distinct type names are kept separate from other objects that have different type names but perhaps identical representations. User-defined data types can be created as subtypes, derived types, enumerated types, record types, and pointer types in Ada. Mechanisms such as subprogram overloading, operator overloading, and explicit type conversion provide the necessary flexibility to write programs within the framework of strong type checking under name equivalence.

Data encapsulation facilities permit definition of data structures in terms of the operations that can be performed on them, and prevent users of a data structure from gaining access to the representation details of the data structure and the routines that manipulate the structure. An abstract data type facility allows the programmer to declare templates for abstract data objects using visible access functions and hidden representation details. Multiple instances of the data structures and associated code can be created using declaration statements; the template is written once and used repeatedly.

A generic facility allows parameterization of source text. Specific entities are created from a generic template by supplying parameter values that are substituted into the template using macro expansion. Packages, tasks, and procedures can be written once and instantiated in various ways for various purposes.

Flexible scoping rules in modern programming languages retain the advantages of nested block structure while overcoming some of the disadvantages. User-defined exception handling allows the programmer to specify actions to be taken in response to system-defined exception conditions, and to specify additional exception conditions and exception handlers.

Concurrency mechanisms in modern programming languages support the increasing role of multiple-processor architectures and distributed systems, as well as increased efficiency on single-processor architectures. Concurrency mechanisms in modern programming languages support concurrent programming at the application level.

At any particular point in time, the features provided by our programming languages reflect our understanding of software and programming. Features available in Ada, for example, reflect a much more sophisticated understanding of programming than those available in FORTRAN IV. However, it will become apparent with experience in using Ada and other modern languages that much remains to be done in the evolution of programming languages to support development and maintenance of software products.

REFERENCES

(ADA83) *Reference Manual for the Ada* Programming Language,* ANSI/ MIL-STD-1815 A, United States Department of Defense, 1983.

(ADD80) Addyman, A. (ed.): ISO/DP7185 - Specification for the Computer Programming Language Pascal (2d draft), *Pascal News,* no. 20, December, 1980.

(DIJ68) Dijkstra, E.: "Co-operating Sequential Processes," in *Programming Languages,* F. Genuys (ed.), Academic Press, London, 1968.

(GHE82) Ghezzi, C. and M. Jazayeri: *Programming Language Concepts,* John Wiley, New York, 1982.

(HOA78) Hoare, C. A. R.: "Communicating Sequential Processes," *Comm. ACM.,* vol. 21, no. 8, August 1978.

(ICH79) Ichbiah, J., et al.: "Rationale for the Design of the Ada Programming Language," *ACM SIGPLAN Notices,* vol. 14, no. 6, June 1979.

(LAM77) Lampson, B., et al.: "Report on the Programming Language Euclid," *ACM SIGPLAN Notices,* vol. 12, no. 2, February 1977.

(NAU63) Naur, P. (ed.): "Revised Report on the Algorithmic Language Algol60," *Comm. ACM,* vol. 6, no. 1, January 1963.

(WIR74) Wirth, N., and K. Jensen: *Pascal User Manual and Report,* Springer-Verlag, Berlin, 1974.

(ZAH74) Zahn, C.: "A Control Statement for Natural Top-Down Structured Programming," Symposium on Programming, Paris, 1974.

*Ada is a registered trademark of the U.S. Government, Ada Joint Program Office

EXERCISES

7.1 Discuss the advantages and disadvantages of structural type equivalence.

7.2 Give examples of static and dynamic type checking in a programming language of your choice.

7.3 Design an experiment to detect the cost of various run-time checks in a programming language of your choice.

7.4 In 1974, Zahn proposed two new "event driven" control constructs (ZAH74):

```
        begin_until EV1,EV2,...EVn;
          STMTS_0;
        end;
         then
           EV1 => STMTS_1;
           EV2 => STMTS_2;
           :::
           EVn => STMTS_n;
         end;
```

and

```
        loop_until EV1,EV2,...EVn;
          STMTS_0;
        end loop;
         then
           EV1 => STMTS_1;
           EV2 => STMTS_2;
           :::
           EVn => STMTS_n;
         end;
```

The begin_until construct specifies execution of statement list STMTS_0, and the loop_until construct specifies repeated execution of STMTS_0. Within STMTS_0, a RAISE EVi construct can appear. Execution of RAISE EVi causes transfer to the corresponding block of code in the then part of the construct. If no raise statement is executed, no code in the then part of the construct is executed.

(a) Translate "if B then S1 else S2" into Zahn's begin_until construct.
(b) Translate the case statement into Zahn's begin_until construct.
(c) Translate "while B loop S end loop" into Zahn's loop_until construct.
(d) Translate "repeat B until S" into Zahn's loop_until construct.

7.5 Compare and contrast pointer variables in PL/1 and Pascal. What are the relative advantages and disadvantages of each approach?

7.6 Write simple Pascal examples to illustrate compile-time, load-time, and run-time type checking violations. Run your examples on a computer and observe the outcomes.

7.7 Define the specification part of an Ada package for a symbol table. Each table entry consists of a symbol and three attribute fields. Desired operations include inserting a new symbol and zero or more attributes, inserting and retrieving selected attributes of a symbol, determining if a given symbol is in the table, and checking for a full table.

7.8 Your symbol table package in Exercise 7.7 is to be placed in a library for use by other programmers. Write the user documentation for the package.

7.9 Convert the symbol table package in Exercise 7.7 to a generic package in which the table size and the types of the symbol attributes are parameters.

7.10 (a) Discuss the pros and cons of the resumption and termination models of exception handling.
  (b) Would you rather write a program using resumption or termination exception handling? Why?
  (c) Would you rather modify a program that uses resumption or termination exception handling? Why?

7.11 Obtain a copy of Appendix F (Implementation Dependent Characteristics) of the reference manual for an Ada implementation. Does the appendix tell you everything you might want to know about the local implementation?

7.12 Write an Ada task to implement a semaphore.

7.13 (GHE82) Most computers provide an indivisible test-and-set machine instruction that can be used for synchronization of concurrent processes. For example, the instruction is called TS on the IBM 360.

TS has two boolean arguments. Execution of TS(X,Y) copies the value of Y into X and sets Y to false.

A set of concurrent processes that must execute some instructions in mutual exclusion can use a global boolean variable, PERMIT, initialized to false, and a local boolean variable X in the following way:

```
repeat TS(X,PERMIT)
until X;
-- instructions to be executed in mutual exclusion
PERMIT := false;
```

A process executes its mutual exclusion instructions by exiting the repeat loop. If PERMIT is true the process falls through the loop. If PERMIT is false, the process stays in the repeat loop until PERMIT is set to true by another process. This latter activity is referred to as "busy waiting."

(*a*) Write code to implement P and V operations using the test-and-set primitive.

(*b*) Why is it important that TS be an indivisible instruction?

7.14 Investigate the external interrupt handling capabilities of a computer of your choice. How are interrupt priorities and disabling of interrupts on this machine reflected in the Ada programming language?

EIGHT

VERIFICATION AND VALIDATION TECHNIQUES

INTRODUCTION

The goals of verification and validation activities are to assess and improve the quality of the work products generated during development and modification of software. Quality attributes of interest include correctness, completeness, consistency, reliability, usefulness, usability, efficiency, conformance to standards, and overall cost effectiveness.

There are two types of verification: life-cycle verification and formal verification. Life-cycle verification is the process of determining the degree to which the work products of a given phase of the development cycle fulfill the specifications established during prior phases. Formal verification is a rigorous mathematical demonstration that source code conforms to its specifications. Validation is the process of evaluating software at the end of the software development process to determine compliance with the requirements (IEE83). Boehm (BOE83) phrases these definitions as follows:

Verification: "Are we building the product right?"
Validation: "Are we building the right product?"

High quality cannot be achieved through testing of source code alone. Although a program should be totally free of errors, this is seldom the case for large software products. Even if source code errors were the only measure of quality, testing alone cannot guarantee the absence of errors in a program. A well known maxim states that the number of bugs remaining in a program is proportional to the number already discovered. This is because one has most confidence in programs with no detected bugs after thorough testing and least confidence in a program with a long history of fixes. The best way to minimize the number of errors in a program is to catch and remove the errors during analysis and design, so that few errors are introduced into the source code. Although source code testing is an important technique for assessing quality, it is only one of several techniques discussed in this chapter. Verification and validation are pervasive concepts, not a set of activities that occur strictly following implementation.

Verification and validation involve assessment of work products to determine conformance to specifications. Specifications include the requirements specifications, the design documentation, various stylistic guidelines, implementation language standards, project standards, organizational standards, and user expectations, as well as the meta-specifications for the formats and notations used in the various product specifications. The requirements must be examined for conformance to user needs, environmental constraints, and notational standards. The design documentation must be verified with respect to the requirements and notational conventions, and the source code must be examined for conformance to the requirements, the design documentation, user expectations, and various implementation and documentation standards. In addition, the supporting documents (user's manual, test plan, principles of operation, etc.) must be examined for correctness, completeness, consistency, and adherence to standards.

Errors occur when any aspect of a software product is incomplete, inconsistent, or incorrect. Three major categories of software errors are requirements errors, design errors, and implementation errors. Requirements errors are caused by incorrect statement of user needs, by failure to completely specify functional and performance requirements, by inconsistencies among the requirements, and by infeasible requirements.

Design errors are introduced by failure to translate the requirements into correct and complete solution structures, by inconsistencies within the design specifications, and by inconsistencies between the design specifications and the requirements. A requirements error or a design error that is not discovered until source code testing can be very costly to correct (recall Figure 2.5). It is thus important that the quality of requirements and design documents be assessed early and often.

Implementation errors are the errors made in translating design specifications into source code. Implementation errors can occur in data declarations, in data referencing, in control flow logic, in computational expressions, in subprogram interfaces, and in input/output operations.

The quality of work products generated during analysis and design can be assessed and improved by using systematic quality assurance procedures, by walkthroughs and inspections, and by automated checks for consistency and completeness. Techniques for assessing and improving the quality of source code include systematic quality assurance procedures, walkthroughs and inspections, static analysis, symbolic execution, unit testing, and systematic integration testing. Formal verification techniques can be used to show, in a rigorous manner, that a source program conforms to its requirements; formal verification also can be used to guide systematic synthesis of source programs. These topics are discussed in subsequent sections of this chapter.

8.1 QUALITY ASSURANCE

Quality assurance is "a planned and systematic pattern of all actions necessary to provide adequate confidence that the item or product conforms to established technical requirements" (IEE83). The purpose of a software quality assurance group is to provide assurance that the procedures, tools, and techniques used during product development and modification are adequate to provide the desired level of confidence in the work products.

Often, software quality assurance personnel are organizationally distinct from the software development group. This adds a degree of impartiality to quality assurance activities, and allows quality assurance personnel to become specialists in their discipline. In some organizations, quality assurance personnel function in an advisory capacity, while in others the quality assurance group actively develops standards, tools, and techniques, and examines all work products for conformance to specifications.

Preparation of a *Software Quality Assurance Plan* for each software project is a primary responsibility of the software quality assurance group. Topics in a *Software Quality Assurance Plan* include (BUC79):

1. Purpose and scope of the plan
2. Documents referenced in the plan
3. Organizational structure, tasks to be performed, and specific responsibilities as they relate to product quality
4. Documents to be prepared and checks to be made for adequacy of the documentation
5. Standards, practices, and conventions to be used
6. Reviews and audits to be conducted
7. A configuration management plan that identifies software product items, controls and implements changes, and records and reports changed status
8. Practices and procedures to be followed in reporting, tracking, and resolving software problems
9. Specific tools and techniques to be used to support quality assurance activities
10. Methods and facilities to be used to maintain and store controlled versions of identified software
11. Methods and facilities to be used to protect computer program physical media
12. Provisions for ensuring the quality of vendor-provided and subcontractor-developed software
13. Methods and facilities to be used in collecting, maintaining, and retaining quality assurance records

Other duties performed by quality assurance personnel include:

1. Development of standard policies, practices, and procedures
2. Development of testing tools and other quality assurance aids
3. Performance of the quality assurance functions described in the *Software Quality Assurance Plan* for each project
4. Performance and documentation of final product acceptance tests for each software product.

More specifically, a software quality assurance group may perform the following functions:

1. During analysis and design, a *Software Verification Plan* and an *Acceptance Test Plan* are prepared. Tables 2.9 and 2.10 illustrate the format of these plans. The verification plan describes the methods to be used in verifying that the requirements are satisfied by the design documents and that the source code is consistent with the requirements specifications and design documentation. The *Source Code Test Plan* (discussed below) is an important component of the *Software Verification Plan*. The *Acceptance Test Plan* includes test cases, expected outcomes, and capabilities demonstrated by each test case. Often, quality assurance personnel will work with the customer to develop a single *Acceptance Test Plan*. In other cases, the customer will develop an *Acceptance Test Plan* independent of the *Quality Assurance Plan*. In either case, an in-house *Acceptance Test Plan* should be developed by quality assurance personnel. Acceptance testing is further discussed in Section 8.6.2. Following completion of the verification plan and the acceptance plan, a Software Verification Review is held to evaluate the adequacy of the plans.
2. During product evolution, In-Process Audits are conducted to verify consistency and completeness of the work products. Items to be audited for consistency include interface specifications for hardware, software, and people; internal design versus functional specifications; source code versus design documentation; and functional requirements versus test descriptions. In practice, only certain critical portions of the system may be subjected to intensive audits.
3. Prior to product delivery, a Functional Audit and a Physical Audit are performed. The Functional Audit reconfirms that all requirements have been met. The Physical Audit verifies that the source code and all associated documents are complete, internally consistent, consistent with one another, and ready for delivery. A *Software Verification Summary* is prepared to describe the results of all reviews, audits, and tests conducted by quality assurance personnel throughout the development cycle.

Quality assurance personnel are sometimes in charge of arrangements for walkthroughs, inspections, and major milestone reviews. In addition, quality assurance personnel often conduct the project post mortem, write the project legacy document, and provide long-term retention of project records. The quality assurance organization can also serve as a focal point for collection, analysis, and dissemination of quantitative data concerning cost distribution, schedule slippage, error rates, and other factors that influence quality and productivity.

Typically, the quality assurance group will work with the development group to derive the *Source Code Test Plan*. As discussed in Section 5.7, a test plan for the source code specifies the objectives of testing (e.g., to achieve error-free operation under stated conditions for a stated period of time), the test completion criteria (to discover and correct a predetermined number of errors, to achieve a specified percent of logical path coverage), the system integration plan (strategy, schedule, responsible individuals), methods to be used on particular modules (walkthroughs, inspections, static analysis, dynamic tests, formal verification), and particular test inputs and expected outcomes.

As discussed in Sections 5.7 and 8.5, there are four types of tests that the source code must satisfy: function tests, performance tests, stress tests, and structure tests. Function tests and performance tests are based on the requirements specifications; they are designed to demonstrate that the system satisfies its requirements. Therefore, the test plan can be only as good as the requirements, which in turn must be phrased in quantified, testable terms.

Functional test cases specify typical operating conditions, typical input values, and typical expected results. Function tests also test behavior just inside, on, and just beyond the functional boundaries. Examples of functional boundary tests include testing a real-valued square root routine with small positive numbers, zero, and negative numbers; or testing a matrix inversion routine on a one-by-one matrix and a singular matrix.

Performance tests are designed to verify response time under varying loads, percent of execution time spent in various segments of the program, throughput, primary and secondary memory utilization, and traffic rates on data channels and communication links.

Stress tests are designed to overload a system in various ways. Examples of stress tests include attempting to sign on more than the maximum number of allowed terminals, processing more than the allowed number of identifiers or static levels, or disconnecting a communication link.

Structure tests are concerned with examining the internal processing logic of a software system. The particular routines called and the logical paths traversed through the routines are the objects of interest. The goal of structure testing is to traverse a specified number of paths through each routine in the system to establish thoroughness of testing.

A typical approach to structure testing is to augment the functional, performance, and stress tests with additional test cases to achieve the desired level of test coverage. Thus, structure tests cannot be designed until the system is implemented and subjected to the predefined test plan. Structure testing and test coverage criteria are discussed in Section 8.5.

Each test case in the *Source Code Test Plan* should provide the following information:

Type of test (function, performance, stress, structure)
Machine configuration
Test assumptions
Requirements being tested
Exact test stimuli
Expected outcome

In some cases, quality assurance personnel will work with development personnel to derive the *Source Code Test Plan*. In other cases, the quality assurance group will merely verify the adequacy of the test plan for the source code. In either case, the test plan is an important work product of the design process, and like all work products, it should be developed in a systematic manner and evaluated by the quality assurance group.

8.2 WALKTHROUGHS AND INSPECTIONS

Walkthroughs and inspections can be used to systematically examine work products throughout the software life cycle. Requirements, design specifications, test plans, source code, principles of operation, user's manuals, and maintenance procedures are some of the items that can be examined in this manner. In a walkthrough session, the material being examined is presented by a reviewee and evaluated by a team of reviewers. The reviewee "walks through" the work product, and reviewers raise questions on issues of concern. A walkthrough is not a project review, but is rather an in-depth examination of selected work products by individuals who are qualified to offer expert opinions. Inspections differ from walkthroughs in that a team of trained inspectors, working from checklists of items to be examined, perform inspections of work products. Walkthroughs and inspections are discussed in turn.

8.2.1 Walkthroughs

A walkthrough team usually consists of a reviewee and three to five reviewers. On one- or two-person projects it may not be cost-effective to assemble a review team; however, the walkthrough technique can be beneficial with only one or two reviewers. In this case a walkthrough formalizes the process of explaining your work to a colleague.

Members of a walkthrough team may include the project leader, other members of the project team, a representative from the quality assurance group, a technical writer, and other technical personnel who have an interest in the project. Customers and users should be included in walkthroughs during the requirements and preliminary design phases, but they are usually excluded from subsequent walkthrough sessions. Higher level managers should not attend walkthroughs. Walkthrough sessions should be held in an open, nondefensive atmosphere. The presence of a vice president or department manager may inhibit the review process.

The goal of a walkthrough is to discover and make note of problem areas. Problems are not resolved during the walkthrough session. They are resolved by the reviewee following the walkthrough session. A follow-up meeting or follow-up memo should be used to inform reviewers of actions taken. The reviewee may work with one or more reviewers to resolve problems, but it is the reviewee's responsibility to ensure that the problems noted during the walkthrough are solved.

Several guidelines should be observed to gain maximum benefit from walkthroughs:

1. Everyone's work should be reviewed on a scheduled basis. This approach ensures that all work products are reviewed, provides a vehicle of communication among team members, and lessens the threat to individual reviewees. In particular, the project leader's technical work should be reviewed. An open, nondefensive attitude by the project leader can establish a healthy atmosphere for reviews.
2. Emphasis should be placed on detecting errors. A walkthrough session should not be used to correct errors. Errors should be noted for subsequent resolution by the reviewee. To this end, one member of the review team should be designated recording secretary for the session.
3. Major issues should be addressed. Although it is sometimes difficult to distinguish between major and minor issues, walkthrough sessions should not degenerate into detailed discussions of minor problems. For example, major issues of code efficiency might be addressed, but minor issues of coding style should be avoided. Some issues are best discussed in private following the walkthrough. One reviewer should be designated as moderator in order to maintain a positive atmosphere and to keep the walkthrough focused on major issues.
4. Walkthrough sessions should be limited to 2 hours. A definite time limit ensures that the meeting will not drag on for several hours. This helps to limit the scope of material to be examined, reinforces the emphasis on major issues, and provides incentive for active participation by the reviewers.

Successful use of walkthroughs is strongly dependent on establishing a positive, nonthreatening atmosphere for the walkthrough sessions. The project leader, the senior programmers, and the walkthrough moderator should receive special training in walkthrough techniques and group dynamics to ensure the correct psychological setting. Other factors that contribute to the success of walkthroughs include emphasizing the detection of major problems, limiting the time duration of each walkthrough, and scheduling walkthroughs for each team member on a regular basis.

Sufficient time for walkthroughs must be allotted in the project schedule. Walkthrough sessions must be regarded as part of each participant's normal workload, rather than as an overload commitment. The time spent in walkthroughs is amply repaid by numerous benefits: errors are caught at the earliest possible time, when they are easiest and least expensive to fix; project team communication is improved; project personnel learn new techniques from one another and new personnel quickly learn project details; motivation is improved; work products come to be viewed as public documents; and team members derive greater job satisfaction from their work.

Walkthroughs must not be used as vehicles for employee evaluation. Over a period of time, the project leader will observe strengths and weaknesses in each team member. In many cases, project assignments can be adjusted to take advantage of each individual's abilities. In some cases, team members will learn from their colleagues and overcome initial weaknesses. In a few cases, reassignment or dismissal of unsuitable personnel may be necessary. In any case, these actions must be based on observations of numerous factors over a period of time, and not on an individual's performance in one or two walkthrough sessions.

8.2.2 Inspections

Inspections, like walkthroughs, can be used throughout the software life cycle to assess and improve the quality of the various work products. Inspection teams consist of one to four members who are trained for their tasks. The inspectors work from checklists of inspection items. Inspections are conducted in a similar manner to walkthroughs, but more structure is imposed on the sessions, and each participant has a definite role to play.

Design and code inspections were first described by Fagan (FAG76). In Fagan's experiment, three separate inspections were performed: one following design, but prior to implementation; one following implementation, but prior to unit testing; and one following unit testing. The inspection following unit testing was not considered to be cost-effective in discovering errors; therefore, it is not recommended.

According to Fagan, an inspection team consists of four persons, who play the roles of moderator, designer, implementer, and tester. Items to be inspected in a design inspection might include completeness of the design with respect to the user and functional requirements, internal completeness and consistency in definition and usage of terminology, and correctness of the interfaces between modules. Items to be inspected in a code inspection might include subprogram interfaces, decision logic, data referencing, computational expressions, I/O statements, comments, data flow, and memory usage.

Actual items examined under the category of subprogram interfaces, for example, might include (MYE79):

1. Are the numbers of actual parameters and formal parameters in agreement?
2. Do the type attributes of actual and formal parameters match?
3. Do the dimensional units of actual and formal parameters match?
4. Are the numbers, attributes, and ordering of arguments to built-in functions correct?
5. Are constants passed as modifiable arguments?
6. Are global variable definitions and usage consistent among modules?

The actual items in the checklist will depend on the implementation language. In a language that enforces separate compilation, many of the error conditions listed above will be checked by type checking across the compilation interfaces. In FORTRAN systems, on the other hand, none of the conditions listed above are checked by the compiler or linker. They are thus candidates for inspection.

In Fagan's initial experiment, the inspection team conducted two 2-hour sessions per day and expended 25 hours per person (100 person-hours total). Of the errors found during development, 67 percent were found before any unit testing was performed. During the first 7 months of operation, 38 percent fewer errors were found in the inspected program than in a similar program produced by a control group using informal walkthroughs. The difference in productivity between the project team using inspections and the control group was negligible. It should be noted that the productivity data included training time for the inspectors.

In a subsequent experiment, Fagan found that 82 percent of all errors discovered during development of a software product were found during design and code inspections. The savings in programmer resources on the project was 25 percent of estimated cost because most errors were found before unit testing. It was also observed that the inspection rate was approximately five times faster for applications programs than for systems programs.

Subsequent experiments have reported 70 percent and greater error removal during design and code inspections (JON78). Given these results, it is difficult to understand why inspections are not routinely used on every software project. Inspections and walkthroughs are particularly valuable for real-time systems, where debugging of execution sequences is difficult due to the nonrepeatability of error situations.

An interesting aspect of inspections is the observation that different programmers tend to make different kinds of characteristic errors. Errors found during an inspection can be cycled back to the programmers who make them, and with this feedback, programmers tend to eliminate those types of errors from their subsequent work, thus improving quality and productivity.

In his paper, Fagan contrasts walkthroughs and inspections, and observes a number of advantages for inspection teams: inspectors have definite roles to play; the moderator, rather than the reviewee, directs the effort; an error checklist is utilized; and detailed error feedback is provided to individual programmers. On the other hand, we observe that walkthroughs improve project team communication and project morale by involving team members in the walkthrough process. In addition, walkthroughs are an excellent educational medium for new team members. Balanced use of both inspections and walkthroughs is recommended.

8.3 STATIC ANALYSIS

Static analysis is a technique for assessing the structural characteristics of source code, design specifications, or any notational representation that conforms to well-defined syntactic rules. The present discussion is restricted to static analysis of source code. In static analysis, the structure of the code is examined, but the code is not executed. Because static analysis is concerned with program structure, it is particularly useful for discovering questionable coding practices and departures from coding standards, in addition to detecting structural errors such as uninitialized variables and mismatches between actual and formal parameters.

Static analysis can be performed manually using walkthrough or inspection techniques; however, the term "static analysis" is most often used to denote examination of program structure by an automated tool (RAM75, MIL75, FOS76, SOF80, GRC83). A static analyzer will typically construct a symbol table and a graph of control flow for each subprogram, as well as a call graph for the entire program. The symbol table contains information about each variable: its type attributes, the statement where declared, statements where set to a new value, and statements where used to provide values.

Figure 8.1 illustrates a code segment and the corresponding control flow graph. The nodes in a control-flow graph correspond to basic blocks of source code, and the arcs represent possible transfers of control between blocks. A basic block of source code has the property that if the first statement in the block is executed, every statement in the block will be executed. In a call graph, the nodes represent program units and the arcs represent potential invocation of one program unit by another.

Given a control-flow graph and a symbol table that contains, for each variable in a subprogram, the statement numbers where the variables are declared, set, and used, a static analyzer can determine data flow information such as uninitialized variables (on some control paths or on all paths), variables that are declared but never used, and variables that are set but not subsequently used (on some paths or on all paths). For example, in Figure 8.1 variable X is uninitialized on path ABC and is set but not used on path ABD.

Static analyzers typically produce lists of errors, questionable coding practices

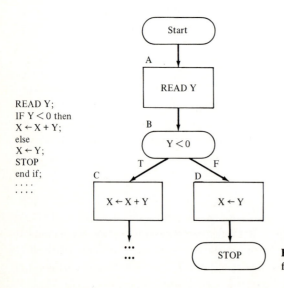

```
READ Y;
IF Y < 0 then
X ← X + Y;
else
X ← Y;
STOP
end if;
. . . .
. . . .
```

Figure 8.1 A code segment and control-flow graph.

Table 8.1 Some static analysis capabilities

Control flow graph

Symbol table for variables (including statement numbers where defined, set, and used)

Call graph (subprograms called by each routine)

Arguments passed to each routine; where called from

Uninitialized variables (on some paths, on all paths)

Variables set but not used (on some paths, on all paths)

Isolated code segments (on some paths, on all paths)

Departures from coding standards (language standards, project standards)

Alignment errors in COMMON blocks (FORTRAN)

Misuse of subprogram parameters: incorrect number of actual parameters, mismatched types between actual and formal parameters, formal output parameters not set by called routine, formal output parameters set but not used by calling routine, actual parameters not used for input or output by called routine

Total number of lines

Total number and location of comment lines

Total number and location of blank lines

Number and location of labels and goto statements

Number and location of system calls

Number and location of literal constants

(anomalies), and departures from coding standards. For instance, a variable that is uninitialized on all paths is a structural error. A variable that is set but not used on any subsequent control path, or a variable that is declared but never used, is not an error, but it is an anomaly that may be symptomatic of an error. Departures from coding standards, such as using non-ANSI FORTRAN constructs, backward GOTO transfers of control, or jumps into loop bodies, can also be detected by static analysis.

Table 8.1 contains a list of typical items that are provided by static analyzers.

There are both practical and theoretical limitations to static analysis. A major practical limitation involves dynamic evaluation of memory references at run time. In higher-level programming languages, array subscripts and pointer variables provide dynamic memory references based on prior computations performed by the program. Static analyzers cannot evaluate subscripts or pointer values; it is thus impossible to distinguish between array elements or members of a list using static analysis techniques. Dynamic test cases are typically used to obtain information that is difficult or impossible to obtain by static analysis techniques.

Major theoretical limitations are imposed on static analysis by decidability theory. Decidability results can be phrased in various ways and have many profound implications. One phrasing states that, given an arbitrary program written in a general purpose programming language (one capable of simulating a Turing machine), it is impossible to examine the program in an algorithmic manner and determine if an arbitrarily chosen statement in the program will be executed when the program operates on arbitrarily chosen input data.

By "algorithmic manner" we mean that it is impossible to write a computer program to perform this task for all possible programs. The term "arbitrary" is used to mean that there are programs and data for which the analysis is possible; however, there exist programs and data for which the analysis is not possible. Furthermore, there is no algorithmic way to identify all programs and data for which the analysis is possible; otherwise the halting problem for Turing machines would be solvable.

Decidability theory thus states that it is not possible to write a static analyzer that will examine an arbitrary program and arbitrary input data and determine whether the program will execute a particular halt statement, or call a particular subroutine, or execute a particular I/O statement, or branch to a given label. It is therefore impossible to perform static analysis on an arbitrary program and automatically derive a set of input data that will drive the program along a particular control path. It is possible, however, to place restrictions on programs so that undecidable issues become decidable. For example, a straight-line program with no branching statements is guaranteed to execute every statement in the program on every execution (excluding overflow, etc.), and static analysis can be used to determine whether a program contains branching statements.

A more interesting case is illustrated in Figure 8.2. Paths ABC and CDE have mutually exclusive conditions; thus, path ABCDE can never be executed. Block E is an unreachable code segment, unless there is another path into the block. In this example, a static analyzer would be able to determine that path ABCDE is not executable (i.e., it is a syntactic path, but not a semantic path). This analysis is possible because the predicates in nodes B and D are linear inequalities when expressed in terms of the input variable Y.

Conjunction of the predicates encountered along an execution path, when expressed in terms of the input variables, forms a "path condition." In Figure 8.2, the path condition for path ABCDE is

$$(Y > 0) \text{ and } (Y < 0)$$

If values for the input variables can be found to satisfy the path condition, program execution using those values will result in traversal of that path. Clearly, there is no value of Y that satisfies the path condition for path ABCDE in Figure 8.2. Thus, the path is not semantically feasible.

Loop tests can be factored into a path condition in the following manner. In a loop construct of the form

$$\text{"for I in M..N loop"}$$

M and N become constraints on the path. If M or N is a constant, that value is used in the set of constraints. For loop constructs of the form

$$\text{while B do S}$$

two paths are formed, one through the body of loop S with predicate B assumed to be true, and one that by-passes S with predicate B assumed to be false.

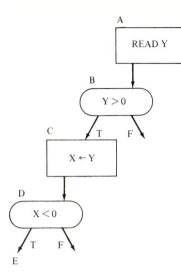

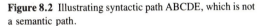

Figure 8.2 Illustrating syntactic path ABCDE, which is not a semantic path.

In general, the problem illustrated in Figure 8.2 is unsolvable, because systems of nonlinear inequalities are unsolvable in the most general case. If path conditions can be expressed as sets of linear inequalities in the input variables, they can be examined algorithmically to determine whether the paths are executable (whether the set of inequalities has a solution). If solutions exist, they represent sets of input data that will drive the program down the paths specified by the corresponding inequalities.

By restricting programs to have only linear path conditions, the problem of automatically deriving test data to drive programs along particular execution paths can be solved using static analysis, symbolic execution, and linear programming techniques. The requirement for linear path conditions is, however, a severe restriction to place on programs and programmers. These issues are examined in greater detail in the following section.

8.4 SYMBOLIC EXECUTION

Symbolic execution is a validation technique in which the input variables of a program unit are assigned symbolic values rather than literal values. A program is analyzed by propagating the symbolic values of the inputs into the operands in expressions. The resulting symbolic expressions are simplified at each step in the computation so that all intermediate computations and decisions are always expressed in terms of the symbolic inputs. For instance, evaluation of an assignment statement results in association of a symbolic expression with the left-hand variable. When that variable is used in subsequent expressions, the current symbolic value is used. In this manner, all computations and decisions are expressed as symbolic values of the inputs.

Figure 8.3 illustrates a program segment and its symbolic execution. Symbolic

PROGRAM   SYMBOLIC EXECUTION

```
READ(B, C);                              B ← b; C ← c;
A := B + C;
X : = A * C;                             B ← b; C ← c;
IF (A ⩽ X) THEN                            A ← b+c;
                                           X ← (b+c)*c;
      : : : : : : : : : : : I              (b+c) ⩽ (b+c)*c

   ELSE IF (B ⩾ 1) OR (B ⩽ −1) THEN
                                          (b ⩾ 1) OR (b ⩽ −1)

      : : : : : : : : : : : II


   ELSE
      : : : : : : : : : : : III
```

Figure 8.3 A Program segment and its symbolic execution.

predicates from the IF statements can be conjoined to form path conditions that describe the constraints under which various segments of code will be executed. Figure 8.4 illustrates path conditions for program segments I, II, and III in Figure 8.3. Figure 8.5 is a plot of the boundaries between regions I, II, and III as functions of symbolic input values b and c. Any literal values of b and c chosen from region I, II, or III will result in execution of code segment I, II, or III.

Symbolic execution can thus be used to derive path conditions that can be solved to find input data values that will drive a program along a particular execution path, provided all predicates in the corresponding path condition are linear

I: $[(b + c) \leqslant (b + c) *c]$
II: $[(b + c) > (b + c) *c]$ AND $[(b \geqslant 1)$ OR $(b \leqslant −1)]$
III: $[(b + c) > (b + c) *c]$ AND $[(−1 < b < +1)]$

Figure 8.4 Symbolic path expressions.

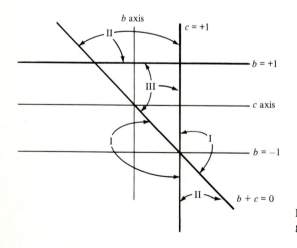

Figure 8.5 Boundaries between regions I, II, and III.

functions of the symbolic input values. When the predicates are nonlinear in the input values, the path condition may or may not be solvable because systems of nonlinear inequalities are in general unsolvable.

In addition to their use in deriving test data, path conditions can be used to show that operations such as division, array referencing, and pointer operations are secure (or unsecure) in particular regions of a program. For example, the boundary b + c = 0 in Figure 8.5 is part of region I. Division by A (symbolic value b + c) may fail in region I; however, division by A in region II or III is safe, provided A is not redefined prior to use in those regions, because b + c = 0 would cause the program to traverse the path into region I; the program will not execute code in regions II and III for literal values of b and c such that b + c = 0.

Program loops can be analyzed using symbolic execution trees. Figure 8.6a illustrates a function that sums elements 1..N of integer array A, provided N is in the range of the array bounds. When the elements of array A are given symbolic values a1, a2, . . . an, symbolic execution of the function results in the symbolic execution tree illustrated in Figure 8.6b.

```
function SUM(A: INTARRAY; N: NATURAL) return INTEGER is
  S: INTEGER := 0;
  I: NATURAL := 1;      SYMBOLIC VALUES
begin                   A1 : a1
  while I <= N loop     A2 : a2
    S := S + A(I);      A3 : a3
    I := I + 1;         :::::
  end loop;             An : an
  return (S);
end SUM;
```

Figure 8.6a An Ada function to sum elements 1..N of array A.

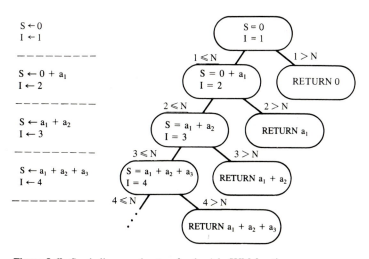

Figure 8.6b Symbolic execution tree for the Ada SUM function.

The computation described by the symbolic execution tree can be expressed in symbolic form as

$$S = \sum_{j=1}^{I-1} Aj$$

this result is the "loop invariant."

A loop invariant summarizes the behavior of a loop, independent of the number of times the loop is traversed. Techniques for proving that a loop invariant is in fact invariant are examined in Section 8.7. Given that the loop invariant in Figure 8.6b is truly invariant, it can be used to show that function SUM returns the desired value. On loop exit, I has the value $N + 1$. Substituting $N + 1$ for I in the invariant results in

$$S = \sum_{j=1}^{(N+1)-1} Aj = \sum_{j=1}^{N} Aj$$

which is the desired result.

The example in Figure 8.6 illustrates the technique of expressing output values as symbolic expressions of input variables. Symbolic output expressions can be examined for computational errors, and used to derive particular input data values that will produce certain desired results under actual test execution.

To summarize, symbolic execution can be used to generate intermediate expressions and output expressions as functions of the input variables, to derive loop invariants, to detect infeasible paths through a program (see Figure 8.2), and to demonstrate the potential for, or lack of potential for, semantic errors in certain regions of the code (division by zero, array reference out of bounds, etc.). In the latter case, the postulated condition (e.g., $Z = 0, I > N$) is conjoined to the path condition. Input values that satisfy the augmented path condition will cause the error. Conversely, if there is no solution to the augmented path condition, the error cannot occur under any set of input values.

Symbolic execution can be performed manually or by an automated tool. Symbolic execution systems have been developed for various programming languages: ATTEST (CLA76) and DISSECT (HOW78) symbolically execute FORTRAN programs, EFFIGY (DAR78) operates on programs written in a subset of PL/1, and SELECT (BOY75) symbolically executes LISP programs. Goals for these experimental systems included automatic generation of output expressions as functions of the input variables and computation paths, detection of infeasible paths through the program, detection of semantic errors in the code, automated generation of test data, informal verification of programs, and derivation of loop invariants.

All these systems are (were) experimental in nature. There are no widely used production versions of symbolic execution systems, although some validation systems have utilized symbolic execution techniques to establish factors such as safe array references (RAM75). Problems to be overcome in symbolic execution include symbolic handling of loops, symbolic evaluation of subscripts and pointers, treatment of nonlinear inequalities in path expressions, and the large amount of detail to be handled.

In the latter regard, many investigators feel that symbolic execution techniques are best applied at the level of functional specifications and design specifications, where the amount of detail to be handled is less. Also, we observe that manual application of symbolic execution is a powerful tool for reasoning about programs.

Finally, we observe that symbolic execution is an important conceptual tool that forms the bridge from testing to formal verification. In Section 8.5, the bridge between testing and symbolic execution is demonstrated in connection with the discussion of domain testing theory, where the intermediate computations must be expressed in terms of the input variables.

The bridge to testing is also apparent when one considers the possibility of supplying some program inputs in literal form and some in symbolic form. If all inputs are literal, the program is being tested. If all inputs are symbolic, the program is being analyzed using symbolic execution techniques. It is thus possible to vary the degree of symbolic execution from none in the pure testing case to all in the pure symbolic case. Often, it is possible to determine the sensitivity of a program to a particular input variable (or combination of variables) by using a symbol value for the variable(s) of interest and literal values for all other inputs.

In Section 8.7, we will see that loop invariants are the essence of formal verification for programs written in procedural programming languages. In this section, we have demonstrated that it is sometimes possible to recognize the general form of a loop invariant using symbolic execution. Thus, the bridge from symbolic execution to formal verification is evident.

8.5 UNIT TESTING AND DEBUGGING

Static analysis is used to investigate the structural properties of source code. Dynamic test cases are used to investigate the behavior of source code by executing the program on the test data. As before, we use the term "program unit" to denote a routine or a collection of routines implemented by an individual programmer. In a well-designed system, a program unit is a stand-alone program or a functional unit of a larger system.

8.5.1 Unit Testing

Unit testing comprises the set of tests performed by an individual programmer prior to integration of the unit into a larger system. The situation is illustrated as follows:

Coding & debugging $\longrightarrow$ unit testing $\longrightarrow$ integration testing

A program unit is usually small enough that the programmer who developed it can test it in great detail, and certainly in greater detail than will be possible when the unit is integrated into an evolving software product. As discussed in Section

5.7, there are four categories of tests that a programmer will typically perform on a program unit:

Functional tests
Performance tests
Stress tests
Structure tests

Functional test cases involve exercising the code with nominal input values for which the expected results are known, as well as boundary values (minimum values, maximum values, and values on and just outside the functional boundaries) and special values, such as logically related inputs, 1×1 matrices, the identity matrix, files of identical elements, and empty files.

Performance testing determines the amount of execution time spent in various parts of the unit, program throughput, response time, and device utilization by the program unit. A certain amount of performance tuning may be done during unit testing; however, caution must be exercised to avoid expending too much effort on fine tuning of a program unit that contributes little to the overall performance of the entire system. Performance testing is most productive at the subsystem and system levels.

Stress tests are those tests designed to intentionally break the unit. A great deal can be learned about the strengths and limitations of a program by examining the manner in which a program unit breaks.

Structure tests are concerned with exercising the internal logic of a program and traversing particular execution paths. Some authors refer collectively to functional, performance, and stress testing as "black box" testing, while structure testing is referred to as "white box" or "glass box" testing. The major activities in structural testing are deciding which paths to exercise, deriving test data to exercise those paths, determining the test coverage criterion to be used, executing the test cases, and measuring the test coverage achieved when the test cases are exercised.

A test coverage (or test completion) criterion must be established for unit testing, because program units usually contain too many paths to permit exhaustive testing. This can be seen by examining the program segment in Figure 8.7. As

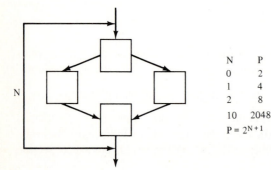

N	P
0	2
1	4
2	8
10	2048

$$P = 2^{N+1}$$

Figure 8.7 Loop paths.

illustrated in Figure 8.7, loops introduce combinatorial numbers of execution paths and make exhaustive testing impossible.

Even if it were possible to successfully test all paths through a program, correctness would not be guaranteed by path testing because the program might have missing paths and computational errors that were not discovered by the particular test cases chosen. A missing path error occurs when a branching statement and the associated computations are accidentally omitted. Missing path errors can only be detected by functional test cases derived from the requirements specifications. Thus, tests based solely on the program structure cannot detect all the potential errors in a source program. Coincidental correctness occurs when a test case fails to detect a computational error. For instance, the expressions (A + A) and (A*A) have identical values when A has the value 2.

Program errors can be classified as missing path errors, computational errors, and domain errors. Tai has observed that N + 1 linearly independent test cases are required to establish computational correctness of a program that performs only linear calculations on N input variables (TAI80). By linear calculations, we mean that all computations are linear functions of the input variables when symbolic input values are propagated throughout the program (perhaps using symbolic execution techniques).

A domain error occurs when a program traverses the wrong path because of an incorrect predicate in a branching statement. White and Cohen have shown that, for very simple programs, domain errors can be detected by test cases that are either on or near the borders of the path domains (WHI80).

The borders of a path domain are determined by the inequalities in the test cases. For example, region III in Figure 8.5 is formed by the borders $b + c = 0$, $b = 1$, and $c = 1$. Domain testing theory requires, among other things, that each border of each domain be determined by a linear predicate having only one relational operator. Other restrictions that must be placed on programs to make domain testing theory valid include (WHI80):

1. Coincidental correctness does not occur for any test case. If a test traverses an incorrect path, the output values are different from the values that would be computed on the correct path.
2. There are no missing paths associated with the path being tested.
3. Each border is produced by a predicate having only one relational operator.
4. Each adjacent path domain computes a function different from the function computed by the path being tested.
5. The border being tested is a linear function of the input variables. If the border is incorrect, the correct border is linear.
6. The input space is continuous rather than discrete.
7. Each test case off the border (each off point) is a small distance, epsilon, from the border.

Under these rather severe restrictions, domain testing theory states that domain errors can be detected as follows:

1. For each border of an N-dimensional domain, errors of magnitude greater than epsilon can be detected if there are N test cases on the border and one test case outside the domain but within epsilon of the border, provided the border is formed by an inequality test ($<$, $<=$, $>$, $>=$).
2. For each border of an N-dimensional space formed by an equality or non-equality test ($=$, $/=$), there must be N + 1 test cases on the border, and two test cases within epsilon of the border. Furthermore, the two off-border points must be on opposite sides of the border, and one of the points on the border must be on the segment connecting the two off points.

Of course, real programs do not satisfy the linearity assumptions of computational or domain testing theory, and so they will require even more test cases than indicated by the theory to detect these types of errors. Testing theory based on simplifying models thus provides insight into the difficulties encountered in testing real programs.

Establishing a test completion criterion is another difficulty encountered in unit testing of real programs. In practice, there are three commonly used measures of test coverage in unit testing: statement coverage, branch coverage, and logical path coverage. These measures are illustrated in Figure 8.8. Using statement coverage as the test completion criterion, the programmer attempts to find a set of test cases that will execute each statement in the program at least once. Using branch coverage as the test completion criterion, the programmer attempts to find a set of test cases that will execute each branching statement in each direction at least once. Logical path coverage acknowledges that the order in which branches are executed during a test (the path traversed) is an important factor in determining the test outcome. Several methods for systematically determining the paths to be tested according to some logical criterion have been proposed (WOO80). Of course, none of these criteria guarantee computational or domain correctness.

Myers has observed that branch testing may not detect all errors in multiple condition predicates (MYE79). The following segment of Ada code illustrates this point:

```
if (X > 3 and then Y  = 2) then
    Z := 1;
endif;
if (X = 4 or else Z > 3) then
    Z := Z + 1;
endif;
```

The test cases (X = 5, Y = 2, Z = 3) and (X = 4, Y = 3, Z = 3) achieve branch coverage by covering the True-False and False-True paths through the segment. Note, however, that the second condition in the second if statement (Z > 3) is not tested by either test case. If, for example, the condition is erroneous and should be (Z <=3), this set of test data will not detect the error.

On the other hand, the test cases (X = 3, Y = 2, Z = 5) and (X = 4, Y = 3, Z = 3) test both conditions in both predicates but fail to achieve branch coverage

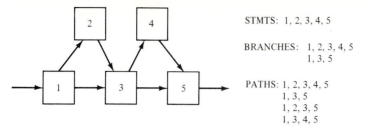

STMTS: 1, 2, 3, 4, 5

BRANCHES: 1, 2, 3, 4, 5
            1, 3, 5

PATHS: 1, 2, 3, 4, 5
      1, 3, 5
      1, 2, 3, 5
      1, 3, 4, 5

Figure 8.8 Coverage measures.

because both tests exercise the False-True path. In order to thoroughly exercise program logic, it is necessary to test all branches and all possible outcomes of multiple conditions in the predicates.

An often used rule of thumb for unit test completion is 85 percent to 90 percent of branch coverage (that is, 85 percent to 90 percent of all branch alternatives have been traversed by the set of unit test cases). This coverage criterion strikes a balance between using an excessive number of test cases and leaving test completion to the intuition of each individual programmer. Typically, functional, performance, and stress tests based on the functional requirements and a programmer's intuition will achieve 60 percent to 70 percent of statement coverage. Adding branch tests to achieve 85 percent to 90 percent branch coverage is thus a significant improvement in test coverage.

It may not be possible to achieve 100 percent of branch coverage because of the difficulties involved in finding input data that will exercise a nested branching statement in a particular way. Also, some code may be exercised only under exception conditions that cannot be duplicated during unit testing.

A technique often used during unit testing is to measure path coverage achieved by functional, performance, and stress tests, and to add additional test cases until the desired level of branch coverage is achieved. Of course, a testing tool is required to determine the paths traversed by individual test cases and by the cumulative set of test cases.

Test completion criteria based on considerations other than path coverage are sometimes used. These criteria typically involve termination of testing when a predetermined (low) rate of error discovery is achieved, or when a predetermined number of errors have been discovered and corrected; for example, when 95 percent of the estimated errors have been discovered and removed. Techniques for estimating the number of errors remaining in a program include predictive models, rules of thumb, error seeding, and trend plotting.

Predictive models are based on statistical theory; they are discussed by Shooman (SHO83). Rules of thumb are based on previous experience. It may be known, for example, that a similar project experienced five errors per hundred lines of source code during testing and the first 6 months of operation. Error seeding is a technique that involves intentional introduction (seeding) of errors into the source code. After some period of time, the number of nonseeded errors discovered during testing is multiplied by the ratio of total seeded errors to seeded errors discovered during testing to produce an estimate of the total number of nonseeded errors remaining in the program.

A trend plot is a graph of errors discovered per unit time versus time; for example, the number of errors discovered per day versus days. Typically the graph will build up to a maximum value and tail off with passing time. One must be cautious, however, to consider the nature and severity of the errors being discovered. Often, the large number of errors found initially are simple and easy to fix. The really tough errors may be the ones that are not discovered until late in testing, when the trend plot might indicate that sufficient testing has already occurred.

Several tools have been developed to support unit testing. They include the SOFTOOL package, RXVP80, the NBS FORTRAN77 Analyzer, and TOOL-PACK (SOF80, GRC83, FTN77, TOO83). These tools provide both static analysis and dynamic tracing capabilities. SOFTOOL and RXVP80 both provide optional structured FORTRAN preprocessors and operate on FORTRAN IV programs, while the NBS Analyzer and TOOLPACK operate on FORTRAN77 programs. Each set of tools provides different, but overlapping, sets of capabilities, and none provides all the capabilities one might desire. Some of the capabilities provided by these tools are listed in Table 8.2 under the categories of static analysis, dynamic tracing, optimization, and test coverage (LIG83).

8.5.2 Debugging

Debugging is the process of isolating and correcting the causes of known errors. Success at debugging requires highly developed problem-solving skills. Commonly used debugging methods include induction, deduction, and backtracking (BRO73, MYE79). Debugging by induction involves the following steps:

1. Collect the available information. Enumerate known facts about the observed failure and known facts concerning successful test cases. What are the observed symptoms? When did the error occur? Under what conditions did it occur? How does the failure case differ from successful cases?
2. Look for patterns. Examine the collected information for conditions that differentiate the failure case from the successful cases.
3. Form one or more hypotheses. Derive one or more hypotheses from the observed relationships. If no hypotheses are apparent, re-examine the available information and collect additional information, perhaps by running more test cases. If several hypotheses emerge, rank them in the order of most likely to least likely.
4. Prove or disprove each hypothesis. Re-examine the available information to determine whether the hypothesis explains all aspects of the observed problem. Do not overlook the possibility that there may be multiple errors. Do not proceed to step 5 until step 4 is completed.
5. Implement the appropriate corrections. Make the correction(s) indicated by your evaluation of the various hypotheses. Make the corrections to a back-up copy of the code, in case the modifications are not correct.
6. Verify the correction. Rerun the failure case to be sure that the fix corrects the

Table 8.2 Testing tool capabilities

Static Analysis
  Incorrect number of arguments in a subroutine call
  Unreachable code segments
  DO loop variable redefined inside the loop
  Modification of dummy arguments in a subprogram
  Function references in conditionally executed expressions
  Identifiers referenced but not set
  Identifiers set but not referenced
  Identifiers referenced and then set
  Identifiers declared by default
  List of routines called by each routine
  List of routines that call each routine
  Identifier cross-references for each program unit
  Identifier cross-references for the entire program
  Total number of statements of each type

Dynamic Tracing
  Trace message for each statement executed
  Routine name printed on entry to and exit from the routine
  Selective tracing capability
  Breakpoints, examination of state, single-step execution

Optimization
  Total time, percent of time, and average time spent in each routine
    Including time in called routines
    Excluding time in called routines
  Comparison of average time on a single run to average time on previous runs
  Total time and percent of time spent executing each statement

Test Coverage
  Number of routines executed cumulatively and executed on this run
  Number of new routines executed on this run
  Number of times each routine was executed cumulatively and on this run
  Number and percent of statements executed cumulatively and on this run
  Number of times each statement was executed cumulatively and on this run .

observed symptom. Run additional test cases to increase your confidence in the fix. Rerun the previously successful test cases to be sure that your fix has not created new problems. If the fix is successful, make the fix-up copy the primary version of the code and delete the old copy. If the fix is not successful, go to step 1.

Debugging by deduction proceeds as follows:

1. List possible causes for the observed failure.
2. Use the available information to eliminate various hypotheses.
3. Elaborate the remaining hypotheses.
4. Prove or disprove each hypothesis.
5. Determine the appropriate corrections.
6. Verify the corrections.

Debugging by backtracking involves working backward in the source code from the point where the error was observed in an attempt to identify the exact point where the error occurred. It may be necessary to run additional test cases in order to collect more information. Techniques for collecting the necessary information are described in the following paragraphs.

Traditional debugging techniques utilize diagnostic output statements, snapshot dumps, selective traces on data values and control flow, and instruction-dependent breakpoints. Modern debugging tools utilize assertion-controlled breakpoints and execution histories.

Diagnostic output statements can be embedded in the source code as specially formatted comment statements that are activated using a special translator option. Diagnostic output from these statements provides snapshots of selected components of the program state, from which the programmer attempts to infer program behavior. The program state includes the values associated with all currently accessible symbols and any additional information, such as the program stack and program counter, needed to continue execution from a particular point in the execution sequence of the program.

A snapshot dump is a machine-level representation of the partial or total program state at a particular point in the execution sequence. A structured snapshot dump is a source-level representation of the partial or total state of a program. The names and current values of symbols accessible at the time of the snapshot are provided.

A trace facility lists changes in selected state components. In its simplest form, a trace will print all changes in data values for all variables and all changes in control flow. A selective trace will trace specific variables and control flow in specific regions of the source text.

A traditional breakpoint facility interrupts program execution and transfers control to the programmer's terminal when execution reaches a specified "break" instruction in the source code. The programmer can typically examine the program state, change values of state components, set new breakpoints, and resume execution in either normal mode or single step mode, perhaps starting at another instruction location.

Assertion-driven debugging. Assertions are logical predicates written at the source-code level to describe relationships among components of the current program state and relationships between program states (e.g., $J < 10$ *and* $A(I) = M$). An assertion violation can alter the execution sequence, cause recording of state component information for later processing, or trap control to the programmer's terminal. Assertion violations that transfer control to the programmer's terminal are called "conditional breakpoints." They become unconditional breakpoints (traditional instruction-dependent breakpoints) under assertions such as $0 = 1$, or FALSE. Conditional breakpoints are state-dependent, while unconditional breakpoints are instruction-dependent. Conditional breakpoints allow the programmer to focus on the nature of the error itself, rather than on instruction locations where the error might have occurred.

An assertion-driven debugging and unit testing tool called ALADDIN is described in (FAI79). ALADDIN is an acronym for Assembly Language Assertion-Driven Debugging Interpreter. ALADDIN is an interactive conditional breakpoint facility for debugging and testing of assembly language programs. If an assertion becomes false during execution of an object program, a breakpoint is executed and control is passed to the user's terminal.

In the ALADDIN system, assertions can be used either for debugging-finding the cause of a known error, or for testing-determining if certain errors are present. Debugging assertions take forms such as

$$\$ \ PC \ > \ 377 \ \$$$

or

$$\$ \ *AC2 \ < \ > \ 177777 \ \$$$

The first example states that the program counter is always greater than 377 (octal). The assertion is violated and a breakpoint will be executed if the machine attempts to execute an instruction in page zero of the machine. The second example states that accumulator 2 does not contain the indicated octal constant. A breakpoint will be executed if a negative "1" in two's complement form is stored in accumulator 2. Furthermore, the breakpoint will occur on the instruction cycle in which the negative 1 is stored in accumulator 2. This pinpoints the exact instruction execution where the error occurred. Speculation of the form "somehow accumulator two is getting a negative 1" is reduced to exact determination of which instruction execution causes accumulator 2 to receive the offending value.

In ALADDIN, testing assertions take the form

$$\$ \ X \ < \ 10; \ Y \ >= \ 0 \ \$$$

or

$$\$ \ X \ + \ Y \ <= \ *AC0 \ \& \ *CBIT \ = \ 1 \ \$$$

The first example states that $X \ < \ 10$ *or* $Y \ >= \ 0$ is true. A breakpoint will be executed on any instruction cycle in which the assertion becomes false (i.e., if $X \ >= \ 10$ *and* $Y \ < \ 0$ occur simultaneously). The second example states that the sum of the values in symbolic locations X and Y is less than or equal to the value in accumulator 0 *and* the carry bit is 1. A breakpoint will be executed if the sum of X and Y exceeds the value in accumulator 0 *or* if the carry bit becomes 0.

In the debugging mode, an assertion facility frees the user from the customary trial and error guessing required to locate the source of an error because the program is interrupted on the instruction cycle in which the error occurs. In the testing mode, only departures from asserted behavior are reported. The programmer does not have to examine dumps and traces to ascertain correct program behavior. The goal of assertion-driven testing is to provide a sufficient set of assertions so that the absence of an assertion violation assures proper functioning of the software being tested.

Execution histories. An execution history is a record of execution events collected from an executing program. The history is typically stored in a data base for post-mortem examination after the program has terminated execution. A traceback facility uses the execution history to trace control flow and data flow both forward and backward in execution time. Control flow and data flow dependencies can be traced either forward or backward in execution time from the current position in the execution history. Interpreting the execution history in reverse order provides the illusion that the program is executing backward in execution time. This permits analysis of how a particular computation was influenced by previous events. This capability is extremely valuable in debugging and testing of nonrepeatable error conditions such as those that arise in real-time processing of external events.

The Extendable Debugging and Monitoring System (EXDAMS) and the Interactive Semantic Modeling System (ISMS) are two examples of debugging and testing facilities that incorporate an execution history collection and display capability (BAL69, FAI75). The structure of the ISMS debugging and testing facility is illustrated in Figure 8.9.

The ISMS scheme utilizes a preprocessor to perform static analysis of the source program and to instrument the source code with history-collecting subroutine calls. A program model is built by the static analyzer and stored in the program data base. The program model contains a copy of the uninstrumented source text, a symbol table for the program identifiers, an execution model of the program, and a cross reference table to interface the execution model to the source text. The execution history is interfaced to the execution model, which is in turn cross referenced to the source text. In this manner program behavior can be presented to the user in source level terms.

In an execution history system, the user is unable to interact directly with the executing program, but instead examines program behavior by interrogating the post-mortem data base. This inability to interact with the executing program characterizes the differences between the two fundamental approaches to debugging and unit testing: interpretation and history collection.

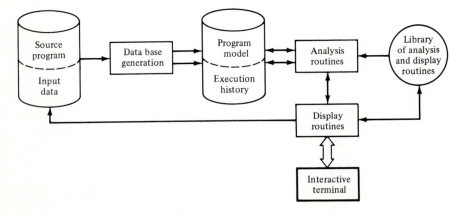

Figure 8.9 Structure of the ISMS Program Testing System.

The execution state of a program at any given point in execution time consists of the values associated with the currently accessible symbols plus the control flow information needed to continue execution from that point. In the execution history approach, only the changes in execution state are recorded as the program executes. This approach is taken to reduce the unreasonable overhead in execution time and memory space that would be required to maintain a complete copy of the execution state at each step in the execution sequence. An execution state is reconstructed from an incremental history of changes by starting at the beginning of the history, in the initial state, and scanning through the history to accumulate the changes that occur up to the desired point in execution time. Other execution states can be derived by scanning forward or backward through the execution history from that point, modifying the state as appropriate.

Interpretive systems typically maintain a complete execution state at each point in execution time. The state is updated at each step in the execution sequence. This method maintains little or no historical information concerning the sequence of execution states.

The relative merits of interpreters and execution histories are evident. An execution history contains a complete set of execution states in incremental form. Thus, summary information can be collected, changes in execution states can be traced either forward or backward in execution time, arbitrarily complex assertions can be checked without preplanning, and flowback analysis can be provided.

On the other hand, the user cannot stop execution at an arbitrary point, change the execution state in various ways, and continue execution as is possible in an interpretive system such as ALADDIN. However, interpreters suffer the disadvantage of not maintaining historical information. When an interpreter is used, it may be necessary to re-execute the entire program to check an assertion involving multiple program states, to collect summary statistics, or to determine control flow and data flow dependencies. Many interpretive systems, including ALADDIN, keep a history log of the last 10 or 20 execution states, which partially alleviates, but does not totally solve, this problem.

8.6 SYSTEM TESTING

System testing involves two kinds of activities: integration testing and acceptance testing. Strategies for integrating software components into a functioning product include the bottom-up strategy, the top-down strategy, and the sandwich strategy. Careful planning and scheduling are required to ensure that modules will be available for integration into the evolving software product when needed. The integration strategy dictates the order in which modules must be available, and thus exerts a strong influence on the order in which modules are written, debugged, and unit tested.

Acceptance testing involves planning and execution of functional tests, performance tests, and stress tests to verify that the implemented system satisfies its requirements. Acceptance tests are typically performed by the quality assurance and/or customer organizations. Depending on local circumstances, the development group may or may not be involved in acceptance testing. Integration testing and acceptance testing are discussed in the following sections.

8.6.1 Integration Testing

Bottom-up integration is the traditional strategy used to integrate the components of a software system into a functioning whole. Bottom-up integration consists of unit testing, followed by subsystem testing, followed by testing of the entire system. Unit testing has the goal of discovering errors in the individual modules of the system. Modules are tested in isolation from one another in an artificial environment known as a "test harness," which consists of the driver programs and data necessary to exercise the modules. Unit testing should be as exhaustive as possible to ensure that each representative case handled by each module has been tested. Unit testing is eased by a system structure that is composed of small, loosely coupled modules.

A subsystem consists of several modules that communicate with each other through well-defined interfaces. Normally, a subsystem implements a major segment of the total system. The primary purpose of subsystem testing is to verify operation of the interfaces between modules in the subsystem. Both control and data interfaces must be tested. Large software systems may require several levels of subsystem testing; lower-level subsystems are successively combined to form higher-level subsystems. In most software systems, exhaustive testing of subsystem capabilities is not feasible due to the combinational complexity of the module interfaces; therefore, test cases must be carefully chosen to exercise the interfaces in the desired manner.

System testing is concerned with subtleties in the interfaces, decision logic, control flow, recovery procedures, throughput, capacity, and timing characteristics of the entire system. Careful test planning is required to determine the extent and nature of system testing to be performed and to establish criteria by which the results will be evaluated.

Disadvantages of bottom-up testing include the necessity to write and debug test harnesses for the modules and subsystems, and the level of complexity that results from combining modules and subsystems into larger and larger units. The extreme case of complexity results when each module is unit tested in isolation and all modules are then linked and executed in one single integration run. This is the "big bang" approach to integration testing. The main problem with big-bang integration is the difficulty of isolating the sources of errors.

Test harnesses provide data environments and calling sequences for the routines and subsystems that are being tested in isolation. Test harness preparation can amount to 50 percent or more of the coding and debugging effort for a software product.

Top-down integration starts with the main routine and one or two immediately subordinate routines in the system structure. After this top-level "skeleton" has been thoroughly tested, it becomes the test harness for its immediately subordinate routines. Top-down integration requires the use of program stubs to simulate the effect of lower-level routines that are called by those being tested.

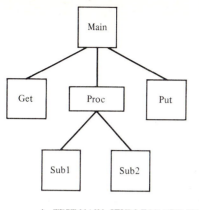

1. TEST MAIN; STUBS FOR GET, PROC, PUT
2. ADD GET; TEST MAIN, GET
3. ADD PROC; STUBS FOR SUB1, SUB2
4. ADD PUT; TEST MAIN, GET, PROC, PUT
5. ADD SUB1
   TEST MAIN, GET, PROC, PUT, SUB1
6. ADD SUB2
   TEST MAIN, GET, PROC, PUT, SUB1, SUB2

Figure 8.10 Top-down integration testing strategy.

Figure 8.10 illustrates integrated top-down integration testing. Top-down integration offers several advantages:

1. System integration is distributed throughout the implementation phase. Modules are integrated as they are developed.
2. Top-level interfaces are tested first and most often.
3. The top-level routines provide a natural test harness for lower-level routines.
4. Errors are localized to the new modules and interfaces that are being added.

While it may appear that top-down integration is always preferable, there are many situations in which it is not possible to adhere to a strict top-down coding and integration strategy. For example, it may be difficult to find top-level input data that will exercise a lower level module in a particular desired manner. Also, the evolving system may be very expensive to run as a test harness for new routines; it may not be cost effective to relink and re-execute a system of 50 or 100 routines each time a new routine is added. Significant amounts of machine time can often be saved by testing subsystems in isolation before inserting them into the evolving top-down structure. In some cases, it may not be possible to use program stubs to simulate modules below the current level (e.g., device drivers, interrupt handlers). It may be necessary to test certain critical low-level modules first. The sandwich testing strategy may be preferred in these situations.

Sandwich integration is predominately top-down, but bottom-up techniques are used on some modules and subsystems. This mix alleviates many of the problems encountered in pure top-down testing and retains the advantages of top-down integration at the subsystem and system level.

Automated tools used in integration testing include module drivers, test data generators, environment simulators, and a library management facility to allow easy configuration and reconfiguration of system elements. Automated module drivers permit specification of test cases (both inputs and expected results) in a descriptive language. The driver tool then calls the routine(s) using the specified test cases, compares actual results with expected results, and reports discrepancies.

Some module drivers also provide program stubs for top-down testing. Test cases are written for the stub, and when the stub is invoked by the routine being tested, the driver examines the input parameters to the stub and returns the corresponding outputs to the routine. Automated test drivers include AUT, MTS, TEST-MASTER, and TPL (HEU74, MTS74, GEN77, PAN78).

Test data generators are of two varieties: those that generate files of random data values according to some predefined format, and those that generate test data for particular execution paths. In the latter category, symbolic executors such as ATTEST can sometimes be used to derive a set of test data that will force program execution to follow a particular control path (CLA76). Test data are generated from formal specifications by the TESTER system (PET76).

There are other tools that can be used to aid derivation of test cases. For example, some static analyzers can identify the minimum number of paths that must be executed in order to achieve coverage of all decision branches in a module.

Environment simulators are sometimes used during integration and acceptance testing to simulate the operating environment in which the software will function. Simulators are used in situations in which operation of the actual environment is impractical. Such situations include development of software for nonexistent machines, simulation of real-time inputs from an expensive to operate or nonexistent system, and situations in which live testing is impossible (e.g., ballistic missile systems). Examples of environment simulators are PRIM (GAL75) for emulating machines that do not exist, and the Saturn Flight Program Simulator for simulating live flight tests (JAC70).

An automated development library consists of a data base that contains all project documentation, source code, object code, test cases, error reports, etc., in machine-readable form. Utility programs such as text editors, compilers, report formatters, and management information tools allow access to and manipulation of materials. Automated library systems include the Software Factory (BRA75), PDS (DAV77), and SCCS (ROC75). Currently, a great deal of interest is being focused on the Ada Programming Support Environments (STO80).

Projects that do not incorporate full-scale development libraries sometimes use validation libraries to maintain code, test plans, test cases, test results, error reports, and test schedule status information. A validation library can be automated or manually maintained. In either case, system integration is greatly eased through use of a central repository for information.

8.6.2 Acceptance Testing

Acceptance testing involves planning and execution of functional tests, performance tests, and stress tests in order to demonstrate that the implemented system satisfies its requirements. It is not unusual for two sets of acceptance tests to be run:

those developed by the quality assurance group and those developed by the customer.

In addition to functional and performance tests, stress tests are performed to determine the limitations of the system. For example, a compiler might be tested to determine the effect of symbol table overflow, or a real-time system might be tested to determine the effect of simultaneous arrival of numerous high-priority interrupts.

Typically, acceptance tests will incorporate test cases developed during unit testing and integration testing. Additional test cases are added to achieve the desired level of functional, performance, and stress testing of the entire system. Tools of special importance during acceptance testing include a test coverage analyzer, a timing analyzer, and a coding standards checker.

A test coverage analyzer records the control paths followed for each test case. The cumulative record is used to establish the extent of test coverage obtained during acceptance testing. Without this tool, it is impossible to establish the extent of test coverage obtained. In large systems, the coverage analyzer may record only the routines called and not the individual statements executed.

A timing analyzer reports the time spent in various regions of the source code under different test cases. It is not unusual for a program to spend 80 to 90 percent of execution time in 20 percent or less of the code. These regions of the code are areas to concentrate on to improve system performance.

Certain coding standards are often stated in the product requirements; for example, no GOTOs, no recursive routines, ANSI FORTRAN constructs, etc. Coding standards may be project-related, customer-related, developer-related, or language-related. Manual inspection is usually not an adequate mechanism for detecting violations of coding standards. Static analyzers and standards checkers can be used to inspect code for departures from standards and guidelines.

8.7 FORMAL VERIFICATION

Formal verification involves the use of rigorous, mathematical techniques to demonstrate that computer programs have certain desired properties. The methods of input-output assertions, weakest preconditions, and structural induction are three commonly used techniques. Each is discussed in turn.

8.7.1 Input-Output Assertions

The method of input-output assertions was introduced by Floyd (FLO67) and refined by Hoare (HOA73) and Dijkstra (DIJ76). Floyd's work was seminal to the entire field of formal verification.

Using input-output assertions, predicates (assertions) are associated with the entry point, the exit point, and various intermediate points in the source code. The predicates, or verification conditions, must be true whenever the associated code is executed. The notation (P) S (R) is used to mean that if predicate P is true prior to executing code segment S, predicate R will be true following execution of S. For example,

$$(1 < i < N) \; i := i + 1 \; (2 < i < N+1)$$

The composition rule of logic permits conjunctions of predicates to be formed along particular execution paths:

(P) S1, (Q) *and* (Q) S2 (R) *implies* (P) S1; S2 (R)

The composition rule permits the following statement: If all the intermediate predicates are true along a particular execution path, the truth of the input assertion (input predicate) will imply the truth of the output assertion (output predicate) for that execution path.

The method of input-output assertions states that if the conjunction of predicates from the input assertion to an output assertion is true, and if the input assertion is satisfied by the input conditions, and if the program terminates after following the execution path of interest, then the output assertion will be true on termination of the program.

Termination is proved by showing that the execution sequence for each loop monotonically decreases (increases) some nonnegative (negative) property on each pass through the loop. Due to the characteristics of the loop, this property must eventually reach a lower (upper) bound, and execution of the loop will terminate. For example, an integer loop counter starts at $N > 0$ and is decremented by 1 until it reaches 0, or it starts at 0 and is incremented by 1 until it reaches $N > 0$.

An example from Floyd's original paper, rewritten in Ada, is illustrated in Figure 8.11 (which is similar to Figure 8.5).

```
function SUM(A: INTARRAY; N: NATURAL) return INTEGER is
    -- N ∈ J +   (J +  is the set of positive integers)
I: NATURAL := 1;
    -- (N ∈ J + ) and (I = 1)
S: INTEGER := 0;
    -- (N ∈ J + ) and (I = 1) and (S = 0)
while I <= N loop
```

$$-- (N \in J +) \text{ and } (I \in J +) \text{ and } (I <= N + 1) \text{ and } S = \sum_{j=1}^{I-1} Aj$$

```
    S := S + A(I);
```

$$-- (N \in J +) \text{ and } (I \in J +) \text{ and } (I <= N) \text{ and } S = \sum_{j=1}^{I} Aj$$

```
    I := I + 1;
```

$$-- (N \in J +) \text{ and } (I \in J +) \text{ and } (2 <= I <= N + 1) \text{ and } S = \sum_{j=1}^{I-1} Aj$$

```
end loop;
```

$$-- (N \in J +) \text{ and } (I = N + 1) \text{ and } S = \sum_{j=1}^{I-1} Aj = \sum_{j=1}^{(N+1)-1} Aj$$

$$-- \text{i.e.;} \quad S = \sum_{j=1}^{N} Aj$$

```
    return (S);
```

Figure 8.11 An Ada function with intermediate assertions.

In practice, it is not necessary to list all the intermediate predicates illustrated in Figure 8.11. The minimal requirement is that a predicate be associated with each innermost nested loop. In Figure 8.11, the loop predicate is

$$S = \sum_{j=1}^{I-1} Aj$$

Loop predicates must be shown to be invariant relations; i.e., a loop invariant must be true independent of the number of times the loop is traversed. In particular, a loop invariant must satisfy the following conditions:

It must be true on loop entry.
It must be true independent of the number of loop traversals.
It must imply the desired condition on loop exit.

The loop invariant in Figure 8.11 satisfies these conditions. It is true on loop entry, when $S = 0$ and $I = 1$:

$$S = \sum_{j=1}^{0} Aj = 0$$

and it implies the desired output predicate, when $I = N + 1$:

$$S = \sum_{j=1}^{(N+1)-1} Aj = \sum_{j=1}^{N} Aj$$

8.7.2 Weakest Preconditions

The loop invariant in Figure 8.11 can be shown to be true independent of the number of loop traversals by the method of weakest preconditions (DIJ76). Given a proposition of the form (P) S (R), P is the weakest precondition for S if it is the weakest condition that will guarantee the truth of R following execution of S. The weakest precondition is expressed as

$$P = wp(S,R)$$

In practice, P is found by working backwards from R. If S is an assignment statement of the form $X := E$, the weakest precondition P is obtained by substituting expression E in place of X everywhere X appears in predicate R:

$$wp(X := E, R) = R(E \rightarrow X)$$

For example,

$$wp(A := B + 3, A = 5) = (A = 5 \text{ with } B + 3 \rightarrow A)$$
$$= (B + 3 = 5) \text{ or } (B = 2)$$

Thus $B = 2$ is the weakest precondition that will ensure $A = 5$ following execution of $A := B + 3$:

$$(B = 2) A := B + 3 (A = 5)$$

Applying the method of weakest preconditions to the example in Figure 8.11, we assume the loop invariant to be true following execution of the loop body and work backwards to show it must also be true prior to execution of the body:

$$wp(S := S + A(I); I := I + 1, S = \sum_{j=1}^{I-1} Aj)$$

$$= wp(S := S + A(I), wp(I := I + 1, S = \sum_{j=1}^{I-1} Aj))$$

$$= wp(S := S + A(I), S = \sum_{j=1}^{I} Aj)$$

$$= (S + A(I) = \sum_{j=1}^{I} Aj)$$

$$= (S = \sum_{j=1}^{I-1} Aj)$$

These arguments, plus the observation that function SUM must return a value in finite time (because I is incremented by 1 on each loop traversal until it reaches N), allow us to conclude that the loop predicate is an invariant relation, and that SUM correctly computes the sum of A(1..N).

There are both practical and theoretical limitations to formal verification by the method of input-output assertions. For example, what happens if S overflows during loop iteration? What if N is not within the bounds of A? What if A is not initialized? What if the data type of A's elements does not allow the " + " operator? Exception handlers can be written and additional preconditions can be specified to handle these situations. Furthermore, the effect of exception handling can be incorporated into the verification process (LUC80).

While treatment of overflow conditions and other exceptions might have been incorporated into our proof, the central point of our discussion is the issue of incomplete specifications. What else might we have forgotten to consider? There is no algorithmic way to ensure that we have thought of everything. It is thus correct to say that we have verified certain properties of the source code under certain assumptions, rather than to say that we have verified the source code for operation under all conditions. In general, formal verification can only reflect the preconditions and intermediate assertions used in the verification process.

Another practical limitation of formal verification is the amount of effort required to verify a program of, say, 500 lines. The verification effort often requires more lines of proof than lines of code, with the attendant possibility of introducing errors into the proof. This concern is somewhat alleviated by automated verification tools, such as the AFFIRM system (MUS80). While the verification process can never be fully automated, due to decidability considerations, an automated aid can reduce the tedium and opportunity for error that exists in manual verification.

The fundamental theoretical limitation of automated techniques for formal verification involves the derivation of loop invariants. Algorithmic derivation of loop invariants for arbitrary programs is an unsolvable problem. There are programs for which loop invariants can be derived automatically, but there are also programs for which automated derivation of loop invariants will fail. Furthermore, there is no algorithm to distinguish between the two classes of programs; otherwise, automated verification would be a decidable problem.

In general, loop invariants must be supplied by the programmer, who must use insight, intelligence, and ingenuity to provide the necessary verification conditions. This limitation and the sheer tedium of formally verifying a large program are the primary reasons many people feel formal verification techniques will never be of practical value in production environments.

We readily agree that there are difficulties to be faced in applying the methods of formal verification; however, there are two fundamental reasons to remain optimistic about formal verification techniques: automated verification aids, and use of formal verification techniques to systematically derive correct programs.

While automated verification systems cannot derive loop invariants for every conceivable program, there are many programs for which loop invariants can be automatically derived. When coupled with techniques such as symbolic execution and interactive dialogues, properly trained, intelligent programmers using automated verification systems can effectively assess and improve the quality of software products (MUS80).

There are two basic approaches to manual use of formal verification techniques. One is to associate assertions with existing source code and verify consistency between code and assertions (which is difficult). The other is to write the assertions first and derive correct code from them (which is usually somewhat easier). The latter technique is illustrated in the following example, in which a SUM function similar to, but not identical to, the one in Figure 8.11 is derived.

Step 1: Write the desired postcondition for the function.

$$\text{return}\left(\sum_{j=1}^{N} Aj\right)$$

Step 2: Postulate an algorithm for the function body.

(In this example, the form of the postcondition suggests a summation loop, which implies an initialization part, a loop invariant, and a loop body.)

```
-- initialization part
-- loop

-- add element Aj; 1 <= j <= N

-- endloop
```
$$-- \text{return}\left(\sum_{j=1}^{N} Aj\right)$$

Step 3: Postulate a loop invariant, based on the postcondition.

$$S = \sum_{j=1}^{I} A_j$$

Step 4: Use the weakest precondition method to derive the loop increment statement L.

(Summation is expressed as $S := S + A(I)$)

$$wp\left(S := S + A(I), \; S = \sum_{j=1}^{I} A_j\right) = \left(S = \sum_{j=1}^{I-1} A_j\right)$$

$$wp\left(L, \; S = \sum_{j=1}^{I-1} A_j\right) = \left(S = \sum_{j=1}^{I} A_j\right)$$

Thus, $L = (I := I + 1)$ satisfies the wp equation.

Step 5: Derive the loop termination condition, B.

(Conjunction of the loop invariant with the negation of the loop termination condition implies the postcondition.)

while B loop
$$-- \left(S = \sum_{j=1}^{I} A_j\right)$$
I := I + 1;
S := S + A(I);
end loop;
$$-- \left(S = \sum_{j=1}^{N} A_j\right)$$

Thus,

$$\left(\left(S = \sum_{j=1}^{I} A_j\right) \; and \; (\text{not } B)\right) \; implies \; \left(S = \sum_{j=1}^{N} A_j\right)$$

or:

$$(\text{not } B) = (I = N)$$

or:

$$(B) = (I \; /= \; N)$$

Step 6: Derive the loop initialization statements.

Loop initialization statements are chosen to satisfy the loop invariant on loop entry. In general, any initial values Io and So for I and S such that

$$0 <= Io <= N \text{ and } So = \sum_{j=1}^{Io} A_j$$

will suffice; Io = 0 and So = 0 are the obvious choices to make function SUM a subprogram of general utility.

Step 7: State the preconditions. A necessary precondition for correct operation of SUM is that A be an integer array having elements 1..N. This condition is expressed in the formal parameter specifications and the exception handler shown below.

Step 8: Write the function in final form.

```
function SUM(A: INTEGER_ARRAY; N: INTEGER) return INTEGER is
     ERROR: exception;
     I: INTEGER := 0;
     S: INTEGER := 0;
begin
     if N not in (1..A'LAST) then raise ERROR;
     while I /= N loop
          I := I + 1;
          S := S + A(I);
     end loop;
     return (S);
exception
     when ERROR =>
     PUT("N out of bounds in function SUM");
     raise ERROR;
end SUM;
```

It is obvious that the process illustrated above is not completely algorithmic in nature. Foresight of the desired result was used, just as it always is in programming. However, the technique of systematically following steps 1–8 formalizes the thought patterns of many programmers. Observe that the program derived above is similar to, but not identical to, the program in Figure 8.11; both are correct implementations of function SUM.

8.7.3 Structural Induction

Structural induction is a formal verification technique based on the general principle of mathematical induction; the induction must be performed on a partially ordered set that is well founded (LEV80). Given set S having the necessary properties and a proposition P to be proved, mathematical induction proceeds as follows:

1. Show P to be true for the minimal element(s) in S.
2. Assume P to be true for each element in S that has an ordinal number less than or equal to N and show P to be true for the N + first element in S.

The set of natural numbers under the ordering relation "$<$" is a commonly used induction set, and many properties of the natural numbers can be proved by induction. For example,

$$\sum_{j=1}^{n} j = n(n + 1)/2$$

Basis(n = 1)

$$\sum_{j=1}^{1} j = 1(1 + 1)/2 = 1$$

Inductive hypothesis Assume

$$\sum_{j=1}^{k} j = n(n + 1)/2 \qquad 0 < k < m + 1$$

Induction Show

$$\sum_{j=1}^{m+1} = (m + 1)(m + 1 + 1)/2$$

$$\sum_{j=1}^{m+1} j = \sum_{j=1}^{m} Aj + (m + 1)$$

$$= m(m + 1)/2 + (m + 1) \qquad \text{(by hypothesis)}$$

$$= (m + 1)(m + 2)/2$$

Structural induction can be applied to recursive programs in a straightforward manner. Consider the Ada function to compute the factorial of natural numbers:

```
function FACTORIAL(N: NATURAL) return NATURAL is
begin
   return(if N = 1 then 1 else N*FACTORIAL(N-1));
end FACTORIAL;
```

Basis(n = 1)

FACTORIAL(1) = 1 (by inspection)

Inductive hypothesis

FACTORIAL(K) = K*(K-1)...*1; $1 <= K <= N$

Induction

FACTORIAL(N + 1)
   = (N + 1)*FACTORIAL(N)
   = (N + 1)*N*(N-1)...1

$$= (N + 1)*N! \text{ (by the inductive hypothesis)}$$

$$= (N + 1)!$$

Structural induction can be used to prove properties of algorithms operating on recursive data structures. Such proofs often use induction on the size of the structure. Consider the LISP-like function APPEND:

```
APPEND(L1,L2)
    if L1 = NIL then L2
    else CONS(CAR(L1), APPEND(CDR(L1),L2));
end APPEND;
```

Function APPEND acccepts two lists, L1 and L2, as its input parameters and returns a list composed of the elements of L1 followed by the elements of L2. NIL denotes an empty list; CONS has two arguments, E and L. CONS constructs a list consisting of element E followed by the elements of list L. CAR returns the first element of a list; and CDR returns all of a list except the first element. To prove that APPEND works correctly, we perform induction on the length of L1.

Basis(L1 = NIL) APPEND(NIL,L2) = L2

Inductive hypothesis Assume APPEND works correctly for all L1 and L2 such that length(L1) <= K; 0 <= K <= N.

Induction Show that APPEND works for all L1 and L2 such that length(L1) = N + 1.

1. If length(L1) = N + 1 then L1 /= NIL; hence APPEND(L1,L2) = CONS(CAR(L1), APPEND(CDR(L1),L2)).
2. length(CDR(L1)) = N; hence APPEND(CDR(L1),L2) works correctly by hypothesis. The result is a list consisting of all elements of L1 except the first, followed by all elements of L2.
3. CONS(CAR(L1),APPEND(CDR(L1),L2)) returns a list consisting of the first element of L1 followed by the remaining elements of L1 followed by the elements of N2; hence APPEND works correctly for length(L1) = N + 1.

An inductive proof of recursive tree traversal can be formulated in a similar manner. Preorder traversal of a binary tree can be specified as follows:

```
procedure PREORDER(T: TREE) is
    begin
        if not EMPTY(T) then
            PRINT(DATA(T));
            PREORDER(LEFT(T));
            PREORDER(RIGHT(T));
        end if;
end PREORDER;.
```

An inductive proof that the traversal algorithm will visit all nodes of the tree in the order: root, left, right can be developed using induction on the number of nodes in the tree.

Basis (N = 0) PREORDER works correctly for a tree that has no nodes.

If the tree has no nodes, EMPTY(T) is true on the first call to PREORDER.

Thus, the routine correctly prints the nodes in PREORDER.

Hypothesis Assume PREORDER works correctly for a tree that has N or fewer nodes.

Induction Assume T is a tree with N + 1 nodes and show that the nodes are printed in preorder.
Then EMPTY(T) is false on the initial call and PRINT(DATA(T)) is executed.
The call to PREORDER(LEFT(T)) works correctly (by hypothesis) because LEFT(T) is a tree that has N or fewer nodes. Even if RIGHT(T) is empty, LEFT(T) is a tree that has N or fewer nodes (N to be exact). By hypothesis, LEFT(T) is traversed in preorder.
A similar argument holds for the call to PREORDER(RIGHT(T)): Even if LEFT(T) is empty, RIGHT(T) is a tree that has N or fewer nodes.

By inspection of the algorithm, it is obvious that the root node is printed first. By hypothesis, the subtrees (which have N or fewer nodes) are printed in preorder. Thus, the algorithm is correct.

The relative ease with which properties of recursive functions can be proved, when compared with iterative algorithms, is a major argument in favor of the functional, or applicative, style of programming (BAC78).

8.8 SUMMARY

A high-quality software product satisfies user needs, conforms to its requirements and design specifications, and exhibits an absence of errors. Techniques for assessing and improving software quality include systematic quality assurance procedures, walkthroughs, inspections, static analysis, symbolic execution, debugging and unit testing, integration testing, acceptance testing, and formal verification. Each technique has its strengths and weaknesses, and no technique is sufficient by itself.

In practice, a combination of techniques is required to assess and improve software quality: static analysis and unit testing provide complementary information concerning source-code structure and behavior; symbolic execution is a natural link between testing and formal verification; inspections, walkthroughs, and quality assurance are procedures that can be used throughout the product life cycle. Formal verification can be used to demonstrate certain logical properties of source programs, and to guide synthesis of logically correct programs.

The primary goals of verification and validation are to assess and improve the quality of the various work products generated during software development and modification. High quality is best achieved by careful attention to the details of systematic planning, analysis, design, and implementation. It is incorrect to view source-code testing as the primary vehicle for quality improvement. High quality cannot be tested into an ill-conceived and badly implemented system. Although testing is an important technique, assessing and improving product quality is a pervasive life-cycle concept, not merely an activity to be performed following system implementation.

REFERENCES

(BAC78) Backus, J.: "Can Programming Be Liberated from the Von Neumann Style? A Functional Style and Its Algebra of Programs," *Comm. ACM,* vol. 21, no. 8, August 1978.

(BAL69) Balzer, R.: "EXDAMS: Extendable Debugging & Monitoring System," *AFIPS Conf. Proc.,* vol. 34, 1969.

(BOE83) Boehm, B.: private communication.

(BOY75) Boyer, R., et al.: "SELECT - A Formal System for Testing and Debugging Programs by Symbolic Execution," *Proceedings 1975 Intl. Conf. on Reliable Software,* published by IEEE, 1975.

(BRA75) Bratman, H.: "The Software Factory," *COMPUTER,* vol. 8, no. 5, 1975.

(BRO73) Brown, A. and W. Sampson: *Program Debugging,* Macdonald Publishing, London, 1973.

(BUC79) Buckley, F.: "A Standard for Software Quality Assurance Plans," *COMPUTER,* vol. 12, no. 8, August 1979.

(CLA76) Clarke, L.: "A System to Generate Test Data and Symbolically Execute Programs," *IEEE Trans. Software Eng.,* vol. SE-2, no. 3, 1976.

(DAR78) Darringer, J. and J. King: "Applications of Symbolic Execution to Program Testing," *COMPUTER,* vol. 11, no. 4, April 1978.

(DAV77) Davis, C., and C. Vick: "The Software Development System," *IEEE Trans. Software Eng.,* vol. SE-3, no. 1, 1977.

(DIJ76) Dijkstra, E.: *A Discipline of Programming,* Prentice-Hall, Englewood Cliffs, N.J., 1976.

(FAG76) Fagan, M.: "Design and Code Inspections to Reduce Errors in Program Development," *IBM Syst. J.,* vol. 15, no. 3, 1976.

(FAI75) Fairley, R.: "An Experimental Program Testing Facility," *IEEE Trans. Software Eng.,* vol. SE-1, no. 4, 1975.

(FAI78) Fairley, R.: "Static Analysis and Dynamic Testing of Computer Software," *COMPUTER,* vol. 11, no. 4, 1978.

(FAI79) Fairley, R.: "ALADDIN: Assembly Language Assertion-Driven Debugging Interpreter," *IEEE Trans. Software Eng.,* vol. SE-5, no. 4, 1979.

(FAI80) Fairley, R.: "Ada Debugging and Testing Support Environments," *ACM SIGPLAN Symp. on the Ada Programming Language, ACM SIGPLAN Notices,* vol. 15, no. 11, November 1980.

(FLO67) Floyd, R.: "Assigning Meanings to Programs," *Proc. of Symp. on Applied Math.,* vol. 19, American Math Society, 1967.

(FOS76) Fosdick, L. and L. Osterweil: "Data Flow Analysis in Software Reliability," *ACM Computing Surveys,* vol. 8, no. 3, 1976.

(FTN77) *FORTRAN77 Analyzer User's Manual,* NTIS Report No. PB83-117101, July 1982.

(GAL75) Gallenson, L., et al.: *PRIM User's Manual,* Information Sciences Institute Report ISI/TM-75-1, University of Southern California, 1975.

(GEN77) General Electric: *Fortran Test Procedure Language-Programmer Reference Manual,* General Electric Corp., 1977.

(GRC83) Data Sheets on RXVP80, General Research Corp., P.O. Box 6770, Santa Barbara, CA 93111.

(HEU74) Heuerman, C., et al.: "Automated Test and Verification," *IBM Tech. Disclosure Bulletin,* vol. 17, no. 7, 1974.

(HOA73) Hoare, C. A. R., and N. Wirth: "An Axiomatic Definition of the Programming Language Pascal," *Acta Informatica,* 2, 1973.

(HOW78) Howden, W.: "DISSECT - A Symbolic Evaluation and Program Testing System," *IEEE Trans. Software Eng.,* vol SE-4, no. 1, 1978.

(IEE83) *IEEE Standard Glossary of Software Engineering Terminology,* IEEE Std. 729-1983, published by the IEEE, New York, NY.

(JAC70) Jacobs, J., and T. Dillon: "Interactive Saturn Flight Program Simulator," *IBM Systems Journal,* vol. 9, no. 2, 1970.

(JOH83) Johnson, M. (ed.): "Proceedings of the ACM SIGSOFT/SIGPLAN Software Engineering Symposium on High-Level Debugging," *ACM Software Engineering Notes,* vol. 8, no. 4, August 1983.

(JON78) Jones, T.: "Measuring Program Quality and Productivity," *IBM Systems Journal,* vol. 17, no. 1, 1978.

(LEV80) Levy, L.: *Discrete Structures of Computer Science,* Wiley, New York, 1980.

(LIG83) Ligett, D.: WINSE Internal Memo on Static and Dynamic Analysis Tools, Wang Institute of Graduate Studies, July, 1983.

(LUC80) Luckham, D., and W. Polak: "Ada Exception Handling: An Axiomatic Approach," *ACM TOPLAS,* vol. 2, no. 2, 1980.

(MYE79) Myers, G.: *The Art of Software Testing,* Wiley-Interscience, New York, 1979.

(MIL75) Miller, E.: *Methodology for Comprehensive Software Testing,* RADC-TR-75-161, General Research Corp., Santa Barbara, CA, 1975.

(MTS74) *Module Testing System (MTS) Fact Book,* Management Systems and Programming Limited, London, England, 1974.

(MUS80) Musser, D.: "Abstract Data Type Specification in the AFFIRM System," *IEEE Trans. Software Eng.,* vol. SE-6, no. 1, January 1980.

(PAN78) Panzl, D.: "Automatic Software Test Drivers," *COMPUTER,* vol. 11, no. 4, 1978.

(PET76) Peterson, R.: "TESTER/1: An Abstract Model for the Automatic Synthesis of Program Test Case Specifications," *Symposium on Computer Software Engineering,* Polytechnic Press, New York, 1976.

(RAM75) Ramamoorthy, C., and S. Ho: "Testing Large Software with Automated Software Evaluation System," *IEEE Trans. Software Eng.,* vol. SE-1, no. 1, January 1975.

(ROC75) Rochking, M.: "The Source Code Control System," *IEEE Trans. Software Eng.,* vol. SE-1, no. 4, 1975.

(SHO83) Shooman, M.: *Software Engineering,* McGraw-Hill, New York, 1983.

(SOF80) *SOFTOOL80: A Comparative Example,* Report No. F005-11-80.1, Softool Corp., Goleta, CA.

(STO80) *"Stoneman": Requirements for Ada Programming Support Environments,* U.S. Department of Defense, 1980.

(TAI80) Tai, K.: "Program Testing Complexity and Test Criteria," *IEEE Trans. Software Eng.,* vol. SE-6, no. 6, November 1980.

(TOO83) *The Toolpack/IST Programming Environment,* Argonne National Labs Report No. ANL/MCS-TM-7, 1983.

(WHI80) White, L. and E. Cohen: "A Domain Strategy for Computer Program Testing," *IEEE Trans. Software Eng.*, vol. SE-6, no. 3, May 1980.

(WOO80) Woodward, M., et al.: "Experience with Path Analysis and Testing of Programs," *IEEE Trans. Software Eng.*, vol. SE-6, no. 3, May 1980.

EXERCISES

8.1 Conduct a structured walkthrough session on some segment of a software project of your choice. Include a moderator and a recording secretary plus two or three people who have knowledge of and interest in the project. Provide participants with copies of relevant material 2 or 3 days before the session. Do not let the session run more than 2 hours.

8.2 (*a*) Compose a design inspection checklist for a software project of your choice. Apply the checklist to the design specifications.

(*b*) Design a code inspection checklist for a real-time software product.

(*c*) Design a code inspection checklist for a scientific application program.

(*d*) Design a code inspection checklist for a data processing application program.

8.3 Apply one or more of your checklists from Exercise 8.2 to a software system of your choice.

8.4 Investigate the software quality assurance procedures in an organization of your choice. Is there a published quality assurance standard? How does it compare with the *IEEE Software Quality Assurance Plan* (BUC79)? Is the quality assurance function in your organization authoritative or advisory?

8.5 Select a small program consisting of a main routine and two to four subprograms. Manually perform static analysis of the code. Generate the information listed in Table 8.1. Observe how certain information (such as the flow graph and symbol table) allows you to generate other information (such as uninitialized variables and variables set but not used). Compare manual static analysis with the code inspection checklists developed in Exercise 8.2.

8.6 Obtain a user's manual for a testing tool such as RXVP80, the NBS Analyzer, or SOFTOOL. What types of information does the tool provide? How difficult is it to use the tool? What machine resources are required?

8.7 If a static analyzer is available in your installation, run it on the program from Exercise 8.5. Compare manual analysis to automated analysis in terms of quantity and quality of information and ease of obtaining that information.

8.8 Manually perform symbolic execution on an individual subprogram.

(*a*) Derive the path condition for each path in the routine.

(*b*) Use symbolic execution trees to derive loop invariants.

(*c*) Use the loop invariants in the path conditions to summarize loop behavior.

(*d*) Find input data values that satisfy the path conditions for various paths through the code.

(*e*) Use the path conditions to derive input data that will cause error conditions such as division by 0 and subscripts out of range.

8.9 (*a*) Derive a set of test cases for a program consisting of three to five routines. Your test cases should include functional, performance, and stress tests.

(*b*) Instrument the program in part a to measure the statements executed under your set of test cases. What percentage of total statements is executed by your set of test cases?

(*c*) Are you confident that the program contains no remaining errors? Why or why not?

8.10 Investigate the debugging facilities provided by your favorite language/computer installation. What additional facilities would be useful for unit-level debugging? For large-scale system debugging?

8.11 Develop a test plan for your term project. The test plan should include:

A description of techniques to be used (inspections, static analysis, symbolic execution, etc.)

Unit test cases (functional, performance, stress, structural)

Unit testing completion criteria
Integration testing strategy
Integration testing schedule
Acceptance tests
Acceptance criteria

8.12 Use the loop invariant in Step 3 of Section 8.7 to verify the correctness of the program in Step 8.

8.13 Follow Steps 1 to 8 in Section 8.7 to synthesize a routine that computes the product of A(1)..A(n).

8.14 Follow Steps 1 to 8 in Section 8.7 to synthesize a routine that computes the quotient Z1 and remainder Z2 of a nonnegative integer X1 and a positive integer X2, such that

$$X1 = Z1*X2 + Z2 \text{ and } (0 <= Z2 <= X2)$$

NINE

SOFTWARE MAINTENANCE

INTRODUCTION

The term "software maintenance" is used to describe the software engineering activities that occur following delivery of a software product to the customer. The maintenance phase of the software life cycle is the time period in which a software product performs useful work. Typically, the development cycle for a software product spans 1 or 2 years, while the maintenance phase spans 5 to 10 years.

Maintenance activities involve making enhancements to software products, adapting products to new environments, and correcting problems. Software product enhancement may involve providing new functional capabilities, improving user displays and modes of interaction, upgrading external documents and internal documentation, or upgrading the performance characteristics of a system. Adaptation of software to a new environment may involve moving the software to a different machine, or for instance, modifying the software to accommodate a new telecommunications protocol or an additional disk drive. Problem correction involves modification and revalidation of software to correct errors. Some errors require immediate attention, some can be corrected on a scheduled, periodic basis, and others are known but never corrected.

It is well established that maintenance activities consume a large portion of the total life-cycle budget (LIE80). It is not uncommon for software maintenance to account for 70 percent of total software life-cycle costs (with development requiring 30 percent). As a general rule of thumb, the distribution of effort for software maintenance includes 60 percent of the maintenance budget for enhancement, and 20 percent each for adaptation and correction.

If maintenance consumes 70 percent of the total life-cycle effort devoted to a particular software product, and if 60 percent of maintenance goes to enhancing the product, then 42 percent of the total life-cycle effort for that product is dedicated to product enhancement. Given this perspective, it is apparent that the product delivered to the customer at the end of the development cycle is only the initial version of the system. Some authors have suggested that the appropriate life-cycle model for software is development → evolution → evolution → evolution ... .

This perspective makes it apparent that the primary goal of software development should be production of maintainable software systems. Maintainability, like all high-level quality attributes, can be expressed in terms of attributes that are built into the product. The primary product attributes that contribute to software maintainability are clarity, modularity, and good internal documentation of the source code, as well as appropriate supporting documents.

It should also be observed that software maintenance is a microcosm of the software development cycle. Enhancement and adaptation of software reinitiates development in the analysis phase, while correction of a software problem may reinitiate the development cycle in the analysis phase, the design phase, or the implementation phase. Thus, all of the tools and techniques used to develop software are potentially useful for software maintenance.

Analysis activities during software maintenance involve understanding the scope and effect of a desired change, as well as the constraints on making the change. Design during maintenance involves redesigning the product to incorporate the desired changes. The changes must then be implemented, internal documentation of the code must be updated, and new test cases must be designed to assess the adequacy of the modification. Also, the supporting documents (requirements, design specifications, test plan, principles of operation, user's manual, cross-reference directories, etc.) must be updated to reflect the changes. Updated versions of the software (code and supporting documents) must then be distributed to various customer sites, and configuration control records for each site must be updated.

All of these tasks must be accomplished using a systematic, orderly approach to tracking and analysis of change requests, and careful redesign, reimplementation, revalidation, and redocumentation of the changes. Otherwise, the software product will quickly degrade as a result of the maintenance process. It is not unusual for a well designed, properly implemented, and adequately documented initial version of a software product to become unmaintainable due to inadequate maintenance procedures. This can result in situations in which it becomes easier and less expensive to reimplement a module or subsystem than to modify the existing version. Software maintenance activities must not destroy the maintainability of software. A small change in the source code often requires extensive changes to the test suite and the supporting documents. Failure to recognize the true cost of a "small change" in the source code is one of the most significant problems in software maintenance.

In subsequent sections of this chapter we discuss development-cycle activities that enhance maintainability, the managerial aspects of software maintenance, configuration management, the role of source-code metrics in maintenance, and tools and techniques for accomplishing maintenance.

9.1 ENHANCING MAINTAINABILITY DURING DEVELOPMENT

Many activities performed during software development enhance the maintainability of a software product. Some of these activities are listed in Table 9.1 and discussed below.

Analysis activities. The analysis phase of software development is concerned with determining customer requirements and constraints, and establishing feasibility of the product. From the maintenance viewpoint, the most important activities that occur during analysis are establishing standards and guidelines for the project and the work products to ensure uniformity of the products; setting of milestones to ensure that the work products are produced on schedule; specifying quality assurance procedures to ensure development of high-quality documents; identifying

Table 9.1 Development activities that enhance software maintainability

Analysis Activities
    Develop standards and guidelines
    Set milestones for the supporting documents
    Specify quality assurance procedures
    Identify likely product enhancements
    Determine resources required for maintenance
    Estimate maintenance costs

Architectural Design Activities
    Emphasize clarity and modularity as design criteria
    Design to ease likely enhancements
    Use standardized notations to document data flow,
        functions, structure, and interconnections
    Observe the principles of information hiding, data
        abstraction, and top-down hierarchical decomposition

Detailed Design Activities
    Use standardized notations to specify algorithms, data
        structures, and procedure interface specifications
    Specify side effects and exception handling for each routine
    Provide cross-reference directories

Implementation Activities
    Use single entry, single exit constructs
    Use standard indentation of constructs
    Use simple, clear coding style
    Use symbolic constants to parameterize routines
    Provide margins on resources
    Provide standard documentation prologues for each routine
    Follow standard internal commenting guidelines

Other Activities
    Develop a maintenance guide
    Develop a test suite
    Provide test suite documentation

product enhancements that will most likely occur following initial delivery of the system; and estimating the resources (personnel, equipment, floor space) required to perform maintenance activities.

Software maintenance may be performed by the developing organization, by the customer, or by a third party on behalf of the customer. In any case, the customer must be given an estimate of the resources required and likely costs to be incurred in maintaining the system. These estimates may exert a strong influence on the feasibility of system requirements, and may result in modifications to the requirements. An estimate of the resources required for maintenance allows planning for and procurement of the necessary maintenance facilities and personnel during the development cycle, and minimizes unpleasant surprises for the customer.

Standards and guidelines. Various types of standards and guidelines can be developed to enhance the maintainability of software. Standard formats for requirements documents and design specifications, structured coding conventions, and standardized formats for the supporting documents such as the test plan, the principles of operation, the installation manual, and the user's manual contribute to the understandability and hence the maintainability of software. The quality assurance group can be given responsibility for developing and enforcing various standards and guidelines during software development. Managers can ensure that milestones are being met, and that documents are being developed on schedule in conjunction with the design specifications and the source code.

Design activities. Architectural design is concerned with developing the functional components, conceptual data structures, and interconnections in a software system. The most important activity for enhancing maintainability during architectural design is to emphasize clarity, modularity, and ease of modification as the primary design criteria. Given alternative ways of structuring a system, the designers will choose a particular structure on the basis of certain design criteria that may be explicitly stated or implicitly understood. The criteria may include coupling and cohesion of modules, efficiency considerations, interfaces to existing software, features in the machine architecture, and other factors discussed in Chapter 5. Explicit emphasis on clarity, modularity, and ease of modification will usually result in a system that is easier to maintain than one designed using efficiency in execution time and minimization of memory space as the primary design criteria.

Design concepts such as information hiding, data abstraction, and top-down hierarchical decomposition are appropriate mechanisms for achieving a clearly understandable, modular, and easily modified system structure. For ease of understanding, and for ease of verifying completeness and consistency of the design, standardized notations such as data flow diagrams, structure charts and/or HIPOs should be used. These forms of design documentation aid the software maintainer who must understand the software product well enough to modify it and revalidate it.

Detailed design is concerned with specifying algorithmic details, concrete data representations, and details of the interfaces among routines and data structures.

Standardized notations should be used to describe algorithms, data structures, and interfaces. Procedure interface specifications should describe the modes and problem domain attributes of parameters and global variables used by each routine. In addition, selectively shared data areas, global variables, side effects, and exception handling mechanisms should be documented for each routine that incorporates those features. A call graph and cross-reference directory should be prepared to indicate the scope of effect of each routine; call graphs and directories provide the information needed to determine which routines and data structures are affected by modifications to other routines.

Implementation activities. Implementation, like design, should have the primary goal of producing software that is easy to understand and easy to modify. Single entry, single exit coding constructs should be used, standard indentation of constructs should be observed, and a straightforward coding style should be adopted. Ease of maintenance is enhanced by use of symbolic constants to parameterize the software, by data encapsulation techniques, and by adequate margins on resources such as table sizes and overflow tracks on disks. In addition, standard prologues in each routine should provide the author's name, the date of development, the name of the maintenance programmer, and the date and purpose of each modification. In addition, input and output assertions, side effects, and exceptions and exception handling actions should be documented in the prologue of each routine. Internal comments in the code should follow the guidelines presented in Table 6.5. Each implemented unit should be accompanied by a program unit notebook, as discussed in Section 6.4.

Supporting documents. There are two particularly important supporting documents that should be prepared during the software development cycle in order to ease maintenance activities. These documents are the maintenance guide and the test suite description. The maintenance guide provides a technical description of the operational capabilities of the entire system, and hierarchy diagrams, call graphs, and cross-reference directories for the system. An external description of each module, including its purpose, input and output assertions, side effects, global data structures accessed, and exceptions and exception handling actions should be specified in the maintenance guide.

Every delivered software product should be accompanied by a test suite. A test suite is a file of test cases developed during system integration testing and customer acceptance testing. The test suite should contain a set of test data and actual results from those tests. When software is modified, test cases are added to the test suite to validate the modifications, and the entire test suite is rerun to verify that the modifications have not introduced any unexpected side effects. Execution of a test suite following software modification is referred to as regression testing.

Documentation for the test suite should specify the system configuration, assumptions and conditions for each test case, the rationale for each test case, the actual input data for each test, and a description of expected results for each test. During product development, the quality assurance group is often given responsibility for preparing the acceptance test and maintenance test suites.

9.2 MANAGERIAL ASPECTS OF SOFTWARE MAINTENANCE

Successful software maintenance, like all software engineering activities, requires a combination of managerial skills and technical expertise. In this section, we discuss some of the managerial concerns of software maintenance. Technical isues in software maintenance are discussed in the following sections.

One of the most important aspects of software maintenance involves tracking and control of maintenance activities. Maintenance activity for a software product usually occurs in response to a change request filed by a user of the product. Change request processing can be described by the following algorithm:

> —software change request initiated
> —request analyzed
> if (request not valid) then
> > —request closed
> else
> > —request & recommendations submitted to change control board
> > if (change control board concurs) then
> > —modifications performed with priority and constraints
> > > established by change control board
> > —regression tests performed
> > —changes submitted to change control board
> > > if (change control board approves) then
> > > > —master tape updated
> > > > —external documentation updated
> > > > —update distributed as directed by change control board
> > > else
> > > > —control board objections satisfied and changes resubmitted
> > > > > to control board
> > else
> > > —request closed

A typical change request form is illustrated in Figure 9.1.

Change requests are usually initiated by users. A change request may entail enhancement, adaptation, or error correction. Major enhancements and major adaptations may require extensive analysis and negotiation with the customer; they are often handled as new development projects rather than as routine maintenance activities.

A change request is first reviewed by an analyst. In some cases, the request may report a user problem that is not caused by the software being maintained. In this situation, the analyst notifies the user and, with the concurrence of the user, closes the change request. Otherwise, the analyst submits to the control board the change

Software Change Request

Initiating Site: _____ Program: _____

Configuration No.: _____

Originator: _____ Date: _____

Description of Request: _____

_____

Date Needed: _____

Authorizing Signature: _____ Orgn: _____ Date: _____

****

REQUEST NO: _____

Analyst: _____ Start Date: _____

Findings: _____

Recommendation: _____

_____

Estimated Resources: Programmer-Hours: _____ Computer: _____

Temporary Fix: _____

Signature: _____ Date: _____

****

Control Board Recommendation

  Reject Request: Rationale _____

  Modify Request: _____

  Fix As Recommended: Priority _____

                Distribution 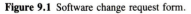_____

  Signature _____ Date: _____

****

Programmer _____ Start Date: _____

Components Modified: _____

Date Test Suite Updated: _____ Date Documents Updated: _____

Resources Required: Programmer-Hours: _____ Computer: _____

Signature: _____ Date: _____

****

Quality Assurance Representative: _____ Date: _____

Source Code Verified: Date: _____

Documentation/Documents Verified: Date: _____

Test Suite Verified: Date: _____

Signature: _____ Date: _____

****

Control Board Release Approval

Signature: _____ Date: _____

Figure 9.1 Software change request form.

request, the proposed fix, and an estimate of the resources required to satisfy the request.

    Emergency troubleshooting and temporary fixes are typically handled on an ad hoc basis by the change analysts and maintenance programmers. Emergency fixes are followed up by a change request, and the permanent modification is approved by the change control board.

Change control board. The change control board reviews and approves all change requests. The board may deny a request, recommend a modified version of the change, or approve the change as submitted. The analyst provides liaison between the change control board and the request initiator. Approved changes are forwarded to the maintenance programmers for action in accordance with the priority and constraints established by the change control board. The software is modified, revalidated, and submitted to the change control board for approval. If the control board approves, the master tapes and external documents are updated to reflect the changes, and the modified software is distributed to user sites as specified by the control board. In the event that the change control board does not approve the modifications performed by the maintenance programmers, the control board objections are addressed by the analysts and programmers and the update is again submitted to the board for approval.

The composition of a change control board, and the formality with which it functions, depend on the nature of the software, the organizational structure, and the particular people involved. A change control board may consist of several high-level managers from both software and nonsoftware areas of the maintenance and user organizations; the board may also call on particular individuals to lend expertise from time to time. On the other hand, the change control board may consist of only an individual maintenance programmer's immediate supervisor or a quality assurance representative.

Important aspects of this structure are the shielding of maintenance programmers from continual interruption by users, and the guidance provided to the programmers and analysts by the change control board. The problem analyst performs user liaison and provides communication between the users, the change control board, and maintenance programmers. The change control board takes into account numerous factors that the maintenance programmers may not be aware of in establishing priorities and constraints for maintenance activities.

Change request summaries. The status of change requests and software maintenance activities should be summarized on a weekly or monthly basis. The summary should report emergency problems and temporary fixes in effect since the last report; new change requests received and their probable disposition; old open requests, along with the status of progress and probable closing date for each; and change requests that have been closed since the last summary report, including a description of each closed request and its disposition.

In addition, a maintenance trends summary should be included in each change request summary; a trends summary is a graph showing the number of new requests and the total number of open requests as a function of time. A maintenance trends summary is illustrated in Figure 9.2.

The change request summary and the maintenance trends summary are valuable sources of information. New change requests can be checked against the change request summary to determine whether similar requests have been received, and if so, the current status of those requests, including suggested temporary fixes. The trends summary provides a concise statement of the maintenance workload; it should distinguish between enhancement requests, adaptation requests, error correction requests, and total requests. New and open error correction requests should be monitored closely to determine whether the software is improving or degrading with passing time.

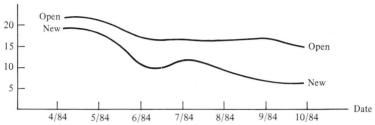

Figure 9.2 Maintenance trend summary program XYZ, 10/9/84.

Quality assurance activities. The primary function of a quality assurance group during software maintenance is to ensure that software quality does not degrade as a result of maintenance activities. In particular, the quality assurance group should conduct audits and spot checks to determine that external documents are properly updated to reflect modifications, that the structure and internal documentation of source code are not being destroyed by quick fixes, that temporary fixes are followed up by change requests and permanent modifications, that test suites are updated to reflect modifications, that physical protection of master tapes and test suites is adequate, that software change requests are resolved in a timely manner, and that the software configuration management plan is being enforced.

A software configuration management plan itemizes the software products to be controlled, specifies the mechanisms of change control, reports changed status of software products, and inventories the versions of software products that are distributed to various user sites. Configuration management tools for software products are discussed in the next section of this chapter.

In many organizations, the quality assurance group monitors change requests, prepares change request summaries, performs regression testing of software modifications, provides configuration management, and retains and protects the physical media for software products. The quality assurance group should be represented on the change control board and should have sign-off authority for new releases of modified software products. Often, the change control board is administered by quality assurance personnel.

Organizing maintenance programmers. Software maintenance can be performed by the development team or by members of a separate organization; there are advantages and disadvantages to both approaches. Members of the development team will be intimately familiar with the product; they will understand the design philosophy of the system, and why it functions as it does. If members of the development team know they will be responsible for maintaining the product, it is likely that they will take great care to design and implement the system to enhance maintainability. On the other hand, they will probably be less careful in preparing the supporting documentation. Also, the developers will most likely be assigned to a new development project while retaining responsibility for maintenance of the released product. Maintenance activities may divert the developers from their new project, resulting in slippage of the new project schedule. Also, maintenance by the developers makes the maintenance activity vulnerable to personnel turnover.

Maintenance by a separate group forces more attention to standards and high-quality documentation. It also has the advantage of releasing the development team to pursue other activities. In addition, the maintenance team can become highly expert on various details of the product because they devote their full attention to the product. However, there is often a morale problem associated with maintenance programming, and, rightly or wrongly, a stigma is often associated with being a "maintenance programmer." Development of new products is generally regarded as being more interesting and more rewarding than maintenance of an existing product.

A desirable method of organizing maintenance programming is to periodically rotate programmers between development and maintenance. There are a number of advantages to this approach: programmers can pursue career paths without fear of getting "stuck" in a dead-end maintenance task; novice programmers can learn new skills from more experienced programmers; the general level of maintenance personnel is raised by periodically rotating outstanding programmers into maintenance tasks; rotating programmers between development and maintenance impresses on software developers the need for high-quality source code and adequate documentation; a greater sense of appreciation for the skills required for both kinds of activities is provided; greater flexibility in staffing is obtained; overall improvement in personnel experience level is gained; and less stigma is attached to performing maintenance tasks.

The primary disadvantage of this approach is the overhead cost incurred in rotating personnel among different tasks. When balanced with the long-term benefits that accrue to personnel rotation, this disadvantage is more than adequately compensated.

Regardless of the manner in which maintenance personnel are organized, it is imperative that at least two people be assigned to each software unit to be maintained. This provides each maintenance programmer with a sounding board for ideas, each programmer can inspect the other's work products, and the organization is protected from dependence on a single individual for maintenance of a particular software product.

9.3 CONFIGURATION MANAGEMENT

Configuration management is concerned with tracking and controlling of the work products that constitute a software product. During product development, the various milestone reviews result in formal acceptance of work products such as the project plan, the requirements specifications, the test plan, the user's manual, the design documentation, and the source code. When a work product passes a milestone review, it is placed under configuration control and any subsequent changes to the work product can be made only with formal agreement of both the customer

Table 9.2 Five laws of program evolution (LEH80)

1. CONTINUING CHANGE
A program undergoes continuing change or becomes progressively less useful. The change process continues until it becomes cost-effective to replace the program with a re-created version.
2. INCREASING COMPLEXITY
As an evolving program is changed, its complexity, which reflects deteriorating structure, increases unless work is done to maintain or reduce the complexity.
3. THE FUNDAMENTAL LAW OF PROGRAM EVOLUTION
Program evolution is subject to a dynamic that makes the programming process, and hence measures of global project and system attributes, self-regulating with statistically determinable trends and invariances.
4. CONSERVATION OF ORGANIZATION STABILITY
The global activity rate in a project supporting an evolving program is statistically invariant.
5. CONSERVATION OF FAMILIARITY
The release content (changes, additions, deletions) of the successive releases of an evolving program is statistically invariant.

and the developer organizations. A work product placed under configuration control is said to have been "baselined" or "benchmarked."

During software maintenance, a configuration management plan and configuration management tools are required to track and control various versions of the work products that constitute a software product. Tracking and controlling multiple versions of a software product is a significant issue in software maintenance. Belady and Lehman have shown that large software products tend to evolve into families of versions, each version being similar to, but different from, other members of the family (BEL79). Belady and Lehman developed five laws of program evolution based on their studies of large-system dynamics. Their five laws are stated in Table 9.2 (LEH80). The first two laws indicate that continuous effort is required to maintain the maintainability of a software product.

Configuration management data bases. Software tools to support configuration management include configuration management data bases and version control library systems. A configuration management data base can provide information concerning product structure, current revision number, current status, and change request history for each product version. The following list is typical of the questions that a configuration management data base should be able to answer (SHI82):

How many versions of each product exist?
How do the versions differ?
Which versions of which products are distributed to which sites?
What documents are available for each version of each product?
What is the revision history of each component of each version of each product?
When will the next revision of a given component of a given version of a product be available?
What hardware configuration is required to operate a specific version of the product?

Which revisions constitute a specific version of the product?
Which versions are affected by a given component revision?
Which versions are affected by a specific error report?
Which errors were corrected in a specific revision?
How many errors were reported/fixed in the past month?
What are the causes of reported product failures?
Which components are functionally similar in which versions?
Is a given old version still used by some users?
What was the configuration of a given version on a given date?

Version control libraries. A version control library may be part of a configuration management data base, or it may be used as a stand-alone tool. A configuration management data base provides a macro view of a product family, while a version control library controls the various files that constitute the various versions of a software product. A version control library system is not a data base and does not contain the information required to answer questions such as those posed above. Entities in a version control library may include source code, relocatable object code, job control commands, data files, and supporting documents. Each entity in the library must carry an identity stamp that includes a version number, date, time, and programmer identity. Operations to be performed on a library include creation of the library, addition and deletion of components, preparation of back-up copies, editing of files, listing of summary statistics, and compilation/assembly of specified versions of the system (JOS78).

The Revision Control System (RCS) is one example of a version control library system (TIC82). RCS treats all files as text, even though they may in fact contain programs, data, and documents. Using RCS, different versions of text files can be created, stored, and retrieved. Changes to versions are logged, and changes can be merged to create versions. Only the differences between successive versions are stored to save the space overhead of storing multiple versions of a file. Perhaps the most important feature of RCS is the access control mechanism. Users of RCS check out files and check them in under control of RCS. When a file is checked out, it is locked so that one user will not accidentally overwrite the changes made by another user of the file.

Effective configuration management systems integrate support tools such as configuration management data bases and version control library systems within the managerial framework of change control described in the previous section.

9.4 SOURCE-CODE METRICS

During the past few years, a great deal of effort has been expended on developing metrics to measure the complexity of source code. Most of the metrics incorporate easily computed properties of the source code, such as the number of operators and operands, the complexity of the control flow graph, the number of parameters and global variables in routines, and the number of levels and manner of interconnection of the call graph. The approach taken is to compute a number, or a set of numbers, that measures the complexity of the code. Thus, a program with measure 10 would be more complex than a program with measure 5.

An overall measure of software complexity, by whatever technique, must account for factors such as the computing environment, the application area, the particular algorithms implemented, the required levels of reliability and efficiency, and the characteristics of product users. Measures based solely on source-code properties do not account for these factors and are thus of limited utility in comparing the complexity of two completely different programs. However, complexity measures based on source-code properties can be used to compare two similar well-versions of the same program. Thus, source-code complexity measures can be used to determine the complexity of a program before and after modification, and used to identify candidate routines for further refinement and rework. Even in these cases, however, one must be careful that programmers do not introduce complexity of a more obscure nature (in the data structures and data access techniques, for example) in order to minimize the properties measured by the particular complexity metrics being used.

Given these precautions, and a thorough understanding of what is and is not measured by source-code metrics, the metrics can be used to indicate that some aspects of software quality are or are not being degraded by maintenance activities. If source-code complexity increases with each subsequent modification, a point may be reached where an initially well-structured, easily understood, and adequately documented software product becomes unmaintainable. The use of automated tools to analyze source code and calculate complexity metrics makes this technique particularly attractive.

Two source-code metrics are discussed in this section: Halstead's effort equation, and McCabe's cyclomatic complexity measure.

Halstead's effort equation. Halstead developed a number of metrics that are computed from easily obtained properties of the source code (HAL77). These properties include the total number of operators in a program, N1; the total number of operands in the program, N2; the number of unique operators in the program, n1; and the number of unique operands, n2. Figure 9.3 illustrates a simple FORTRAN routine and the associated values of N1, N2, n1, and n2.

Halstead defines several quantities using these numbers. For example, program length N is defined as N1 + N2; (N1 + N2 = 50 in Figure 9.3). Halstead's estimator of program length is:

$$N = n1 \log 2 \ n1 + n2 \log 2 \ n2$$

For the example in Figure 9.3,

$$N = 10(3.2) + 7(2.8) = 52.9$$

Program volume is defined as

$$V = (N1 + N2) \log 2 \ (n1 + n2)$$

```
SUBROUTINE SORT (X, N)
DIMENSION X(N)
IF (N .LT. 2) RETURN
DO  20  I = 2,N
     DO 10 J = 1,I
     IF (X(I) .GE. X(J)) GO TO 10
     SAVE = X(I)
     X(I)   = X(J)
          X(J)   = SAVE
10       CONTINUE
20  CONTINUE
     RETURN
     END
```

Operand	Count		Operator	Count
1 X	6		1 End of statement	7
2 I	5		2 Array subscript	6
3 J	4		3 =	5
4 N	2		4 IF ()	2
5 2	2		5 DO	2
6 SAVE	2		6 ,	2
$n_2 = 7$ 1	1		7 End of program	1
	$22 = N_2$		8 .LT.	1
			9 .GE.	1
			$n_1 = 10$ GO TO 10	1
				$28 = N_1$

Figure 9.3 Operator and operand count for a FORTRAN routine.

and language level (the level of language abstraction) is

$$L = (2*n2)/(n1*N2)$$

Program effort is defined as V/L:

$$E = (n1*N2*(N1 + N2)*log2(n1 + n2)) / (2*n2)$$

Program effort is interpreted to be the number of mental discriminations required to implement the program. Alternatively, it can be interpreted as the effort required to read and understand a program. Experiments by Curtis and colleagues have shown that Halstead's effort metric is well correlated with the observed effort required to debug and modify small programs (CUR79). Program effort thus appears to be a measure of interest for software maintenance.

An interesting application of Halstead's metrics is in detecting similarity of programs (GRI81). One similarity detector uses the total number of operators and operands, the number of unique operators and operands, the number of lines, the number of variables declared, the number of variables used, and the total number of control constructs. Experience with the detector indicates that it is quite effective in detecting identical, but disguised, homework solutions in programming courses.

McCabe's cyclomatic metric. McCabe has observed that the difficulty of understanding a program is largely determined by the complexity of the control flow graph for that program (MCC76). The cyclomatic number V of a connected graph G is the number of linearly independent paths in the graph. V(G) is computed as follows:

$$V(G) = E - n + 2p$$

where E is the number of edges
n is the number of nodes
p is the number of connected components

V(G) is 5 for the example illustrated in Figure 9.4. The dashed line in Figure 9.4 connecting output node f to input node a is added to produce a connected graph (every node can be reached from every other node).

McCabe observes that for a structured program with single entry, single exit constructs, V equals the number of predicates plus one. Also, provided G is planar, V is equal to the number of regions in G.

An upper bound of 10 is recommended by McCabe as the maximum complexity for the control graph of an individual routine. (One permissible exception is a large case statement with numerous independent cases.) Cyclomatic complexity in the range of 3 to 7 is typical of well-structured routines.

In his paper, McCabe reports strong correlation between cyclomatic complexity, ease of testing, and the reliability of routines. Curtis has found that Halstead's effort metric correlates more strongly with ease of debugging and modification than does McCabe's cyclomatic number.

During the implementation phase, one might use source-code metrics to identify routines that are candidates for further refinement and rewriting. During maintenance, the complexity metrics can be used to track and control the complexity level of modified routines.

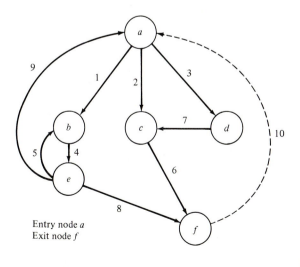

Entry node *a*
Exit node *f*

$$V(G) = 9 - 6 + 2 = 5$$

Figure 9.4 A control-flow graph and cyclomatic complexity calculation.

9.5 OTHER MAINTENANCE TOOLS AND TECHNIQUES

Because software maintenance is a microcosm of software development, the activities that a software maintainer may become involved in span the entire spectrum of software engineering. The maintainer may analyze change requests; negotiate with users; formulate recommended solutions for the change control board, including cost estimates and priorities; debug software; provide temporary fixes and emergency repairs; redesign, modify, and revalidate software; update external documentation and master tapes; retain and protect physical media; perform configuration control; and provide liaison and user training for software product users.

In some organizations, the software maintainer is supported by analysts who provide user liaison and formulate recommendations to the change control board, by a training organization that trains users, by technical writers who update the supporting documents, and by quality assurance personnel who revalidate modified software, perform configuration management, and maintain physical media. In the ad hoc approach to software maintenance, the maintenance programmer performs all of these activities without the benefit of a change control board to provide guidance (see Section 9.2).

Automated tools to support software maintenance include technical support tools and managerial support tools. Tools to support the technical aspects of software maintenance span the spectrum from analysis and design tools to implementation tools to debugging and testing tools. Automated tools of special importance for software maintenance are itemized in Table 9.3. They include text editors, debugging aids, cross-reference generators, linkage editors, comparators, complexity metric calculators, version control systems, and configuration management data bases.

A text editor permits rapid, efficient modification of source programs, test data, and supporting documents. Text editors can be used to insert and replace segments of source code, internal comments, test data, and supporting documents; to systematically change all occurrences of an identifier or other textual string; to locate all references to a given identifier or other string of text; and to save both old and new versions of a routine, test file, or document. A syntax-directed text editor can be used to preserve the structure of source code, and an intelligent text editor can ensure that all cross references in the supporting documents are correctly updated.

Table 9.3 Automated tools for software maintenance

Text editors
Debugging aids
Cross-reference generators
Linkage editors
Comparators
Complexity metric calculators
Version control systems
Configuration management data bases

Debugging aids provide traps, dumps, traces, assertion checking, and history files to aid in locating the causes of known errors. System-level cross-reference generators provide cross-reference listings for procedures calls, statement usage, and data references. Cross-reference directories provide the calling structure (the call graph) of who calls whom and from where, and procedure names and statement numbers where formal parameters, local variables, and global variables are defined, set, and used.

A linkage editor links together object modules of compiled code to produce an executable program. Linkage editors can be used by a maintenance programmer to configure a system in various ways, and to link selectively recompiled modules into a software system. Linkage editors for Ada programs provide consistency checking of parameter lists between calling and called routines, cross-references of all system-level names, and incremental recompilation and linkage of modified routines.

A comparator compares two files of information and reports the differences. Comparators can be used during maintenance to compare two versions of a source program, a test suite, a file of test results, or two versions of a supporting document. Use of a comparator allows the maintenance programmer to pinpoint differences between versions, to determine whether a modification has achieved a desired result, and to determine whether adverse side effects have been introduced by a modification.

Source-code complexity metrics were discussed in Section 9.4. Use of complexity metrics requires automated tools to compute the measures of interest. The complexity of source code can be compared before and after a modification is made to determine whether complexity, as measured by the metrics utilized, has increased as a result of the modification.

Version control systems and configuration management data bases were discussed in Section 9.3. They can be used to track the history of each module in a system by recording which modules and which versions of which modules comprise which system releases. These tools can also be used to associate source modules with object modules, to record which versions use which modules, and to provide system protection by preventing updates to master files that have not been approved by the change control board. Also, a version control system can coordinate experimental versions of a system when several maintenance programmers are simultaneously modifying the same module or subsystem.

Other aspects of change control that can be supported by automated tools include change request processing, periodic status reporting, change control board recommendations, quality assurance tracking, and updating of historical data.

9.6 SUMMARY

Software maintenance activities involve making enhancements to software products, adapting products to new environments, and correcting problems. It is not uncommon for maintenance to consume more that 50 percent of the total life-cycle budget for a software product. The systematic activities and high-quality work products produced during product development pay large dividends during maintenance. Some of the most important activities for enhancing maintainability during product development were discussed.

Software maintenance, like software development, requires a combination of managerial control and technical expertise. Both aspects of software maintenance were discussed. An algorithm for tracking and controlling maintenance activities was presented. The foci for management of software maintenance are change request forms, change request summaries, and a change control board that approves product changes and provides configuration management for various product versions and user sites. Typical change request forms and change request summaries were illustrated and discussed, and techniques for organizing maintenance programmers were described.

Automated tools for software maintenance include both technical and managerial tools. Automated tools of particular importance for software maintenance include text editors; debugging aids; cross-reference generators; linkage editors; comparators; version control libraries; configuration management data bases; and tools to support machine-processable change request forms, interactive access to change requests, and change request summaries and other configuration management reports.

Because software maintenance is a microcosm of software development, the tools, techniques, and activities of software maintenance span the entire product life cycle. Difficulties encountered in software maintenance and the social stigma attached to software maintenance are largely due to lack of systematic planning for software maintenance during the development process, the failure of programmers and managers to properly organize for software maintenance activities, and failure to provide the necessary tools and techniques for software maintenance.

Planning for maintenance, developing the software product to enhance maintainability, proper organization of maintenance programmers and maintenance activities, and provision of maintenance tools can result in vast improvements in software quality, programmer productivity, and programmer morale.

REFERENCES

(BEL79) Belady, L., and M. Lehman: "The Characteristics of Large Systems," in *Research Directions in Software Technology*, P. Wegner, ed., MIT Press, Cambridge, Mass., 1979.

(CUR79) Curtis, B., et al.: "Third Time Charm: Stronger Prediction of Programmer Performance by Software Complexity Metrics," *Proceedings of the Fourth ICSE*, Munich, September 1979.

(FEL79) Feldman, J.: "Make - A Program for Maintaining Computer Programs," *Software Practice and Experience*, April 1979.

(GLA81) Glass, R., and R. Noiseux: *Software Maintenance Guidebook*, Prentice-Hall, Englewood Cliffs, N.J., 1981.

(GRI81) Grier, S.: "A Tool that Detects Plagarism in Pascal Programs," *ACM SIGCSE Bulletin*, vol. 13, no. 1, February 1981.

(HAL77) Halstead, M.: *Elements of Software Science*, Elsevier, New York, 1977.

(JOS78) Josephs, W.: "A Mini-Computer Based Library Control System," Proceedings of the Software Quality and Assurance Workshop, *ACM Software Engineering Notes*, vol. 3, no. 5, November 1978.

(LEH80) Lehman, M.: "On Understanding Laws, Evolution, and Conservation in the Large-Program Life Cycle," *The Journal of Systems and Software*, vol. 1, no. 3, 1980.

(LIE80) Lientz, B., and E. Swanson: *Software Maintenance Management: A Study of the Maintenance of Computer Application Software in 487 Data Processing Organizations*, Addison-Wesley, Reading, Mass., 1980.

(MCC76) McCabe, T.: "A Complexity Measure," *IEEE Trans. on Software Eng.*, vol. SE-2, no. 4, December 1976.

(SHI82) Shigo, O., et al.: "Configuration Control for Evolutional Software Products," *Proceedings of the Sixth ICSE*, Tokyo, Japan, 1982.

(TIC82) Tichy, W.: "Design, Implementation, and Evaluation of a Revision Control System," *Proceedings of the Sixth ICSE*, Tokyo, Japan, 1982.

TEN

SUMMARY

INTRODUCTION

We have defined software engineering as the technological and managerial discipline concerned with systematic production and maintenance of software products that are developed and modified on time and within cost estimates. A software product, in contrast to software developed for personal use, has multiple developers, users, and maintainers. Most often, the developers, users, and maintainers are distinct entities.

Software engineering is based on the foundation areas of computer science, management science, economics, communication skills, and the engineering approach to problem solving. The primary goals of software engineering are to improve the quality of software products and to increase the productivity and job satisfaction of software engineers.

A software product consists of several deliverable items in addition to the source code. Typical deliverables include a user's manual, a software verification report, a test suite, the program unit notebooks, a maintainer's guide, installation instructions, and training materials. Systematic development of a software product also requires development of several internal working documents (internal work products) that may or may not be included in the package of deliverable items. These documents include the *Product Definition;* the *Project Plan;* the *Software Requirements Specification;* the customer contract; the design documentation; the quality assurance plan; resource tracking and control reports; internal audit reports; individual progress reports; minutes from walkthroughs, inspections, and project review meetings; and the project legacy document.

Development of these work products typically proceeds in phases, progressing from plans to requirements to design to implementation to integration and acceptance. The completion of a phase is a major milestone in the project life cycle and results in formal acceptance of the associated work products, which become the baseline documents for that phase of the project. After a document is baselined, subsequent changes are made only with the agreement of all concerned parties.

It is important to distinguish the phasing of work products from the phasing of activities that produce the work products. Techniques such as prototyping, iterative enhancement, building of successive versions, and early delivery of pilot versions to test sites may be used within any particular phase of the effort as an aid to development of the work products for that project phase. Conducting project activities within a phased framework of milestones and baseline work products assures an orderly development process, and keeps all concerned parties focused on the appropriate issues at the appropriate times. Failure to separate issues of concern and premature involvement in implementation details are the most pervasive problems in software engineering.

This chapter summarizes the work activities, work products, milestones, and issues of concern discussed in the preceding chapters of the text.

10.1 PLANNING AND COST ESTIMATION

Planning and cost estimation were the topics of Chapters 2 and 3. Planning is an essential, yet often neglected, phase of a software project. Work products from the planning phase include the *Product Definition* and the *Project Plan*. The primary components of a *Product Definition* are a concise definition of the problem to be solved, a statement of the goals for the system and the project, identification of user characteristics, a statement of the functions to be performed by the system, the solution strategy, priorities for product features, and the product acceptance criteria.

Essential components of a *Project Plan* include the life-cycle model to be used, the organizational structure, preliminary estimates of staffing and resource requirements, a preliminary cost estimate, a preliminary development schedule, and specifications for the project monitoring and control mechanisms. The life-cycle model defines the terminology, milestones, and work products for the project. The organizational structure includes the work breakdown structure for the project, statements of work for each element in the work breakdown structure, and the management structure and team structure to be used on the project. Possible management structures include the project format, the functional format, and the matrix format. Team structures include the democratic team, the hierarchical team, and the chief programmer team. Management by objectives and written job descriptions derived from the statements of work are effective techniques for assigning and tracking work responsibilities among project personnel.

The staffing, resource, cost, and development schedule estimates are labeled preliminary during the planning phase because the project is often not well understood at this time. A series of increasingly accurate estimates should be prepared during the early phases of a software project.

Cost estimation is the least precise activity in software engineering. All cost estimation techniques are based on extrapolations of historical data. The fundamental difficulties in cost estimation involve determining the size and scope of the project during the planning phase, and deciding how to extrapolate past performance to the present project.

The two fundamental approaches to cost estimation are the top-down and bottom-up approaches. The top-down approach focuses on the cost of performing the various functional activities associated with a software project, such as planning, management, development, quality assurance, configuration management, publications, machine resources, and product integration. The bottom-up approach focuses on estimating the cost of developing each component in the software product and summing those costs to arrive at an overall estimate. In practice, both approaches should be used and the differences reconciled.

Techniques for estimating the cost of a software product include expert judgment, pricing to win the contract, and algorithmic cost estimation. Models for algorithmic cost estimation are typically macro-oriented or micro-oriented. The SLIM approach, developed by Putnam, is a macro model based on the Rayleigh curve approximation to project staffing. The COCOMO model, developed by Boehm, is a micro model in which effort multipliers are used to adjust an estimate based on delivered lines of source code. The multipliers account for factors such as the abilities of individual personnel, product complexity, available time, and the level of technology utilized. The macro approach of Putnam accounts for these factors in a single constant multiplier that is determined from past performance on similar projects.

The Project Feasibility Review is the milestone review for the *Product Definition* and the *Project Plan*. The outcome of a feasibility review can be termination of the project, approval of the project, or more study by the planning team.

10.2 SOFTWARE REQUIREMENTS DEFINITION

Chapter 4 was concerned with defining the technical requirements for a software product. Major topics included the format and content of a *Software Requirements Specification,* formal specification techniques, and requirements languages and processors. The goal of requirements definition is to produce a complete and consistent specification of the technical requirements for a software product, using formal notations as appropriate.

The essential components of a *Software Requirements Specification* are a brief product overview and summary, specification of the external interfaces and data flows, the functional requirements, the performance requirements, exception handling, and the acceptance criteria for the software product.

Techniques for specifying the functional requirements for a software product can be categorized as relational and state-oriented. Relational notations include implicit equations, recurrence relations, algebraic axioms, and regular expressions.

Relational notations can be used to specify the desired functional behavior without indicating an implementation technique. On the one hand, this provides maximum flexibility for the product designer. On the other hand, it provides no guidance to the designer.

State-oriented notations discussed include decision tables, event tables, transition tables, finite state mechanisms, and Petri nets. All of these notations incorporate the concepts of state and state transition. They provide guidance to the designer and can be viewed as notations for specifying functional requirements, or as notations for specifying high-level external design of the software product. In practice, the boundary between functional specification and external design is imprecise.

Formal notations are concise and unambiguous, and support formal analysis of completeness and consistency of the requirements specifications. Use of formal notations also allows formal reasoning about various characteristics of the software product being specified.

Languages and processors for requirements specification discussed in Chapter 4 include PSL/PSA, RSL/REVS, SADT, SSA, and GIST. The processors allow interactive development of requirements, produce various types of formatted reports, and provide diagnostic messages concerning completeness and consistency of the requirements. SADT and SSA do not have automated processors, but are nevertheless useful notations.

Most languages for requirements analysis are in fact analysis and design tools, in that they incorporate notations for describing process structure and algorithmic details. Automated tools for requirements analysis must be used with some discipline to prevent requirements from becoming entangled with design and implementation concerns.

The Software Requirements Review is the milestone associated with requirements definition. Work products to be reviewed include the *Software Requirements Specification* and a preliminary version of the *User's Manual*. As with the feasibility review, the outcome may be cancellation of the project, redirection of the project, additional work on the requirements document, or acceptance of the requirement specification.

10.3 SOFTWARE DESIGN CONCEPTS

Various concepts of software design were covered in Chapter 5. Topics discussed included fundamental concerns, modules and modularization criteria, design notations, design techniques, detailed design considerations, design considerations for real-time and distributed systems, test plans, walkthroughs and inspections, and design guidelines.

Design activities include external design, architectural design, and detailed design. Each activity involves different issues, and different notations are appropriate to support the differing activities. The variety of notations and techniques discussed in Chapter 5 reflects both the diversity of design issues and the diversity of viewpoints concerning the design process. For instance, the data flow approach to software design (structured design) views the conversion of data flow diagrams into structure charts as a major concern of the designer. On the other hand, the data structure approach (Jackson design) views the structure of input and output data files, and the derivation of program structure based on the file structures, to be the central issues. Both views of design are valid, and neither is more "correct" than the other, although each is probably best suited to particular classes of design problems.

Knowing when the detailed design is detailed enough, and when to start converting the design into an implementation, is an issue of concern to software designers. Our rule of thumb is to consider the design complete when programmers familiar with the implementation language, but unfamiliar with the user requirements, can implement the system working from the design specifications alone.

There are typically two milestone reviews during software design: the Preliminary Design Review and the Critical Design Review. The preliminary review is held near the end of architectural design and prior to detailed design, while the critical review is held near the completion of detailed design and prior to implementation.

Work products reviewed in a Preliminary Design Review include the requirements, the preliminary user's manual, the external design specifications, and the architectural design specifications. Work products reviewed during the Critical Design Review include all the work products reviewed during the prior reviews, but special emphasis is placed on the detailed design specifications and the test plan.

The exact timing of these reviews depends on the particular project, because detailed design of some modules and subsystems may occur in parallel with architectural design of other product components. Similarly, implementation may overlap completion of detailed design. However, the trend should be from external design to architectural design to detailed design to implementation. As always, a successful milestone review focuses attention on the proper activities at the proper time and results in baseline documents for the following activities.

10.4 IMPLEMENTATION ISSUES

Chapter 6 presented a discussion of structured coding techniques, coding style, implementation standards and guidelines, and documentation guidelines. The primary goal of product implementation is development of source code that is easy to read and easy to understand. Clarity of source code eases debugging, testing, and modification of a software product. These activities consume a large portion of most software budgets. We observed that most of the difficulties encountered during implementation are caused by inadequate analysis and design. Given adequate design documentation, implementation of a software product should be a straightforward, low stress, highly efficient process.

The basic tenet of structured coding is use of single entry, single exit constructs. When a program is written using only single entry, single exit constructs, the dynamic flow of execution will match the static structure of the source text. This allows one to understand program behavior by reading the code from start to end, as written. Strict adherence to single entry, single exit program constructs raises concerns for the time and space efficiency of the code. In some cases, single entry, single exit programs will require repeated code segments or repeated subroutine calls. Strict adherence to single entry, single exit would prevent premature loop exits and branching to exception handling code.

Our philosophy of structured coding is to adhere to single entry, single exit constructs in the majority of situations, but to violate single entry, single exit as common sense dictates. In particular, forward transfers of control to a local region of the program do not usually interfere with clarity and ease of understanding. It is not our intent to encourage poor coding style, but to acknowledge the realities of implementation. This view should not be taken as a license to substitute goto statements for careful thought and redesign.

Adherence to implementation standards and guidelines by all programmers on a project results in a product of uniform quality. Standards were defined as those concerns that can be checked by an automated tool, while determining adherence to a guideline requires human interpretation. Several conditions must be observed to obtain voluntary adherence to standards and guidelines. These conditions were discussed, and it was observed that the psychological atmosphere established by the project leader and the senior programmers is crucial to obtaining voluntary adherence to standards and guidelines.

Supporting documents for the implementation phase include all baselined work products of the analysis and design phases and the program unit notebooks. A program unit is the unit of work assigned to an individual programmer. The format and content of program unit notebooks was discussed. Finally, guidelines for the documentation prologues in individual routines and compilation units and internal commenting conventions were discussed.

The major milestone for product implementation is successful integration of source code components into a functioning system. There are, however, several intermediate milestones that typically occur prior to integration. For example, before a routine can be placed in the library for the evolving system, it may be required that the routine be inspected by an inspection team, or reviewed in a walkthough session, or tested to a given level of test coverage. Product integration typically occurs in carefully planned stages, with successful completion of each stage providing an intermediate milestone. The ultimate milestone for product implementation is successful demonstration of product capabilities on the customer's acceptance tests.

10.5 MODERN LANGUAGE FEATURES

Chapter 7 presented features of modern programming languages that can be used to improve the quality of source code and increase the productivity of programmers. Features discussed included type checking rules, separate compilation, user defined data types, data abstraction, scoping rules, exception handling, and concurrency models. Ada, PL/1, Pascal, and FORTRAN were used to illustrate the various concepts.

The major issue in type checking is flexibility versus security. Strongly typed languages provide maximum security, while automatic type coercion provides maximum flexibility. The modern trend is to augment strong type checking with features that increase flexibility while maintaining the security of strong type checking. In Ada, these features include explicit type conversion, operator overloading, subprogram overloading, and derived types.

Separate compilation allows retention of program modules in a library. The modules are linked into the software system, as appropriate, by the linking loader. The distinction between independent compilation, as in FORTRAN, and separate compilation, as in Ada, is that type checking across compilation-unit interfaces is performed by a separate compilation facility, but not by an independent compilation facility.

User-defined data types, in conjunction with strong type checking, allow the programmer to model and segregate entities from the problem domain using a different data type for each type of problem entity. This is in contrast to FORTRAN, where many different object types from the problem domain must all be represented as REALs or INTEGERs.

Scoping rules are concerned with accessibility of named entities in various regions of a program. Modern concepts of information hiding and data abstraction are contrary to the traditional nested block structure scoping rules. The trend in modern programming languages is toward creation of flat structures and explicit naming of the visibility and access rights of various program units.

The two basic models of exception handling are the resumption and termination models. PL/1 utilizes the resumption model, in which a program is allowed to continue execution from the point of an exception following the exception handling actions. Ada utilizes the termination model, in which a program must terminate the unit in which the exception occurs following the exception handling actions. In Ada, an exception unit is a block, procedure, or task. A primary motivation for blocks in Ada is to limit the scope of an exception condition. It was shown in Chapter 7 that the termination model of exception handling improves program clarity and allows formal reasoning about the behavior of programs that incorporate exception handling.

Concurrency issues are addressed in Chapters 5 and 7 of the text. With the advent of multiprocessors and distributed computing systems, it is becoming increasingly important for the software engineer to understand concurrent processing techniques. The three fundamental mechanisms of concurrency, namely, shared variables, asynchronous message passing, and synchronous message passing, were discussed briefly. The Ada rendezvous mechanism was illustrated.

10.6 VERIFICATION AND VALIDATION TECHNIQUES

Life-cycle verification is the process of determining the degree to which the work products of a given phase of the development cycle fulfill the specifications of prior phases. Formal verification is a rigorous, mathematical demonstration that source code conforms to its requirements. Validation is concerned with evaluating a software product at the end of the development process to determine compliance with the product requirements. The primary goals of verification and validation activities are to assess and improve the quality of the intermediate work products and deliverable items in a software project.

Techniques for verification and validation discussed in Chapter 8 include quality assurance procedures, walkthroughs and inspections, static analysis, symbolic execution, unit testing and debugging, system testing, and formal verification. A major theme of Chapter 8 is that quality cannot be tested into source code. High quality is best achieved by continuous verification of the work products as they evolve.

Quality assurance activities can be extremely effective for assessing and improving the quality of work products. In some organizations, the quality assurance group exerts authoritative influence on software projects, while in others quality assurance is performed in an advisory capacity. The effectiveness of the quality assurance group is strongly dependent on the working relationship that exists between the quality assurance group and the product development group.

Walkthroughs and inspections can also be extremely effective, again depending on the psychological atmosphere in the organization. Walkthroughs and inspections should be used as opportunities to detect errors without finger pointing or assignment of blame. Their effectiveness can be quickly compromised if they are allowed to deteriorate into name-calling sessions. Inspections appear to be more effective at finding errors, but team communication, education, and morale are best served by walkthroughs.

Static analysis tools are effective mechanisms for locating structural errors in source code and design documentation, for detecting anomalous situations, and for detecting departures from standards. One problem with static analysis is that the tools tend to produce large numbers of warning messages that do not necessarily denote error conditions. Programmers quickly tire of the tedium of investigating numerous warning messages that do not in fact denote errors.

The major concerns of unit testing are development of effective test cases and the completion criterion against which the tests are conducted. Function tests and performance tests are developed during the design phase; they are based on the requirements specification. Stress tests are designed to intentionally overload or break the system. Structure tests are concerned with examining the logical structure of the code. Unit testing is the primary opportunity for thoroughness of testing, because systems become too complex for thorough testing when the modules are integrated together.

Testing theory indicates the futility of attempting to detect all errors through testing alone. Exhaustive testing of all paths is seldom feasible, and even if it is feasible, it does not guarantee detection of missing path errors, computational errors, or domain errors. These considerations re-emphasize the need for systematic analysis and design and for continuous verification of work products so that errors are removed prior to implementation. Despite the inadequacies of testing it is nevertheless desirable to execute a systematically derived set of test cases to gain increased confidence in the software product.

Testing is the process of executing test cases with the intent of exposing errors.

Debugging is the process of locating and correcting the cause of a known error. Debugging tools and techniques include dumps, traces, breakpoints, assertions, and history collection. Effective debugging requires highly developed problem solving skills.

The major concerns of integration testing are developing an incremental strategy that will limit the complexity of interactions among components as they are added to the system, developing an implementation and integration schedule that will make the modules available when needed, and designing test cases that will demonstrate the viability of the evolving system.

Formal verification is often dismissed as impractical for application to large software products. Problems cited include the amount of effort required, the opportunity for error in the verification process, and the level of sophistication required of the programmer. There are at least two reasons to remain optimistic about future prospects for formal verification technology. One is the use of formal verification techniques to guide systematic synthesis of algorithms, and the other is the advent of automated verification tools. A verification tool can never totally automate the process of formal verification because of decidability limitations, but verification tools can automate much of the verification process, thus reducing the amount of effort required and reducing the chance of introducing errors into the verification process.

The final point in Chapter 8 is a demonstration of the ease of proving various properties of functional programs, when compared with procedural programs. At this point, one can only speculate on new programming paradigms such as logic programming and transformation-based programming that may in the future ease many of our concerns for verification and validation.

10.7 SOFTWARE MAINTENANCE

Software maintenance is a catch-all phrase used to denote the various modification activities that occur following product release. Modifications are made in order to enhance, adapt, and correct errors in software products. Maintenance is a microcosm of software development, in that modification of the product may involve reanalysis, redesign, reimplementation, revalidation, and updating of supporting documents. Because maintenance typically consumes more than half of the life-cycle budget for a software product, major benefits accrue during software maintenance from the systematic activities pursued during product development.

Maintenance issues discussed in Chapter 9 include development activities that enhance maintainability of the product, managerial aspects of maintenance, configuration management, source code metrics, and other tools and techniques for software maintenance.

Software maintenance, like all software engineering activities, requires both managerial and technical expertise. Managerial concerns during the software maintenance phase involve the change control board, change request procedures, quality assurance activities, and techniques for organizing maintenance programmers.

Configuration management is a pervasive concern throughout the development and maintenance cycles of a software product life cycle. When work products pass their milestone reviews, they are typically placed under configuration control. Subsequent changes to the work products require a formal change mechanism. Work products that have not yet been baselined may exist in several versions. Tracking and controlling various versions of a software product is the major problem of configuration management during software maintenance.

Configuration management is particularly important during the maintenance phase because most software products are distributed to multiple sites and exist in multiple versions and releases. Tools to aid configuration management include configuration management data bases and version control libraries.

Maintaining the quality of a software product through successive cycles of modification and updating is an issue of fundamental concern during software maintenance. The quality of a software product can quickly degrade due to patches and quick fixes if great care is not taken to ensure that coding style and documentation standards are maintained and that the supporting documents are updated to reflect the changes. Two techniques for maintaining product quality are formal quality assurance procedures and source code metrics. The roles of these techniques were discussed in Chapter 9.

Difficulties encountered in the maintenance phase and the social stigma attached to maintenance programming are typically caused by failure to plan the maintenance activity during product development, failure to properly organize the maintenance activity, and failure to provide the necessary tools, techniques, and resources for maintenance.

Planning for maintenance, developing the product with an eye to maintenance, organizing the maintenance activity and the maintenance programmers, and providing good maintenance tools can greatly improve software quality, programmer productivity, and programmer morale.

10.8 CONCLUSION

The pervasive concerns of software engineering are software quality, programmer productivity, and increased job satisfaction for software engineers. The fundamental goal of software engineering is to provide methods, tools, and techniques that will allow competent people to do a competent job. On the one hand, the gurus and wizards of software will eschew systematic techniques; on the other hand, systematic techniques will never transform incompetence into expertise. That leaves the vast middle ground of sincere, competent professionals to benefit from systematic approaches to software engineering.

The fundamental problems in software engineering are control of complexity, the lack of physical constraints and boundaries in software, and the tendency to mix concerns that belong on different levels of abstraction. In addition, there are few, if any, universally accepted methods, tools, techniques, or notations in software engineering. This is due to the immaturity and diversity of the software engineering discipline. Lack of standardized techniques for software project management is also indicative of the immaturity of our discipline. However, we must remember that the technology of software is truly in its infancy when compared with other technological disciplines.

Prospects for the future include maturation of the discipline, with an accompanying improvement in methods, tools, and techniques, and new programming paradigms that will represent radical departures from the Von Neumann model of computation. Regardless of new developments, it will always be necessary to first analyze the problem, plan a solution strategy, design a solution, implement and validate the solution, prepare supporting documents and documentation, and modify and update the system as the environment and the users' needs evolve. Thus, the basic problem-solving paradigm of software engineering appears to be sound.

Finally, we observe that software engineering is a people-intensive activity. Software is developed by people for use by other people. Software engineering is a new and rapidly evolving professional discipline. The hallmarks of a profession are advanced training based on well-established intellectual foundations; an apprenticeship period to gain practical experience within the profession; methods, tools, and techniques specifically developed for use by practitioners of the profession; and the attitude of professionalism. We are hopeful that this text has imparted some of the methods, tools, and techniques of software engineering, and most especially that it has enhanced your aspirations and helped to raise your level of professionalism.

APPENDIX

TERM PROJECTS

Software engineering is concerned with the methods, tools, and techniques used to develop and maintain computer software. An appreciation for, and understanding of, software engineering concepts is best gained by applying them to a real software project. This appendix describes the format and schedule for a term project and suggests some projects.

Participation as a member of a software development team is an essential component of the term project. Project teams of three or four members per team should be organized. Different teams may develop different products, or each team may develop a different component of a large system, or multiple teams may develop identical subsystems needed by other teams and "sell" their versions of the needed subsystem to the other teams for course points (HOR77).

Each team must have an organizational structure. Possible structures are the democratic team, the chief programmer team, or the hierarchical team (see Chapter 2). Regardless of the organizational structure chosen, it is essential that each team have a well-defined team structure, and that each team have a designated leader at all times.

Each team member should maintain a log of time spent on course activities. The log should be broken into categories such as reading, preparing specifications, attending meetings, writing code, debugging and testing, etc. Each entry in the log should be annotated with comments. At the end of the semester, the log will provide you with a valuable perspective, and it will help your instructor to improve the course.

A list of suggested term projects is provided below. Your instructor may choose to have all teams working on the same project, or your team may be encouraged to define your own project. In selecting a project, the following issues should be considered:

Is it too ambitious or not ambitious enough?
Are the goals of the project clearly understood?
Can the project be expanded or reduced later if necessary?
Can the project be split into subtasks for each team member?

Your instructor will provide assistance in answering these questions.

At least three versions of your system should be planned: a prototype version that demonstrates basic features and provides an architectural skeleton for further development; a modest version that provides nominal functionality; and an enhanced version that incorporates all the desired features, but probably cannot be completed within the resource and time constraints.

At the discretion of your instructor, it is suggested that the following documents be prepared during the project:

1. A System Definition consisting of a Product Definition and a Project Plan.
2. A Software Requirements Specification.
3. A design document consisting of external design, architectural design, and detailed design specifications.
4. A test plan.
5. A User's Manual.
6. A properly documented, debugged, and tested program.
7. A project legacy document

Suggested formats for these documents follow:

System Requirements
 I. Product Definition
   Problem statement
   Functions to be provided
   Processing environment: hardware/software
   User characteristics
   Solution strategy
   Product features: prototype/modest/enhanced versions
   Acceptance criteria
   Sources of information
   Glossary of terms
 II. Project Plan
   Life-cycle model: terminology/milestones/work products

Team structure
Development schedule: milestones and reviews
Programming languages and development tools
Documents to be prepared
Manner of demonstration
Sources of information
Glossary of terms

Software Requirements Specification
    Section 1: Product overview and summary
    Section 2: Development/operating/maintenance environments
    Section 3: External interfaces and data flows
        User displays and report formats
        User command summary
        High-level data flow diagrams
        Logical data sources and sinks
        Logical data stores
        Logical data dictionary
    Section 4: Functional specifications
    Section 5: Performance requirements
    Section 6: Exception conditions/exception handling
    Section 7: Early subsets and implementation priorities
    Section 8: Foreseeable modifications and enhancements
    Section 9: Acceptance criteria
        Functional and performance tests
        Documentation standards
    Section 10: Design guidelines (hints and constraints)
    Section 11: Sources of information
    Section 12: Glossary of terms

Design Document
  I. External Design Specifications
        User displays and report formats
        User command summary
        Detailed data flow diagrams
        Logical data stores
        Logical data dictionary
        Logical format of data files and data bases
 II. Architectural Design Specifications
        Structure diagrams
        Parameter specifications
        Logical data structures
        Functional descriptions

III. Detailed Design Specifications
        Subprogram interface specifications
        Documentation prologue for each routine
        Pseudocode for each routine
        Physical data structure and data file specifications
        Packaging specifications

User's Manual
  I. Introduction
        Product rationale and overview
        Terminology
        Basic features
        Summary of display and report formats
        Outline of the manual
 II. Getting Started
        Sign-on
        Help mode
        Sample run
III. Modes of Operation
        Commands/displays/options
IV. Advanced Features
 V. Command Syntax and System Options

Test Plan
  I. Functional Tests
        Nominal inputs—expected results
        Boundary conditions—minima and maxima
        Logically related inputs—correct and incorrect relations
        Special values—empty files, 1×1 matrices
        Default initial values
 II. Performance Tests
        Response time/execution time/throughput
        Memory/channel/bus utilization
III. Stress Tests
        Intentional attempts to break system
IV. Structural Tests
        Designed to achieve a required level of test coverage

Each test case should provide the following information:
  Type of test: functional/performance/stress/structural
  Machine configuration
  Test assumptions
  Requirements being tested
  Exact test stimuli
  Expected outcome (be precise)

Source-Code Documentation

Each subprogram should contain a standard prologue, as described in Chapter 6, and the internal commenting guidelines presented in Chapter 6 should be observed.

Project Legacy
  Section 1: Project description
  Section 2: Initial expectations
  Section 3: Current status of the project
  Section 4: Remaining areas of concern
  Section 5: Activities/time log(s)
  Section 6: Technical lessons learned
  Section 7: Managerial lessons learned
  Section 8: Recommendations to future projects

Term Project Schedule

Week 1 Organize teams.
Week 2 Project proposals due.
Week 3 Preliminary requirements for the prototype, the modest version, and the enhanced version due.
Week 4 Final requirements document for the prototype and the modest version due.
          Preliminary version of the user's manual for the modest version due.
          Software requirements review held.
Week 5 External and architectural design specifications for the prototype due.
          Detailed design and implementation of prototype begins.
          Test plan for prototype begun.
Week 6 Preliminary design review held.
Week 8 Prototype implementation completed.
          Prototype demonstrated.
Week 9 External and architectural design specifications for the modest version due.
          Test plan for modest version begun.
Week 10 Detailed design specifications for modest version due.
          Critical design review held.
          Implementation of modest version begun.
Week 11 Test plan for modest version completed and reviewed.
Week 12 Second draft of user's manual for modest version due.
          Debugging and unit testing of modest version begun.
Week 13 Implementation of modest version completed.
          Integration testing begun.
Week 14 Final version of user's manual for modest version due.
          Integration testing completed.
Week 15 Acceptance testing of modest version.
          Demonstration of modest version.

Final version of requirements, design specifications, and test plan for modest version due.

Requirements and external design and architectural design specifications for enhanced version due.

Project legacy document due.

SUGGESTED TERM PROJECTS

The following suggested term projects are based on the author's experience in teaching software engineering and on project suggestions by Professor Elaine Kant (KAN81). All of the projects described here are open-ended. Be careful to define your prototype, modest version, and enhanced version of the product so that functional and performance capabilities can be easily moved between different versions of the system as the project evolves.

The list of suggested projects follows:

1. An interactive text editor for general-purpose text editing.
2. A special-purpose editor for editing Pascal programs. Special commands should be provided to insert skeleton statement templates for procedure headings, if-then-else statements, while loops, etc. The editor should not allow construction of syntactically invalid programs.
3. A student registration program to manage course requests, and handle student class scheduling, classroom scheduling, student registration status, class lists for instructors, room use sheets, add/drop requests, and summary reports.
4. A program for computer-aided instruction. The subject might be Pascal programming, selected topics in mathematics, or data structures (use your imagination). The system should provide interactive lessons, a scoring system, analysis of error patterns, and a history file for each student.
5. A database system to maintain bibliographies. System capabilities should include adding new categories, adding entries and associated keywords to existing categories, and searching by keywords in other fields. Provide a user query language.
6. A database system for maintaining voting records of members of congress. The system should keep, for each district, the name and party affiliation of the representative, date of election, and a set of (user-determined) votes on specific bills and issues. There should be a facility to determine how each member of congress rates on any particular set of issues (e.g., the environment, ERA, or defense). There should be various ways to print this information (perhaps using a query language) and to deal with members of congress who win or lose elections, resign, die, etc.
7. A prototype simulation of a small, low-cost computing engine that one might find for sale to the average consumer in the foreseeable future. It could be for adults or children; it might perform a common, routine task now performed

manually, or it might be a game. The "Spell and Speak" system from Texas Instruments would be a candidate.

8. A program to manage a board game such as Clue, checkers, bridge, Othello, backgammon, chess, or Go. The prototype version might be a board manager for people competitors. The second version of the program might be augmented to make the computer one of the competitors. Alternatively, programs for games such as Adventure, or Dungeons and Dragons in which the computer is the Dungeon Master, might be developed.

9. A program to detect similarities in programs written by students in introductory programming classes. Measures of similarity might include number of unique operators in a program, number of unique operands, total operators, total operands, total lines of code, variables declared, variables used, and total number of control statements. The analyzer and report generator should be independent of the student programming language.

10. An on-line recipe file and meal planner. The program should compute the overall nutritional value of a meal, summarize the necessary ingredients, maintain an inventory of material on hand, and estimate cost. It should also be able to suggest meals given commands such as "use ground beef" or "do not use eggs or milk."

11. An automated bank teller to keep track of accounts and let users perform authorized transactions such as move money between accounts, make deposits and withdrawals, pay bills, etc. The system should provide displays similar to those in actual teller machines. It should be secure and reliable. Consider multiple machines, simultaneous deposits and withdrawals, bank manager functions, and backup systems.

12. A manuscript processing system that checks spelling and diction, and identifies parts of speech. The system should compute a "fog" index for the manuscript and provide summary information, such as average sentence length, number and percent of compound sentences, use of commas, number of paragraphs, etc.

13. A personal finances manager to balance your checkbook, keep track of bills, match receipts to credit card statements, do tax computations, and provide summary reports of various kinds.

14. An interpreter and an interactive debugger for (a subset of) Pascal or some other programming language. Provide debugging features such as breakpoints, source-code modification, assertion checking, step-mode operation, conditional tracing, and displays of control flow and data flow.

15. A simulator with logic debugging aids for a computer such as the 8080, PDP-11, or M68000. Provide fancy displays. Investigate the possibility of attaching simulated real time devices to the machine simulator.

16. A calendar maintainer to schedule your time. Send reminders through the computer mail system, coordinate activities with other people's calendars, and display parts of the calendar on demand (such as "display today's schedule," "display next week," or "schedule one hour per week for the next four weeks starting at 10 a.m.").

17. A terminal reservation system for the terminal room. This is an automated sign-up sheet for a collection of terminals (and possibly other resources). People should be able to express preferences for various times. The system should include facilities for administrators to collect and print statistics on usage, as well as a scheduling algorithm to ensure fair distribution of resources among users. It should be easy to change the scheduling algorithm.

18. A program to analyze the NFL playoff situation, which has a complex set of tie-breaking rules for resolving various situations that can arise. One portion of the system would be an evaluator to determine the playoff choices given the end of season scenario. The rules should be implemented so that they can be easily changed. The user interface might be very simple, or it might provide a query language capable of answering questions such as "If Denver loses to Chicago, what must occur for Denver to enter the playoffs?" Incremental improvement might include the ability to guess, based on the season so far, how some future games might be decided or which games might be crucial for a given team.

19. A software cost estimation program for estimating resources required to develop software products. The system might be based on the COCOMO model or the SLIM model described in Chapter 3.

20. A string-handling package for Pascal. The system should provide dynamic allocation of variable-length character strings, with an explicit or automatic allocation mechanism. In addition to managing storage, the package should provide facilities for operations on strings, such as copying, catenating, comparing, sorting, searching, matching, etc.

Other possibilities for term projects are limited only by your imagination. Good candidates are software tools to support software engineering activities. These might include analysis and functional specification tools, design tools, testing and maintenance tools, or management tools such as a cost estimation tool or a PERT chart system.

Projects involving command interpreters, syntax-driven text editors, and general menu-handling systems are quite feasible. Projects such as poetry or music composers, natural language translators, or theorem provers require great care that your team not waste time deciding what to do or which of many possible approaches to pursue.

Again, we remind you to define three versions of your system: a prototype that will illustrate basic capabilities, a modest version that can easily be completed in the time available, and an enhanced version that provides all the features you would desire in the product. When you are working against a fixed deadline (such as the end of the semester), it is highly desirable for your system to have been specified and designed so that functionality can be moved between versions without sacrificing documentation, testing, or code quality. On the other hand, it is also very nice to have a plan for additional work if your project goes better than anticipated.

REFERENCES

(HOR77) Horning, J., and D. Wortman: "Software Hut: A Computer Program Engineering Project in the Form of A Game," *IEEE Trans. Software Eng.,* vol. SE-3, no. 4, July 1977.

(KAN81) Kant, E.: "A Semester Course in Software Engineering," *ACM Software Engineering Notes,* vol. 6, no. 4, August 1981.

INDEXES

NAME INDEX

Page numbers for References are in *italic*.

SUBJECT INDEX